365 days with **Spurgeon**

Volume
3

A further collection of daily
readings from sermons preached by
Charles Haddon Spurgeon
from his Metropolitan Tabernacle Pulpit

Day One

© Day One Publications 2005
First printed 2005

ISBN 1-84625-006-4

9 781846 250064 >

Unless otherwise stated, all Scripture quotations are from
the Authorised Version Crown Copyright

British Library Cataloguing in Publication Data available

Published by Day One Publications
Ryelands Road, Leominster, HR6 8NZ
☎ 01568 613 740 FAX 01568 611 473
email—sales@dayone.co.uk
web site—www.dayone.co.uk
North American—e-mail—sales@dayonebookstore.com
North American web site—www.dayonebookstore.com

Chief Sub-Editor: David Simm
Designed by Steve Devane and printed by Gutenberg Press, Malta

Dedication

In memory of Gordon Buchanan,
a Christlike Crusader leader,
who introduced me to the study of God's Word
at the Crusader Hall in Nottingham Road, Wandsworth Common,
where Spurgeon preached in the early 1870s
in preparation for the foundation of Trinity Road Chapel,
Upper Tooting.

'Blessed is that ministry of which Christ is all!' Thus wrote C.H. Spurgeon. It is no wonder, therefore, that his ministry was singularly blessed both during his lifetime and now over one hundred and ten years later.

Charles Haddon Spurgeon
photographed around 1870

Once again, the Christian public is indebted to Dr. Terence Crosby for another selection of daily readings from the sermons of the great preacher. If the success of the previous two volumes is anything to go by, then this one will have an equally significant impact on Christians all over the world.

It is vital that we engage with the many theological issues of today, when the seemingly once orthodox are leading many to question the very doctrines that form the foundation of Gospel truth. How carefully one has to read erstwhile reliable authors. The mind must be constantly engaged, discerning what is profitable, what is erroneous and what is of dubious benefit. How calming and restful it is, then, to take a daily dose of Spurgeon, to swallow it slowly and to cherish the taste of it through the day. Spurgeon never leaves a bitter or unpleasant taste in the soul, nor does he trouble the mind with unseemly questions. His is not, what has been termed recently, 'implicit Calvinism.' His is of the explicit sort. The doctrines of grace permeate his exposition of true experimental religion, using 'experimental' in the Puritan sense of the word. These daily readings will not only engage the mind in fruitful meditation, but rightly digested will stir the affections and warm the heart towards Christ. Surely this is a primary ongoing need in the life of every child of God. The following quotation from A.W. Pink can so readily be applied to Spurgeon: 'The one who most profits me is the one whose ministry brings most of the awe of a holy and sovereign God on my heart, who discovers to me my sinfulness and failures, who conveys most light on the path of duty, *who makes Christ most precious to me,* who encourages me to press forward along the narrow way.' (Italics added)

As the sermons from which the extracts in this volume are taken were being preached, lots of things were happening, many of which have been forgotten, some of which were to have long-term repercussions for the future. In 1867, there were reports of Fenian outrages in Ireland and

Photograph taken from Charles Ray, *The Life of Charles Haddon Spurgeon* (London: Passmore and Alabaster, 1903): p. 318.

Manchester, Stanley Baldwin was born, Marx's *Das Kapital* (Vol. 1) was published, and Pope Pius XI announced his intention to hold an ecumenical council. In sport, 'The Queensbury Rules' governing boxing came into force. The following year d'Israeli became prime-minister only to resign and be succeeded that same year by Mr Gladstone; Charles Darwin's *The Variation of Animals and plants under Domestication* was published; the first regular Trades Union Congress was held in Manchester. The year 1869 saw the introduction by Cardinal Manning to the First Vatican Council of a definition of papal infallibility, which dogma was promulgated the following year. Spurgeon's interest in social and political happenings are often alluded to in his sermons and these years were particularly significant in the life of the nation and the churches. 1871 saw an Act of Parliament legalising labour unions. The 'Jehovah's Witnesses' first appeared in that year, also did Darwin's, *The Descent of Man*. The religious scene was being seriously affected by the emergence of these developments. The pursuit of pleasure saw the opening of Barnum's *'The Greatest Show on Earth'* in Brooklyn, New York, and the circus was born. Bank Holidays were introduced in England and Wales and the F.A. Cup was established. So much was happening and the western world was changing rapidly. People's interests were moving from a God-conscious world to the self-interest world. Life was to be enjoyed but without daily recourse to the Giver of all good things. Enjoyment was to be found elsewhere. In 1872, the first international soccer game was played between England and Scotland.

What a comfort it must have been, in these changing times, for the faithful members of the Metropolitan Tabernacle to sit under the ministry of God's Word so regularly! What they heard we can still read, and souls in many nations are still being reached by the pulpit ministry of 'The Prince of Preachers'. We must be grateful to God for the service Terence Crosby has rendered to the church. To some, these readings may be familiar, to you who read them for the first time, may they whet your appetite for more of C.H. Spurgeon. Times change, people come and go, but the value of these sermon extracts are timeless and will reward prayerful contemplation. In his introduction, Terence makes mention of the fact that Spurgeon found it 'far easier to deliver his sermons than to write' a page of preface to the annual volume! For this present writer, to pen this foreword is an honour and a privilege and is a far easier task than that to which the compiler of this volume has devoted his energies. We, the readers, will certainly benefit from his labours. No doubt Terence's achievement in this work, and our joy in reading it on a daily basis, will be further enhanced as the Glory is given to him who alone is worthy, even our Great King Jesus Christ.

David J Ellis
Stowmarket, May 2005

The first two volumes of 365 Days with Spurgeon have conveniently coincided with well-defined periods in his early ministry. Volume one covered his years at New Park Street and volume two continued with the first six years of his ministry at the Metropolitan Tabernacle, concluding at the point at which it was closed for renovation work. This third volume includes readings from the five sermons (nos. 742–746) preached at the Agricultural Hall, Islington from 24 March to 21 April 1867 during the closure and covers the next six years of Spurgeon's ministry at the Metropolitan Tabernacle from 28 April 1867 (no. 747) to 4 May 1873 (no. 1110), thus reaching more or less the half-way point of his ministry in London, which began on 28 April 1854 and concluded on 7 June 1891 (no. 2208). In contrast to the previous two volumes a reading has been allocated to 29 February taken from a sermon preached on Thursday 29 February 1872 (no. 1042), the first of only three 29 February sermons in the 63 volumes of the New Park Street and Metropolitan Tabernacle Pulpits; the others were on a Sunday in 1880 (nos. 1525 & 2663).

Unlike in the previous volume of 365 Days with Spurgeon there was no real change to the format of the sermons covered by this volume. The next major innovation was the inclusion of the numbers of the hymns accompanying each sermon, but that practice did not begin until 8 June 1873 (no. 1116), just outside the scope of this volume. However, for his first thirteen volumes (1855–1867) Spurgeon had written a brief preface in which he had reviewed the year's ministry; in volumes 3 to 7 and 9 he had named specific sermons which had been specially blessed by God. The preface to volume 13 begins 'Far easier does the preacher find it to deliver ten sermons, than to write a page of preface to the annual volume' and from volume 14 the preface was dropped! There are therefore no more references to particularly blessed sermons.

Once again the majority of the readings have been allocated to coincide with the actual dates on which the sermons were preached. Where there is duplication of dates for various reasons, readings have been displaced, as far as possible, to an adjacent day in the same month. The five Agricultural Hall sermons have been brought together in a single sequence. Just over one seventh of the sermons are undated and these have been allocated to unrepresented dates in such a way as to produce some thematic continuity and several short topical series after the manner of Spurgeon, who was averse to preaching a series of any great length. The increased number of undated sermons coincided with the first major interruptions to Spurgeon's ministry resulting from the illnesses which were to plague him for the rest of his life. Particularly touching are the sick notes and letters from Spurgeon attached to nos. 903, 907, 984, 988, 991, 993–995, 997, 1024 and 1080, nearly all of these being undated sermons.

Each reading indicates Spurgeon's sermon-title and text; where it has been necessary to abbreviate exceptionally long texts, the full text has still been listed in the Scripture Index. The suggested further readings and footnotes for meditation have been added by the arranger, but on 41 days part or the whole of Spurgeon's own further readings (which are mentioned at the end of most of these sermons) have been incorporated and are identified as such. The reader's attention has also been drawn to contemporary topics of personal, national and international interest to which Spurgeon occasionally referred. As in previous volumes of 365 Days with Spurgeon there has been a minimum of sympathetic updating of the original material to remove antiquated language and terminology. Where necessary Spurgeon's Scripture quotations (probably from memory) have been corrected to remove any inaccuracies.

I would like to thank all at Day One for their encouragement and assistance during the compilation of this volume. Special thanks are due to John Roberts, David Simm and Digby James, also to David Ellis for producing an excellent introduction at very short notice. As always, the Evangelical Library provided the relevant volumes of the Metropolitan Tabernacle Pulpit on long loan. But most of all, in words which appeared at the start of each of Spurgeon's volumes, 'To the one God of Heaven and earth, in the Trinity of his sacred persons, be all honour and glory, world without end. Amen.'

Terence Peter Crosby
Wandsworth, London

Life in Christ

'Because I live, ye shall live also.' John *14:19*
SUGGESTED FURTHER READING (Spurgeon): Colossians 3:1–4

This truth instructs us in many ways: let us hint at three. It instructs us to admire the condescension of Christ. Look at the two pronouns, 'ye' and 'I'; shall they ever come into contact? Yes, here they stand in close connection with each other. 'I'—the I AM, the Infinite; 'ye'—the creatures of an hour; yet I, the Infinite, come into union with you, the finite; I, the Eternal, take up you, the fleeting, and I make you live because I live. What? Is there such a bond between me and Christ? Is there such a link between his life and mine? Blessed be his name! Adored be his infinite condescension! It next demands of us abundance of gratitude. Apart from Christ we are dead in trespasses and sins; look at the depth of our degradation! But in Christ we live, live with his own life. Look at the height of our exaltation, and let our thankfulness be proportioned to this infinite of mercy. Measure if you can from the lowest hell to the highest heaven, and so great let your thankfulness be to him who has lifted you from death to life. Let the last lesson be, see the all-importance of close communion with Jesus. Union with Christ makes you live; keep up your enjoyment of that union, that you may clearly perceive and enjoy your life. Begin this year with the prayer, 'Nearer to thee, my Lord, nearer to thee.' Think much of the spiritual life and less of this poor carnal life, which will so soon be over. Go to the source of life for an increase of spiritual life. Go to Jesus. Think of him more than you have done, pray to him more; use his name more believingly in your supplications. Serve him better, and seek to grow up into his likeness in all things. Make an advance this year. Life is a growing thing. Your life only grows by getting nearer to Christ.

FOR MEDITATION: The start of a new year is a good time to examine your relationship with Christ. Have you been raised with him (Colossians 3:1), is your life hidden with him (Colossians 3:3) and are you going to appear with him (Colossians 3:4)? Or have you really got nothing to do with him (Ephesians 2:12)?

N.B. This was the last of many new year's motto texts provided by 'a venerable clergyman of the Church of England' for the use of Spurgeon and others.

SERMON NO. 968

Assured security in Christ

'I know whom I have believed, and am persuaded that he is able to keep that which I have committed unto him against that day.' 2 Timothy 1:12
SUGGESTED FURTHER READING: Proverbs 3:1–8

Young people, you cannot do better than early in life entrust your future with the Lord Jesus. Many children at home appear to be very excellent, many lads before they leave their father's house are amiable and commendable in character; but this is a rough world, and it soon spoils the graces that have been nurtured in the conservatory of home-life. Good boys very often turn out very bad men; and girls who were so lovely and pure at home have been known to become very wicked women. O children, your characters will be safe if you trust them with Jesus. I do not say you will be rich if you trust Christ, nor that you will prosper after the manner of men, but I do say that you shall be happy in the best sense of that word, and that your holiness shall be preserved through trusting yourself with Jesus. I pray that you may be led to desire this, especially any of you who are leaving your father's house, or are setting up in business on your own account; commit yourselves to God. This first Sabbath of a new year, what time is more suitable for beginning aright! O may the Holy Spirit softly whisper in your ear reasons that shall persuade you to give yourselves to Christ. My own testimony is that you cannot do a wiser or a better thing. What happiness my soul has known in resting on my Lord. I wish you knew it. I would not cease to be a Christian, if I might be made a king or an angel. No character can be to me so suitable or so happy as that of a humble dependant upon the faithful love of my redeeming Lord. O come and trust him, dear young friends!

FOR MEDITATION: Trusting in Christ is the only way to avoid a misspent youth (Ecclesiastes 11:9–12:1); it is also the only way to guard against a misspent middle age and a misspent old age (Ecclesiastes 11:8).

SERMON NO. 908

Jesus Christ immutable

'Jesus Christ the same yesterday, and to day, and for ever.' Hebrews 13:8
SUGGESTED FURTHER READING: Philippians 3:1–11

I have preached from this text before, but we need not be at all afraid of preaching from the same text twice; the word is inexhaustible, it may be trodden in the winepress many times, and yet run with generous wine. We ought not to hesitate to preach a second time from a passage, any more than anyone would be ashamed to put down the same bucket twice at the village well, or feel aggrieved at sailing twice down the same river; for there is always a freshness about gospel truth, and though the matter may be the same, there are ways of putting it in fresh light, so as to bring new joy to those who meditate upon it. Moreover, what if we should repeat our teachings concerning Christ? What if we should hear over and over again the same things 'touching the King'? We can afford to hear them. Repetitions concerning Jesus are better than varieties upon any other subject; we would sooner hear again and again the precious truths which glorify our Lord Jesus, than listen to the most eloquent orations upon any other theme in all the world. There are a few works of art and wonders of creation which you might gaze upon every day in your life, and yet not weary of them. A great architect tells us there are only a few buildings of this kind, but he instances Westminster Abbey as one; and everyone knows who has ever looked upon the sea, or upon the Niagara Falls, that look as often as you may, though you see precisely the same object, yet there are new tints, new motions of the waves, and new flashings of the light, which forbid the least approach of monotony, and give to the assembling of the waters an ever-enduring charm. Even thus is it with that sea of all delights which is found in the dear Lover of our souls.

FOR MEDITATION: Spurgeon had preached the same message about the same Christ from the same text on the same date eleven years earlier (3 January 1858)—see no. 170 in *365 Days with Spurgeon Vol. 1*. Beware of all who try to introduce another Jesus (2 Corinthians 11:4) and another gospel (Galatians 1:6–9).

SERMON NO. 848

Creation's groans and the saints' sighs

'We know that the whole creation groaneth and travaileth in pain together until now. And not only they, but ourselves also, which have the firstfruits of the Spirit, even we ourselves groan within ourselves, waiting for the adoption, to wit, the redemption of our body.' Romans 8:22–23
SUGGESTED FURTHER READING: 2 Corinthians 5:1–10

The other night, just before Christmas, two men who were working very late, were groaning in two very different ways, one of them saying, 'Ah, there's a poor Christmas day in store for me; my house is full of misery.' He had been a drunkard, a spendthrift, and had not a penny to bless himself with, and his house had become a little hell; he was groaning at the thought of going home to such a scene of quarrelling and distress. Now, his fellow workman, who worked beside him, as it was getting very late, wished himself at home, and therefore groaned. A shopmate asked, 'What's the matter?' 'Oh, I want to get home to my dear wife and children. I have such a happy house; I do not like to be out of it.' The other might have said, 'Ah, you pretend to be a happy man, but here you are groaning.' 'Yes,' he could say, ' and a blessed thing it would be for you if you had the same thing to groan after that I have.' So the Christian has a good Father, a blessed, eternal home, and groans to get to it; but there is more joy even in the groan of a Christian after heaven, than in all the mirth, merriment, dancing and lewdness of the ungodly when their mirth is at its greatest height. We are like the dove that flutters and is weary, but, thank God, we have an ark to go to. We are like Israel in the wilderness and are footsore, but, blessed be God, we are on the way to Canaan. We are like Jacob looking at the wagons and, the more we look at the wagons, the more we long to see Joseph's face; but our groaning after Jesus is a blessed groan, for

"'Tis heaven on earth, 'tis heaven above,
To see his face, and taste his love.'

FOR MEDITATION: The Christian groans in anticipation of a groan-free future in heaven, that totally groan-free zone (Revelation 21:3–4); the unbeliever ought to groan in expectation of a future full of groaning in the most user-unfriendly hell imaginable (Matthew 13:41–42,49–50).

The man greatly beloved

'*O man greatly beloved, fear not: peace be unto thee, be strong, yea, be strong.*' Daniel 10:19

SUGGESTED FURTHER READING: Daniel 6:1–16

There was one crowning token of God's love to Daniel, and that is the perfect consistency of his life all through. Daniel seems to me to be as nearly as possible a perfect character. If any one should ask me for what peculiar virtue I count him to be famous, I should hardly know how to reply. There is a combination in his character of all the excellencies. Neither do I think I could discover anything in which he was deficient. Sinner he was, doubtless, before the eye of God; he is faultless towards man. His was a well-balanced character. There is an equilibrium maintained between the divers graces, even as in John's character, which is also exceedingly beautiful. There is perhaps a touch of loveliness about the character of John, a tender softness that we do not find in Daniel; there is somewhat more of the lion in the prophet and of the lamb in the apostle, but still they are each of them perfect after his kind. All through Daniel's life you do not find a flaw; there is no breakdown anywhere. There was a great occasion in which he might have broken down, but God helped him through it. There he was, a business man for a long lifetime, a man bearing the burden of state, and yet never once any accusation of any wrongdoing could be brought against him. A man of large transactions will usually be chargeable with something or other of wrong performed through his subordinates, even if he himself should be strictly upright; but here was a man rendered by grace so upright and so correct in all that he did, that nothing could be brought against him even by his enemies, except concerning his religion. A great mark of grace this, an ensign of piety far too rare. Many are Christians and will, we hope, creep into heaven, but, alas, the less said about their inconsistencies the better. It is a special mark of a man greatly beloved, when he is consistent from the beginning to the end through the grace of God.

FOR MEDITATION: It is a mark of godliness when accusers are forced to resort to lies (Matthew 5:11; 1 Peter 2:12,15; 3:16–17). Blamelessness is a qualification required by church leaders (1 Timothy 3:2,10; Titus 1:6–7) so that their opponents cannot use the truth to level accusations against them (Titus 2:7–8). Christ is as always our perfect example (1 Peter 2:19–23).

SERMON NO. 1089

A holy celebration

'It is a night to be much observed unto the LORD.' Exodus 12:42
SUGGESTED FURTHER READING: Isaiah 45:18–23

I want you to remember now those blessed days when we began to live spiritually. I think we might date our existence from that time. When we count up our birthdays, we ought always to reckon that amongst them. To leave that out seems to be leaving out the one that makes all the others worth having. I remember a man's tombstone on which was inscribed 'Here lies one who died a child three years old at the age of eighty.' You are only as old as the number of years you have lived unto God. All the rest you might wish to be wiped out; indeed the blood of Christ has wiped them out, and you are alive from the dead, new-born souls. Let the time of your second birth be a season to be remembered before the Lord. Important results will flow to you from the preservation of this memorial. It will humble you and foster the grace of humility. Have you become an old experienced Christian, my brother? Go back to the hole of the pit whence you were digged. While I stand here preaching to a great many of you, I feel brought down to my proper bearings when I recollect how I sat, at about the age of fifteen, a poor trembling sinner, under the galleries of a Primitive Methodist meeting-house, and heard Christ preached and came to him. O that ever I should live to preach the gospel to you! I feel humbled at the very thought of it. You great professors, get back to the cross again! There is nothing about which to vaunt yourselves after all. Look to the hole of the pit whence you were digged: remember what you were when God met with you, and recollect what you would have been if he had not met with you.

FOR MEDITATION: It is right to put the past behind us and look to the future (Philippians 3:13–14), but Christians ought to remember their pre-conversion hopelessness (Ephesians 2:11–12) and their post-conversion first love for the Lord (Revelation 2:4–5). 'Bless the Lord, O my soul, and forget not all his benefits' (Psalm 103:2); can you thank God for the benefits of his salvation (Psalm 103:3–5)? Spurgeon never forgot how God saved him on 6 January 1850.

The glorious Master and the swooning disciple

'And when I saw him, I fell at his feet as dead. And he laid his right hand upon me, saying unto me, Fear not.' Revelation 1:17
SUGGESTED FURTHER READING: Daniel 10:1–19

Was not John beloved of the Lord Jesus? Did he not also know the Saviour's love to him? Yes, but for all that, he was afraid, or else the Master would not have said to him, 'Fear not.' That fear originated partly in a sense of his own weakness and insignificance in the presence of the divine strength and greatness. How shall an insect live in the furnace of the sun? How can mortal eyes behold unquenched the light of Deity, or mortal ears hear that voice which is as many waters? We are such infirmity, folly and nothingness that, if we have but a glimpse of omnipotence, awe and reverence prostrate us to the earth. Daniel tells us that when he saw the great vision by the river Hiddekel, there remained no strength in him, for his comeliness was turned in him into corruption, and he fell into a deep sleep upon his face. John also at that time perhaps perceived more impressively than ever the purity and immaculate holiness of Christ: and, being conscious of his own imperfection, he felt like Isaiah when he cried 'Woe is me! for I am undone; because I am a man of unclean lips ... : for mine eyes have seen the King, the LORD of hosts.' Even his faith, though fixed upon 'THE LORD OUR RIGHTEOUSNESS', was not able to bear him up under the first surprising view of uncreated holiness. Surely his feelings were like those of Job when he said, 'I have heard of thee by the hearing of the ear: but now mine eye seeth thee. Wherefore I abhor myself, and repent in dust and ashes.' The most spiritual and sanctified minds, when they fully perceive the majesty and holiness of God, are so greatly conscious of the great disproportion between themselves and the Lord, that they are humbled and filled with holy awe, and even with dread and alarm. The reverence which is commendable is pushed by the infirmity of our nature into a fear which is excessive, and that which is good in itself is made deadly unto us.

FOR MEDITATION: Walking in the fear of the Lord goes hand in hand with enjoying the comfort of the Holy Spirit (Acts 9:31; Romans 8:13–15). Being utterly terrified of God should be and one day will be the preserve of those who will not trust and obey him (Psalm 53:1,5; Hebrews 10:27,31).

Rest, rest

'Come unto me, all ye that labour and are heavy laden, and I will give you rest. Take my yoke upon you, and learn of me; for I am meek and lowly in heart: and ye shall find rest unto your souls. For my yoke is easy, and my burden is light.' Matthew 11:28–30

SUGGESTED FURTHER READING: Numbers 12:1–13

If I actively labour for Christ I can only find rest in the labour by possessing the meek spirit of my Lord; for if I go forth to labour for Christ without a meek spirit, I shall very soon find that there is no rest in it, for the yoke will chafe the skin of my shoulder. Somebody will begin objecting that I do not perform my work according to his liking. If I am not meek I shall find my proud spirit rising at once, and shall be for defending myself; I shall be irritated, or I shall be discouraged and inclined to do no more, because I am not appreciated as I should be. A meek spirit is not apt to be angry, and does not soon take offence; therefore if others find fault, the meek spirit goes working on, and is not offended; it will not hear the sharp word, nor reply to the severe criticism. If the meek spirit be grieved by some cutting censure and suffers for a moment, it is always ready to forgive and blot out the past, and go on again. The meek spirit in working only seeks to do good to others; it denies itself; it never expects to be well treated; it does not aim at being honoured; it never seeks itself, but purposes only to do good to others. The meek spirit bows its shoulder to the yoke, and expects to have to continue bowing in order to keep the yoke in the right place for labour. It does not look to be exalted by yoke-bearing; it is fully contented if it can exalt Christ and do good to his chosen ones. Remember how meek and lowly Jesus was in all his service, and how calmly, therefore, he bore with those who opposed him.

FOR MEDITATION: Meekness is an important part of Christian character (Galatians 5:23; Ephesians 4:2; Colossians 3:12; 1 Timothy 6:11; Titus 3:2; James 3:13). It should be particularly evident in our dealings with others whenever we are involved in counselling (Galatians 6:1), correcting (2 Timothy 2:25) or witnessing (1 Peter 3:15).

SERMON NO. 969

Voices from the excellent glory

'And lo a voice from heaven, saying, This is my beloved Son, in whom I am well pleased.' Matthew 3:17
'and behold a voice out of the cloud, which said, This is my beloved Son, in whom I am well pleased; hear ye him.' Matthew 17:5
'Father, glorify thy name. Then came there a voice from heaven, saying, I have both glorified it, and will glorify it again.' John 12:28
SUGGESTED FURTHER READING: Mark 4:9–24

God has three times with audible voice spoken out of heaven to bear witness to Jesus. These are historical facts. Then receive *with assured conviction* the truth to which God bears witness. The Man of Nazareth is the Son of the Highest; the Son of Mary is the Saviour appointed to bear human sin; he is the way of salvation, the only way. Doubt not this truth; accept the Saviour, for God declares that he is well pleased in him. Hear him then *with profound reverence*, accept the teaching and invitations of Jesus not as the mere utterances of fallible men, but as the instructions and the loving expostulations of God. Respect every word and command of Christ. Listen to him as spirits listen to the voice of the Most High when they bow before the throne; he says, 'Come unto me, all ye that labour and are heavy laden, and I will give you rest', hear him and lovingly obey the command. Hear him *with unconditional obedience*. God attests him as being sent from heaven. 'Whatsoever he saith unto you, do it.' Since he bids you believe him, be not unbelieving. He has told us to say in his name, 'He that believeth and is baptized shall be saved.' Despise not that double command. Attend, sinner, for the Son of God speaks to you. Trust and be baptized, and you will be saved. There stands the gospel stamped with the authority of deity; obey it now. May the Holy Spirit lead you to do so. Hear him, lastly, *with joyful confidence*. If God has sent Jesus, trust him; if he bears the glory of God's seal upon him, joyfully receive him. You who have trusted him, trust him better from this day forth. Leave your souls confidently in the hand of him of whom Jehovah, thrice speaking out of heaven, declares that he is the only Saviour.

FOR MEDITATION: Words spoken by God to instruct the apostles were for our attention too (John 17:20; 2 Peter 1:17–19; 1 John 1:1–5). Observing all Christ commanded begins by becoming his disciple (Matthew 28:19–20).

Unsound spiritual trading

'All the ways of a man are clean in his own eyes; but the LORD *weigheth the spirits.'* Proverbs 16:2

SUGGESTED FURTHER READING (Spurgeon): Psalm 51:1–19

Let us pray that instead of thinking our ways clean, we may know them to be foul, may mourn over them, and may learn to see them as God sees them, as crooked ways and wrong ways in themselves, not to be boasted of, but to be remembered with shame and confusion of face. Blessed is he who is delivered from any rejoicing in himself. Happy is that man who can see no speck of soundness in his own flesh, but who feels that the leprosy of sin has covered him without and within from head to foot. And, brethren, if we come to such deep humiliation of spirit, the next word is this: let us go together to the great salvation which God has provided in the person of Christ Jesus. Come, linking hand in hand, saint and sinner, now all sinners consciously, let us stand and see where sin has pierced the body of the blessed Substitute with yonder bleeding wounds. Let us read the lines of grief written upon that blessed face; let us gaze into the depth of his soul filled with an ocean of anguish, lashed to a tempest of suffering; let us believe that he suffered in our stead, and so roll our sin and our sinfulness on him. Jesus, accept a sinner, a poor sinner still; though these twenty years I have known thy name, yet still as the chief of sinners I come to thee. Brothers and sisters, we are never safer, I am sure, never healthier, never in a better frame than when we are flat down on the ground before the cross. When you feel yourself to be utterly unworthy, you have hit the truth. When you think you are doing something and are rich and flourishing, you are poor, and naked, and miserable; but when you are consciously weak and sinful, then you are rich. When you are weak you are strong; but, O God, save us from letting our ways seem clean in our own sight. May we weigh our spirits by the help of thy Spirit, and condemn ourselves that we may not be condemned of the Lord.

FOR MEDITATION: The most blameless men in the Bible were more than ready to confess their own sinfulness voluntarily to God (Nehemiah 1:6; Daniel 9:4–5,20). Do you try to hide your sinfulness from God? It won't do you any good (Psalm 32:3; Proverbs 28:13).

SERMON NO. 849

Lingerers hastened

'And while he lingered, the men laid hold upon his hand ... the LORD *being merciful unto him: and they brought him forth, and set him without the city.' Genesis 19:16*
SUGGESTED FURTHER READING (Spurgeon): Psalm 92:1–15

Messengers of God must plainly tell lost souls their condition and their danger, as these angels did. 'Up, get you out of this place,' said they, 'for the LORD will destroy this city.' If you really long to save men's souls, you must tell them a great deal of disagreeable truth. The preaching of the wrath of God has come to be sneered at nowadays, and even good people are half ashamed of it; a weak sentimentality about love and goodness has hushed plain gospel expostulations and warnings. But if we expect souls to be saved we must declare, unflinchingly with all affectionate fidelity, the terrors of the Lord. 'Well,' said the Scottish lad when he listened to the minister who told his congregation that there was no hell, or at any rate only a temporary punishment, 'I need not come and hear this man any longer, for if it be as he says, it is all right, and if it be not as he says, then I must not hear him again, because he will deceive me.' 'Knowing therefore the terror of the Lord,' says the apostle Paul, 'we persuade men.' Let not modern squeamishness prevent plain speaking concerning everlasting torment. Are we to be more gentle than the apostles and wiser than the inspired preachers of the word? Until we feel our minds overshadowed with the dread thought of the sinner's doom we are not in a fit frame for preaching to the unconverted. We shall never persuade men if we are afraid to speak of the judgment and the condemnation of the unrighteous. None was so infinitely gracious as our Lord Jesus Christ, yet no preacher ever uttered more faithful words of thunder. It was he who spoke of the place 'where their worm dieth not, and the fire is not quenched.' It was he who said, 'And these shall go away into everlasting punishment.' It was he who spoke concerning that man in hell who longed for a drop of water to cool his tongue. We must be as plain as Christ was.

FOR MEDITATION: The church has not been authorised to make sinners feel comfortable outside of Christ, but to point out their need and to point them to the one who can give them rest (Matthew 11:28). When it comes to sin, the Spirit-filled preacher does not soft-pedal (Micah 3:8).

Good earnests of great success

'And the word of God increased; and the number of the disciples multiplied in Jerusalem greatly; and a great company of the priests were obedient to the faith.' Acts 6:7

SUGGESTED FURTHER READING: 2 Timothy 3:10–17

God forbid that we should know anything among men save Jesus Christ and him crucified! Look to him—not to the priest, not to your good works, not to your prayers, not to your church-goings or your chapel-goings, but to Christ Jesus exalted. Look to him in faith, and God is willing to forgive you, able to forgive you, to receive you, to make you his children, and for ever to glorify you with himself. We must have much more of this plain preaching, and not only plain preaching but plain teaching. Sunday-school teachers, *you* must teach this same gospel. Many Sunday-school teachers do not. A certain denomination has made the confession that after having had their schoolrooms crowded with children, they do not know that any of those children have afterwards come to be attendants at the places of worship. Miserable confession! Miserable teachers must they be! And have we not known teachers who believed in the doctrines of grace, and upstairs in the chapel they would have fought earnestly for them, but downstairs in the schoolroom they have twaddled to the little children in this kind of way—'Be good boys and girls; keep the Sabbath; do not buy sweets on a Sunday; mind your fathers and your mothers; be good, and you will go to heaven'!—which is not true, and is not the gospel; for the same gospel is for little children as for grown-up men, not 'Do this and live,' which is after the law that was given by Moses, but 'Believe and live,' which is according to the grace and truth that came by Jesus Christ. Teachers must instil the gospel, the whole gospel, and nothing but the gospel, if they are to see the salvation of their classes, for without this no great thing will be done.

FOR MEDITATION: The Lord Jesus Christ takes it seriously when children are led astray (Matthew 18:6). Those who teach children can be just as guilty as those who tempt children. Never despise a child's ability to take in spiritual truth (Matthew 18:10; 21:16).

N.B. In this sermon Spurgeon referred to the unanimous appointment of his brother James on the previous Thursday to serve with him as co-pastor.

SERMON NO. 802

The two yokes

'Thus saith the LORD; Thou hast broken the yokes of wood; but thou shalt make for them yokes of iron.' Jeremiah 28:13
SUGGESTED FURTHER READING: 2 Samuel 12:1–14

Adam wore an easy yoke in Paradise: he broke it. He and his posterity have had to wear yokes of iron ever since. Death has come into the world with all its train of woes. Whenever a child of God, a true child of God, turns aside from the right path under pressure of temptation, he is always made to feel that after he has broken the yoke of wood, he must wear a yoke of iron. John Bunyan's illustration will serve me well here. The two pilgrims, Christian and Hopeful, when they went on their way, came to a place where the road was full of flints that cut their feet, and there were thorns and briers in the way; and by-and-by one of them said, 'Here is a meadow on the other side of the hedge, and if we were just to pass through the gap we might save a corner: it would be sure to come out in the way again, and so we should be certain to avoid the rough places.' Bunyan well describes how, when they got into By-path Meadow, the night and the flood overtook them, and they wished to find the road again, longing for it, rough though it had been. But Giant Despair laid hold of them, took them to his dungeon, and beat them within an inch of their lives, and it was only by mighty grace that they escaped. Take care, Christian! Though you should not utterly perish, you may often have to go with broken bones through a sin. Remember David's sin, his repentance, his life of sorrow and how he went to his grave halting still as a consequence of his crimes. Do not, therefore, shrink from Christian duty because it is onerous. Never, Christian, turn aside from the straight road, the highway of rectitude, because it threatens you with shame or loss. That first loss will be vastly less than the after-losses you will incur by seeking to avoid it.

FOR MEDITATION: Jesus described his yoke as easy and commands us to take it upon ourselves (Matthew 11:29–30). We only make rods for our own backs when we submit ourselves to other forbidden yokes such as being 'unequally yoked together with unbelievers' (2 Corinthians 6:14) and 'the yoke of bondage' to legalism (Galatians 5:1).

A call to holy living

'What do ye more than others?' Matthew 5:47
SUGGESTED FURTHER READING: Genesis 39:1–23

The ungodly man says, 'Well, I do not commit any act of fornication; you do not hear me singing a lascivious song,' and saying that, he feels content: but the Christian's Master expects us to carry the point a great deal further. An unchaste look is a crime to us, and an evil thought is a sin. It shocks me beyond measure when I hear of professedly Christian people who fall into the commission of immodest actions, not such as are called criminal in common society, but loose, fleshly, and full of lasciviousness. I beseech you, all of you, in your conversation with each other, avoid anything which has the appearance of impurity in this respect. Looks and gestures step by step lead on to fouler things, and sport which begins in folly ends in lewdness. Be as chaste as the driven snow; let not an immodest glance defile you. We do not like to say much about these things; they are so delicate, and we tremble lest we should suggest what we would prevent; but, by the tears of Jesus, by the wounds of Jesus, by the death of Jesus, hate 'even the garment spotted by the flesh.' Avoid everything that savours of unchastity. Flee youthful lusts as Joseph did. Run any risk sooner than fall into uncleanness, for it is a deep pit, and the 'abhorred of the Lord shall fall therein.' Strong temptation lies in wait for the young in a great city like this, but let the young man learn of God to cleanse his way, by 'taking heed thereto according to' God's word. May you all be kept from falling and be presented 'faultless before the presence of his glory with exceeding joy'. You are not to be commonly chaste; you are to be much more than that: the very look and thought of impurity are to be hateful to you. Help us, O Spirit of God.

FOR MEDITATION: Even Christians need reminding to steer well clear of immorality (Acts 15:20,29; 1 Corinthians 6:18; 10:8; Ephesians 5:3; Colossians 3:5; 1 Thessalonians 4:3). Even a godly leader can slip into the ungodliest behaviour by small stages. Remember David and Bathsheba—he saw her, he sought information about her, he sent for her and then he sinned with her (2 Samuel 11:2–4).

The lost silver piece

'Either what woman having ten pieces of silver, if she lose one piece, doth not light a candle, and sweep the house, and seek diligently till she find it? And when she hath found it, she calleth her friends and her neighbours together, saying, Rejoice with me; for I have found the piece which I had lost. Likewise, I say unto you, there is joy in the presence of the angels of God over one sinner that repenteth.' Luke 15:8–10
SUGGESTED FURTHER READING: Hebrews 12:22–13:2

She 'calleth her friends and her neighbours together' to share her joy. I am afraid that we do not treat our friends and neighbours with quite enough respect, or remember to invite them to our joys. Who are they? I think the angels are here meant; not only the angels in heaven, but those who are watching here below. Note well, that when the shepherd took home the lost sheep, it is written, 'joy *shall be in heaven* over one sinner that repenteth,' but it does not mention heaven here, nor speak of the future, but it is written, 'there *is* joy in the presence of the angels of God'. Now, the church is on earth, and the Holy Spirit is on earth; when there is a soul saved, the angels down below, who keep watch around the faithful and who are therefore our friends and neighbours, rejoice with us. Do you not know that angels are present in our assemblies? For this reason the apostle Paul tells us that the woman has her head covered in the assembly. He says, 'because of the angels', for they love order and decorum. The angels are wherever the saints are, beholding our orders and rejoicing in our joy. When we see conversions we may bid them rejoice too, and they will praise God with us. I do not suppose the rejoicing ends there; for as angels are always 'ascending and descending upon the Son of man', they soon convey the tidings to the hosts above, and heaven rejoices over one repenting sinner. The joy is a present joy; it is a joy in the house, in the church in her own sphere; it is the joy of her neighbours who are round about her here below. All other joy seems swallowed up in this.

FOR MEDITATION: Angels observe new birth with great joy. They rejoiced at the creation of the world (Job 38:4–7), they rejoiced at Christ's coming into the world (Luke 2:10–14) and they rejoice at the conversion of sinners (Luke 15:10). Have you given them any joy?

SERMON NO. 970

The putting away of sin

'Now once in the end of the world hath he appeared to put away sin by the sacrifice of himself.' Hebrews 9:26
SUGGESTED FURTHER READING: Micah 7:18–20

When Pompey was killed, Julius Caesar obtained possession of a large casket containing correspondence carried on with Pompey. In it there were probably letters from Caesar's followers making overtures to Pompey, and had Caesar read them he could have been so angry with many of his friends that he would have put them to death. Fearing this, he took the casket and destroyed it without reading a single line. What a splendid way of putting away and annihilating all their offences against him! He could not be angry, for he did not know that they had offended. He consumed all their offences and destroyed their iniquities to treat them all as if they were innocent and faithful. The Lord Jesus Christ has made just such an end of our sins. Does not the Lord know our sins then? Yes, in a certain sense, and yet he declares, 'their sins and iniquities will I remember no more.' In one sense God cannot forget, but in another he declares that he remembers not the sins of his people, but has cast them behind his back; 'in that time, saith the Lord, the iniquity of Israel shall be sought for, and there shall be none; and the sins of Judah, and they shall not be found'. An accusing spirit might have said to Caesar, 'Do you not know that Caius and Florus were deeply involved with your enemy, Pompey?' 'No,' he could reply, 'I know nothing against them.' 'But in that casket there is evidence.' 'There remains no casket,' rejoins the hero, 'I have destroyed it.' The metaphor fails because it does not set forth the perfectly legal way in which Jesus has made an end of sin by suffering its penalty. Justice has been satisfied, punishment has been meted out for every sin of ours if we are believers; and all has been accomplished, not by an evasion of law, but by a fulfilment of it, meeting justice face to face, satisfying vengeance and putting away sin.

FOR MEDITATION: God can put your sins as far away from you as east is from west (Psalm 103:12) and behind his back (Isaiah 38:17). He can blot them out as a thick cloud (Isaiah 44:22) and cast them into the depths of the sea (Micah 7:19), but only if you are trusting in Christ who bore them in his body on the cross (Isaiah 53:5–6; 1 Peter 2:24).

SERMON NO. 911

Nearness to God

'But now in Christ Jesus ye who sometimes were far off are made nigh by the blood of Christ.' Ephesians 2:13
SUGGESTED FURTHER READING: Hebrews 10:4–22

A key-phrase of the text is 'by the blood of Christ.' If it be asked what power lies in the blood to bring us nigh, it must be answered, first, that the blood is the symbol of covenant. Always in Scripture when covenants are made, victims are offered and the victim becomes the place and ground of approach between the two covenanting parties. The blood of our Lord Jesus Christ is expressly called 'the blood of the everlasting covenant,' for God comes in covenant near to us by the blood of his only begotten Son. Every man whose faith rests upon the blood of Jesus slain from before the foundation of the world, is in covenant with God, and that covenant becomes to him most sure and certain because it has been ratified by the blood of Jesus Christ, and therefore can never be changed or disannulled. The blood brings us near in another sense, because it is the taking away of the sin which separated us. When we read the word 'blood' as in the text, it means mortal suffering; we are made nigh by the griefs and agonies of the Redeemer. The shedding of blood indicates pain, loss of energy, health, comfort and happiness; but it goes further still—the term 'blood' signifies death. It is the death of Jesus in which we trust. We glory in his life, we triumph in his resurrection, but the ground of our nearness to God lies in his death. The term 'blood', moreover, signifies not a mere expiring, but a painful, ignominious and penal death, a death not brought about by the decay of nature, or the arrows of disease, but caused by the sharp sword of divine vengeance. The word, in fact, refers directly to the crucifixion of our Lord. We are brought nigh to God specially and particularly by a crucified Saviour pouring out his life's blood for us.

FOR MEDITATION: Sin is the only cause of our separation from God (Isaiah 59:2; Romans 3:23); its removal by the blood of Christ crucified is the only means of bringing us back to God (Hebrews 10:19,22; 1 Peter 3:18).

SERMON NO. 851

A personal application

'But now once in the end of the world hath he appeared to put away sin by the sacrifice of himself.' Hebrews 9:26
SUGGESTED FURTHER READING: John 1:9–13

What are you resting in at the present moment? Have you been saying in your soul, 'I am the child of Christian parents; I have never gone into profanity, or open sin; it must be all right with me'? Or have you said in your heart, 'I was christened in my infancy; I have been confirmed; I have paid due attention to the ceremonials of my church, and therefore I am saved'? Or have you said, 'I have kept the commandments from my youth up; I have neither wronged man nor blasphemed God'? I tell you solemnly that these grounds of confidence are utterly worthless. If you could have been saved by your baptism, do you think Christ would have died? If your good works could have opened the gates of heaven for you, do you think that the Christ of God himself would have bled for sinners? If it had been possible for your godly ancestry to have lifted you to the skies, do you suppose that Jesus Christ would have been 'obedient unto death, even the death of the cross'? All other confidence which begins, proceeds and ends with anything else save the person and the work of Jesus, will deceive you in the hour of death and at the day of judgment, and therefore I say to you, do not for a moment entertain it; away with it, confide in it no longer! If I saw you trusting yourself upon a bridge which I knew would snap in the centre when your weight came fairly upon it, I should not be unkind, but only following the instincts of humanity in warning you not to trust in it. And I do so warn you now that other refuge there is none save in Christ Jesus; if you seek another refuge you insult God, you do despite to Jesus Christ and you cast yourself into a tenfold jeopardy, for he that does not believe in Jesus Christ must be lost.

FOR MEDITATION: Read the parable Jesus told to some who were trusting in their own righteousness (Luke 18:9–14). The apostle Paul had more reason than anybody else to have confidence in himself, but he wisely rejected it all as worthless so that he could enjoy God's righteousness through trusting in Christ (Philippians 3:4–9). What precisely are you resting in?

SERMON NO. 962

The arrows of the bow broken in Zion

'There brake he the arrows of the bow, the shield, and the sword, and the battle.' Psalm 76:3
SUGGESTED FURTHER READING: Acts 8:1–8

The more the church has been opposed, the more brightly glorious has she shone forth. God was in the midst of her and helped her; he helped her, and that right early. Our pulse beats fast and our blood grows hot when we read of the persecutions of old pagan Rome. And when we turn to the story of the Reformation and see the hunted ones among the Alps, the Huguenots driven out of France, our own Lollards and the Covenanters of Scotland, we feel proud to belong to such a race of men, we glory in their lineage, and are amazed that the policy of persecution should so long have been considered by shrewd, sharp-witted men, when it ought to have been clear to them that in every case in which they persecuted the church, it multiplied the more exceedingly. God has indeed broken 'the arrows of the bow, the shield, and the sword, and the battle' by sustaining his people in times of persecution. The church has also been assailed with deadly errors. There is scarcely a doctrine of our holy faith which has not been denied. Every age produces a new crop of heretics and infidels. Just as the currents of the times may run, so does the stream of infidelity change its direction. We have lived long enough, some of us, to see three or four species of atheists and deists rise and die, for they are shortlived, an ephemeral generation. We have seen the church attacked by weapons borrowed from geology, ethnology and anatomy, and then from the schools of criticism fierce warriors have issued, but she survives all her antagonists. She has been assailed from almost every quarter, but the fears that tarry in the church today are blown to the wind tomorrow; the church has been enriched by the attacks, for her divines have set to work to study the points that were dubious, to strengthen the walls that seemed a little weak, and so her towers have been strengthened, and her bulwarks consolidated.

FOR MEDITATION: In the face of countless enemies Christians 'are more than conquerors through him that loved us' (Romans 8:37), because he is both stronger (Luke 11:22) and greater (1 John 4:4) than Satan, our very worst opponent.

SERMON NO. 791

Prayer certified of success

'And I say unto you, Ask, and it shall be given you; seek, and ye shall find; knock, and it shall be opened unto you. For every one that asketh receiveth; and he that seeketh findeth; and to him that knocketh it shall be opened.' Luke 11:9–10

SUGGESTED FURTHER READING: Nehemiah 1:1–11

All varieties of true prayer shall meet with responses from heaven. Observe that these varieties of prayer are put on an ascending scale. It is said first that we ask: I suppose that refers to the prayer which is a mere statement of our wants, in which we tell the Lord that we want this and that, and ask him to grant it to us. But as we learn the art of prayer we go on further to seek: which signifies that we marshal our arguments and plead reasons for the granting of our desires, and we begin to wrestle with God for the mercies needed. And if the blessing does not come, we then rise to the third degree, which is knocking: we become importunate; we are not content with asking and giving reasons, but we throw the whole earnestness of our being into our requests, and practise the text which says 'the kingdom of heaven suffereth violence, and the violent take it by force.' So the prayers grow from asking (which is the statement) to seeking (which is the pleading) and to knocking (which is the importuning); to each of these stages of prayer there is a distinct promise. He that asks shall have; what more did he ask for? But he that seeks, going further, shall find, shall enjoy, shall grasp and shall know that he has obtained; and he who knocks shall go further still, for he shall understand, and to him shall the precious thing be opened. He shall not merely have the blessing and enjoy it, but he shall understand it and shall 'comprehend with all saints what is the breadth, and length, and depth, and height'. If you only ask you shall receive, if you seek you shall find, if you knock it shall be opened, but in each case according to your faith shall it be unto you.

FOR MEDITATION: Asking, seeking and knocking all sound very straightforward and simple, but we so often fail to obtain because we seek for ourselves without even bothering to ask God in the first place, or pursue selfish ends when we eventually get round to asking (James 4:2–3).

SERMON NO. 1091

How can I obtain faith?

'So then faith cometh by hearing, and hearing by the word of God.'
Romans 10:17

SUGGESTED FURTHER READING: John 4:7–29

Suppose that you are labouring under a very serious disease, and a physician professes to heal you. You are quite willing to believe in him, but you cannot blindly follow any man, for there are thousands of quacks and impostors. You want to know something about him. Now, in what way would you go to work to get faith in him? How would faith be likely to come to you? It would come by hearing. You hear him speak, and you perceive that he understands your case, for he describes exactly all your symptoms, even those which only you and a skilful physician know. You feel already some confidence in him. He next describes to you as much of the method of cure as you can comprehend, and it seems to you to be very reasonable, and moreover suitable to the requirements of your case. His proposal commends itself to your best judgment, and you are already a stage nearer submission to his mode of operation. Then you enquire as to the man's character; you find that he is no mere pretender, but an authorised, skilful, long-established practitioner, well known for truthfulness, uprightness, and every good quality. Moreover, suppose in addition to this he charges you nothing whatever, but does everything gratis, having evidently no motive of gain, but being altogether disinterested, moved only by real pity for you and a kind desire to remove your pain and save your life. Can you any longer refuse to believe and submit? But if, in addition to all this, he shows you his case-book and bids you read case after case similar to your own in which he has affected perfect cure, and if some of these are your own acquaintances, if they are people whom you know and esteem, surely you will not insult him by saying, 'I wish I could believe you;' but you will be unable to help trusting him, unless you are unwilling to be cured. Faith, in such a case, does not depend upon the will at all; you are convinced by hearing, and you become a believer. In the same way faith comes by hearing.

FOR MEDITATION: Jesus came only for those who admit that they need him to be the Physician of their souls, but even they have to answer his call to repentance (Luke 5:31–32). It is not enough to know that you ought to see a doctor.

The open fountain

'In that day there shall be a fountain opened to the house of David and to the inhabitants of Jerusalem for sin and uncleanness.' Zechariah 13:1
SUGGESTED FURTHER READING: 2 Corinthians 6:14–7:1

It will happen as we grow older and make progress in the Christian life, that we shall discover every day some fresh degree of defilement acquired by our pilgrimage through a sinful world. Do you ever go to rest a single night without feeling that you have been in miry places during the day, and that there is fresh dust upon the garment, new soil upon the feet? Remember every night that there is a fountain opened. Today's sins can be as easily put away as yesterday's sins, and today's sinfulness, which I feel unconquerable for the moment, can be conquered still. I can go to Christ again and say, 'Let thy blood kill this sin of mine and soften my heart into tenderness and holiness once more.' The fountain is still open, and no man can shut it. I know that you in business, coming into contact with the world, must sometimes encounter some very trying circumstances. When perhaps you thought all would be plain sailing you meet with terrible storms. Though minded to live in peace, you fall into a sort of wrestling match with ungodly men; you are obliged to stand up for your own, and you try to do so with moderation of temper, yet your spirit becomes ruffled; and you have to say afterwards, when undergoing self-examination, 'I do not know that I did exactly what I ought to have done; besides, my quiet walk with Christ has been broken by this strife with the sons of men. "Woe is me, that I sojourn in Mesech, that I dwell in the tents of Kedar!"' Beloved, there is a fountain open; go again by simple faith and look to Jesus once again and you will find fresh pardon, and the grace which restores the heart to its repose in Jesus. Your inner life will be again refreshed as you wash in the life-restoring fount prepared for you.

FOR MEDITATION: Even if we practise separation from the world and walk in the light, we still need to be cleansed from sin by the blood of the Lord Jesus Christ (2 Corinthians 6:17–7:1; 1 John 1:7). But deliberately walking in darkness and loving the ways of the world is a denial of the faith (1 John 1:6; 2:15).

SERMON NO. 971

The glorious hereafter and ourselves

'Now he that hath wrought us for the selfsame thing is God, who also hath given unto us the earnest of the Spirit.' 2 Corinthians 5:5
SUGGESTED FURTHER READING: Ephesians 1:11–23

Everything the Holy Spirit works in us is an earnest of heaven. When the Holy Spirit brings to us the joys of hope, this is an earnest. While singing some glowing hymn about the New Jerusalem, our spirit shakes off all her doubts and fears, and anticipates her everlasting heritage. When we enjoy the full assurance of faith, and read our title clear to mansions in the skies, when faith, looking simply to the finished work of Christ, knows whom she has believed, and is persuaded that he is able to keep that which she has committed to him, this is an earnest of heaven. Is not heaven security, confidence, peace? The security, confidence and peace which spring from faith in Jesus Christ are part and parcel of the heaven of the blessed. Heaven is the place of victory, and, my dear friends, when we are victorious over sin, when the Holy Spirit enables us to overcome some propensity, to get down our anger, to crush our pride, to mortify the flesh with its affections and lusts, then in that conscious victory over sin we enjoy an earnest of the triumph of heaven. And once more, when the Holy Spirit gives us to enjoy fellowship with Jesus Christ and with one another, when in the breaking of bread we feel the union which exists between Christ and his members, we have a foretaste of the fellowship of heaven. Do not say then that you know nothing of what heaven is. 'Eye hath not seen, nor ear heard, neither have entered into the heart of man, the things which God hath prepared for them that love him. But God hath revealed them unto us by his Spirit:' spiritual natures do know what heaven is, in the sense of knowing from the drop what the river must be like and of understanding from the ray what the sun must be. Its fulness you cannot measure, its depth you cannot fathom, its unutterable bliss you cannot tell; but still you know what character the glory will be.

FOR MEDITATION: In the life of the Christian on earth 'the fruit of the Spirit is love, joy, peace, longsuffering, gentleness, goodness, faith, meekness, temperance' (Galatians 5:22–23). But as yet the Christian still has only 'the first-fruits of the Spirit' (Romans 8:23) and can look forward in hope of an even better future in eternity.

Constancy and inconstancy—a contrast

'Then shall we know, if we follow on to know the LORD: his going forth is prepared as the morning; and he shall come unto us as the rain, as the latter and former rain unto the earth. O Ephraim, what shall I do unto thee? O Judah, what shall I do unto thee? for your goodness is as a morning cloud, and as the early dew it goeth away.' Hosea 6:3–4

SUGGESTED FURTHER READING (Spurgeon): Luke 8:4–15

The most lasting Christians appear to be those who have seen their inward disease to be very deeply seated and loathsome, and after a while have been led to see the glory of the healing hand of the Lord Jesus as he stretches it out in the gospel. I am afraid that in much modern religion there is a want of depth on all points; they neither deeply tremble nor greatly rejoice; they neither much despair nor much believe. Beware of pious veneering! Beware of the religion which consists in putting on a thin slice of godliness over a mass of carnality. We must have thoroughgoing work within; the grace which reaches the core and affects the innermost spirit is the only grace worth having. To put all in one word, a want of the Holy Spirit is the great cause of religious instability. Beware of mistaking excitement for the Holy Spirit, or your own resolutions for the deep workings of the Spirit of God in the soul. All that nature ever paints God will burn off with hot irons. All that nature ever spins he will unravel and cast away with the rags. You must be born from above; you must have a new nature wrought in you by the finger of God himself, for of all his saints it is written, 'we are his workmanship, created in Christ Jesus'. But I fear there is everywhere a want of the Holy Spirit. There is much getting up of a tawdry morality, barely skin-deep, much crying 'Peace, peace,' where there is no peace, and very little deep heart-searching anxiety to be thoroughly purged from sin. Well-known and well-remembered truths are believed without an accompanying impression of their weight; hopes are flimsily formed, and confidences ill-founded, and it is this which makes deceivers so plentiful.

FOR MEDITATION: Patient perseverance is a far more reliable indicator of genuine Christian faith (Luke 8:15; John 8:31; James 1:25) than short-lived 'conversions' (Mark 4:16–19) which resemble a quick look in the mirror (James 1:23) or a quickly forgotten bath (2 Peter 2:20–22).

SERMON NO. 852

Mary Magdalene

'Mary Magdalene, out of whom he had cast seven devils.' Mark 16:9
SUGGESTED FURTHER READING (Spurgeon): John 20:11–18

When Jesus said 'Mary', I can imagine that the word brought up all her history before her mind, her demoniac days, when her distracted mind was tossed on fiery billows, her happy days, when she sat at her Master's feet and caught his blessed words, the times when she had seen his miracles and wondered, and when she had given him of her substance, and had been glad to minister unto him. If we love Jesus much and cannot be content without him, we too may expect to hear him in the secret of our soul, calling us by name. He will say 'I have called thee by thy name; thou art mine.' Then Mary Magdalene had such a manifestation of Christ's glory as no other woman ever had. It has been beautifully remarked by one of our dear brethren in the ministry (Rev. Alexander Moody Stuart, in his book *The three Marys*), that the expression, 'Touch me not' shows to us that Mary had gone further in communion than most of us ever think of going, because she had drawn as near to Jesus as she might be allowed to go. Jesus said 'Touch me not'. You and I need not be afraid of his saying that to us; we do not make it necessary. We are at such a distance that he would have to say 'Come near, and nearer still;' but as for Mary, her heart was so knit to Christ that she approached so near to him in love, that the Lord knew she could not bear any more and that her higher joys must be reserved for a higher sphere, and therefore he bade her pause. Besides, he would have her know that he was her Lord and Master as well as her friend. Affection must not degenerate into familiarity: he must be reverenced as well as loved. Very different was his dealing with Thomas. He commanded him to touch. Thomas was such a weak thing; he needed that help, but Mary did not need it; her heart was knit to him and leapt for joy, and Jesus, having given her as much joy as she could hold, stayed her hand.

FOR MEDITATION: We ought to draw near to God (Psalm 73:28; Hebrews 10:22; James 4:8); but bear in mind that Moses was not allowed to draw too near, even when God called him by name (Exodus 3:4–5). Knowing God should not be confused with over-familiarity.

Questions of the day and the question of the day

'*What think ye of Christ?*' *Matthew* 22:42
SUGGESTED FURTHER READING: Romans 13:1–7

'Unto Caesar the things which are Caesar's;' to maintain order, to repress crime, to preserve individual liberty, to protect each man's rights, this is Caesar's business. To teach us religion? Is Caesar to do that? God forbid, for what religion will Caesar teach us? Is he a Pagan? He will enforce idolatry. Is he a Papist? He will ordain Popery. Is he an atheist? He will establish infidelity. Remember the days of Queen Mary and see what Caesar is capable of when he meddles with religion. It is none of Caesar's business to deal with our consciences, neither will we ever obey Caesar in any matter which touches conscience. He may make what laws he will about religion, but by our loyalty to God we pour contempt on Caesar when he usurps the place of God. He is no more to us than the meanest beggar in the street if he goes beyond his legitimate authority. To Caesar, Caesar's; politics to politicians; obedience, cheerful and prompt, to civil rulers: to God, and to God only, the things that are God's; and what are these? Our hearts, our souls, our consciences. Man himself is the coin upon which God has stamped his image and superscription (though, alas, both are sadly marred), and we must render to God our manhood, our wills, our thoughts, our judgments, our minds, our hearts. Consciences are for God. Any law that touches a conscience is null and void ipso facto, for the simple reason that kings and parliaments have no right to interfere in the realm of conscience. Conscience is under law to none but God. We do not believe in liberty of conscience towards God. We are bound towards him to believe what he tells us and to do what he bids us; but liberty of conscience in respect to all mankind is the natural right of every man of woman born, and it ought to be tenderly respected.

FOR MEDITATION: Christians ought to be models of civil obedience (1 Peter 2:13–15), but fearing God should take priority over honouring the king (1 Peter 2:17). When we are expected to render unto Caesar the things which are God's, 'We ought to obey God rather than men.' (Acts 5:29).

SERMON NO. 1093

For the troubled

'Thy wrath lieth hard upon me, and thou hast afflicted me with all thy waves.' Psalm 88:7

SUGGESTED FURTHER READING: 2 Corinthians 1:3–7

Our sufferings are of great service to us when God blesses them, for they help us to be useful to others. It must be a terrible thing for a man never to have suffered physical pain. You say, 'I should like to be that man.' But, unless you had extraordinary grace, you would grow hard and cold, you would get to be a sort of cast-iron man, breaking other people with your touch. No, let my heart be tender, even be soft, if it must be softened by pain, for I would gladly know how to bind up my fellow's wound. Let my eye have a tear ready for my brother's sorrows even if, for that to be so, I should have to shed ten thousand for my own. An escape from suffering would be an escape from the power to sympathise, and that ought to be deprecated beyond all things. Luther was right when he said that affliction was the best book in the minister's library. How can the man of God sympathise with the afflicted ones, if he knows nothing at all about their troubles? I remember a hard miserly fellow, who said that the minister ought to be very poor, so that he might have sympathy with the poor. I told him I thought he ought to have a turn at being very rich too, so that he might have sympathy with the very rich; and I suggested to him that perhaps, upon the whole, it would be handiest to keep him somewhere in the middle, so that he might the more easily range over the experience of all classes. If the man of God who is to minister to others could always be robust, it would perhaps be a loss; if he could always be sickly, it might be equally so; but for the pastor to be able to range through all the places where the Lord suffers his sheep to go, is doubtless to the advantage of the flock. And what it is to ministers, that it will be to each one of you, according to his calling, for the consolation of the people of God.

FOR MEDITATION: Our ability to weep with those who weep (Romans 12:15) is enhanced by our own experiences of suffering (2 Corinthians 1:4; Hebrews 5:2). Because of his own sufferings the Lord Jesus Christ is especially qualified to help us and sympathise with us (Hebrews 2:18; 4:15).

Faith's dawn and its clouds

'And straightway the father of the child cried out, and said with tears, Lord, I believe; help thou mine unbelief.' Mark 9:24
SUGGESTED FURTHER READING: John 20:24–31

This poor man did not say, 'Lord, I believe, but have some doubts,' and mention it as if it were a mere matter of common intelligence which did not grieve him. No, he said it with tears; he made a sorrowful confession of it. It was not the mere statement of a fact, but it was the acknowledgment of a fault. With tears he said, 'Lord, I believe' and then acknowledged his unbelief. Learn then always to see unbelief in Christ in the light of a fault. Never say, 'This is my infirmity,' but say, 'This is my sin.' In the Church of God there has been too much of regarding unbelief as though it were a calamity commanding sympathy, rather than a fault demanding censure as well. I am not to say to myself, 'I am unbelieving, and therefore I am to be pitied.' No, 'I am unbelieving, and therefore I must blame myself for it.' Why should I disbelieve my God? How dare I doubt him who cannot lie? How can I mistrust the faithful promiser who has added to his promise his oath, and over and above his promise and his oath has given his own blood as a seal, 'that by two immutable things, in which it was impossible for God to lie, we might have a strong consolation'. Chide yourselves, you doubters. Doubts are among the worst enemies of your soul. Do not entertain them. Do not treat them as though they were poor forlorn travellers to be hospitably entertained, but as rogues and vagabonds to be chased from your door. Fight and slay them, and pray God to help you kill and bury them and not even to leave a bone or a piece of a bone of a doubt above ground. Doubting and unbelief are to be abhorred and to be confessed with tears as sins before God. We need pardon for doubting as much as for blasphemy. We ought no more to excuse doubting than lying, for doubting slanders God and makes him a liar.

FOR MEDITATION: Unbelief is the companion of perversity (Matthew 17:17–21). It is evil, destructive and a bad example to follow (Hebrews 3:12,19; 4:6,11). The best thing to do with unbelief is to resist it as Abraham did (Romans 4:20).

The power of Christ illustrated by the resurrection

'For our conversation is in heaven; from whence also we look for the Saviour, the Lord Jesus Christ: who shall change our vile body, that it may be fashioned like unto his glorious body, according to the working whereby he is able even to subdue all things unto himself.' Philippians 3:20–21
SUGGESTED FURTHER READING: Acts 9:1–22

There is no man in this world so fallen, debased, depraved, and wilfully wicked, that Jesus cannot save him—not even among those who live beyond the reach of ordinary ministry. He can bring the heathen to the gospel, or the gospel to them. The wheels of providence can be so arranged that salvation shall be brought to the outcasts; even war, famine and plague may become messengers for Christ, for he too rides upon the wings of the wind. There lived some few years ago in Perugia, in Italy, a man of the loosest morals and the worst conceivable disposition. He had given up all religion, he loathed God, and he had arrived at such a desperate state of mind that he had conceived an affection for the devil, and endeavoured to worship the evil one. Imagining Satan to be the image and embodiment of all rebellion, free-thinking and lawlessness, he deified him in his own mind and desired nothing better than to be a devil himself. On one occasion, when a Protestant missionary had been in Perugia preaching, a priest happened to say in this man's hearing that there were Protestants in Perugia and that the city was being defiled by heretics. 'And who do you think Protestants are?' said he. 'They are men who have renounced Christ and worship the devil.' A gross and outrageous lie was this, but it answered far other ends than its author meant. The man, hearing this, thought, 'Then I will go and meet with them, for I am much of their mind;' and away he went to the Protestant meeting in the hope of finding an assembly who propagated lawlessness and worshipped the devil. He there heard the gospel and was saved. Behold in this and in ten thousand cases equally remarkable, the ability of our King to subdue all things unto himself.

FOR MEDITATION: Consider the great abilities of Christ. He is able to subdue everything to himself (Philippians 3:21), he is able to succour the tempted (Hebrews 2:18) and he is able to save to the uttermost all who come to God by him (Hebrews 7:25). But he does not force his great abilities upon those who deliberately persist in unbelief (Matthew 13:58; Mark 6:5–6).

SERMON NO. 973

Method and music, or the art of holy and happy living

'And whatsoever ye do in word or deed, do all in the name of the Lord Jesus, giving thanks to God and the Father by him.' Colossians 3:17

SUGGESTED FURTHER READING: Ephesians 4:17–24

We should do all under the sanction of the Lord Jesus as our exemplar. It is an admirable course for us all to pursue, if when we find ourselves in circumstances of perplexity we ask ourselves the question, 'What would Jesus Christ have done if he were in my circumstances?' The answer to that question is the solution to your difficulty. Whatever he would have done, it will be safe enough for you to do. It is certain that he would not have been unbelieving, equally certain that he would not have done a wrong thing to deliver himself. We are also sure that he would not have been impatient, rebellious or despairing, nor would he have grown wrathful or morose. Well then, I know what I must *not* be; it may be possible to learn my positive as well as my negative behaviour from the same guide. By turning over the pages of the evangelists I shall be able to discover some portion of the Saviour's life very like my own; what he was in that situation I must ask for grace that I may be, and I shall certainly be led in the path of wisdom. The royal rule for a Christian is not what is fashionable, for we are not to be conformed to this world, not what is gainful, for the pursuit of gain would lead us to run greedily in the way of Balaam for reward, not that which is generally prescribed in society, for full often the prescriptions of society are antagonistic to the teachings of Christ, not even the conduct of professors, for too many even among them walk as Paul tells us 'even weeping, that they are the enemies of the cross of Christ:' alas, my brethren, the current holiness of the church falls far below the scriptural standard; neither are the common rules of action among professors such as we could safely follow. A safe example is to be found nowhere but in the life of Jesus Christ himself; even the holiest of men are to be followed only as far as they follow Christ, but no further.

FOR MEDITATION: Consider the negative example of the Lord Jesus Christ in 1 Peter 2:21–23. He did not sin, no guile was in his mouth, he did not revile those who reviled him and he did not threaten his persecutors. Negatives like these can have enormous positive implications (Romans 13:9,10).

A sermon for the most miserable of men

'My soul refused to be comforted.' Psalm 77:2
SUGGESTED FURTHER READING: Psalm 42:1–11

Barnabas, the son of consolation, would be hard pressed to cheer the victims of depression when their fits are on them. The oil of joy is poured out in vain for those heads upon which the dust and ashes of melancholy are heaped. Brethren, at such times the unhappy should wisely consider whether their disturbed minds ought not to have rest from labour. In these days, when everybody travels by express and works like a steam-engine, the mental wear and tear are terrible, and the advice of the Great Master to the disciples to go into the desert and rest awhile is full of wisdom and ought to have our earnest attention. Rest is the best, if not the only medicine for men occupied in mental pursuits and subject to frequent depression of spirit. Get away, you sons of sadness, from your ordinary vocations for a little season if you possibly can, and enjoy quiet and repose; above all, escape from your cares by casting them upon God: if you bear them yourself, they will distract you, so that your soul will refuse to be comforted; but if you will leave them to God and endeavour to serve him without distraction, you will overcome the drooping tendency of your spirits and you will yet compass the altar of God with songs of gladness. Let none of us give way to an irritable, complaining, mournful temperament. It is the giving way which is the master-mischief, for it is only as we resist this devil that it will flee from us. Let not your *heart* be troubled. If the troubles outside the soul toss your vessel and drive her to and fro, yet, at least, strain every nerve to keep the seas outside her, lest she sink altogether. Cry with David, 'Why art thou cast down, O my soul? And why art thou disquieted within me?' Never mourn unreasonably. Question yourself about the causes of your tears; reason about the matter till you come to the same conclusion as the psalmist, 'Hope thou in God; for I shall yet praise him'.

FOR MEDITATION: Despondency has afflicted great men of God (Ecclesiastes 2:18–20; 2 Corinthians 1:8). What a difference is made by renewed hope in God (Psalm 43:5; 146:5; 2 Corinthians 1:9–10).

Always, and for all things

'Giving thanks always for all things unto God and the Father in the name of our Lord Jesus Christ.' Ephesians 5:20

SUGGESTED FURTHER READING: Psalm 50:14–23

The position of our text in the epistle is worthy of observation. It follows the precept with regard to sacred songs, in which believers are bidden to speak to themselves and one another in psalms and hymns and spiritual songs, singing and making melody in their hearts to the Lord. If they cannot be always singing they are always to maintain the spirit of song. If they must of necessity desist at intervals from outward expressions of praise, they ought never to refrain from inwardly giving thanks. The apostle Paul, having touched upon the act of singing in public worship, here points out the essential part of it, which lies not in classic music and thrilling harmonies but in the melody of the heart. Thanksgiving is the soul of all acceptable singing. Note also that our text immediately precedes the apostle's exhortation to believers concerning the common duties of ordinary life. The saints are to give thanks to God always, and then to fulfil their duties to their fellow men. The apostle writes, 'submitting yourselves one to another in the fear of God.' He then adds the various branches of holy walking which belong to wives and to husbands, to children and to parents, to servants and to masters; so that it would seem that thanksgiving is the preface to a holy life, the foundation of obedience and the vestibule of sanctity. He who would serve God must begin by praising God, for a grateful heart is the mainspring of obedience. We must offer the salt of gratitude with the sacrifice of obedience; our lives should be anointed with the precious oil of thankfulness. As soldiers march to music, so while we walk in the paths of righteousness we should keep step to the notes of thanksgiving. Larks sing as they mount; so should we magnify the Lord for his mercies while we are winging our way to heaven.

FOR MEDITATION: If, as Spurgeon says, thanksgiving is the preface to a holy life, the foundation of obedience and the vestibule of sanctity, is it any surprise that the companions of unthankfulness and ingratitude make for unpleasant reading (Romans 1:21; 2 Timothy 3:2–5)?

Nearer and dearer

'I sleep, but my heart waketh: it is the voice of my beloved that knocketh, saying, Open to me, ... I have put off my coat; how shall I put it on? I have washed my feet; how shall I defile them? My beloved put in his hand by the hole of the door, ... I rose up to open to my beloved; ... I opened to my beloved; but my beloved had withdrawn himself, and was gone: ... I sought him, but I could not find him.' Song of Solomon 5:2–6
SUGGESTED FURTHER READING: Revelation 3:1–6

'A little folding of the hands to sleep'. I fear that there are thousands of God's children who are awake enough to know that they are asleep, convinced enough of their wrong to know that they are wrong and to hope that they will one day be better, but, alas, they continue in the same unhallowed condition. May I invite every believer to make a strict examination of his own spiritual state. My brother, you may be sleeping due to great worldly prosperity, for nothing tends to slumber more surely than a gentle rocking in the cradle of luxury. On the other hand, you may be sleeping because of overwhelming sorrow, even as the twelve fell asleep when our Lord was in the garden. Some make a downy pillow of their wealth, but others fall asleep in their poverty, like Jacob with a stone for his pillow. To be surrounded with constant worldly occupation, to be oppressed with many cares in business, this is to pass through the enchanted ground; and happy is the man who has grace enough to overcome the influence of his position. Now, if your heart today is sufficiently awake to tell you that you are not living as near to God as you were some years ago, that you have not the love for him you once had, that your warmth and zeal for Christ has departed from you, I beseech you, hear the voice of Jesus Christ: 'As many as I love, I rebuke and chasten: be zealous therefore, and repent.' 'Repent, and do the first works'. Turn unto your Saviour now, that this very day before the sun goes down you may rejoicingly exclaim, 'I found him whom my soul loveth: I held him, and would not let him go'.

FOR MEDITATION: The unconverted are spiritually dead and sound asleep and must wake up (Ephesians 5:14). Christians are spiritually alive, but have to make the effort to stay awake (Romans 13:11; 1 Corinthians 15:34; 1 Thessalonians 5:6; Revelation 3:2).

SERMON NO. 793

The alarum

'I myself will awake early.' Psalm 57:8
SUGGESTED FURTHER READING (Spurgeon): 1 Thessalonians 5:1–11

'Will awake'. This is a world in which most men nowadays are alive to their temporal interests. If in these pushing times any man goes to his business in a sleepy, listless fashion, he very soon finds himself on an ebb-tide with all his affairs aground. The wide-awake man seizes opportunities or makes them, and thus those who are widest awake usually come to the front. Years ago affairs moved like the broad-wheel waggon, very sleepily, with sober pause and leisurely progression, and then the son of the snail had a chance; but now, when we almost fly, if a man would succeed in trade, he must be all alive and all awake. If it be so in temporals, it is equally so in spirituals, for the world, the flesh and the devil are all awake to compete with us; and there is no resolution that I would more earnestly commend to each one of the people of God than this one: 'I will awake; I will awake at once; I will awake early, and I will pray to God that I may be kept awake, that my Christian existence may not be dreamy, but that I may be to the fullest degree useful in my Master's service.' If this were the resolve of each, what a change would come over the Christian church! I long to see the diligence of the shop exceeded by the closet, and the zeal of the market excelled by the church. Each Christian is alive: but is he also awake? He has eyes, but are they open? He has lofty possibilities of blessing his fellow men, but does he exercise them? My heart's desire is that none of us may feel the dreamy influence of this age, which is comparable to the enchanted ground, but that each of us may be watchful, wakeful, vigorous, intense, fervent.

FOR MEDITATION: If we are not properly awake in the first place, it will not be possible for us to sing for joy (Isaiah 26:19), to stand up (Isaiah 51:17) or to see Christ's glory (Luke 9:32). Sleepy Christianity never achieves much good.

The only atoning priest

'But this man, after he had offered one sacrifice for sins for ever, sat down on the right hand of God; from henceforth expecting till his enemies be made his footstool. For by one offering he hath perfected for ever them that are sanctified.' Hebrews 10:12–14
SUGGESTED FURTHER READING: 2 Thessalonians 2:13–17

God's people are described in the text as 'them that are sanctified' and you must beware of misunderstanding that word as though it meant those who are made perfectly holy in character. The word implies an inward work of grace, but it means a great deal more. The passage should be read 'he hath perfected for ever them that *are being sanctified*', for it is in the present in the Greek. The text is not to be made to say that those who are perfectly sanctified are perfected; that would be a commonplace, self-evident truth. But the great high priest perfected for ever those who are being sanctified. Sanctification means primarily the setting apart of a people by God to be holy to himself. Election is sanctification virtually; all God's people were sanctified—set apart and made holy to the Lord—in the eternal purpose and sovereign decree before the earth ever was. Christ has by his death perfected all who were sanctified or set apart in election. This purpose of sanctification is carried out further when those set apart are called out by grace. When effectual grace separates men from the world by conversion and regeneration, they then become, in another sense, the sanctified; they are set apart even as Christ set himself apart, dedicated to God's service and separated from sinners. As the work which began at regeneration is continued and carried on in them, they are in another aspect sanctified; they are realising in themselves that sanctification or dedication to God, which was theirs from before the foundation of the world. The text relates not only to those in heaven who are perfectly sanctified, but also to all who were set apart in the purposes of grace, in that as far as their pardon and justification are concerned, Christ perfected them for ever when he offered up himself without spot unto God.

FOR MEDITATION: Being set apart for God of necessity involves being set apart from ungodliness (1 Corinthians 6:9–11; 1 Thessalonians 4:3; 2 Timothy 2:21–22). To what extent, if any, are you sanctified?

SERMON NO. 1034

Compassion for souls

'She went, and sat down over against him a good way off, as it were a bowshot; for she said, Let me not see the death of the child. And she sat over against him, and lift up her voice, and wept.' Genesis 21:16
SUGGESTED FURTHER READING: 2 Corinthians 5:11–6:2

If we did really know what souls are, and what it is for them to be cast away, those of us who have done very little or nothing would begin to work for Christ directly. It is said in an old story that a certain king of Lydia had a son who had been dumb from birth, but when Lydia was captured, a soldier was about to kill the king, when the young man suddenly found his tongue and cried out, 'Soldier, would you kill the king?' He had never spoken a word before, but his astonishment and fear gave him speech. I think if you had been dumb to that moment, if you indeed saw your own children and neighbours going down into the pit, you would cry out, 'Though I never spoke before, I will speak now. Poor souls, believe in Christ, and you shall be saved.' You do not know how such an utterance as that, however simple, might be blessed. A very little child once found herself in company with an old man in his eighties, a fine old man who loved little children and who took the child upon his knee. Turning round to him, the little one said, 'Sir, I got a grandpa just like you, and my grandpa love Jesus Christ. Does you?' He said, 'I was eighty-four years of age and had always lived among Christian people, but nobody ever thought it worth his while to say as much as that to me.' That little child was the instrument of the old man's conversion. He knew he had not loved the Saviour, and he began to seek him, and in his old age he found salvation. If as much as that is possible for a child, it is possible for you. If you love Jesus, burst the bonds of timidity or, it may be, supineness; snap all fetters, and from this day feel that you cannot bear to think of the ruin of a soul, and must seek its salvation if there be in earth or heaven ways and means by which you can bring a blessing to it.

FOR MEDITATION: There is a time to keep silence (Ecclesiastes 3:7), but not when we are supposed to be God's messengers to others. God has ways of enabling his people to break their guilty silence (2 Kings 7:9; Psalm 39:1–3; Jeremiah 20:9; Ezekiel 33:8).

SERMON NO. 974

Work in us and work by us

'Whereunto I also labour, striving according to his working, which worketh in me mightily.' Colossians 1:29
SUGGESTED FURTHER READING: 1 Corinthians 9:24–27

Our life is in Scripture represented as a race. In such foot-races as were witnessed among the Greeks, in every case the man spent all the strength there was in him, and underwent a training beforehand that he might be fit for the contest. It sometimes happened, and indeed not seldom, that men fell dead at the winning-post through their extreme exertions. Running to heaven is such running as that; we are to strain every nerve. We shall require all the power we have and more, in order to win that incorruptible crown which now glitters before the eye of our faith. If we are so to run that we may obtain, we shall have no energy to spare, but shall spend it all in our heavenly course. Not unfrequently the apostle compares our spiritual life to a boxing match; if the terms in the original Greek were translated into pure vernacular English, they would remind us very much of a boxing ring and of the place where wrestlers strive for the mastery. We are told by scholars that the Greek word in that notable passage, 'I keep under my body', alludes to the getting of the antagonist's head under the arm and dealing it heavy blows. So the flesh must be mortified. The wrestlers in the Greek and Roman games strained every muscle and sinew; there was no part of the body that was not brought into action to overthrow their adversary. For this they agonised often till blood would spurt from the nostrils and veins would burst. Such in a spiritual sense must be the agony of a Christian if he is to overcome temptation and subdue the power of sin. It is no child's play to win heaven. Though saved through the power of Christ's blood and with the energy of his Holy Spirit within us, yet we have no time to loiter, no space in which to trifle; you and I must 'labour, striving according to his working, which worketh in me mightily.'

FOR MEDITATION: The Christian life has been described as fighting a good fight (1 Timothy 6:12) and running a race according to the rules (2 Timothy 2:5) and with patience (Hebrews 12:1). The apostle Paul excelled in both disciplines (2 Timothy 4:7). Resist the temptations to stop fighting (Psalm 78:9; Hebrews 10:32–39) and to stop running well (Galatians 5:7).

Fire—the want of the times

'I am come to send fire on the earth; and what will I, if it be already kindled?' Luke 12:49
SUGGESTED FURTHER READING: 2 Kings 17:24–40

All through this world of ours the gospel will burn up with unquenchable fire everything that is evil, and leave nothing but that which is just and true. Of all things under heaven, the most intolerant is the gospel of Jesus Christ. 'What,' say you, 'intolerant?' Yes, I say, intolerant. The gospel enables us to proclaim liberty of conscience to all men; the gospel wields no temporal sword; it asks for no cannon balls to open the gates of a nation to its ministry: the true gospel prepares no dungeon and no rack; it asks not Peter's sword to cut off Malchus' ear: but while it gives enfranchisement from all bondage, it demands obedience to itself. Within its own realm its power is absolute; its arguments cut and kill error; its teachings lay low every proud hope and expose every false way. The gospel is merciful to the sinner, but merciless to sin. It will not endure evil, but wars against it to overturn it and to set up a throne for him whose right it is to reign. The gospel of Jesus Christ will never join hands with infidelity or Popery. It will never enter into league with idolatry. It cannot be at peace with error. False religions can lie down side by side with one another, for they are equally a lie and there is a brotherhood between them, but the true religion will never rest until all superstitions are utterly exterminated, and until the banner of the King eternal, immortal, invisible, shall wave over every mosque and minaret, temple and shrine. Fire cannot be made tolerant of that which can be consumed; it will burn the stubble until the last particle is gone, and the truth of God is of the same kind.

FOR MEDITATION: False religions and false imitations of Christianity may need to resort to force to win over others, but the Christian's enemies, weapons and armour are spiritual, not physical (2 Corinthians 10:3–6; Ephesians 6:10–13). Paul had every confidence in the power of the gospel message (Romans 1:16; Ephesians 6:15,19–20). Do you?

SERMON NO. 854

The monster dragged to light

'Sin, that it might appear sin, working death in me by that which is good; that sin by the commandment might become exceeding sinful.' Romans 7:13

SUGGESTED FURTHER READING: 1 John 5:13–21

There is a depth of meaning in the expression, 'Sin, that it might appear sin'—as if the apostle could find no other word so terribly descriptive of sin as its own name. He does not say, 'Sin, that it might appear like Satan.' No, for sin is worse than the devil, since it made the devil what he is. Satan as an existence is God's creature, and this sin never was; its origin and nature are altogether apart from God. Sin is even worse than hell, for it is the sting of that dreadful punishment. Anselm used to say that if hell were on one side, and sin on the other, he would rather leap into hell, than willingly sin against God. Paul does not say, 'Sin, that it might appear madness.' Truly it is moral insanity, but it is worse than that by far. It is so bad that there is no name for it but itself. One of our poets who wished to show how evil sin looks in the presence of redeeming love, could only say,

'When the wounds of Christ exploring, Sin doth like itself appear.'

If you need an illustration of what is meant, we might find one in Judas. If you wanted to describe him, you might say he was a traitor, a thief and a betrayer of innocent blood, but you would finish up by saying, 'he was a Judas.' That gives you all in one: none could match him in villainy. If you wished a man to feel a horror of murder, you would not wish murder to appear to him as manslaughter, or as destruction of life, or as mere cruelty, but you would want it to appear as *murder*; you could use no stronger expression. So here, when the Lord turns the strong light of his eternal Spirit upon sin and reveals it in all its hideousness and defilement, it appears to be not only moral discord, disorder, deformity or corruption, but neither more nor less than sin.

FOR MEDITATION: Do you dislike preachers going on about sin? The Bible is full of it. Unless we understand that sin is so appalling and that we are all guilty of it (Romans 3:23; 5:12), we will never begin to comprehend the wonder of God's love in sending Christ to die to save sinners from their sin (Matthew 1:21; Romans 5:8; 1 Timothy 1:15).

Jesus and the lambs

'He shall gather the lambs with his arm, and carry them in his bosom.'
Isaiah 40:11
SUGGESTED FURTHER READING: Matthew 18:5–14

The divine gentleness of our Master has been shown in *the solemn curses with which he effectually guarded the little ones.* Observe how sharp they are! 'But whoso shall offend one of these little ones which believe in me, it were better for him that a millstone were hanged about his neck, and that he were drowned in the depth of the sea.' To offend is to put a stumbling block in the way. How solemn is that warning, 'Take heed that ye despise not one of these little ones'! He must have loved them, or he would not have set such a hedge of fire around them. How many of *the promises are made on purpose for the weak.* I shall not repeat them, because your own study of the word of God must have shown you how the gracious word is framed to the peculiar condition of distress and weakness under which the lambs are suffering. The Holy Spirit with divine art brings home to the heart promises which had never else appeared to be so full of grace. Brethren, the Lord Jesus Christ's tenderness to his people is further shown in this, that *what he requires of them is easy.* 'Take my yoke upon you, and learn of me; ... For my yoke is easy, and my burden is light.' He does not command the babes to preach. He does not send the weak believers to the forefront of the battle, as David did to Uriah, that they may be slain: he gives them no other burden than this, that they will trust him, and give him all their heart. A yoke, how easy! He shows his gentleness, moreover, in that *he accepts the least service that these little ones may offer.* A faint prayer, a sigh, a tear—he will receive all these as much as the most eloquent pleadings of an Elijah. The broken alabaster box and the ointment poured out shall be received, though they come from one who has no former character with which to back the gift; the two mites shall not be disowned. The best work sincerely done out of love to Jesus in dependence upon him, he accepts most cheerfully and thus shows to us his real tenderness for the lambs.

FOR MEDITATION: God's gentleness and tenderness towards his people (Luke 1:78; James 5:11) ought to inspire us to go and do likewise (2 Corinthians 10:1; Ephesians 4:32). Sadly, it doesn't always happen (Matthew 18:26–30).

SERMON NO. 794

The King feasting in his garden

'I am come into my garden, my sister, my spouse: I have gathered my myrrh with my spice; I have eaten my honeycomb with my honey; I have drunk my wine with my milk: eat, O friends; drink, yea, drink abundantly, O beloved.' Song of Solomon 5:1
SUGGESTED FURTHER READING: Isaiah 43:1–7

Permit me to call your attention to those many great little words, which are yet but one—I refer to the word 'my'. Observe that eight or nine times it is repeated. Here is the reason for the solace which the bridegroom finds in his church. Does he walk in the church as men do in a garden for pleasure? Then he says, 'I am come into *my* garden'. Does he talk with his beloved? It is because he calls her '*my* sister, *my* spouse'. Does he love her prayers and praises? It is because they never would be prayed or praised if he had not created these fruits of the lips. He says not, 'I have gathered *your* myrrh with *your* spice;' no, viewed as ours these are poor things, but viewed as his they are most acceptable—'I have gathered *my* myrrh with *my* spice'. So if he finds any honey in his people, any true love in them, he first put it there. 'I have eaten *my* honeycomb with *my* honey'. Yes, and if there be any joy and life in them to make his heart glad, he calls it '*my* wine with *my* milk'. When I read these words and thought of our Lord being fed by us, I could almost have cried out, 'Lord, when saw we thee an hungered, and fed thee? or thirsty, and gave thee drink?' 'Dost thou find any satisfaction in us? Surely, our goodness extendeth not to thee. Whence should we give thee anything to eat?' Yet he declares it, and we may blushingly believe him and praise his name, for surely if he found it so, it is because he made it so. If he has got anything out of us, he must first have put it in us; if he sees 'of the travail of his soul', it is because the travail came first.

FOR MEDITATION: Without faith it is impossible to please God (Hebrews 11:6), but there seems to be no limit to the pleasure he takes in those who fear him and who place their hope in him (Psalm 147:11).

The real presence, the great want of the church

'It was but a little that I passed from them, but I found him whom my soul loveth: I held him, and would not let him go, until I had brought him into my mother's house, and into the chamber of her that conceived me. I charge you, O ye daughters of Jerusalem, by the roes, and by the hinds of the field, that ye stir not up, nor awake my love, till he please.' Song of Solomon 3:4–5

SUGGESTED FURTHER READING (Spurgeon): John 15:1–11

Whenever you have Christ, please remember that you are able to hold him. She who held him in the Song was no stronger than you are; she was but a feeble woman, poorly fed under the Old Testament dispensation; you have drunk the new wine of the new covenant, and you are stronger than she. You can hold him, and he will not be able to go from you. 'How,' say you, 'shall I be able to hold him?' Have you grasped him? Is he with you? Now, then, hold him fast by your faith; trust him implicitly, rest in him for every day's cares, for every moment's ills. Walk by faith and he will walk with you. Hold him also with the grasp of love. Let your whole heart go out towards him. Embrace him with the arms of mighty affection; enchain him with ardent admiration. Lay hold upon him by faith and clasp him with love. Be also much in prayer. Prayer casts a chain about him. He never leaves the heart that prays. There is a sweet perfume about prayer that always attracts the Lord; wherever he perceives it rising up to heaven, there will he be. Hold him, too, by your obedience to him. Never quarrel with him. Let him have his way. He will stop in any house where he can be master; he will stay nowhere where some other will lord it over him. Watch his words; be careful to obey them all. Be very tender in your conduct, so that nothing grieves him. Show to him that you are ready to suffer for his sake. I believe that where there is a prayerful, careful, holy, loving, believing walk towards Jesus, the fellowship of the saint with his Lord will not be broken, but it may continue for months and years. There is no reason, except in ourselves, why fellowship with Jesus should not continue.

FOR MEDITATION: Christ promises to abide in us, on condition that we abide in him (John 15:4–7; 1 John 3:24). For some other practical thoughts on what it means to abide in him read Psalm 15, 1 John 2:10,24 and 2 John 9.

SERMON NO. 1035

The parable of the wedding feast

'The kingdom of heaven is like unto a certain king, which made a marriage for his son, ... saying, Tell them which are bidden, Behold, I have prepared my dinner: my oxen and my fatlings are killed, and all things are ready: come unto the marriage.' Matthew 22:2,4
SUGGESTED FURTHER READING: Isaiah 25:6–9

The generous method by which God honours Christ is set forth here under the form of a banquet. I noted Matthew Henry's way of describing the objects of a feast, and with the alliteration of the Puritans he says, 'A feast is for love and for laughter, for fulness and for fellowship.' It is even so with the gospel. It is for *love*; in the gospel, sinner, you are invited to be reconciled to God, you are assured that God forgives your sins, ceases to be angry, and would have you reconciled to him through his Son. Thus love is established between God and the soul. Then it is for *laughter*, for happiness, for joy. Those who come to God in Christ Jesus and believe in him, have their hearts filled with overflowing peace; this calm lake of peace often lifts up itself in waves of joy. It is not to sorrow but to joy that the great King invites his subjects, when he glorifies his Son Jesus. It is not that you may be distressed, but delighted, that he bids you believe in the crucified Saviour and live. A feast, moreover, is for *fulness*. The hungry, famished soul is satisfied with the blessings of grace. The gospel fills the whole capacity of our manhood. There is not a faculty of our nature which is not made to feel its need supplied when the soul accepts the provisions of mercy; our whole manhood is satisfied with good things and our youth is renewed like the eagles. 'For I have satiated the weary soul, and I have replenished every sorrowful soul.' To crown all, the gospel brings us into *fellowship* with the Father and his Son Jesus Christ. In Christ Jesus we commune with the sacred Trinity. God becomes our Father and reveals his paternal heart. Jesus manifests himself unto us as he does not unto the world, and the communion of the Holy Spirit abides with us.

FOR MEDITATION: Consider the four objects of a feast—love (Song of Solomon 2:4), laughter (Proverbs 15:15), fulness (Isaiah 25:6; John 7:37–38), fellowship (Revelation 3:20). All four are in the Saviour's description of the Father welcoming home the prodigal son (Luke 15:20–24). How many of them describe your relationship with God?

SERMON NO. 975

Sinners bound with the cords of sin

'His own iniquities shall take the wicked himself, and he shall be holden with the cords of his sins.' Proverbs 5:22
SUGGESTED FURTHER READING: Luke 12:13–21

It has long been a mystery who was the man in the iron mask. We believe that the mystery was solved some years ago by the conjecture that he was the twin brother of Louis XIV, King of France, who, fearful lest he might have his throne disturbed by his twin brother, whose features were extremely like his own, encased his face in a mask of iron and shut him up in the Bastille for life. Your body and your soul are twin brothers. Your body, as though it were jealous of your soul, encases it in an iron mask of spiritual ignorance, lest its true features, its immortal lineage should be discovered, and shuts it up within the Bastille of sin, lest getting liberty and discovering its royalty, it should win the mastery over the baser nature. But what a wretch was that Louis XIV to do such a thing to his own brother! How brutal, how worse than the beasts that perish! But, sir, what are you if you do this to your own soul merely that your body may be satisfied and that your earthly nature may have a present gratification? Do not be so unkind, so cruel to yourself. But yet this sin of living for the mouth and living for the eye, this sin of living for what you shall eat and what you shall drink and with what shall you be clothed, this sin of living by the clock within the narrow limits of the time that ticks by the pendulum, this sin of living as if the earth were all and there was nothing beyond—this is the sin that holds this City of London, and holds the world, and binds it like a martyr to the stake to perish, unless it be set free.

FOR MEDITATION: It is important to pay attention to our bodies (Romans 12:1; 1 Corinthians 6:13–20; Ephesians 5:29), but even more urgent to take care for our souls (Matthew 10:28; 16:26; 1 Peter 2:11; 3 John 2).

N.B. This sermon mentions a recent visit by 'Italy's liberator', assumed to mean Victor Emmanuel II. An undated follow-up sermon on deliverance from the bondage of sin begins with a reference to this very sermon and is entitled 'Victor Emmanuel, emancipator' (no. 986—see 3 June). Spurgeon had similarly referred to a visit by the Italian patriot Garibaldi on 17 April 1864 (see *365 Days with Spurgeon vol. 2*).

Every-day usefulness

'And he brought him to Jesus.' John 1:42
SUGGESTED FURTHER READING: 1 John 1:1–4

Perhaps somebody will be saying, 'How did Andrew persuade Simon Peter to come to Christ?' Two or three minutes may be spent in answering that enquiry. He did so, first, by narrating his own personal experience; he said, 'We have found the Messias'. What you have experienced of Christ, tell to others. He did so next by intelligently explaining to him what it was he had found. He did not say he had found someone who had impressed him, but did not know who he was; he told him he had found Messiah, that is, Christ. Be clear in your knowledge of the gospel and your experience of it, and then tell the good news to those whose souls you seek. Andrew had power over Peter because of his own decided conviction. He did not say, 'I hope I have found Christ,' but 'I have found him.' He was sure of that. Get full assurance of your own salvation. There is no weapon like it. He that speaks doubtingly of what he would convince another, asks that other to doubt his testimony. Be positive in your experience and your assurance, for this will help you. Andrew had power over Peter because he put the good news before him in an earnest fashion. He did not say to him, as though it were a common-place fact, 'The Messiah has come'; no, he communicated it to him as the most weighty of all messages with, I do not doubt, becoming tones and gestures—'We have found the Messias, which is ... the Christ.' Now then, brethren and sisters, to your own kinsfolk tell your belief, your enjoyments, and your assurance; tell all judiciously, with assurance of the truth of it, and who can tell whether God may not bless your work?

FOR MEDITATION: In spiritual terms conveying the facts (1 John 1:2–3) in an earnest, gentle and reverent manner (2 Corinthians 5:20; 1 Peter 3:15) carries far more weight than employing the latest evangelistic techniques and gimmicks.

Divine love and its gifts

'*Now our Lord Jesus Christ himself, and God, even our Father, which hath loved us, and hath given us everlasting consolation and good hope through grace, comfort your hearts, and stablish you in every good word and work.*' 2 Thessalonians 2:16,17
SUGGESTED FURTHER READING: Psalm 46:1–11

The eternal love of God is the great fountain and source from which proceed all the spiritual blessings which we enjoy. If you stand at the source of a great river like the Thames, you see nothing there but a tiny rivulet, the fact being that we speak of that little brook as the source of the river only as a matter of courtesy. It is only a very partial source; a great river derives its volume of water from a thousand streams and is sustained by the whole of the watershed along which it flows. The imaginary fountain-head of a river is therefore only a small affair; but suppose the Thames had never borrowed from a single stream in all its course, but welled up at once a full-grown river from some one fountain-head. What a sight it would be! Now the mercy of God to us in Christ Jesus owes nothing to any other stream; it leaps in all its fulness from the infinite depths of the love of God to us, and if in contemplation you can travel to that great deep, profound and unfathomable, and see welling up all the floods of covenant grace, which afterwards flow on for ever to all the chosen seed, you have before you that at which angels wonder. If it would be marvellous to see one river leap up from the earth full-grown, what would it be to gaze upon a vast spring from which all the rivers of the earth should at once come bubbling up, a thousand of them born at a birth? What a vision it would be! Who can conceive it? And yet the love of God is that fountain from which all the rivers of mercy which have ever gladdened our race—all the rivers of grace in time and of glory hereafter—take their rise. My soul, stand at that sacred fountain-head, and adore and magnify for ever and ever 'God, even our Father, which hath loved us'.

FOR MEDITATION: The breadth, length, depth and height of Christ's love are far beyond human knowledge and measurement, yet Christians can enjoy the ability to comprehend and know it (Ephesians 3:18–19)! Is this something to which you long to aspire?

Joshua's vision

'And it came to pass, when Joshua was by Jericho, that he lifted up his eyes and looked, and, behold, there stood a man over against him ... : and Joshua went unto him ... And Joshua fell on his face to the earth, and did worship ... and the captain of the LORD'S *host said unto Joshua, Loose thy shoe from off thy foot; for the place whereon thou standest is holy.' Joshua 5:13–15*
SUGGESTED FURTHER READING: Ephesians 4:25–5:4

'Put off thy shoes from off thy feet'. Joshua, perhaps. had not felt what a solemn thing it was to fight for God, to fight as God's executioner against condemned men. He must put off his shoes, therefore. We can never expect a blessing if we go about God's work flippantly. I shudder when I see any sitting at the Lord's table who can indulge in light remarks or in wandering thoughts on so solemn an occasion. What have you to do here not having on a wedding garment? There are some of us whose besetting sin is levity of spirit. Cheerfulness we are to cultivate, but we must beware lest levity becomes a cankerworm to our graces. Seek a quiet and sober spirit. To seek to save souls from going down to the pit is no pastime; to talk of Jesus is no trifle. We do not meet to pray in sport; we do not gather together in supplication as a mere matter of form. Angels are in our midst observing us; the King himself is here. How would you behave if you actually saw Jesus with your eyes? If I were to vacate the pulpit and the crucified One stood here, stretching out his pierced hands and looking down upon you with the mild radiance of his sovereign love, how would you feel? Ask to feel just so, for he is here. Faith can perceive him. Ask to feel just so at this present moment, and so to go out to your work today and all the remaining days of your life as a servant of God who is standing in the presence of his Lord upon holy ground, and who cannot therefore afford to trifle, since he has solemn work to do, and means to do it in his Master's name.

FOR MEDITATION: If foolish talking and jesting are to be put away from every Christian's mouth (Ephesians 5:4), there can be no place for such irreverence when Christians assemble in Christ's name and in Christ's presence (Matthew 18:20). Everything should 'be done decently and in order.' (1 Corinthians 14:40).

SERMON NO. 795

Joshua's obedience

'Observe to do according to all the law, ... turn not from it to the right hand or to the left.' Joshua 1:7
SUGGESTED FURTHER READING: Nehemiah 8:9–9:5

One good brother said that when he went up the Rhine, he never looked at the rocks or the old castles or the flowing river; he was so taken up with other things! To me nature is a looking-glass in which I see the face of God. I delight to 'Look through nature up to nature's God.' But that was all unholiness to him. I do not understand those who look upon this material world as though it were a very wicked place and as if there were here no trace whatever of the divine hand and no proofs of the divine wisdom, nor manifestations of the divine care. I think we may delight ourselves in the works of God, find much pleasure in them, and get much advanced towards God himself by considering his works. That to which I have thus referred is one extreme. There are others who are all froth and levity, who profess to be Christians, and yet cannot live without the same amusements as worldlings; they must be now at this party, and then at that, never comfortable unless they are making jokes and following after all the levities and frivolities of the world. The first extreme is a pardonable weakness, in which there is much that is commendable, but this is a detestable one, of which I can say nothing good. The Christian should steer between the two. He should be cheerful, but not frivolous. He should be sustained and happy under all circumstances, have a friendly and kindly word for all, and be a man among men as the Saviour was, willing to sit at the banquet and to feast and rejoice with those that do rejoice, but still heavenly-minded in it all, feeling that a joy in which he cannot have Christ with him is no joy, and that places of amusement where he cannot take his Lord with him are no places of amusement, but scenes of misery to him. He should be constantly happy and rejoicing, and yet at the same time should display a deep solemnity of spirit which removes far from him everything that is sacrilegiously light and trifling.

FOR MEDITATION: The opposite of foolish jesting is not being miserable but thankful (Ephesians 5:4). Holiness and joy go together—the fruit of the Holy Spirit includes joy (Romans 14:17; Galatians 5:22; 1 Thessalonians 1:6). Do you thank God for his good gifts (1 Timothy 4:3–4)?

SERMON NO. 796

Precious deaths

'Precious in the sight of the LORD *is the death of his saints.'* Psalm 116:15
SUGGESTED FURTHER READING: Acts 21:7–14

We love the people of God; they are exceedingly precious to us and, therefore, we are too apt to look upon their deaths as a very grievous loss. We would never let them die at all if we could help it. If it were in our power to confer immortality upon our beloved Christian brethren and sisters, we should surely do it, and to their injury we should detain them here in this wilderness, depriving them of a speedy entrance into their inheritance on the other side of the river. It would be cruel to them, but I fear we should often be guilty of it. We should hold them here a little longer, and a little longer yet, finding it hard to relinquish our grasp. The departures of the saints cause us many a pang. We fret; alas, also, we even repine and murmur. We count that we are the poorer because of the eternal enriching of those beloved ones who have gone over to the majority and entered into their rest. Be it known that while we are sorrowing, Christ is rejoicing. His prayer is, 'Father, I will that they also, whom thou hast given me, be with me where I am;' in the advent of every one of his own people to the skies he sees an answer to that prayer, and is therefore glad. He beholds in every perfected one another portion of the reward for the travail of his soul, and he is satisfied in it. We are grieving here, but he is rejoicing there. Sorrowful are their deaths in our sight, but precious are their deaths in his sight. We sit down to mourn our full and yet, meanwhile, the bells of heaven are ringing for the bridal feast above, the streamers are floating joyously in every heavenly street and the celestial world keeps holiday because another heir of heaven has entered upon his heritage. May this correct our grief. Tears are permitted to us, but they must glisten in the light of faith and hope. 'Jesus wept', but Jesus never repined.

FOR MEDITATION: The extended life of other believers may be better for us, but we must beware of being selfish when God chooses to do what is better for them (Philippians 1:21–24).

N.B. A footnote to this sermon records that 'Rev. W. Dransfield, a beloved elder of the church at the Tabernacle, died February 15th, full of years.'

The wedding garment

'And when the king came in to see the guests, he saw there a man which had not on a wedding garment: and he saith unto him, Friend, how camest thou in hither not having a wedding garment? And he was speechless.' Matthew 22:11–12
SUGGESTED FURTHER READING (Spurgeon): Jude 17–25

The wedding garment represents anything which is indispensable to a Christian, but which the unrenewed heart is not willing to accept, anything which the Lord ordains to be a necessary attendant of salvation against which selfishness rebels. Hence it may be said to be Christ's righteousness imputed to us, for many nominal Christians kick against the doctrine of justification by the righteousness of the Saviour and set up their own self-righteousness in opposition to it. To be found in Christ, not having our own righteousness, which is of the law, but the righteousness which is of God by faith, is a prominent badge of a real servant of God, and to refuse it is to manifest opposition to the glory of God and to the name, person and work of his exalted Son. But we might say that the wedding dress is a holy character, the imparted righteousness which the Holy Spirit works in us and which is equally necessary as a proof of grace. I would remind you of the dress which adorns the saints in heaven. They 'have washed their robes, and made them white in the blood of the Lamb.' Their robes once needed washing; this could not be said of the righteousness of the Lord Jesus Christ; that was always perfect and spotless. It is clear that the figure is sometimes applied to saints in reference to their personal character. Holiness is always present in those who are loyal guests of the great King, for without holiness 'no man shall see the Lord'. Too many pacify themselves with the idea that they possess imputed righteousness, while they are indifferent to the sanctifying work of the Spirit. They refuse to put on the garment of obedience and reject the white linen which is the righteousness of saints. Thus they reveal self-will, enmity to God and non-submission to his Son.

FOR MEDITATION: How are you approaching God? In the garments of salvation and the robe of righteousness he provides for all who trust in Christ (Isaiah 61:10) or in the filthy rags of your own imaginary self-righteousness (Isaiah 64:6)?

SERMON NO. 976

Precious, honourable, beloved

'Since thou wast precious in my sight, thou hast been honourable, and I have loved thee.' Isaiah 43:4
SUGGESTED FURTHER READING: 1 Peter 2:12–18

We can never think of the human soul but as a very precious and priceless thing. If that be the case, how honourable all men become as objects of our zeal! 'Honour all men' says the apostle Peter, a text I do not hear quoted half so often as that other, 'Honour the king.' Do not forget the second, but take equal care of the first. There is, because of its spiritual and immortal nature, a dignity about the soul of the meanest man, which no degree of poverty or degradation can altogether take away. The harlot in the streets, how few will care for her! But, tender hearts, as you look on the poor fallen one, say, 'Since your soul was precious in my sight as an immortal spirit, you have been no longer despised and trampled on, but I have loved you as my Saviour loved you, and for his sake I esteem your soul as an honourable, priceless thing.' Do not think of the thousands in prison today as though they were just so much filth to be got rid of. Do not think, above all, of the great mass of the needy and pauperised classes of society as though they were a mere encumbrance of the common welfare, the mere rubbish to be swept away and laid in heaps in the workhouse or on foreign shores. No, they are precious; as precious are their souls as yours. Think of them in that respect, and honour the immortal spark that is in them, the manhood that God has been pleased to create; honour that and, as you honour it, love it and prove your love by praying that God will save it, by using every instrument within your power to recover it from its ruin and to bring it back to the great God to whom it belongs.

FOR MEDITATION: 'Honour all men' includes not only the obvious ones such as parents (Exodus 20:12), the elderly (Leviticus 19:32), husbands and wives (Esther 1:20; 1 Peter 3:7), one another (Romans 12:10), widows (1 Timothy 5:3), elders (1 Timothy 5:17), masters (1 Timothy 6:1) and rulers (1 Peter 2:17), but also those we would usually consider less honourable (1 Corinthians 12:23). Amazement at the honour bestowed by God upon mankind should help us to do it (Psalm 8:4–5).

The importunate widow

'And he spake a parable unto them to this end, that men ought always to pray, and not to faint; ... shall not God avenge his own elect, which cry day and night unto him, though he bear long with them?' Luke 18:1–7
SUGGESTED FURTHER READING: 1 Thessalonians 5:12–18

Our Lord means that believers should exercise a universality of supplication—we ought to pray at all times. There are no canonical hours in the Christian's day or week. We should pray from daybreak to midnight, at such times as the Spirit moves us. We should pray in all conditions, in our poverty and in our wealth, in our health and in our sickness, in the bright days of festival and in the dark nights of lamentation. We should pray at the birth and pray at the funeral, we should pray when our soul is glad within us by reason of abundant mercy, and we should pray when our soul draws nigh unto the gates of death by reason of heaviness. We should pray in all transactions, whether secular or religious. Prayer should sanctify everything. The Word of God and prayer should come in over and above the common things of daily life. Pray over a bargain, pray over going into the shop and coming out again. Remember in the days of Joshua how the Gibeonites deceived Israel because Israel enquired not of the Lord, and be not deceived by a plausible temptation, as you may be if you do not come daily to the Lord, saying, 'Guide me: make straight a plain path for my feet, and lead me in the way everlasting.' You will never err by praying too much; you will never make a mistake by asking God's guidance too often; but you will find this to be the gracious illumination of your eyes, if in the turning of the road where two paths, which seem equally right, meet, you will wait a moment and cry unto God, 'Guide me, O thou great Jehovah.' 'Men ought always to pray'.

FOR MEDITATION: Praying always is linked to standing firm in the Christian fight (Ephesians 6:13,18). The apostle Paul proved it. He was always praying (Romans 1:9; Philippians 1:4; Colossians 1:3,9; 2 Thessalonians 1:11) and did not faint under severe pressures (2 Corinthians 4:1,8–9,16). Unlike the unjust judge who had no concern for the widow in her battle with her adversary (Luke 18:2–3), God cares for his people as they do battle with their adversary the devil (1 Peter 5:7–8).

SERMON NO. 856

Good cause for great zeal

'We have maintenance from the king's palace, and it was not meet for us to see the king's dishonour.' Ezra 4:14
SUGGESTED FURTHER READING: 1 Corinthians 5:1–13

Dishonour may come from those who live in our own house. I charge you that are parents to see to this. Do not tolerate anything in those over whom you have control that would bring dishonour to God. Remember Eli: he did not restrain his sons, and they behaved shamefully. Because they were not restrained, God overthrew Eli's house and did such terrible things 'at which both the ears of every one that heareth it shall tingle.' Joshua said, 'as for me and my house, we will serve the Lord.' We cannot impart to our children new hearts, but we can see to it that there shall be nothing within our gates that is derogatory to Jesus Christ. But you cannot control your children, you say. Then the Lord have mercy upon you! It is your business to do it, and you must do it, or else you will soon find they will control you; and no one knows what judgment will come from God upon those who suffer sin in children to go unrebuked. No, if we are maintained from the king's palace, let us not see the king's dishonour. Let the same holy jealousy animate us among those who wish to be united with us in church fellowship. It is the duty of every church to try to guard the honour and dignity of King Jesus against unworthy persons, who would intrude themselves into the congregation of the saints, those who 'are called, and chosen, and faithful.' We are deceived, and always shall be, for the church never was infallible; but still let no negligence of our practice supplement the infirmity of our judgment. Because ungodly men will creep in unawares, we are not, therefore, to connive at their entrance. To allow persons to come to the communion-table who do not even profess to be born again, is a clear act of treason against the King of kings. To receive into our membership persons of unhallowed life, unchaste, unrighteous, of licentious life and lax doctrine, such as know not the truth as it is in Jesus, would be to betray the trust with which Christ has invested us. That must not be.

FOR MEDITATION: Causing or allowing God's holy name to be dishonoured is bad enough, but it also degrades the believer and encourages unbelievers to blaspheme (Romans 2:23–24; 1 Corinthians 5:1–2; 1 Timothy 5:8).

Spots in our feasts of charity

'These are spots in your feasts of charity, when they feast with you, feeding themselves without fear.' Jude 12
SUGGESTED FURTHER READING: Mark 14:26–50

Should not the departures from the faith of some professors put us on our guard against our own special temptations? I do not know how each one of you is employed in life, but this I know, that there is a precipice near every man's foot and a snare in every man's path. You may not fall into the temptation which besets me, and I may never fall into that which besets you, but there is a lure for every bird, a bait for every fish. I would have you specially take heed of those things in regard to which you have ventured to the very verge. There are some things which are allowable up to a point; beware of going beyond that point, and beware of often going close to it, for the temptation is to go a little further. Edged tools, long handled, wound at last. Beware of extraordinary temptations; watch against them. A child would generally stand on his feet in a gust of wind if he knew it was coming; but when the wind happens to come round a corner furiously, he may be taken off his feet. Mind you are well ballasted by prayer every morning before your vessel puts out to sea, or, carrying the quantity of sail you do, you may be blown over upon the waves to your perpetual shipwreck. Watch constantly against those things which are thought to be no temptations. The most poisonous serpents are found where the sweetest flowers grow, and when Cleopatra would have an asp to poison herself, it was brought in a basket of fair flowers. Beware of arrows shot from a golden bow, or by a woman's hand. 'Watch and pray, that ye enter not into temptation'. I feel as if I could go round among you, and take every one by the hand, and say, 'My brother and my sister, will ye also go away?' If you would answer, 'No, we will follow the Lamb whithersoever he goeth,' then I would reply in my Master's words, 'And what I say unto you I say unto all, Watch.'

FOR MEDITATION: Our spiritual enemies are always watching us and looking for opportunities to attack us. We need to stay one step ahead of them and imitate their tactics, by watching them watching us (Genesis 4:7; Luke 20:20,23; Acts 20:30–31; 1 Peter 5:8).

Wonders

'And praise the name of the LORD *your God, that hath dealt wondrously with you.' Joel 2:26*
SUGGESTED FURTHER READING: Daniel 4:1–4,28–37

In the church we are permitted to expect wonders. We are too much in the habit of going to the assembly for worship, and sitting down and hearing sermons, and if half-a-dozen are converted we are astonished; but we ought to expect thousands to be converted! If the church ever has faith enough to expect great things, she will see great things. When the church falls upon dark times and error mars her beauty, we may expect God to work wonders to purify and exalt her. In the darkest medieval times God found his witnesses, and when the light threatened to die out, then Luther came, a man raised up by God, and a train of glorious men followed behind him. Never tremble, never despair, never be afraid. 'The Lord of hosts is with us; the God of Jacob is our refuge.' We worship the God of wonders, 'Who only doeth wondrous things.' We have a Saviour of wonders; 'his name shall be called Wonderful,' and did not Peter call him 'Jesus of Nazareth, a man approved of God among you by miracles and wonders and signs'? Then the Holy Spirit also works wonders. He came at first with rushing wind and cloven tongues and miraculous gifts, and even now his wonders have not ceased: they have only become spiritual instead of physical, but the Spirit of God is working mightily now. God has worked wonders for us, far beyond all human ability, wonders which we could not perform, wonders that we did not deserve, wonders that we could not have expected, wonders that we could not have imagined, wonders which even now that they have happened we cannot comprehend, and wonders for which we shall never be able to praise God sufficiently throughout eternity, though we spend our whole existence in wondering and adoring the wonder-working God! 'How great are his signs! and how mighty are his wonders!'

FOR MEDITATION: All sorts and conditions of people have praised God for the wonders he has performed for them personally—David (Psalm 40:5), the Jews (Psalm 126:2–3), Nebuchadnezzar (Daniel 4:2), the virgin Mary (Luke 1:49), the demoniac (Luke 8:39). 'Consider how great things he hath done for you.' (1 Samuel 12:24)

SERMON NO. 1098

What and whence are these?

'And one of the elders ... said to me, These are they which came out of great tribulation.' Revelation 7:13–14
SUGGESTED FURTHER READING: 2 Thessalonians 1:1–7

The saints in heaven needed trial like others. The word 'tribulatio' was used by the Romans to signify a threshing instrument. When they beat out the corn from the straw, they called it 'tribulatio'; and so tribulation is sent to us to separate our chaff from our wheat. Since the same tribulation happened to those who are now in heaven, we infer that they needed it as much as ourselves. To what end do men need tribulation? They often require it to arouse them; and yonder saints who serve God day and night in his temple, once slept as others do, and needed to be bestirred. Were they not apostles who slept in Gethsemane? Were they not three of the chief of the apostles who slumbered within a stone's cast of their Master in his agony? The best of men are prone to slumber and need to be awakened by the buffetings of sorrow. They needed trial to chasten them. What son has God ever had, except his firstborn and well-beloved, that did not need chastening? Inasmuch as we are all sinners, we have need in our Father's house to suffer from the rod. They needed tribulation as we do to loosen them from the earth, else they would have struck their roots into this poor soil and tried to live as if this world were their portion. Affliction was also necessary to develop their graces, even as spices need bruising to bring forth their smell, and rose leaves require distilling to draw forth their sweetest perfume. They required adversity to educate them into complete manhood, for they too were once babes in grace. It is in the gymnasium of affliction that men are modelled and fashioned in the beauty of holiness, and all their spiritual powers are trained for harmonious action.

FOR MEDITATION: Tribulation is the believer's companion on the journey to God's kingdom (Acts 14:22). It cannot separate us from his love (Romans 8:35), so need not divert us (1 Thessalonians 3:3–4). Christ's peace (John 16:33) can help us rejoice during it (Romans 5:1–3) as God comforts us (2 Corinthians 1:4; 7:4). How do you react to tribulation?

N.B. This topic was prompted by the recent death and burial of Rev. W. Dransfield (see 18 February).

SERMON NO. 1040

All fulness in Christ

'For it pleased the Father that in him should all fulness dwell.' Colossians
1:19
SUGGESTED FURTHER READING: John 1:14–18

There is a fulness in Christ Jesus which the seeking sinner should behold
with joyfulness. What do you need, sinner? You need all things, but
Christ is all. You need power to believe in him; he gives power to the
faint. You need repentance; he was exalted on high to give repentance as
well as remission of sin. You need a new heart: the covenant runs thus, 'A
new heart also will I give you, and a new spirit will I put within you'. You
need pardon; behold his streaming wounds, wash and be clean. You need
healing; he is 'the Lord that healeth thee.' You need clothing; his
righteousness shall become your dress. You need preservation; you shall
be preserved in him. You need life; he has said, 'Awake thou that sleepest,
and arise from the dead, and Christ shall give thee light.' He came that
we might have life. You need—but the catalogue is too long for us to read
through. Be assured that though you pile up your necessities till they rise
like Alps before you, yet the all-sufficient Saviour can remove all your
needs. You may confidently sing—

'Thou, O Christ, art all I want;
More than all in thee I find.'

This is true also of the saint as well as the sinner. Child of God, you are
saved, but your needs are not therefore removed. Are they not as
continuous as your heart-beats. When are we not in need, my brethren?
The more alive we are to God, the more we are aware of our spiritual
necessities. He who is 'blind, and naked' thinks himself to be 'rich, and
increased with goods,' but let the mind be truly enlightened, and we feel
that we are completely dependent upon the charity of God. Let us be
glad, then, as we learn that there is no necessity in our spirit which is not
abundantly provided for us in the all-fulness of Jesus Christ.

FOR MEDITATION: We can be filled with the fulness of God (Ephesians
3:19)! 'The Lord is my shepherd; I shall not want ... my cup runneth over'
(Psalm 23:1,5). Paul proved it (Philippians 4:11–13,18) and so can we
(Philippians 4:19) if we fear the Lord and seek him (Psalm 34:9–10).

SERMON NO. 978

The two builders and their houses

'And the rain descended, and the floods came, and the winds blew, and beat upon that house; and it ...' Matthew 7:25 & 27
SUGGESTED FURTHER READING: Job 1:13–2:10

Trials will come to profession, whether it be true or false. If I do not mistake the reference in the text to rain, floods and winds, these trials will be of three sorts at least. The rain typifies *afflictions from heaven*. God will send you adversities like showers, tribulations as many as the drops of the dew. Between now and heaven, professor, you will feel the pelting storm. Like other men, your body will be sick; or if not, you shall have trouble in your house; children and friends will die, or riches will take to themselves wings and fly like an eagle towards heaven. You must have trials from God's hand; and, if you are not relying on Christ, you will not be able to bear them. If you are not by real faith one with Jesus Christ, even God's rain will be too much for you. But there will also arise *trials from earth*—'the floods came'. In former days the floods of persecution were more terrible than now, but persecution is still felt; and if you are a professor, you will have to bear a measure of it. Cruel mockings are still used against the people of God. The world no more loves the true church today than it did in the olden times. Can you bear slander and reproach for Jesus? Not unless you are firmly rooted and grounded. In the day of temptation and persecution the rootless plants of the stony ground are withered away. There will also come *mysterious trials* typified by 'the winds'. The prince of the power of the air will assail you with blasphemous suggestions, horrible temptations or artful insinuations. He knows how to cast clouds of despondency over the human spirit; he can attack the four corners of the house at once by his mysterious agency; he can tempt us in various ways at the same time, and drive us to our wits' end. Woe to you, then, unless you have something better than the mere sand of profession by which to hold!

FOR MEDITATION: The trials of our faith will be unpleasant in and of themselves, but the outcome will be valuable and wonderful for all who pass the test (James 1:2–4,12; 1 Peter 1:6–7). Not every profession of faith passes the test (Matthew 13:20–21).

The fulness of Jesus the treasury of saints

'Of his fulness have all we received, and grace for grace.' John 1:16
SUGGESTED FURTHER READING: Hebrews 1:1–14

'Of his fulness have all we received'; we know that this is none other than
that august personage whom John calls 'The Word', or the speech of
God, so called because God in nature has revealed himself, as it were,
inarticulately and indistinctly, but in his Son he has revealed himself as a
man declares his inmost thoughts, by distinct and intelligible speech.
Jesus is to the Father what speech is to us; he is the unfolding of the
Father's thoughts, the revelation of the Father's heart. He that has seen
Christ has seen the Father. 'Would you have me see you?' said Socrates,
'then speak;' for speech reveals the man. Would you see God? Listen to
Christ, for he is God's Word, revealing the heart of deity. Lest, however,
we should imagine Jesus to be a mere utterance, a mere word spoken and
forgotten, our apostle is particularly careful that we should know that
Jesus is a real and true person, and therefore tells us that the divine Word,
out of whose fulness we have received, is most assuredly God. No
language can be more distinct. He ascribes to him the eternity which
belongs to God: 'In the beginning was the Word'. He expressly claims
divinity for him: 'the Word was God.' He ascribes to him the acts of
God: 'without him was not any thing made that was made.' He ascribes
to him self-existence, which is the essential characteristic of God: 'In him
was life'. He claims for him a nature peculiar to God: 'God is light, and
in him is no darkness at all', and the Word is 'the true Light, which
lighteth every man that cometh into the world.' No writer could be more
explicit in his utterances; and beyond all question he sets forth the proper
deity of the Blessed One of whom we must all receive if we would obtain
eternal salvation.

FOR MEDITATION: In the Old Testament 'thus saith the Lord GOD' (Isaiah
7:7) was limited to the words and actions of his prophets (Hebrews 1:1).
In the New Testament 'thus saith the Lord God' is not only seen in the
words and actions of the Lord Jesus Christ, but also embodied in his
whole person (Hebrews 1:2–3; 1 John 1:1–2).

A persuasive to steadfastness

'For we are made partakers of Christ, if we hold the beginning of our confidence stedfast unto the end.' Hebrews 3:14
SUGGESTED FURTHER READING: 1 John 2:15–25

Are we made partakers of Christ? Many think they are who are not. There is nothing more to be dreaded than a supposed righteousness, a counterfeit justification, a spurious hope. Better, I sometimes think, to have no religion than to have a false religion. I am quite certain that the man is much more likely to be saved who knows that he is 'wretched, and miserable, and poor, and blind, and naked', than the man who says, 'I am rich, and increased with goods'. It is infinitely better to take the road to heaven doubting than to go in another direction presuming. I am far more pleased with the soul that is always questioning, 'Am I right?' than with him who has drunk the cup of arrogance till he is intoxicated with self-conceit and says, 'I know my lot; the lines have fallen to me in pleasant places; there is no need for self-examination in my case.' Brethren, be assured of this; all are not partakers of Christ: all the baptised are not partakers of Christ: all churchmen are not partakers of Christ: all dissenters are not made partakers of Christ: all members of the church are not made partakers of Christ: all ministers, all elders, all bishops are not made partakers of Christ. All apostles were not made partakers of Christ. One of them, Christ's familiar friend, who kept the little purse which held all the Master's earthly store, lifted up his heel against him, betrayed him with a tender treacherous kiss, and became the son of perdition. He was a companion of Christ, but not a partaker of him. Am *I* made a partaker of Christ? Multiply the question till each individual among you makes it his own.

FOR MEDITATION: This was the first of only three sermons in the Metropolitan Tabernacle Pulpit preached on 29 February. Nobody would expect to find today's date in the calendar except during a Leap Year, but so many take for granted their place in Christ and his kingdom. Not every one who addresses Jesus as Lord and claims to serve him is the genuine article (Matthew 7:21–23).

SERMON NO. 1042

Special protracted prayer

'And it came to pass in those days, that he went out into a mountain to pray, and continued all night in prayer to God.' Luke 6:12
SUGGESTED FURTHER READING: Ezra 8:21–32

If you enter upon a new enterprise, or engage in something that is weightier and more extensive than what you have done before, select a night or a day, and set it apart for special communion with the Most High. If you are to pray, you must work, but if you are to work, you must also pray. If your prayer without your work will be hypocrisy, your work without your prayer will be presumption; so see to it that you are specially in supplication when specially in service. Balance your praying and working. To anyone who asks me, 'When should I give myself especially to a protracted season of prayer?' I would answer that these occasions will frequently occur. You should certainly do this when about to join the church. The day of your public profession of your faith should be altogether a consecrated day. I recollect rising before the sun to seek my Master's presence on the day when I was buried with him in baptism. It seemed to me a solemn ordinance not to be lightly undertaken, or flippantly carried out, a duty which, if done at all, should be performed in the most solemn and earnest manner. What is baptism without fellowship with Christ? To be buried in baptism, but not *with him*, what is it? I would say to young people who are joining the church now, mind that you do not do it thoughtlessly, but in coming forward to enlist in the army of Christ, set apart a special season for self-examination and prayer. When you arrive at any great change of life, do the same. Do not enter upon marriage, or upon emigration, or upon starting in business, without having sought a benediction from your Father who is in heaven. Any of these things may involve years of pain or years of happiness to you; seek, therefore, to have the smile of God upon what you are about to do.

FOR MEDITATION: The Lord Jesus Christ took time to pray before taking important decisions (Luke 6:12–13) and before undertaking the most important part of his work on earth (Matthew 26:36–44). Taking time to pray beforehand can save a lot of wasted time and effort later (Mark 9:28–29; James 4:2).

SERMON NO. 798

The man of sorrows

'A *man of sorrows, and acquainted with grief.*' Isaiah 53:3
SUGGESTED FURTHER READING: Luke 22:39–46

With grief he had an *intimate* acquaintance. He did not know merely what it was in others, but it came home to himself. We have read of grief, we have sympathised with grief, we have sometimes felt grief: but the Lord felt it more intensely than other men in his innermost soul; he, beyond us all, was conversant with its dark depths. He knew the secret of the heart which refuses to be comforted. He had sat at grief's table, eaten of grief's black bread, and dipped his morsel in her vinegar. By the bitter waters of Marah he dwelt. He and grief were close friends. It was a *continuous* acquaintance. He did not call at grief's house sometimes to take a tonic by the way, neither did he sip now and then of the wormwood and the gall, but the bitter cup was always in his hand, and ashes were always mingled with his bread. Not only forty days in the wilderness did Jesus fast; the world was ever a wilderness to him, and his life was one long Lent. I do not say that he was not, after all, a happy man, for deep down in his soul benevolence always supplied a living spring of joy to him. There was a joy into which we are one day to enter, 'the joy of the Lord', 'the joy that was set before him' for which he 'endured the cross, despising the shame'; but that does not at all take away from the fact that his acquaintance with grief was continuous and intimate beyond that of any man who ever lived. It was indeed a *growing* acquaintance with grief, for each step took him deeper down into the grim shades of sorrow. As there is a progress in the teaching of Christ and in the life of Christ, so there is also in the griefs of Christ. The tempest loomed darker and darker. His sun rose in a cloud, but it set in congregated horrors of heaped-up night, till in a moment the clouds were suddenly rent in sunder and, as a loud voice proclaimed, 'It is finished', a glorious morning dawned where all expected an eternal night.

FOR MEDITATION: 'Behold and see if there be any sorrow like unto my sorrow … wherewith the Lord hath afflicted me' (Lamentations 1:12). In Gethsemane the apostles were sorrowful (Luke 22:45), but Jesus exceedingly so (Matthew 26:37–38) 'even unto death'. Remember that it was our griefs and our sorrows resulting from our sins that he endured on the cross (Isaiah 53:4–5).

SERMON NO. 1099

Another royal procession

'Tell ye the daughter of Sion, Behold, thy King cometh unto thee, meek, and sitting upon an ass, and a colt the foal of an ass.' Matthew 21:5
SUGGESTED FURTHER READING: Luke 19:37–48

Christ's compassion did not permit him to keep back the tidings of future punishment. He said, 'For the days shall come upon thee, that thine enemies shall cast a trench about thee, and compass thee round, and keep thee in on every side, and shall lay thee even with the ground, and thy children within thee; and they shall not leave in thee one stone upon another.' I have noted that in genuine revivals the preachers of God's truth are not backward in preaching the threatenings, as well as the promises. We are told that men are drawn to Christ by love, and the statement is true; but, at the same time, knowing 'the terror of the Lord,' we are to persuade men and not to keep back from them the evil tidings. Even Christ with weeping eyes and tender heart does not hesitate to tell Jerusalem of its coming destruction, and I believe it is a token that Christ is in the church when those terrible things of his are not kept back to please the popular taste, when there is no attempt to cut them down and moderate them, in order to make the wrath to come look less terrible than it is. It must be thundered out, 'except ye repent, ye shall all likewise perish.' It must be told the sinner that if he goes on in his iniquity, he shall be driven away from hope and salvation, 'where their worm dieth not, and the fire is not quenched.' Christ is not present in an unfaithful church, and this is a point upon which some churches grow very unfaithful. We must deliver the whole truth, the dark side as well as that which smiles with mercy, and Christ is not present unless it be so. The sympathy of Jesus led him, as it should lead us, to be lovingly honest with men.

FOR MEDITATION: God's judgments can follow hard upon attempts to hush them up (1 Kings 22:6–8,12–18,34–36; Isaiah 30:9–14). It is futile to cry 'Peace, peace' to the unsaved 'when there is no peace' (Jeremiah 6:13–15), but wonderful when God says it to those he is saving (Isaiah 57:19).

N.B. This sermon's title alludes to an event on 27 February 1872 when Queen Victoria, the Prince and Princess of Wales, the Court and Parliament processed in state to St Paul's Cathedral for a national thanksgiving service for the recovery of the Prince of Wales after a serious typhoid attack.

Faith and regeneration

'Whosoever believeth that Jesus is the Christ is born of God: and every one that loveth him that begat loveth him also that is begotten of him.'
1 John 5:1
SUGGESTED FURTHER READING: Matthew 21:1–17

Do I this day believe that Jesus is the great Prophet anointed of God to reveal to me the way of salvation? Do I accept him as my teacher, and admit that he has the words of eternal life? If I so believe, I shall obey his gospel and possess eternal life. Do I accept him to be henceforth the revealer of God to my soul, the messenger of the covenant, the anointed Prophet of the Most High? But he is also a priest. Now, a priest is ordained from among men to offer sacrifices; do I firmly believe that Jesus was ordained to offer his one sacrifice for the sins of mankind, by the offering of which sacrifice once for all he has finished atonement and made complete expiation? Do I accept his atonement as an atonement for me, and receive his death as an expiation upon which I rest my hope for forgiveness of all my transgressions? Do I in fact believe Jesus to be the one sole, only propitiating priest, and accept him to act as priest for me? If so, then I have in part believed that Jesus is the Anointed. But he is also King, and if I desire to know whether I possess the right faith, I further must ask myself, 'Is Jesus, who is now exalted in heaven, who once bled on the cross, now King to me? Is his law my law? Do I desire entirely to submit myself to his government? Do I hate what he hates, and love what he loves? Do I live to praise him? Do I, as a loyal subject, desire to see his kingdom come and his will done on earth as it is in heaven?' My dear friend, if you can heartily and earnestly say, 'I accept Jesus Christ of Nazareth to be Prophet, Priest and King to me, because God has anointed him to exercise those three offices, and in each of these three characters I sincerely trust him,' then, dear friend, you have the faith of God's elect, for it is written, 'Whosoever believeth that Jesus is the Christ is born of God'.

FOR MEDITATION: Prophets, priests and kings were unreliable mediators between God and man in Old Testament times (Ezekiel 22:25–30), and are just as unreliable today, but the Lord Jesus Christ uniquely fulfils this role (1 Timothy 2:5–6): as prophet (Hebrews 1:1–2; Ephesians 2:13,17), priest (Hebrews 7:25–27) and prince (Acts 5:31).

SERMON NO. 979

Noah's flood

'The flood came, and took them all away.' Matthew 24:39
SUGGESTED FURTHER READING: Genesis 7:1–23

All who were in the ark were safe. Nobody fell out of that divinely-appointed refuge; nobody was dragged out; nobody died in it; nobody was left to perish in it. All who went in came out unharmed. They were all preserved in it; they were all safely brought through the dreadful catastrophe. The ark preserved them all, and so will Jesus Christ preserve all who are in him. Whoever may come to him shall be secure. None of them shall perish, neither shall any pluck them out of his hand. Think what strange creatures they were that were preserved! Why, there went into that ark unclean animals two and two. May God bring some of you who have been like unclean animals unto Christ; great swine of sin, you have wandered furthest in iniquity and defiled yourselves, yet when the swine were in the ark they were safe, and so shall you be. You ravens, you black ravens of sin, if you fly to Christ he will not cast you out, but you shall be secure. If electing love shall pick you out, and effectual grace shall draw you to the door of that ark, it shall be shut upon you and you shall be saved. Within that ark there was the timid hare, but its timidity did not destroy it; there was the weak cony, but despite its weakness, in the ark it was completely safe. There were to be found such slow-moving creatures as the snail, some darkness-loving creatures like the bat, but they were all safe; the mouse was as safe as the ox, the snail was as safe as the greyhound, the squirrel was as secure as the elephant, and the timid hare was as safe as the courageous lion—safe, not because of what they were, but because of where they were, namely in the ark.

FOR MEDITATION: Noah in the ark is a picture of all who are in Christ. God sent him in (Genesis 7:1), God shut him in (Genesis 7:16) and God saved him in the ark (Genesis 8:1). But Noah had to obey God's call and enter the ark (Genesis 7:7,13). Suppose he hadn't! We have to come to Christ and be in Christ before he can keep his promises never to cast us out and never to condemn us (John 6:37; Romans 8:1).

Sincerity and duplicity

'Hereby we do know that we know him, if we keep his commandments. He that saith, I know him, and keepeth not his commandments, is a liar, and the truth is not in him.' 1 John 2:3–4
SUGGESTED FURTHER READING: Matthew 7:15–23

A minister may say that he is sent of God, and yet be a wolf in sheep's clothing. A man may say that he unites himself to the church of God, but he may be no better than a hypocrite and an alien, who has no part in her fellowship. We may say that we pray, and yet never a prayer may come from our hearts. We may say to our fellow men that we are Christians, and yet we may never have been born again, never have obtained the precious faith of God's elect, never have been washed in the blood of Jesus Christ. As you would not be satisfied with merely saying that you are rich, as you want the title-deeds of the broad acres, as you want to hear the coins chink in your box, as you want the real thing and not the mere saying of it, so, I pray you, do not put up with the mere profession of religion. Do not be content with a bare assertion, or think that is enough, but seek to have your own profession verified by the witness of heaven, as well as by that of your own conscience. It is not written, 'He that *says* that he believes shall be saved,' but 'He that believeth and is baptized shall be saved'. It is not said, that he who *says* he has confessed his sins shall be forgiven, but 'whoso confesseth and forsaketh them shall have mercy.' Mere sayers, though they say, 'Lord, open to us', and assert that Christ did eat in their streets, shall have for an answer, 'I never knew you: depart from me, ye that work iniquity.' Let us not be deceived, duped and taken in by any notion that saying so makes it so; take heed lest with a flattering tongue you impose on your own soul. Standing in view of that eye which penetrates the inmost heart, may we learn to distinguish between the mere profession and the full possession of real grace and vital godliness.

FOR MEDITATION: We can claim that we have fellowship with God (1 John 1:6), that we have no sin and have not sinned (1 John 1:8,10), that we know God (1 John 2:4), that we are in the light (1 John 2:9) and that we love God (1 John 4:20) without a single word of it being true. Jacob claimed to be Esau (Genesis 27:19,24), but that could never turn him into Esau. He fooled Isaac, but we can never fool God.

SERMON NO. 922

Perseverance without presumption

'I give unto them eternal life; and they shall never perish, neither shall any man pluck them out of my hand.' John 10:28
SUGGESTED FURTHER READING: Hebrews 6:11–20

'They shall never perish'. I am very thankful for this word, because there have been some who have tried to do away with the force of the entire passage—'neither shall any man pluck them out of my hand.' 'No,' they have said, 'but they may slip between the fingers and, though they cannot be plucked out, yet they may go out of their own accord.' But here is a short sentence that puts all such thoughts out of the question—'they shall never perish'—in his hands or out of his hands, under any supposition whatever—'they shall never perish'. Observe that there is no restriction here; it includes all time—'they shall *never* perish'. Are they young believers with strong passions and weak judgment? Have they little knowledge, small experience and tender faith? May they not die while they are yet lambs and perish while they are so feeble? 'They shall never perish'. But in middle life, when men too often lose the freshness of early grace, when the love of their espousals may perhaps have lost its power, may they not get worldly? May they not, somehow or other, then be led aside? 'They shall never perish'. Perish they would, could worldliness destroy them; perish they would, could evil utterly and entirely get the mastery of grace, but it shall not. 'They shall never perish'. But may they not grow older and yet not wiser? May they not be surprised by temptation, as so many have been in times when they have become carnally secure, because they thought their experience had made them strong? 'They shall never perish,' neither if they are beginners, nor if they have all but finished their course. 'They shall never perish'. It shuts out all time and all reference to time, by taking the whole range of possible periods into the one word 'never'. 'They shall *never* perish'.

FOR MEDITATION: Having eternal life instead of perishing is the experience of whosoever truly trusts in the Lord Jesus Christ (John 3:15–16). Not believing and not continuing in the faith are danger signs of never having belonged to Christ at all (John 10:26; 1 John 2:19).

Jesus the example of holy praise

'I will declare thy name unto my brethren: in the midst of the congregation will I praise thee. Ye that fear the LORD, *praise him.'* Psalm 22:22–23

SUGGESTED FURTHER READING: Ephesians 5:15–20

Praise God *vocally*. I hate to enter a place of worship where half-a-dozen sing to the praise and glory of themselves, and the rest stand and listen. I like that good old plan of everybody singing, singing his best, singing carefully and heartily. If you cannot sing artistically, never mind; you will be right enough if you sing from the heart and pay attention to it, and do not drawl out like a musical machine that has been set going and therefore runs on mechanically. With a little care the heart brings the art, and the heart desiring to praise will by-and-by train the voice to time and tune. I would have our service of song to be of the best. I care not for the fineries of music and the prettiness of chants and anthems. As for instrumental music, I fear that it often destroys the singing of the congregation, and detracts from the spirituality and simplicity of worship. If I could crowd a building by the fine music which some churches delight in, God forbid that I should touch it; but let us have the best and most orderly harmony we can make. Let the saints come with their hearts in the best humour and their voices in the best tune, and let them take care that there be no slovenliness and discord in the public worship of the Most High. Take care to praise God also *mentally*. The grandest praise that floats up to the throne is that which arises from silent contemplation and reverent thought. Sit down and think of the greatness of God, his love, his power, his faithfulness and his sovereignty, and as your mind bows prostrate before his majesty, you will have praised him, though not a sound shall have come from you. Praise God also by your *actions*, your sacrifice to him of your property, your offering to him week by week of your substance. This is true praise and far less likely to be hypocritical than the mere thanksgiving of words. 'Ye that fear the Lord, praise him'.

FOR MEDITATION: God is offended by the idle songs of those who ignore him (Isaiah 5:11–12; Amos 6:4–6). He can be displeased with the gatherings and songs of his people (Amos 5:21–23). In our singing God is not looking for our ability to entertain others, but for right hearts, spirituality and understanding (Psalm 57:7–9; 1 Corinthians 14:15; Colossians 3:16).

SERMON NO. 799

Good news for the lost

'For the Son of man is come to seek and to save that which was lost.'
Luke 19:10
SUGGESTED FURTHER READING: John 8:1–11

There occurred not long ago an instance of the world's relentless cruelty
to those whom it is fashionable to brand with dishonour. A person, who
had perhaps fallen into sin in her earlier days, was restored to a
respectable position; she was received in society among the noblest, but
on a sudden dastardly lips revealed a secret and a sin committed far back
was raked up against her; henceforth the world put away the woman,
never asking her if she had repented, or taking her after-conduct into
consideration. The world is so pure, chaste and immaculate that it shut
out the erring one as if she had been a leper. Though itself reeking with
foulest abominations, society feigns a virtuousness pure as the lily and
chaste as the snow. The world is cold, hard and cruel towards a certain
class of offenders. It receives into its embraces men who are, every inch of
them, unclean; but a betrayed, deceived, broken-hearted woman, the
world shakes off as if she were a viper. This is the society which boasts its
gallantry! This is the just, fair-dealing world! It caresses its noble rakes,
but casts off the most penitent among the betrayed. Hypocritical, canting
world! Hollow, lying world, to pretend to a virtue which you do not
know! Rail not at the inconsistencies of religious men while your own are
so glaring! Cruel tyrant, learn mercy and do justice, before you become a
judge of the servants of the Lord. Now, 'the Son of man is come to seek
and to save' those whom the world puts outside its camp. The world says,
'Shame on her; we will not speak to her;' but Christ Jesus says, 'I have
come to pardon her and to restore her, and she shall love me much,
because much has been forgiven her!'

FOR MEDITATION: God will not despise a broken and contrite heart (Psalm
51:17), but stands by his people when they are despised and rejected of
men (Nehemiah 4:4; Isaiah 49:7; 60:14; Matthew 18:10). The Lord Jesus
Christ endured the very same treatment (Isaiah 53:3) and still regards it
as directed at him when his people are rejected (Luke 10:16).

Pray without ceasing

'Pray without ceasing.' 1 Thessalonians 5:17
SUGGESTED FURTHER READING: Jonah 1:1–6

One thing implied in the text is that a Christian has no right to go into any place where he could not continue to pray. Pray without ceasing? Then I am never to be in a place where I could not pray without ceasing. Hence many worldly amusements without being particularised may be judged and condemned at once. Certain people believe in ready-made prayers, cut and dried for all occasions and, at the same time, they believe persons to be regenerated in baptism though their lives are anything but Christian; ought they not to provide prayers for all circumstances in which these, the dear regenerated but graceless sons and daughters of the church, are found? As, for instance, a pious collect for a young prince or nobleman who is about to go to a shooting-match, that he may be forgiven for his cruelty towards those poor pigeons who are only badly wounded and made to linger in misery, as also a prayer for a religious and regenerated gentleman who is going to a horse-race, and a collect for young people, who have received the grace of confirmation, upon their going to the theatre to attend a very questionable play. Could not such special collects be made to order? You revolt at the idea. Well then, have nothing to do with that upon which you cannot ask God's blessing; have nothing to do with it, for if God cannot bless it, you may depend upon it the devil has cursed it. Anything that is right for you to do you may consecrate with prayer, and let this be a sure gauge and test to you; if you feel that it would be an insult to the majesty of heaven for you to ask the Lord's blessing upon what is proposed to you, then stand clear of the unholy thing. If God does not approve, neither must you have fellowship with it.

FOR MEDITATION: Are you involved in activities upon which you feel you cannot really pray for God's blessing? Actions carried out in prayerless doubt and disobedience are divorced from faith and amount to one thing—sin (Romans 14:23). In the suggested further reading Jonah proved it the hard way.

Christ the glory of his people

'A light to lighten the Gentiles, and the glory of thy people Israel.' Luke
2:32
SUGGESTED FURTHER READING: Romans 9:1–5

We must read this passage literally, for so Simeon intended it. The Lord
Jesus Christ, though once despised and rejected by his own countrymen,
is the great honour and splendour of God's people Israel. It is reckoned
an honour to a nation when eminent persons are born of its stock and
lineage; but Israel can claim the palm above all lands, for she can say that
our Lord sprang out of Judah. Put together all the heroic and famous
names of Greece and Rome; add all the literary splendours of Germany,
and the flashing beauties of France; combine with these the blazing fame
of Milton and Shakespeare, of Bacon and of Newton in our own land—
and all countries put together cannot compass so great a glory of
manhood as can the nation of the Jews, for they can claim not so much
Moses, David and the prophets, as Jesus of Nazareth, the King of the
Jews, in whom 'dwelleth all the fulness of the Godhead bodily.' If
mention be made of Egypt and Babylon, or Philistia and Tyre, saying
'this man was born there', the answer shall be concerning Zion, 'The Son
of Man was born in her.' It ill behoves us ever to speak slightingly of the
Jew. It ill behoves the Christian church to despond concerning the
conversion of the seed of Israel, or to be so indifferent as she sometimes
is to the conversion of Israel. Brethren, the day will come when the veil
shall be taken from the eye and the hardness from the heart, and
Abraham's sons shall behold the true Messiah and accept him as their
glory and their all. In that day, after the long time of winter, how bright
the summer will be! If their casting away brought the Gentiles so much
blessing, what will their gathering together be 'but life from the dead?'
After so long an alienation, how ravishing and delightful will be the
reconciliation between the Bridegroom and his ancient spouse!

FOR MEDITATION: Like every other nation the Jews have produced things
which are spiritually worthless (Mark 7:3–7; Philippians 3:5–8; Titus
1:13–14), but we ought to honour them as the channel through whom
God sent to us the Saviour (John 4:22; Romans 9:5).

Hidden manna

'Thy words were found, and I did eat them; and thy word was unto me the joy and rejoicing of mine heart: for I am called by thy name, O Lord God of hosts.' Jeremiah 15:16
SUGGESTED FURTHER READING: Psalm 119:97–112

A young man who had never read his Bible was led to conversion by the gift of a bookmark, presented to him by a relative. The gift was made upon the condition that it should be put into his Bible, but should never stop two days in one place. He meant to shift it and not to read the book, but his eye glanced on a text; after a while he became interested, by-and-by he was converted, and then the bookmark was moved with growing pleasure. Some professors cannot say that they shift their bookmark every day. Probably of all the books printed, the most widely circulated and the least read volume is the word of God. Books about the Bible are read, I fear, more than the Book itself. Would we see all these parties and sects if people studiously followed the teaching of inspiration? The Word is one; whence these many creeds? We cry, 'the Bible alone is the religion of Protestants'; but it is not true of half the Protestants. Some overlay the Bible with the Prayer-book and kill its living meaning; others read through the spectacles of a religious leader and follow man's gloss rather than God's text. Few indeed come to the pure fount of gospel undefiled. A second-hand religion suits most, for it spares them the trouble of thinking, which to many is a labour too severe; while to be taught of man is so much easier than to wait upon the Holy Spirit for instruction. Remember the words of Psalm 119 and make them your own. 'I will delight myself in thy statutes: I will not forget thy word.' 'How sweet are thy words unto my taste! Yea, sweeter than honey to my mouth!' 'Thy testimonies have I taken as an heritage for ever: for they are the rejoicing of my heart.' 'Mine eyes prevent the night watches, that I might meditate in thy word.' 'My soul hath kept thy testimonies; and I love them exceedingly. I have kept thy precepts and thy testimonies: for all my ways are before thee.'

FOR MEDITATION: God's word is truth and cannot be broken (John 10:35; 17:17). What man says about God's word is not always reliable (2 Peter 3:16) and needs to be checked against the Scriptures (Acts 17:11). Is the Bible your final authority for what you believe and do?

Backsliding healed

'I will heal their backsliding.' Hosea 14:4
SUGGESTED FURTHER READING: Jeremiah 3:20–25

There is consolation in the very fact that the Lord here looks upon the grievous sin of backsliding under the image of a disease. It is not said, 'I will pardon their backsliding', which is included in the term, but 'I will heal' it, as though he said, 'My poor people, I do remember that they are but dust; they are liable to a thousand temptations through the fall, and they soon go astray, but I will not treat them as though they were rebels; I will look upon them as patients and they shall look upon me as a physician.' There is consolation in the very fact that God should condescend for Jesus's sake thus to look upon our loathsome, abominable, ill-deserving, hell-deserving sin as being not so much a condemning iniquity in his sight as a disease upon which he looks, pitying us that we should endure the power of it. And then observe that, having looked at backsliding as a disease, he does not say, 'I will put this diseased one away.' Under the legal dispensation he who had leprosy or any contagious disease must be put without the camp, but it is not here said, 'I will banish them for their backsliding.' My dear friends, if we had been put out of God's church, and if we had never been allowed again to come to his table, we confess we have richly deserved to have it so, but it is not so written here. It is not, 'I will put them in quarantine; I will expel them out of the goodly land and from amongst my people', but 'I will heal their backsliding'. Much less does he say, 'I will destroy them because of their backsliding.' Some will have it that God's people may sin, partially and finally, so as never to be the Lord's beloved again; they sin themselves out of the covenant; but we have not so learned Christ, neither have we so understood the Fatherhood of our God.

'Whom once he loves, he never leaves,
But loves them to the end.'

FOR MEDITATION: Jesus likened the salvation of sinners to the healing of the sick (Mark 2:17). If he can heal us from the terminal disease of sin when we first return to him (1 Peter 2:24–25), he can just as surely heal us and receive us again when we return to him from later backslidings.

Why am I thus?

'I delight in the law of God after the inward man: but I see another law in my members, warring against the law of my mind, and bringing me into captivity to the law of sin which is in my members.' Romans 7:22–23
SUGGESTED FURTHER READING: Matthew 16:13–23

I knew a man once who, in attending a prayer-meeting, felt his heart much lifted up in the ways of God, drew very near to his heavenly Father, held sweet communication with Christ, and enjoyed much of the fellowship of the Spirit. Little did he think that the moment the prayer-meeting was over somebody in the congregation would insult and bitterly affront him. Because he was taken unawares his anger was roused and he spoke unadvisedly with his tongue. He had better have held his peace. I believe that if that man had been met at any other time, he would have taken the insult without resenting it or making any reply whatever, for he was of a tolerably quiet temper. But he had been unwarned and so was unguarded. The very love shed abroad in his heart caused the animosity he encountered to shock his feelings the more. He had been so near heaven that he expected everybody present to have had thoughts in harmony with his own; he had not reckoned upon being assailed then. When there is most money in the house, then is the likeliest time for thieves to break in; and when there is most grace in the soul, the devil will try, if he can, to assault it. Pirates were not accustomed to attack vessels when they went out to fetch gold from the Indies: they always waylaid them when they were coming home, with the view of getting rich spoil worth the capture. If you have enjoyed a sermon, if you have got near to God in prayer, if the Scriptures have been very precious to you, you may expect just then that the dragon that sleeps within will wake up and disturb the peaceful calm of your soul.

'We should suspect some danger nigh,
Where we possess delight.'

FOR MEDITATION: Christ's followers will be attacked and tempted by his enemies just as he was (John 15:18–20). The nearer we are to him, the more likely we are to get hit by attacks upon his cause. Our spiritual highs can be precarious times for us (1 Corinthians 10:12; Galatians 6:1), as Peter proved (Matthew 16:17,23).

The centurion's faith and humility

'The centurion sent friends to him, saying unto him, Lord, trouble not thyself: for I am not worthy that thou shouldest enter under my roof. Wherefore neither thought I myself worthy to come unto thee: but say in a word, and my servant shall be healed.' Luke 7:6–7
SUGGESTED FURTHER READING (Spurgeon): Matthew 8:5–13

Your sense of your unworthiness, if it be properly used, should drive you to Christ. You are unworthy, but Jesus died for the unworthy. Jesus did not die for those who profess to be by nature good and deserving, for the healthy have no need of a physician; but it is written, 'in due time Christ died for the ungodly.' 'Christ died for our' what? 'Excellencies and virtues'? No; 'Christ died for our sins according to the scriptures'. We read that 'Christ also hath once suffered for sins, the just for' whom? 'For the just'? By no means—'the just for the unjust, that he might bring us to God'. Gospel pharmacy is for the sick; gospel bread is for the hungry; gospel fountains are open to the unclean; gospel water is given to the thirsty. You who need not shall not have; but you who want it may freely come. Let your huge and painful needs impel you to fly to Jesus. Let the vast cravings of your insatiable spirit compel you to come to him in whom all fulness dwells. Your unworthiness should act as a wing to bear you to Christ, the sinner's Saviour. It should also have this effect upon you—it should prevent you raising those scruples and making those demands which so hinder some persons from finding peace. The proud spirit says, 'I must have signs and wonders, or I will not believe. I must feel deep convictions and horrible tremors or I must quake because of dreams or threatening texts applied to me with awful power.' But, unworthy one, if you are truly humbled, you will not dare to ask for these; you will have done with demands and stipulations and you will cry, 'Lord, give me but a word, speak but a word of promise, and it shall be enough for me. Do but say to me, "Thy sins are forgiven": give me but half a text, give me one kind assuring word to sink my fears again, and I will believe it and rest upon it.'

FOR MEDITATION: Christ died to justify the uncircumcised (Romans 3:30; Colossians 2:13), the ungodly (Romans 4:5; 5:6), the unjust (1 Peter 3:18) and the unrighteous (1 John 1:9), but not those who go on in their unbelief (John 3:18).

An old-fashioned conversion

'Lo, all these things worketh God oftentimes with man, to bring back his soul from the pit, to be enlightened with the light of the living.' Job 33:29–30

SUGGESTED FURTHER READING: Jeremiah 23:23–32

In the days of Elihu dreams were much more frequently the way in which God spoke (see Job 33:14–16), for there were few messengers from God to interpret his mind, no openly declared gospel, and few assemblies for instruction by hearing the word; there was then no written word of God. They had no inspired books at all, so that, lacking the Bible and the frequent ministrations of God's servants, the Lord was pleased to supply their deficiencies by speaking to men in the visions of the night. We must not expect the Lord to return to the general use of so feeble an agency now that he employs others which are far more effectual. It is much more profitable for you to have the word in your houses which you can read at all times and to have God's ministers to proclaim clearly the gospel of Jesus, than it would be to have to depend upon visions of the night. The means outwardly may have changed, but still, whether it be by the dream at night or by the sermon on the Sabbath, the power is just the same, namely in the word of God. If God speaks to men in dreams, he says nothing more and nothing different from what he says in the written word. If any say, 'I have dreamed this or that,' and it be not in the Scriptures, away with their dreams! If anything occurs in your own mind in a vision which is not already revealed in the Book of God, put it away; it is an idle fancy not to be regarded. Woe to that man whose religion is the baseless fabric of dreams; he will one day wake up to find that nothing short of realities could save him. We have 'a more sure word of prophecy; whereunto ye do well that ye take heed, as unto a light that shineth in a dark place'.

FOR MEDITATION: Even in the Old Testament warnings were given about the unreliability of dreams (Ecclesiastes 5:3,7). Under the law dreamers who diverted God's people from his ways were to be punished by death (Deuteronomy 13:1–5). Now that God has spoken to us even more clearly through his Son (Hebrews 1:2) and the New Testament, we have even less excuse for taking our stand on dubious visions which may cause us to depart from God (Colossians 2:18–19).

SERMON NO. 1101

Mercy's master motive

'For my name's sake will I defer mine anger, and for my praise will I refrain for thee, that I cut thee not off.' Isaiah 48:9
SUGGESTED FURTHER READING: Psalm 130:1–8

Truly the Lord's love does accomplish great moral wonders. Even among men forgiveness is often more potent than punishment. I have heard it related of a soldier at Woolwich, that he had frequently been drunk and disorderly; though he had been very frequently imprisoned and otherwise punished for his offences, he was incorrigible. On one occasion he had incurred the severe penalty of the lash and expected to receive it. He had no excuse to offer and did not pretend to make any. He was sullen and obdurate. At last the commanding officer said to him, 'We cannot do anything with you; we have imprisoned you; we have flogged you; yet we cannot improve you. There is only one thing we have never done with you, and that we are going to try; we forgive you.' The culprit broke down at once. Hard as he was, this new treatment overcame him. That word 'You are fully forgiven,' broke him down far more than the cat-o'-nine-tails; he was never an offender again. To many a soul that has been very obstinate against God, even to persecuting the followers of the Lord Jesus, the Lord has by the Holy Spirit said, 'I have loved thee with an everlasting love; I gave my Son to die for thee; I laid thy sins on him, and now I freely forgive thee, and take thee to be my child, my well-beloved.' Then how speedily the heart dissolves and the rebellious will surrenders.

'I yield—by mighty love subdued,
Who can resist its charms?
And throw myself, by wrath pursued,
Into my Saviour's arms.'

God grant that in many a case this may be true at this moment.

FOR MEDITATION: Even on a human level the kindness of others towards us is a powerful deterrent against wronging them in return (Genesis 39:8–9). How much more should God's kindness lead us to repentance from our sin (Romans 2:4). Mercy rather than vengeance is also God's prescription for us towards those who wrong us (Romans 12:19–20).

The old way of the wicked

'Hast thou marked the old way which wicked men have trodden? Which were cut down out of time, whose foundation was overflown with a flood: which said unto God, Depart from us: and what can the Almighty do for them?' Job 22:15–17
SUGGESTED FURTHER READING: 2 Chronicles 33:1–13

'Why will ye die?' Why will you choose a path that even now gives you no rest? Why select a way which hereafter shall fill you with eternal misery? Tarry awhile and ask yourself whether it be well to fling away your everlasting hope and ruin yourself for present wilfulness! Pause awhile! That sickness of yours from which you have just recovered, that loss of property which has made you so sorrowful, that dire affliction which you see in a beloved wife, all these are bars and chains. Will you overleap them, will you go steeple-chase to hell? Oh, sorry exertion for so miserable an end! No, let mercy arrest you. God's hand is out upon the bridle now, he reins up your horse, he thrusts back the steed upon its haunches; will you heed your Maker, will you let your conscience listen to his voice? Stay on the plains of mercy. If you break through this warning, you may have another and another, but the further the road is travelled the fewer the barricades and impediments become, till the last part of that tremendous road which leads down to death is all smooth as glass, and a soul may take a dreadful glissade, as down the steep sides of an Alpine mountain, and so glide into hell without the soul being disturbed. The Lord may give you up and then, like the train of which we read the other day in the newspapers, when the engine had become overpowered by the weight and the brakes were of no further use, the whole will run down the tremendous decline to destruction. God permits the last end of many men to be just such an awful descent. Put the brakes on this morning, seek to arrest the growing force of your lusts and the growing tendency towards evil, and may God's Spirit make use of the words which the text has suggested to us, to make you come to a dead halt and be saved by faith in Jesus!

FOR MEDITATION: Sometimes, if we ignore God's kindness towards us, he may allow calamity to befall us so that we are brought to our senses and back to him (2 Chronicles 33:10–13; Jonah 1:17–2:1; Luke 15:14–17). Has God needed to resort to extreme measures to attract your attention?

SERMON NO. 859

Carried by four

'And behold, men brought in a bed a man which was taken with a palsy: and they sought means to bring him in, and to lay him before him. And when they could not find by what way they might bring him in because of the multitude, they went upon the housetop, and let him down through the tiling with his couch into the midst before Jesus.' Luke 5:18–19

SUGGESTED FURTHER READING: 1 Corinthians 9:19–23

Mr Hartley in his Travels says: 'When I lived at Aegina I used to look up not infrequently at the roof above my head, and contemplate how easily the whole transaction of the paralytic might take place. The roof was made in the following manner:- a layer of reeds, of a large species, was placed upon the rafters; on these a quantity of heather was strewed; on the heather earth was deposited, and beaten down into a solid mass. Now, what difficulty would there be in removing first the earth, next the heather, and then the reeds? Nor would the difficulty be increased, if the earth had a pavement of tiling laid upon it. No inconvenience could result to the persons in the house from the removal of the tiles and earth; for the heather and reeds would stop anything that might otherwise fall down, and would be removed last of all.' To let a man down through the roof was a device most strange and striking, but it only gives point to the remark which we have to make here. If we want to have souls saved, we must not be too squeamish and delicate about conventionalities, rules and proprieties, for 'the kingdom of heaven suffereth violence'. We must make up our minds to this: 'Smash or crash, everything shall go to pieces which stands between the soul and its God: it matters not what tiles are to be taken off, what plaster is to be digged up, or what boards are to be torn away, or what labour, or trouble, or expense we may be at; the soul is too precious for us to stand upon nice questions. If by any means we may save some, is our policy. Skin for skin, all that we have is nothing comparable to a man's soul.'

FOR MEDITATION: Soul-seeking and soul-winning involves the salvation of the lost (Luke 19:10) from death (James 5:20). Saving sinners by 'pulling them out of the fire' (Jude 23) is not a description of a pastime or hobby, but of something far more serious and urgent.

Nathanael and the fig tree

'Jesus saw Nathanael coming to him, and saith of him, Behold an Israelite indeed, in whom is no guile! Nathanael saith unto him, Whence knowest thou me? Jesus answered and said unto him, Before that Philip called thee, when thou wast under the fig tree, I saw thee. Nathanael answered and saith unto him, Rabbi, thou art the Son of God.' John 1:47–49
SUGGESTED FURTHER READING: Acts 10:1–33

Though all have sinned and deserve the wrath of God, yet all unconverted men are not precisely in the same condition of mind in reference to the gospel. In the parable of the sower we are taught that before the good seed fell upon the field at all, there was a difference in the various soils; some of it was stony ground, another part was thorny, a third was trodden hard like a highway, while another plot is described by our Lord as 'good' ground. Although in every case the carnal mind is enmity against God, yet there are influences at work which in many cases have mitigated, if not subdued, that enmity. While many took up stones to kill our Lord, there were others who heard him gladly. While to this day thousands reject the gospel, there are others who receive the word with joy. These differences we ascribe to God's preparatory grace; we believe, however, that the subject of these differences is not aware that grace is at work upon him; neither is it precisely grace in the same form as saving grace, for the soul under its power has not yet learned its own need of Christ, or the excellency of his salvation. There is such a thing as a preparatory work of mercy on the soul, making it ready for the yet higher work of grace, even as the ploughing comes before the sowing. We read in the narrative of the creation that before the divine voice said, 'Let there be light', 'darkness was upon the face of the deep.' Yet it is added, 'And the Spirit of God moved upon the face of the waters.' Even so in the darkness of human nature, where as yet no ray of living light has shone, the Spirit of God may be moving with secret energy, making the soul ready for the hour when the true light shall shine.

FOR MEDITATION: Seeking souls are not the only ones who need God's preparatory grace. A work of grace is required in the soul-winner as well. Consider the preparation of Ananias (Acts 9:10–16) and Peter (Acts 10:9–16,28) for witnessing, while God was respectively preparing Saul and Cornelius for their conversions.

SERMON NO. 921

Broken bones

'Make me to hear joy and gladness; that the bones which thou hast broken may rejoice.' Psalm 51:8
SUGGESTED FURTHER READING: Isaiah 1:1–8

When a heart is broken with repentance, the gangrene of remorse is most urgent to enter it; when the spirit is humbled, the gangrene of unbelief covets the opportunity to take possession of the man; when the heart is really emptied and made to feel its own nothingness, then the demon despair beholds a dark cavern in which to fix its horrible abode. It is a dreadful thing to have the faith broken, the hope broken and the love broken, and the entire man, as it were, reduced to a palpitating mass of pain. It is a dreadfully dangerous condition to be in; alas, when men have sinned and have been made to suffer afterwards, how often have they turned to their sins again with greater hardness of heart than ever! With many, the more they are smitten the more they revolt. When 'the whole head is sick, and the whole heart faint' and they seem to be nothing 'but wounds, and bruises, and putrifying sores' through the afflictions they have suffered, yet they return to their idols still and the more they are chastened the more they revolt. Think, I pray you, how many professors have backslidden and have been chastened, but have continued in their backsliding until they have gone down to hell! I did not say children of God, but professors; and how do you know that you are not mere professors yourselves? My friend, if you are living in known sin at this time and are happy in it, you have great cause to tremble. If you can go on from day to day, and from week to week, in neglected prayer and neglected reading of the word, if you can live without the means of grace in the weekdays, if you are cold and indifferent towards our Lord and Master, if you are altogether becoming worldly, covetous, vain, and fond of levity and the things of this world, and yet are at ease, you have grave cause to suspect that you are not one of the true children of the living God.

FOR MEDITATION: Mere realisation of sin can lead to the fearful dead-ends of remorse (Matthew 27:3–5) and regret (Hebrews 12:16–17). Only when accompanied by true repentance does it lead to the wide open door of forgiveness (Luke 24:47; Acts 5:31), eternal life (Acts 11:18) and salvation (2 Corinthians 7:10).

SERMON NO. 861

The woman which was a sinner

'And, behold, a woman in the city, which was a sinner, when she knew that Jesus sat at meat in the Pharisee's house, brought an alabaster box of ointment, and stood at his feet behind him weeping, and began to wash his feet with tears, and did wipe them with the hairs of her head, and kissed his feet, and anointed them with the ointment.' Luke 7:37–38
SUGGESTED FURTHER READING *(Spurgeon)*: Psalm 116:1–19

Love—*its source*: it bubbles up as a pure stream from the well-head of grace. 'She loved much', but it was because much had been forgiven. There is no such thing as mere natural love to God. The only true love which can burn in the human heart towards the Lord is that which the Holy Spirit himself kindles. If you truly love the God who made and redeemed you, you may be well assured that you are his child, for none but his children have any love to him. Its *secondary cause* is faith. Luke 7:50 tells us 'Thy faith hath saved thee'. Our souls do not begin with loving Christ, but the first lesson is to trust. Many penitents attempt this difficult task; they aspire to reach the stair-head without treading the steps; they insist on reaching the pinnacle of the temple before they have crossed the threshold. First trust Christ for the pardon of your sin: when your sins are forgiven, love shall flash to your heart as the result of gratitude for what the Redeemer has done for you. Grace is the source of love, but faith is the agent by which love is brought to us. *The food* of love is a sense of sin and of forgiveness. If we felt more deeply the guilt of our past lives, we should love Jesus Christ better. If we had a clearer sense that our sins deserve the deepest hell, that Christ suffered what we ought to have suffered in order to redeem us from our iniquities, we should not be such cold-hearted creatures. We are perfectly monstrous in our lack of love to Christ, but the true secret of it is a forgetfulness of our ruined and lost natural estate, and of the sufferings by which we have been redeemed from that condition. O that our love might feed itself this day and find a renewal of its strength in remembering what sovereign grace has done.

FOR MEDITATION: God's love towards us provided God with motives for action (John 3:16; Galatians 2:20). We do not love him naturally (1 John 4:10); our love towards God has to be prompted by his loving actions towards us (Psalm 116:1; 1 John 4:19). Do you love God? Why?

SERMON NO. 801

The conditions of power in prayer

'And whatsoever we ask, we receive of him, because we keep his commandments, and do those things that are pleasing in his sight. And this is his commandment, That we should believe on the name of his Son Jesus Christ, and love one another, as he gave us commandment. And he that keepeth his commandments dwelleth in him, and he in him.' 1 John 3:22–24
SUGGESTED FURTHER READING (Spurgeon): Isaiah 1:10–20

If you sincerely seek mercy of God through Jesus Christ you shall have it. Whatever may have been your previous condition of life, if you now penitently seek Jehovah's face through the appointed Mediator, he will be found of you. If the Holy Spirit has taught you to pray, hesitate no longer, but hasten to the cross and there rest your guilty soul on Jesus. Qualifications for the sinner's first prayer I know of none except sincerity; but we must speak in a different way to those of you who are saved. You have now become the people of God, and while you shall be heard just as the sinner would be heard and shall daily find the needful grace which every sinner receives in answer to prayer, yet you are now a child of God and you are under a special discipline peculiar to the regenerated family. In that discipline answers to prayer occupy a high position and are of eminent use. There is something for a believer to enjoy over and above bare salvation; there are mercies, blessings, comforts and favours which render his present life useful, happy and honourable, and these he shall not have irrespective of character. They are not vital matters with regard to salvation; those the believer possesses unconditionally, for they are covenant blessings; but we now refer to the honours and the delicacies of the house. If you neglect the conditions appended to these, your heavenly Father will withhold them from you. The essential blessings of the covenant of grace stand unconditioned; the invitation to seek for mercy is addressed to those who have no qualifications whatever except their need: but come inside the divine family as saved men and women, and you will find that other choice blessings are given or withheld according to our attention to the Lord's rules in his family.

FOR MEDITATION: The same Lord who promises the gift of salvation to every one who calls upon him (Romans 10:13) also warns his people not to expect anything else from him if they ask wrongly (James 1:6–7; 4:3).

SERMON NO. 1103

Glorious predestination

'For whom he did foreknow, he also did predestinate to be conformed to the image of his Son, that he might be the firstborn among many brethren.' Romans 8:29
SUGGESTED FURTHER READING: Romans 11:1–6

It is asserted that the Lord foreknew who would repent, believe in Jesus and persevere in a consistent life to the end. This is readily granted, but a reader must use very powerful magnifying glasses before he will be able to discover that sense in the text. Upon looking carefully at my Bible again I do not perceive such a statement. Where are those words which you have added—'Whom he did foreknow to repent, to believe, and to persevere in grace'? I do not find them in the English version or in the Greek original. If I could so read them the passage would certainly be very easy and would greatly alter my doctrinal views; but, as I do not find those words there, I do not believe in them. However wise and advisable a human interpolation may be, it has no authority with us; we bow to holy Scripture, but not to glosses which theologians may choose to put upon it. No hint is given in the text of foreseen virtue any more than of foreseen sin and, therefore, we are driven to find another meaning. We find that the word 'know' is frequently used in Scripture not only for knowledge, but also for favour and love. Our Lord Jesus Christ will say in the judgment concerning certain persons, 'I never knew you', yet in a sense he knew them, for he knows every man; the wicked as well as the righteous; but there the meaning is, 'I never knew you so as to feel any favour towards you.' See also John 10:14–15 and 2 Timothy 2:19. In Romans 11:2 we read, 'God hath not cast away his people which he foreknew', where the sense evidently has the idea of fore-love; and it is so to be understood here. Those whom the Lord looked upon with favour as he foresaw them, 'he also did predestinate to be conformed to the image of his Son'.

FOR MEDITATION: Events are seen and foreseen (Acts 2:31; Galatians 3:8), but God's people themselves are known and foreknown (1 Peter 1:2). Before God told him, Jeremiah was unaware of the relationship he already had with God before his birth (Jeremiah 1:5); the same is true of all who come to faith in Christ, as the apostle Paul discovered for himself (Galatians 1:15).

SERMON NO. 1043

Mourning at the sight of the crucified

'And all the people that came together to that sight, beholding the things which were done, smote their breasts, and returned.' Luke 23:48
SUGGESTED FURTHER READING: John 16:16–28

You and I are not in the same condition as the multitude who had surrounded Calvary; for at that time our Lord was still dead, but now he is risen indeed. There were yet three days from that Thursday evening (for there is much reason to believe that our Lord was not crucified on Friday) in which Jesus must dwell in the regions of the dead. Our Lord, therefore, so far as human eyes could see him, was a proper object of pity and mourning and not of thanksgiving; but now, beloved, he ever lives and gloriously reigns. No charnel house confines that blessed body. He saw no corruption; for the moment when the third day dawned, he could no longer be held with the bonds of death, but he manifested himself alive unto his disciples. He tarried in this world for forty days. Some of his time was spent with those who knew him in the flesh; perhaps a larger part of it was passed with those saints who came out of their graves after his resurrection; but certain it is that he is gone up as the first-fruit from the dead; he is gone up to the right hand of God, even the Father. Do not bewail those wounds; they are gleaming with heavenly splendour. Do not lament his death: he lives no more to die. Do not mourn that shame and spitting:—

'The head that once was crowned with thorns,
Is crowned with glory now.'

Look up and thank God that 'death hath no more dominion over him.' 'He ever liveth to make intercession for us', and he shall shortly come with angelic bands surrounding him, to judge the living and the dead. The argument for joy overshadows the reason for sorrow.

FOR MEDITATION: It was the reports and sightings of the risen Christ which brought joy to sorrowing women and to frightened apostles (Matthew 28:8; Luke 24:41; John 20:20). If he had never risen from the dead, they and we would have had to remain the most miserable of people (1 Corinthians 15:17–19).

SERMON NO. 860

The ascension of Christ

'Wherefore he saith, When he ascended up on high, he led captivity captive, and gave gifts unto men. ... And he gave some, apostles; and some, prophets; and some, evangelists; and some, pastors and teachers; for the perfecting of the saints, for the work of the ministry, for the edifying of the body of Christ.' Ephesians 4:8,11–12

SUGGESTED FURTHER READING (Spurgeon): Psalm 68:1–19

Did you notice in Psalm 68:18 the words, 'Thou has received gifts for men; yea, for the rebellious also'? When the Lord went back to his throne, he had thoughts of love towards rebels still. The spiritual gifts of the church are for the good of the rebels as well as for the building up of those who are reconciled. Sinner, every true minister exists for your good, and all the workers of the church have an eye to you. There are one or two promises connected with our Lord's ascension which show his kindness to you: 'I, if I be lifted up from the earth, will draw all men unto me.' An ascended Saviour draws you—run after him. Here is another word: 'Him hath God exalted'—to curse? No—'to give repentance to Israel, and forgiveness of sins.' Look up to the glory into which he has entered; ask for repentance and forgiveness. Do you doubt his power to save you? Here is another text: 'he is able also to save them to the uttermost that come unto God by him, seeing he ever liveth to make intercession for them.' Surely he has gone to heaven for you as well as for the saints. You ought to take good heart and put your trust in him at this happy hour. How dangerous it will be to despise him! They who despised him in his shame perished. Jerusalem became a field of blood because it rejected the despised Nazarene. What will it be to reject the King, now that he has taken to himself his great power? Remember that this same Jesus who has gone up to heaven 'shall so come in like manner' as he was seen to go up into heaven. His return is certain, and your summons to his bar equally certain; but what account can you give if you reject him? O come and trust him this day.

FOR MEDITATION: We all have cause to be grateful to God for his patient, merciful and forgiving attitude towards the rebellious (Isaiah 65:1–2; Daniel 9:5,9), but the ascended Lord Jesus Christ acts an as advocate with the Father only on behalf of those who come to him in repentance for their rebelliousness (1 John 1:9; 2:1).

SERMON NO. 982

Prepare to meet thy God

'Prepare to meet thy God, O Israel.' Amos 4:12
SUGGESTED FURTHER READING: Revelation 6:12–17

Think awhile upon whom you have to meet! You must meet *your God*! That is, you must meet *offended justice* whose laws you have broken, whose penalties you have ridiculed; justice righteously indignant, with its sword drawn, you must confront. You must be examined by *unblinded omniscience*. Him who has seen your heart, read your thoughts, jotted down your affections and remembered your idle words, you must meet. *Infinite discernment* you must meet, those eyes that never yet were duped, the God who will see through the veils of hypocrisy and all the concealments of formality. There will be no making yourself out to be better than you are before him. You must meet him who will read you as a man reads a book. You must meet with *unsullied holiness*. You have not always found yourself happy on earth when you have been with holy men; you could not act out your natural impulses in their presence; they were a check upon you; but what must it be to meet the infinitely holy God? You will have to meet with *insulted mercy*, and perhaps this will be the most dreadful meeting of the whole, when your conscience will remind you that you were invited to repent, urged to lay hold of Christ and bidden to be saved, but you would not be persuaded. O sinner, by so much as God is patient with you now, by so much will he be angry with you then. They who slight the warnings of his grace shall feel the terrors of his wrath. To none shall it be so hard to meet God in justice as to those who would not meet him in grace; vengeance takes the place of slighted mercy. God grant that you may never know what it is to meet insulted love, rejected mercy and tenderness turned to wrath!

FOR MEDITATION: Under the old covenant God gave his people a place in which they could safely meet with him (Exodus 25:21–22). He has now given us a person in whom we can come to him (John 14:6) and whom believers will gladly meet at his second coming (1 Thessalonians 4:17). But to meet God outside of Christ will be most appalling (Hebrews 10:31).

N.B. Spurgeon's choice of subject was affected on the previous evening when he was called out to a dying girl who had long attended the Metropolitan Tabernacle. 'I know I do love Jesus,' she said as she died.

SERMON NO. 923

The stone rolled away

'The angel of the Lord descended from heaven, and came and rolled back the stone from the door, and sat upon it.' Matthew 28:2
SUGGESTED FURTHER READING: John 5:19–29

The resurrection acts much in the same manner as the pillar which Jehovah placed between Israel and Egypt; it was darkness to Egypt, but it gave light to Israel. All was dark amidst Egypt's hosts, but all was brightness and comfort amongst Israel's tribes. So the resurrection is a doctrine full of horror to those who know not Christ and trust him not. What have they to gain by resurrection? Happy were they could they sleep in everlasting annihilation. What have they to gain by Christ's resurrection? Shall he come whom they have despised? Is he living whom they have hated and abhorred? Will he bid them rise? Will they have to meet him as a Judge upon the throne? The very thought of this is enough to smite through the loins of kings today; but what will the fact of it be when the clarion trumpet startles all the sons of Adam from their last beds of dust? Oh, the horrors of that tremendous morning, when every sinner shall rise and the risen Saviour shall come in the clouds of heaven and all the holy angels with him! Truly there is nothing but dismay for those who are on the evil side of that resurrection stone. But how great the joy which the resurrection brings to those who are on the right side of that stone! How they look for his appearing with ecstasy growing daily! How they build upon the sweet truth that they shall arise and see their Saviour with their eyes! I would have you ask yourselves today on which side of that boundary stone you are. Have you life in Christ? Are you risen with Christ? Do you trust alone in him who rose from the dead? If so, do not fear: the angel comforts you and Jesus cheers you; but if you have no life in Christ, but are dead while you live, let the very thought that Jesus is risen strike you with fear and make you tremble, for tremble well you may at what awaits you.

FOR MEDITATION: Scripture does not say much about the resurrection body of the unsaved, but their fate cannot be any better than that of the unnamed rich man in Hades who 'lift up his eyes, being in torments' (Luke 16:23) and who cried out 'cool my tongue; for I am tormented in this flame' (Luke 16:24). The saved will be free from all tears in their eyes, crying and pain (Revelation 21:4). Which group will you be joining?

SERMON NO. 863

Israel's God and God's Israel

'There is none like unto the God of Jeshurun, who rideth upon the heaven in thy help, and in his excellency on the sky. The eternal God is thy refuge, and underneath are the everlasting arms.' Deuteronomy 33:26–27
SUGGESTED FURTHER READING: 1 Kings 19:1–8

What a grand day that was for Elijah when he saw the fire come down upon his bullock in answer to his prayer, and he cried in holy wrath, 'Take the prophets of Baal; let not one of them escape.' I think I see the grim pleasure in the prophet's face as he saw them taken to the brook and slain. Behold his exhilaration as he binds up his loins and runs before Ahab's chariot, keeping pace with the monarch's horses, with an agility in which soul and body joined. And then what happens a day or two afterwards? In the wilderness all alone, he has fled from a woman's face and you hear him cry, 'take away my life; for I am not better than my fathers.' Yes, the man who was never to die at all prayed that he might die. Just so, high exaltations involve deep depressions. But what was under Elijah when he fell down in that fainting fit under the juniper tree? Why, underneath were the everlasting arms. So shall it be with you who are called thus to fall into the depths of depression; the eternal arms shall be lower than you are. Brethren, there are many such occasions in which the spirit sinks sometimes through a sense of sin, through disappointments, through desertions of friends, through beholding the decay of the Lord's work, through a lack of success in ministry, or a thousand other mischiefs which may all cast us low, even as low as Jonah who said he 'went down to the bottoms of the mountains;' but when Jonah went to the lowest, underneath him were the everlasting arms; and when the earth with her bars was about him for ever and the weeds were wrapped about his head, he came up again, because still lower than him was the hand of God: the everlasting arms were underneath him still.

FOR MEDITATION: The arms of the almighty God are strong to rule, but a safe refuge for his lambs (Isaiah 40:10–11). Remember how gently the Lord Jesus Christ took up children in his arms (Mark 9:36; 10:16). Everlasting consolation, good hope and comfort (2 Thessalonians 2:16–17) are available to all who are 'Safe in the arms of Jesus'.

SERMON NO. 803

Spring

'As the earth bringeth forth her bud, and as the garden causeth the things that are sown in it to spring forth; so the Lord GOD will cause righteousness and praise to spring forth before all the nations.' Isaiah 61:11
SUGGESTED FURTHER READING: Psalm 65:9–13

We have never been able to agree with the theory that nature once started, works of itself like a clock which has been wound up. We believe that its operations conform to certain laws, but there must be some power to carry out the laws, or else they would be a dead letter. Everything that exists is a continuous emanation from the Most High, and everything that is done anywhere in the world, God lends the strength and gives the power whereby it is done. If we were to see performed in a single moment the turning of one grain of wheat into a full-grown ear, we should exclaim, 'wonderful!' and regard it as a miracle! But if God is pleased to take some few months in performing the same operation, it is no less wonderful. If spring came but once in a century, what wonder it would excite in all hearts! If it had happened once only, it would be considered to be the crown of miracles, and sceptics would ridicule those who believed in its possibility; yet God creates our harvests as surely as if there had never been a harvest before, and he forms our ripe fields by his omnipotence as truly even as he fashioned man in the garden of Eden, perfect at once! God is alive and God is at work; he has not taken himself into his secret chambers and shut the door behind him to leave us orphans in the world and the earth without a ruler and friend! He works everywhere, in the deepest caverns of the sea and among the highest pinnacles of the heavens: and there, he works among the violets of yonder bank and the primroses which peer forth from amidst the withered leaves around the underwood of the copse, and there also, where the bees begin to hum, the lark to sing and the lambs to play. It is God who sends 'Spring, the Awakener,' to fill the earth with flowers. He does it all!

FOR MEDITATION: The god of Deism who creates the world and leaves it to run without his further intervention is not the God of the Bible! The true and living God who created all things (Acts 14:15) has continued to visit his creation (Psalm 65:9), doing good and providing us with rain, seasons and food (Leviticus 26:4; Psalm 104:27–28; 145:15–16; Acts 14:17). Are you grateful to him?

SERMON NO. 1104

Loosing the shoe-latchet

'One mightier than I cometh, the latchet of whose shoe
to unloose.' Luke 3:16
SUGGESTED FURTHER READING: Luke 7:36–50

In small things lie the crucibles and the touchstones. A
come to the Sunday worship, but it is not every hypocrit
prayer-meetings, or read the Bible in secret, or speak
things of God to the saints. These are less things, so
therefore they neglect them and so condemn themselve
deep religion prayer is loved: where religion is shallow o
worship are cared for. You shall find the same true in other things. A man
who is no Christian will very likely not tell you a downright lie by saying
that black is white, but he will not hesitate to declare that whity-brown is
white—he will go to that length. Now, the Christian will not go halfway
to falsehood; he scorns to go an inch on that road. He will no more cheat
you out of twopence, than he would out of two thousand pounds. He
will not rob you of an inch any more than of a mile. It is in the little that
the genuineness of the Christian is made to appear; the Goldsmiths' Hall
mark is a small affair, but you know true silver by it. There is a vast deal
of difference between the man who gladly bears Christ's shoes and
another who will not stoop to anything which he thinks beneath him.
Even a Pharisee will ask Christ to his house to sit at meat with him and is
willing to entertain a great religious leader at his table; but it is not
everyone who will stoop down and unloose his shoes, for that very
Pharisee who made the feast neither brought him water to wash his feet,
nor gave him the kiss of welcome; he proved the insincerity of his
hospitality by forgetting the little things.

FOR MEDITATION: The Lord Jesus Christ had no time for those who
publicly paraded their big deeds (Matthew 6:1–2,5,7,16). What his people
do in secret means far more to him (Matthew 6:4,6,18). Faithfulness or
unfaithfulness in the smallest of things speaks volumes (Luke 16:10).

The old man crucified

'Knowing this, that our old man is crucified with him.' Romans 6:6
SUGGESTED FURTHER READING: Galatians 5:13–6:1

Crucifixion was a lingering death. Our old nature has not been put to death by the sword, or stoning, or burning; it has been crucified; this will bring on a sure death in time, but it is slow. A man crucified often lived for hours and days and, I have read, even for a week. Our old man will linger on his cross as long as we are alive on earth. Each one of our sins has a horrible vitality about it. 'As many lives as a cat,' John Bunyan said unbelief had; and the same may be said of every sin within us; it is crucified, but it is not wholly dead. Expect to have fight with sin, till you sheathe your sword and put on your crown. I speak with great respect to my dear friends who wear the honourable insignia of old age, but they may let one who is a child compared to them remind them that old age does not bring with it such a weakening in the man to sin, as to permit them to cease from watchfulness. When passions cannot be indulged, they often rage the more furiously; and if one sin be driven out by change of life, another will often labour to possess the soul in its place. Alas that men should ever begin to trust to their experience or their acquired prudence, for then they are the most likely persons to fall into sin. Your lusts are crucified, but they live, and there is vitality enough in them to make you rue the day, if the nails of grace do not hold them fast and keep the demons to their tree of doom.

FOR MEDITATION: The Christian has crucified the flesh (Galatians 5:24) and is crucified unto the world (Galatians 6:14), but is still repeatedly warned to beware of the ongoing influences of both the flesh and the world (Romans 13:14; Galatians 5:13,16; Titus 2:12; 1 Peter 2:11; 1 John 2:15–16).

SERMON NO. 882

Good news for loyal subjects

'He must reign.' 1 Corinthians 15:25
SUGGESTED FURTHER READING: Romans 7:13–25

The text occurs in that memorable chapter concerning the resurrection and it especially points to death. 'For he must reign, till he hath put all enemies under his feet. The last enemy that shall be destroyed is death.' Now, beloved believer, you are called to fight daily with sin, and here is your consolation—Jesus must reign. The Christ in you must bruise Satan under your feet. His atonement has for ever destroyed the damning power of your sins. Christ reigns supreme on the milk-white throne of mercy as the pardoning God. Even so Jesus must reign over the active power of sin within your heart, for his death is the double death of sin; he has pierced its heart and nailed its hands and feet; 'sin shall not have dominion over you'. Jesus, the King of kings, must hold his court in the castle-yard of your heart, and all your powers and passions must do him cheerful homage. Most sweet prince, thou shalt wear thy royal robes in the coronation chamber of my affections; thou shalt reign over my quick imperious temper. He shall put his foot on the neck of my pride and shall command my every thought and wish. Where I cannot rule, Jesus can. Rebellious lusts own the spell of the cross, and indwelling sin falls like Dagon before that ark. Jesus has made us kings and priests that we may reign over the triple monarchy of our nature—spirit, soul and body—and that by our self-conquest he may be undisputed sovereign of the isle of man. You who are contending with your corruptions, push on the war, for he must reign. Corruption is very strong, but Christ is stronger, and grace must 'reign through righteousness unto eternal life by Jesus Christ our Lord.' I think I hear you groaning, 'O wretched man that I am! Who shall deliver me from the body of this death?' Listen to the answer; it rings like a sweet Sabbath bell—'I thank God through Jesus Christ our Lord.'

FOR MEDITATION: Christ must reign and 'he shall reign' (Luke 1:33; Romans 15:12; Revelation 11:15). Sin and death have not disappeared, but have they ceased to reign over you? Have they been succeeded by the reign of God's grace in your life (Romans 5:17,21; 6:12–14)?

SERMON NO. 807

Jesus only

'And when they had lifted up their eyes, they saw no man, save Jesus only.' Matthew 17:8
SUGGESTED FURTHER READING: Psalm 73:21–28

I do desire for my fellow Christians and for myself, that more and more the great object of our thoughts, motives and acts may be 'Jesus only.' I believe that whenever our religion is most vital, it is most full of Christ. Moreover, when it is most practical, downright and common sense, it always gets nearest to Jesus. I can bear witness that whenever I am in deeps of sorrow, nothing will do for me but 'Jesus only.' I can rest in some degree in the externals of religion, its outward escarpments and bulwarks, when I am in health; but I retreat to the innermost citadel of our holy faith, namely, to the very heart of Christ, when my spirit is assailed by temptation, or besieged with sorrow and anguish. What is more, my witness is that whenever I have high spiritual enjoyments, rich, rare and celestial, they are always connected with 'Jesus only'; other religious things may give some kind of joy, and joy that is healthy too, but the most sublime and divine of all joys must be found in 'Jesus only.' In short, I find if I want to labour much, I must live on 'Jesus only'; if I desire to suffer patiently, I must feed on 'Jesus only'; if I wish to wrestle with God successfully, I must plead 'Jesus only'; if I aspire to conquer sin, I must use the blood of 'Jesus only'; if I pant to learn the mysteries of heaven, I must seek the teachings of 'Jesus only.' I believe that anything which we add to Christ lowers our position, and that the more elevated our souls become, the more nearly like what they are to be when they shall enter into the region of the perfect, the more completely everything else will sink and die out; and Jesus, 'Jesus only', will be first and last, the Alpha and Omega of every thought of head and pulse of heart. May it be so with every Christian!

FOR MEDITATION: Do you share the single-mindedness of those who wanted to see Jesus (Luke 19:2–4; John 12:20–21)? We cannot do better than meditate on Jesus Christ and him crucified; this was the unique aim of the apostle Paul's preaching (1 Corinthians 2:2) and the sole object of his glorying (Galatians 6:14).

SERMON NO. 924

Life's ever-springing well

'The water that I shall give him shall be in him a well of water springing up into everlasting life.' John 4:14
SUGGESTED FURTHER READING (Spurgeon): Romans 8:9–11

How about this matter? How fares it with you? Have you this life within you? I do not ask whether you have been baptised. I make no enquiry whether you have taken communion lately. Have you within you a life which only God can give? Is your religion only a thing of saying prayers, reading chapters and singing hymns, or is it a life? Suppose there were no churches, no chapels, no sermons, no assemblies for worship, would you still be a Christian? Have you a secret something within you which cannot be weighed in the scales, nor measured, nor comprehended in the balance, a mystery which the eagle's eye has not seen and which the lion's whelps have not discerned, a secret inner life which philosophy cannot detect and which carnal reason will not perceive, but which is most sure and true, the incorruptible seed within your soul? Have you a life within you, strange, unearthly and supernatural? Do your prayers come from within? Do your praises well up from the deeps of your spirit? Have you had personal dealings with God? Have you ever told him your sins out of a broken heart? Have you looked to Jesus with a tearful but believing eye and for yourself rested on him? Remember, as surely as this book was written by the finger of God, so true is it that you can never enter heaven unless you have within your own heart the Holy Spirit dwelling there, and unless you be yourself renewed in the spirit of your mind. 'Except ye be converted, and become as little children, ye shall not enter into the kingdom of heaven.' 'Ye must be born again.' How is it with you? God help you to search yourself, and give you a just and true deliverance.

FOR MEDITATION: Thinking that we have eternal life is a total deception unless we come to Christ to receive eternal life (John 5:39–40); but if we have trusted in him, we can actually know that we have eternal life (1 John 5:13).

Apostolic exhortation

'Repent ye therefore, and be converted, that your sins may be blotted out, when the times of refreshing shall come from the presence of the Lord.'
Acts 3:19
SUGGESTED FURTHER READING: Ezekiel 18:27–32

Perhaps there is no better definition of repentance than that which is given in our little children's hymn-book:—

'Repentance is to leave the sins we loved before,
And show that we in earnest grieve, by doing so no more.'

Repentance is a discovery of the evil of sin, a mourning that we have committed it, a resolution to forsake it. It is, in fact, a change of mind of a very deep and practical character, which makes the man love what once he hated, and hate what once he loved. Conversion means a turning round, a turning from and a turning to—a turning from sin to holiness, from carelessness to thought, from the world to heaven, from self to Jesus, a complete turning. The word here translated 'be converted', is not so in the Greek; it is really, 'Repent … and convert', or rather, 'Repent … and turn'. It is an active word. When the demoniac had the devils cast out of him, I may compare that to repentance; but when he put on his clothes and was no longer naked and filthy, but 'clothed, and in his right mind', I may compare that to conversion. When the prodigal was feeding the pigs and suddenly began to consider and to come to himself, that was repentance. When he set out and left the far country and went to his father's house, that was conversion. Repentance is a part of conversion. It is, perhaps, the gate or door to it. It is that Jordan through which we pass when we turn from the desert of sin to seek the Canaan of conversion. Regeneration is the implanting of a new nature, and one of the earliest signs of that is a faith in Christ, a repentance from sin, and a consequent conversion from evil to good.

FOR MEDITATION: Repentance never stands alone but alongside a turning from sin (Ezekiel 18:30) to God (Acts 26:20), faith in the Lord Jesus Christ (Mark 1:15; Acts 20:21) and fruit in a transformed life (Matthew 3:8; Acts 26:20). Have you repented? God commands all to repent (Acts 17:30).

SERMON NO. 804

The heart of Jesus

'I am meek and lowly in heart.' Matthew 11:29
SUGGESTED FURTHER READING: 1 Peter 2:18–3:2

Matthew Henry says that there are only three men in the Bible whose faces are said to have shone, Moses, Jesus and Stephen, and all these were meek men. God will not make angry men's faces shine; rather do they gather blackness. If anything can put a divine glow on a Christian's face, it is a readiness to forgive. If you are ready to forgive, you possess one of the sweetest beauties of the Redeemer's character. The power of meekness is wonderful if we would but believe it. There is no power in anger; after all, 'the wrath of man worketh not the righteousness of God.' Stoop to conquer: submit to overcome. Holy Mr Dodd when reproving a profligate was assailed by him in his anger, and two of the good man's teeth were knocked out; simply wiping the blood from his mouth, the man of God said, 'And I will cheerfully allow you to knock out all the rest if you will but mind what I have said, and seek the salvation of your soul.' His opponent felt that there was something in the good man which he did not possess, and he was won to a better mind. A woman who had previously been terribly quarrelsome was converted. Her husband persecuted her cruelly for her religion; one day in his passion he struck her on the face so as to knock her to the ground; she simply rose and said, 'But, my husband, if it would do you any good and bring you to Christ, I would be willing to be struck again.' 'Woman,' he said, 'these religious people have made a wonderful change in you, or you would not have spoken so gently; go where you will from now on.' Nothing conquers like meekness, not the meekness which is pretended, but real gentleness.

FOR MEDITATION: Persecution and evil should not be repaid in kind with cursing and vengeance but with the more noble reaction of goodness (Romans 12:14–21). This was the Master's approach and he expects his disciples to follow his example (1 Peter 2:20–21). Learn the lesson of Proverbs 15:1.

Joy in a reconciled God

'And not only so, but we also joy in God through our Lord Jesus Christ, by whom we have now received the atonement.' Romans 5:11
SUGGESTED FURTHER READING (Spurgeon): Isaiah 12:1–6

Joy in God is the happiest of all joys. There are other sweets, but this is the virgin honey dropping fresh from the comb. Joy in God is also a most elevating joy. Those who joy in wealth grow avaricious, while those who joy in their friends too often lose nobility of spirit; but he who boasts in God grows like God. It is a solid joy, and he who joys in God has good reasons for rejoicing. He has arguments which will justify his joy at any time. He who rejoices in God shall never be confounded or ashamed, world without end. It is an abiding joy. If I rejoice in the sun, it sets; if in the earth, it shall be burnt up; if in myself, I shall die; but to triumph in One who never fails and never changes, but lasts for ever, this is lasting joy. In a word, it is celestial joy. It flows like the river of God which rises at the foot of his throne and waters the celestial streets, while trees on either side bear all manner of fruits. Blessed is the man whose nature strikes its roots deep into the banks of this river; he 'bringeth forth his fruit in his season; his leaf also shall not wither; and whatsoever he doeth shall prosper.' The only sad reflection is that there are so many who know nothing about joy in God. They could never gaze upon the stars and say, 'My God, thou hast made all these, and I love thee; I love thee not as I fancy thou art, but as thou hast said thou art in the Scripture; I would not alter thy nature if I could; I would not tempt thee by saying, "Do not this or that;" whatever thou doest I admire, for I am reconciled to thee, and I joy in thee.'

FOR MEDITATION: Things may fail us (Habakkuk 3:17) and people may forsake us (Psalm 27:10; Isaiah 49:15; 2 Timothy 4:10,16), but God has promised to do neither to his people (Deuteronomy 31:6,8; Hebrews 13:5) and keeps his word (2 Timothy 4:17). Can you still rejoice in him when everything seems to go wrong (Habakkuk 3:18)?

Covenant blessings

'A new heart also will I give you.' Ezekiel 36:26
SUGGESTED FURTHER READING: Romans 2:25–29

Man's attempts to improve human nature begin from without; the theory is that the work will deepen till it reaches that which is within. Theirs is an outward ointment for an inward disease, a bandage upon the skin to stop the bleeding of the heart. Miserable physicians are they all. Their remedies fail to eradicate the deep-seated maladies of humanity. God's way of dealing with men is the reverse. He begins within and works towards the exterior in due course. A man who sees the signs of disease and operates upon the symptoms, but never looks to the root of the mischief, is a mere quack. It is very possible that by potent poisons he may check unpleasing indications, but he may kill the man in doing so; but the wise physician looks to the fountain of the disease, and if it be possible to touch the core and centre of it, he leaves the symptoms to right themselves. If your watch is out of order, the watchmaker does not consider it sufficient to clean the silver case or to remove dust from the face, but he looks within and discovers that this wheel is broken, this cog out of order, or the main spring in need of renewal; he is not much concerned about setting the hands accurately at first, for he knows that the external manifestations of the correct time will follow from setting the time-keeping machinery within to rights. Look at brooks and rivulets which have been allowed to be blackened into foul sewers; if we want to have them purged it is of small avail to cast chemicals into the stream; the only remedy is to forbid the pollution and demand that factories shall not poison us wholesale, but consume their waste products in some other manner. The voice of common sense bids us go to the original cause of the defilement and deal with it at its sources. That is just what God does when he saves a sinner; he begins at the origin of the sinner's sin and deals with his heart.

FOR MEDITATION: The Pharisees were experts at treating outward symptoms while ignoring the inner disease. Jesus, the Great Physician, had harsh words for them (Matthew 15:11–20; 23:25–28; Luke 11:39–41). Have you asked and trusted him to cleanse you from your sinful heart? Read how King David approached God for inward cleansing (Psalm 51:2,6,10,17).

Individual sin laid on Jesus

'All we like sheep have gone astray; we have turned every one to his own way; and the LORD *hath laid on him the iniquity of us all.'* Isaiah 53:6
SUGGESTED FURTHER READING: 1 Corinthians 6:9–11

This thought has charmed me beyond measure. Here were Lot's sins, scandalous sins, I cannot mention them; they were very different from David's sins. Black sins, scarlet sins were those of David, but David's sins are not at all like those of Manasseh; the sins of Manasseh were not the same as those of Peter—Peter sinned in quite a different track; and the woman that was a sinner, you could not liken her to Peter, neither if you look to her character could you set her side by side with Lydia; nor if you think of Lydia, can you see her without discovering a great divergence between her and the Philippian jailer. They are all alike—they have all 'gone astray'; but they are all different—they 'have turned every one to his own way'. But here is the blessed gathering up of them all—the Lord has caused to meet on the Redeemer, as in a common focus, the iniquity of them all; and up yonder Manasseh's song joins sweetly with that of the woman who was a sinner, and Lydia, chaste but yet needing pardon, sings side by side with Bathsheba and Rahab; while David takes up the strain with Samson and Gideon, and these with Abraham and Isaac, all differently sinners. The atonement meets every case. We always think that man a quack who advertises a medicine as healing every disease, but when you come to the great gospel medicine, the precious blood of Jesus Christ, you have there in very deed what the old doctors used to call a *catholicon*, a universal medicine which meets every case in its distinctness, and puts away sin in all its separateness of guilt as if it were made for that sin, and for that sin alone.

FOR MEDITATION: Faith in Christ crucified results in the forgiveness of all our sins (1 John 1:7,9), but failure to trust in him prevents any of them from being forgiven (John 8:24). Jesus said that faith gave the scandalous sinners of his day entry to God's kingdom, while unbelief kept the religious and respectable outside (Matthew 21:31–32).

SERMON NO. 925

Away with fear

'Fear thou not; for I am with thee: be not dismayed; for I am thy God: I will strengthen thee; yea, I will help thee; yea, I will uphold thee with the right hand of my righteousness.' Isaiah 41:10
SUGGESTED FURTHER READING: Luke 1:5–25

It is usually sinful to be afraid and dismayed, because such a state of mind almost always results from unbelief. Have you ever thought what a great sin unbelief is? We talk about it and confess it, but we do not sufficiently consider the deep heinousness of it. We will confess unbelief of God without a blush, and yet nothing could make us acknowledge dishonesty to man. Tell me which of these two is the worse fault. Is not unbelief a robbery of God, a treason felony against him? If I were in conversation with any one of you, and you should say to me, 'Sir, I cannot believe you,' nothing you could say would sting me more. It is a very strong thing to say to anyone, 'I cannot believe you.' Why, if there were two of the lowest men or women fighting in a street quarrel, and one of them said to the other, 'I cannot believe a word you say,' the worst slut would feel the insult. Every truthful man feels that he has a right to be believed. He speaks upon the honour of an honest man, and if you say, 'I cannot believe you,' and even begin to lament that you have no faith in him, the reflection is not upon yourself, but on the person you cannot believe. And shall it ever come to this, that God's own children shall say that they cannot believe their God? Oh, sin of sins! It takes away the very Godhead from God, for if God be not true, he is not God; and if he be not fit to be believed, neither is he fit to be adored, for a God whom you cannot trust you cannot worship. Oh, God-killing traitor, you sin of unbelief! May we be delivered from it, and not think it light or trifling, but shake it off from us as Paul shook off the viper into the fire.

FOR MEDITATION: Unbelief is the mark of the unbeliever, but it is out of place when displayed by Christians. Jesus rebuked his disciples for their unbelief (Matthew 17:20; Mark 16:14; John 20:27), but was more than willing to help a stranger who confessed it to him (Mark 9:24). Unbelief is an evil we must guard against (Hebrews 3:12–13).

SERMON NO. 930

Deep calleth unto deep

'Deep calleth unto deep.' Psalm 42:7
SUGGESTED FURTHER READING: Romans 5:15–21

I would never for a moment attempt to make out the abyss of the fall to be less deep than it is; it is bottomless. The miseries of mankind cannot be exaggerated. Could our tears for ever flow, could we be turned each one into a Jeremiah, yet could we never weep enough for the slain of the daughter of our people. Human misery is deep beyond expression. But what shall I say? How shall I speak? Where shall I find words to express the delight of my soul, that I have such a truth to tell you? There is a deep which answers to the deep of human ruin, and it is the deep of divine grace. There can be no evil in man which the infinite mercy of God cannot overcome. Behold God himself incarnate in the person of the Nazarene! Behold the Son of God spending on earth a life of service and of condescension! Behold him dying a death of ignominy and pain! The atonement of Christ is such a Red Sea that all the Egyptians of a believer's sins shall be drowned therein. There is such virtue in the redemption offered up by Christ, that it meets the full extent of the guilt which any sinner who seeks him may have incurred. Moreover, to meet the obstinacy and depravity of our hearts, behold how 'Deep calleth unto deep'! God's eternal Spirit has condescended to dwell in these hearts of ours. He quickens death into life; he fills the thirsty soul with waters of divine grace; he turns the stone to flesh, and makes the adamant palpitate with tenderness. Blessed be his name; he has done wonders in our souls. He has brought Christ home to our hearts, and made us willing to rejoice in Christ and to be saved by him. Myriads of spirits before the throne attest the fact that the grace of God is deeper than the depths of our sin, higher than the heights of our rebellion, broader and longer than the breadths and lengths of our depravity. O, the exceeding riches of the grace of God! 'O the depth' said the apostle Paul; and we may well say the same.

FOR MEDITATION: The depth of Christ's love is beyond human comprehension (Ephesians 3:17–19) and no depth can separate the Christian from it (Romans 8:39). Have you cried to him from the depths of your sin for forgiveness (Psalm 130:1–4)? God can cast your sins into the depths of the sea (Micah 7:19).

SERMON NO. 865

Resurrection with Christ

'But God, who is rich in mercy, for his great love wherewith he loved us, even when we were dead in sins, hath quickened us together with Christ, (by grace ye are saved).' Ephesians 2:4–5
SUGGESTED FURTHER READING: Acts 26:1–25

I sat one day at a public dinner opposite a gentleman of the gourmand species, who seemed a man of vast erudition as to wines, spirits and all the viands of the table; he judged and criticised at such a rate that I thought he ought to have been employed by our provision merchants as taster in general. He had finely developed lips and he smacked them frequently. His palate was in a fine critical condition. He was also as proficient in the quantity as in the quality, and disposed of meats and drinks in a most wholesale manner. His retreating forehead, empurpled nose and protruding lips made him, while eating at least, more like an animal than a man. At last, hearing a little conversation around him on religious matters, he opened his small eyes and his great mouth, and delivered himself of this sage utterance—'I have lived sixty years in this world, and I have never felt or believed in anything spiritual in all my life.' The speech was a needless diversion of his energies from the roast duck. We did not need him to tell us that. I for one was quite clear about it before he spoke. If the cat under the table had suddenly jumped on a chair and said the same thing, I should have attached as much importance to the utterance of the one as to the declaration of the other; and so, by one sin in one man and another in another man, they betray their spiritual death. Until a man has received the divine life, his remarks thereon, even if he is an archbishop, count for nothing. He knows nothing about it according to his own testimony; then why should he go on to try to beat down with sneers and sarcasms those who solemnly confess that they have such a life, and that this life has become real to them, so real that the mental life is made to sink into a subordinate condition compared with the spiritual life which reigns within the soul?

FOR MEDITATION: Through his faith the believer still speaks even after his death (Hebrews 11:4), whereas the unconverted are spiritually dead even while they still live and speak (1 Timothy 5:6).

'The Lord is risen indeed'

'Why seek ye the living among the dead? He is not here, but is risen: remember how he spake unto you when he was yet in Galilee.' Luke 24:5–6
SUGGESTED FURTHER READING: Matthew 28:1–20

What amazing news these good women received:- 'He is not here, but is risen'. This was amazing news to his enemies. They said, 'We have killed him; we have put him in the tomb; it is all over with him.' A-ha! Scribe, Pharisee, Priest, what have you done? Your work is all undone, for he is risen! It was amazing news for Satan. He no doubt dreamed that he had destroyed the Saviour, but he is risen! What a thrill went through all the regions of hell! What news it was for the grave! Now was it utterly destroyed, and death had lost his sting! What news it was for trembling saints—'The Lord is risen indeed'. They plucked up courage and they said, 'The good cause is the right one still and it will conquer, for our Christ is still alive at its head.' It was good news for sinners. It is good news for every sinner. Christ is alive; if you seek him, he will be found by you. He is not a dead Christ to whom I point you today. He is risen and 'he is able also to save them to the uttermost that come unto God by him'. There is no better news for sad, distressed, desponding and despairing men than this—the Saviour lives, able still to save and willing to receive you to his tender heart. This was glad news for all the angels and all the spirits in heaven, glad news indeed for them. And this day it shall be glad news to us, and we will live in the power of it by the help of his Spirit, and we will tell it to our brethren that they may rejoice with us, and we will not despair any longer. We will give way no more to doubts and fears, but we will say to one another, 'He is risen indeed'; therefore let our hearts be glad.

FOR MEDITATION: Read again Matthew 28:1–10. On the very first Easter Sunday the women had a concerned expectation (vv. 1–5), received a concise explanation (v. 6), undertook a convincing exploration (v. 6), displayed confident expressions (vv. 7–8) and enjoyed a confirming experience (vv. 9–10). Does the resurrection of Christ have any of these effects upon you?

SERMON NO. 1106

The model home mission and the model home missionary

'Who went about doing good.' Acts 10:38
SUGGESTED FURTHER READING (Spurgeon): Matthew 9:35–10:15

Whatever you do, do it thoroughly, do it heartily. If it be worth doing at all, it is worth doing well; for such a Master there must be no second-rate work, and with such a gracious reward before you there must be no offering of that which costs you nothing. You must throw yourselves into whatever you undertake for Jesus. Will you now take one word which is often used by Mark as a motto for yourselves? The idiom of the gospel of Mark is 'straightway'. He is always saying of Christ that straightway he did this, and straightway he did that. Now, if you have work for Christ before your eye, straightway hasten to do it. Most Christians miss the honour they might have in service by waiting till a more convenient season. Do something tonight before you go to bed, if it be only the giving away of a tract. Do something as each moment flies. If hitherto you have not been a worker, begin now, or if you have been a worker up till now, do not pause, but end the evening with another good word to sister, child or friend. Evermore breath out consecration to Christ. And let me bid you, dear friends, if you love my Lord and Master, to have comfort in trying to serve him, because there is an all-sufficient power which you may obtain for this service. Our Lord is declared in the same verse as our text to be one who was anointed 'with the Holy Ghost and with power'. That same Holy Spirit is given to the church, and that same power lingers in the assemblies of the faithful. Ask for this anointing and pray that, as in this verse we are told that 'God was with' Jesus, so God may be with you. Remember last Sunday evening's text [see 10 April]— 'Fear thou not; for I am with thee: be not dismayed; for I am thy God: I will strengthen thee; yea, I will help thee; yea, I will uphold thee with the right hand of my righteousness.'

FOR MEDITATION: The Lord Jesus Christ did not give people over-ambitious projects when they began to follow him. The former demoniac was sent home to his friends and began there (Mark 5:19–20); Andrew first found his brother (John 1:41). Jerusalem was the starting-point for the apostles; the ends of the earth would come later (Acts 1:8). What immediate forms of outreach are available to you?

SERMON NO. 929

The unwearied runner

'They shall run and not be weary.' Isaiah 40:31
SUGGESTED FURTHER READING: 2 Samuel 18:19–32

Running is a pace which indicates fulness of alacrity. If your servant has an errand to do for you and he creeps along the road, it is probably because he is unwilling; but if he is thoroughly willing, he is usually forward and quick in all his movements. When Abraham saw the three men, strangers, passing by his tent-door, 'he ran to meet them' and 'ran unto the herd' to fetch a calf and killed it; by quickening his pace, the patriarch showed how welcome they were. When Eliezer came to the well, we find that Rebekah 'hasted' and 'ran' to draw water for him and for the camels; her readiness to do an act of kindness was indicated by the pace which she used. When young Samuel thought that Eli called him by night, he arose and we read that 'he ran unto Eli, and said, Here I am; for thou calledst me.' Now, there ought, in the service of our God, always to be a holy promptness and alacrity. I dare say you have noticed, in the gospel according to Mark, how Mark so often uses about our Lord the words 'straightway' and 'immediately'. Mark's is the gospel which describes Christ as a servant, and it is one of the attributes of a good servant that he is prompt at once to do his lord's bidding. Our blessed Saviour straightway did whatever he had undertaken to do. We ought to be ready in the Master's service, and to say at once without demur, 'Here am I; send me.' Foul scorn is it that soldiers of the cross should ever require to be flogged to the battle as the Persian monarch's slaves were in the days of the invasion of Greece; every man among us should be as David, who ran forward to the giant eager for the fray, or as Elisha, who 'left the oxen, and ran after Elijah,' or as Philip, who ran to meet the chariot of the Ethiopian.

FOR MEDITATION: You probably steer well clear of those whose 'feet run to evil' (Proverbs 1:15–16; Isaiah 59:7), but can you truthfully echo the words of the Psalmist who said he would run in the way of God's commandments and who did not delay to keep them (Psalm 119:32,60)?

A young man's vision

'Your young men shall see visions.' Acts 2:17
SUGGESTED FURTHER READING: John 1:35–51

Those who do not serve God at home are of no use anywhere. It is all very well to talk about what you would do if you could speak to the Hindus. Nonsense! What do you do when you are in the streets of Whitechapel? You will be of no use whatever in Calcutta, unless you are of use in Poplar or Bermondsey. The human mind is the same everywhere. Its sins may take another form, but there are just the same difficulties in one place as in another. It is all very well for you to turn into a sort of Don Quixote in imagination and dream of what you would do, if you went out upon a spiritual campaign as a heavenly knight-errant, tilting against windmills; just try your hand at the conversion of that young man who sits next to you in the pew. See what you can do for Jesus Christ in the shop. See whether you can serve your Master in that little Bible class of which you are a member. Rest assured that no missionary ardour really burns within that man who does not love the souls of those who live in the same house and dwell in the same neighbourhood. Give me that man for a missionary of whom it is said that, when he took a lodging in a house, all the other inhabitants were brought to God within six months; or one who was a son whose father was unconverted, but who gave the Lord no rest until he saw his parent saved; or one who was a tradesman who, while he was pushing his business earnestly, always found time to be an evangelist. That is the man who will maintain missionary fervour alive at home, and that is the man who will help to promote missionary effort abroad.

FOR MEDITATION: There is nothing wrong in having aspirations to serve God (1 Timothy 3:1), but one of the most important qualifications is faithfulness in the smaller task (Luke 16:10). Failure at home is almost inevitably going to be mirrored by failure in the wider sphere of God's church (1 Timothy 3:5). Barnabas and Saul were already faithful workers (Acts 11:25–26) before God called them to special missionary work (Acts 13:1–2).

The sine qua non [i.e. the indispensable condition]

'Jesus answered him, If I wash thee not, thou hast no part with me.' John 13:8
SUGGESTED FURTHER READING: Colossians 3:5–15

Included in this feet-washing, I believe, is the continual sanctification which faith in Jesus Christ carries on within us by the power of the Holy Spirit. If a man professes to be a Christian, and is not in his walk and conversation holier than other men, that man's profession is vain. There are some who seem to think that we are to come to Christ as sinners and then, having believed in him, we are to live as we did before. But, my brethren, it is not so. Christ saves his people *from* their sins. When you hear the complaints of God's servants concerning their temptations and their indwelling sins, you are not to conclude that sin has dominion over them, or that they have not overcome sin, or that they are not other men than they once were. No, my brethren, I believe the holier a man becomes the more he mourns over the unholiness which remains in him; but he is in very truth a far better man, a spiritual and holy man. If Jesus does not wash you so that you become godly and upright, you may depend upon it that you have no part in him. If he does not wash that tongue and cleanse away those angry, idle or filthy words, if he does not wash that hand and render it impossible for it to perform a dishonest or unchaste act, if he does not wash that foot and render it impossible for it to carry you to the haunts of vice and criminal amusement, you have no part in him. It is all worthless for unconverted persons to be baptised and come to his table, for if he has not sanctified you in some measure, he has not justified you. If you are not a changed man, neither are you a saved man, and if you do not aspire after holiness, neither need you hope that you shall have a part in the heaven of the blessed. 'If I wash thee not, thou hast no part with me.'

FOR MEDITATION: Any teaching which contains a loophole allowing room for ongoing unholiness is not according to Christ (Ephesians 4:17–20), but sheer vanity (Ephesians 5:5–6); the faith it promotes is in itself impure and defiled (James 1:26–27).

Rest

'For we which have believed do enter into rest.' Hebrews 4:3
SUGGESTED FURTHER READING: Joshua 21:43–22:6

Consider the Christian's rest. He was led by Moses, the law, out of the Egypt of sin into the wilderness of conviction and seeking after God; and now Jesus, the true Joshua, has led him into perfect acceptance and peace; and since the discomforts of conviction and the troubles of unpardoned sin are over, he sits down under the vine and fig tree of the gracious promise and rejoices in Christ Jesus. Think of Canaan as a type of the peace which God's people at this present time by faith enjoy. So also is the Sabbath. That is a blessed standing ordinance, reminding believers of their delightful privileges. Work during the six days, for it is your duty—'Six days shalt thou labour'; but on the Sabbath enjoy perfect rest, both in body and in soul. Yet look to the higher meaning of the Sabbath, and learn to cease from your own works. If you were to be saved by works, you must work without a moment's pause, for you could never complete the toil, since absolute perfection would be demanded. But when you come to Christ, your works are finished; there is no hewing of wood nor drawing of water; there is no keeping of commandments with a view to merit, no toilsome tugging at ceremonials and ordinances with a view to acceptance. 'It is finished' is the silver bell that rings your soul into a marriage of peace and joy in Christ Jesus. Take care, believer, that you live in a perpetual Sabbath of rest in the finished work of your ascended Lord. Remember that your legal righteousness is complete; you have ceased from your own works as God did from his; and let none provoke you to go back to the old bondage of the law, but stand fast in the blessed liberty of grace, rejoicing in the perfect work of your Substitute and Surety.

FOR MEDITATION: Our daily work should illustrate our service to God (Ephesians 6:5–7; Colossians 3:22–24). But does your lifestyle also illustrate your rest of faith in the salvation he has provided for you in his Son? The Sabbath of rest was used by God to test the faith of the Israelites (Exodus 16:22–30); what does your use of the Lord's Day say about you?

Bringing the king back

'Now therefore why speak ye not a word of bringing the king back?'
2 Samuel 19:10
SUGGESTED FURTHER READING: Luke 19:11–27

Be instant in season and out of season for your Master, that he may be glorified in you. 'Oh, I could not do much,' says one. Then do what you can. No one flower makes a garden, but altogether the fair blossoms of spring create a paradise of beauty. Let all the Lord's flowers contribute in their proportion to the beauty of the garden of the Lord. 'But I am so unused to it.' Then, my brother, that is a very powerful reason why you should do twice as much, so as to make up for your past idleness. 'Oh, but I am afraid nothing would come of it.' What has that to do with you? God has promised a blessing, and if the blessing should not come in your day, yet, if you have done what the Master bade you, you will not be blamed for lack of success. 'Sir,' asks another, 'will you give me some work to do?' No, I will not; for if you are good for anything you will find it for yourself. In such a place as London, for people to go to their minister to know what they are to do seems to me to be the height of absurdity. What work can you do? Put your hand out and begin, for there is plenty within reach. Your own unconverted child, whose face you kiss tonight, is to be the first object of your labours. Begin to educate your family for Christ, and pray for the salvation of your own household. What spheres you may find in the neighbourhoods where you live! They swarm with immortal souls and abound in sin; the fields are white unto the harvest. Some of you may not be able to work by using your tongue; then use your purses. Use whatever God has given you; only, I pray you, never let it be said that you do not speak 'a word of bringing the king back.'

FOR MEDITATION: In Thessalonica the early Christians were all accused of 'saying that there is another king, one Jesus' (Acts 17:7). The accusation was certainly true of the apostle Paul wherever he went (Acts 19:8; 20:25; 28:23,31), but could it be levelled against you?

SERMON NO. 808

A call to worship

'And the inhabitants of one city shall go to another, saying, Let us go speedily to pray before the LORD, *and to seek the* LORD *of Hosts: I will go also.' Zechariah 8:21*
SUGGESTED FURTHER READING: Psalm 84:1–12

The text says, 'Let us go speedily to pray'; by which is meant, I suppose, that when the time came to pray, they were punctual; they were not laggards; they did not come into the assembly late; they did not drop in one by one after the service had begun, but they said, 'Let us go speedily'. They looked up to their clocks and said, 'How long will it take us to walk so as to be there at the commencement? Let us start five minutes before that time lest we should not be able to keep up the pace, and should by any means reach the door after the first prayer.' I wish latecomers would remember David's choice. You remember what part he wished to take in the house of God: he was willing to be a doorkeeper, and that not because the doorkeeper has the most comfortable berth, for that is the hardest post a man can choose, but he knew that doorkeepers are the first in and the last out, and so David wished to be first at the service and the last at the going away. How few would be of David's mind! It has been said that Dissenters in years gone by placed the clock outside the meeting-house, so that they might never enter late, but the modern Dissenters place the clock inside, that their preachers may not keep them too long. There is some truth in the remark, but it is not to our honour. Let us mend our ways and say to one another in the language of the text, 'Let us go speedily to pray before the Lord'. Let us go with quick feet. If we go slowly to market, let us go quickly to meeting; if we are slow on weekdays, let us go quickly on the Sabbath. Let us never keep Jesus Christ waiting; we shall do if we are not in time, for he is sure to be punctual, even if only two or three are met together in his name.

FOR MEDITATION: Paul told the Corinthians that all aspects of their meetings should be conducted 'decently and in order' (1 Corinthians 14:40). He rebuked those who started too early without waiting for others (1 Corinthians 11:21,33). What would he have said about those who habitually turn up after or even well after the publicised starting time?

The Master's profession—the disciples's pursuit

'I have preached righteousness in the great congregation: lo, I have not refrained my lips, O LORD, thou knowest. I have not hid thy righteousness within my heart; I have declared thy faithfulness and thy salvation: I have not concealed thy lovingkindness and thy truth from the great congregation.' Psalm 40:9–10

SUGGESTED FURTHER READING: Jeremiah 1:1–8

It may be that you are one of those who ought to become a missionary; it may be that you ought to dedicate your life to some work for God either at home or abroad. Well, if it be so, do not mistake your path in life. We do not urge you to rush into the ministry, much less into foreign ministry, unless you are called to it, for that is the very last place for a man to be in who is not called to the work. Act as a Christian young man for once in your life by asking God whether it is your vocation to bear the cross of Christ into lands where as yet it is unknown. Surely, whatever answer you may feel called upon to give, you will be ready for it. You will be willing to give yourself up to the very hardest form of service to which you may be called. I should like you, then, to be sure about this at the outset lest you should in the turn of the road miss the path and so not be able to say at the last, 'I have preached righteousness in the great congregation: lo, I have not refrained my lips, O Lord, thou knowest. I have not hid thy righteousness within my heart; I have declared thy faithfulness and thy salvation: I have not concealed thy lovingkindness and thy truth from the great congregation.' I should not like you, if meant by the gifts of God to be a great missionary, to die a millionaire. I should not like it, were you fitted to be a missionary, that you should drivel down into a king; for what are all your kings, nobles, stars, garters, diadems and tiaras, when you put them all together, compared with the dignity of winning souls for Christ, with the special honour of building for Christ, not on another man's foundation, but preaching Christ's gospel in regions yet far beyond?

FOR MEDITATION: The missionary mandate is both general and specific. Every Christian is called to do something (Matthew 28:19–20), but some are called to do something specific (Acts 13:2). There is no harm in following Paul's example by asking God what he wants you to do (Acts 9:6; 22:10), as long as you are also willing to say 'Thy will be done' (Matthew 6:10).

SERMON NO. 977

The triumph of Christianity

'All the ends of the world shall remember and turn unto the LORD: and all the kindreds of the nations shall worship before thee.' Psalm 22:27
SUGGESTED FURTHER READING: Luke 24:44–53

The conversion of the nations follows the usual rule, and by no means differs from the conversion of men at home. It is a remembering, a turning to the Lord, and a worshipping of him. They turn to Christ, they look to him and are lightened; and then, straightway, they begin to adore and reverence him who has saved them. It is clear then that we are to seek the salvation of the nations by using the ordinary means. If we expect to see them saved in some extraordinary way differing from what we have hitherto seen, we shall be disappointed and we shall be led into practical mistakes. We have nothing to do in foreign lands, but just what the apostle did in Asia Minor and what we are doing here; we are to preach Jesus Christ and him crucified. I do not believe that any race of men needs a peculiar gospel or a novel mode of administering it. There may be different styles of preaching; God will give us those; but there need be no other mode of action than the apostolic one—'they that were scattered abroad went every where preaching the word.' The mode prescribed in the marching orders of our grand Captain is this: 'Go ye into all the world, and preach the gospel to every creature', not found schools, nor debate with sceptics, nor civilise, but 'preach the gospel'. Do this to every creature and the sure results will follow in one place as in another; men shall remember, shall turn unto the Lord and shall worship him. Dear unconverted person, the very best means for your conversion are being employed now; and therefore, I would have you remember that if these fail, neither would you be converted 'though one rose from the dead.' This deserves your solemn consideration and I beseech you to lay it to heart.

FOR MEDITATION: The missionary method is as worldwide as the missionary mandate. All nations are to be taught Christ's commandments (Matthew 28:19–20) that they must repent (Luke 24:47) and trust in Christ (Romans 1:5; 16:26). God's method was first tested on the Day of Pentecost (Acts 2:5) and will one day be proved to have been successful in every nation (Revelation 5:9; 7:9).

SERMON NO. 1047

Marah; or, the bitter waters sweetened

*'They could not drink of the waters of Marah, for they were bitter: ...
and the* LORD *showed him a tree, which when he had cast into the waters,
the waters were made sweet.' Exodus 15:23,25*
SUGGESTED FURTHER READING: Acts 4:1–12

I liken the world that lies in darkness to a thirsty caravan gathered
around Marah's well where the water is too bitter to drink. High are the
Andes, lofty the Himalayas, but the woes of mankind are higher still. The
Ganges, the Indus and other mighty streams pour their floods into the
ocean; but what mighty deep could contain the torrents of human grief?
A very deluge is the sorrow as well as the sin of man. The heathen know
nothing of the healing tree cut down of old, which still has power to
sweeten mortal misery. You know it, you have your trials, and you
surmount them by the appeals you make to your Lord and by the power
of his consolations; but these sons of darkness have your griefs and more,
but not your Comforter. For them the flood, but not the ark; the tempest,
but not the refuge. And you have that which would cheer them: no doubt
passes across your mind as to the gospel. These are wavering times in
which some professors and teachers almost believe that the gospel is only
one theory of many and will have to stand its test and, in all probability,
will fail as many human systems of thought have done. You think not so;
you believe that God's gospel is truth, a revelation of Jehovah. Heaven
and earth may pass away, but not his word, his Christ, his decree, his
covenant. You know that you have a tree that can heal the bitter
fountains. No doubt comes across your mind as to that: what then? By
common humanity, much more by the tender movements of the grace of
God upon your souls, I entreat you to present this remedy to those who
who need it so much. Will anything suffice as substitute for it? Is there
anywhere on earth another healing tree beside that which fell beneath the
axe at Calvary? Are there other leaves 'for the healing of the nations'?

FOR MEDITATION: Read the missionary message in 1 Peter 2:24—Christ's
death on the tree for our sins can heal us spiritually. This message came first
to Israel (Acts 5:30–31); their reluctance to accept it and be healed opened
the way for Gentiles to hear it (Acts 28:27–28). Forgiveness of sins is for
every one in every nation who trusts in Christ crucified (Acts 10:35,39,43).

SERMON NO. 987

Martha and Mary

'Martha received him into her house. And she had a sister called Mary, which also sat at Jesus' feet, and heard his word. But Martha was cumbered about much serving, and came to him, and said, Lord, dost thou not care that my sister hath left me to serve alone?' Luke 10:38–40
SUGGESTED FURTHER READING: Joshua 1:1–9

We must not be so active as to neglect communion, nor so contemplative as to become unpractical. In the chapter from which our text is taken we have several lessons on this subject. The seventy disciples returned from their preaching tour flushed with the joy of success; and our Saviour, to refine that joy and prevent its degenerating into pride, bids them rather rejoice that their names were written in heaven. He conducted their contemplations to the glorious doctrine of election, that grateful thoughts might sober them after successful work. He bids them consider themselves as debtors to the grace which reveals unto babes the mysteries of God, for he would not allow their new position as workers to make them forget that they were the chosen of God and therefore debtors. Our wise Master next returns to the subject of service and instructs them by the memorable parable of the good Samaritan and the wounded man; and then as if they might vainly imagine philanthropy, as it is the service of Christ, to be the only service of Christ, he brings in the two sisters of Bethany, the Holy Spirit meaning thereby to teach us that while we ought to abound in service and to do good abundantly to our fellow men, yet we must not fail in worship, in spiritual reverence, in meek discipleship and in quiet contemplation. While we are practical like the seventy, practical like the Samaritan and practical like Martha, we are also, like the Saviour, to rejoice in spirit and say, 'I thank thee, O Father', and we are also, like Mary, to sit down in quietude and nourish our souls with divine truth.

FOR MEDITATION: Seeking God earnestly and knowing him is vital to serving him properly. David taught Solomon this lesson (1 Chronicles 28:9) and some later kings of Judah proved it (2 Chronicles 19:3–4; 31:20–21; 34:3); 'the people that do know their God shall be strong, and do exploits.' (Daniel 11:32)

SERMON NO. 927

Waters to swim in

'Waters to swim in.' Ezekiel 47:5
SUGGESTED FURTHER READING: Philippians 1:3–14

The text does not speak about waters to float in, though this is essential.
Many people never get beyond that floating period, and they conclude
that they are safe and all is well because they fancy their heads are above
water; whereas the man who is really taught of God goes on from the
floating to the swimming. Now swimming is an active exercise. The man
progresses as he strikes out. He makes headway. He dives and rises: he
turns to the right, he swims to the left, he pursues his course, he goes
whithersoever he wills. Now, the holy word of God and the gospel are
'waters to swim in'. Many of you only know what it is to float. You are
resting in the truth of God for your salvation, but making no advance in
heavenly things. Beloved, let us learn to swim in those waters; I mean, let
us learn to trust God in active exertions for the promotion of his
kingdom, to trust him in endeavours to do good. How blessedly our
friend George Muller of Bristol swims! What a master swimmer he is! He
has had his feet off the bottom many years, and as he swims he draws
along behind him some 2,500 orphan children, whom, by God's grace, he
is saving from the floods of sin and bringing, we trust, safe to shore. Dear
brother, dear sister, could you not swim too? 'Oh, but I have no money.'
You want to walk, I see. 'But I have very slender gifts compared with
what I need.' Cannot the Lord give you gifts and graces? Will you not
trust him? Dear brother, are you called to serve God in a very difficult
sphere of labour? Cannot you go on? 'I have nobody to help me.' Oh, I
see you are all for walking on the bottom. Brethren, it is 'waters to swim
in'. Cannot you swim without any help except the help of the All in all?

FOR MEDITATION: Physical challenges posed by deep waters have on more
than one occasion been overcome by the faith of God's people (Hebrews
11:7,29), but have proved overwhelming when faith has been lacking
(Matthew 8:24–26; 14:29–31). Spiritually the assurance of God's presence
makes all the difference (Isaiah 43:2). Peter's willingness to launch out
into the deep at Christ's word resulted in the promise that he would
advance to becoming a fisher of men (Luke 5:4–5,10).

Tearful sowing and joyful reaping

'He that goeth forth and weepeth, bearing precious seed, shall doubtless come again with rejoicing, bringing his sheaves with him.' Psalm 126:6
SUGGESTED FURTHER READING: Colossians 1:1–8

Sunday-school teachers, if you go forth as the text tells you, you shall not be without fruits. I have heard many discussions amongst my brethren about whether or not every earnest labourer may expect to have fruit. I have always inclined to the belief that such is the rule, and though there may be exceptions and perhaps some men may be rather a 'savour of death unto death' than 'of life unto life', yet it seems to me that if I never won souls I would sigh till I did and would break my heart over them if I could not break their hearts; if they would not be saved and were not saved, I would almost cry with Moses, 'blot me, I pray thee, out of thy book'. Though I can understand the possibility of an earnest sower never reaping, I cannot understand the possibility of an earnest sower being content not to reap. I cannot comprehend any one of you Christian people trying to win souls and not having results, and being satisfied without results. I can suppose that you may love the Lord and may have been trying your best for years unsuccessfully, but then I am sure you feel unhappy about it. I can not only suppose that to be the case, but I am thankful that you are unhappy. I hope the unhappiness will increase with you, till at last in the anguish of your spirit you shall cry like Rachel, 'Give me children, or else I die.' Then you will be the very person described in the text: you go forth weeping, bearing seed that is precious to you; and you must have results; you must come again rejoicing, bringing your sheaves with you.

FOR MEDITATION: As 'a man of sorrows and acquainted with grief' the Lord Jesus Christ would see the fruit 'of the travail of his soul' and 'be satisfied' (Isaiah 53:3,11). The fruitful ministry of the apostle Paul was likewise marked by tears and sorrows (Acts 20:19,31; Romans 9:2; 2 Corinthians 2:4; Philippians 2:27; 3:18). A cold-hearted mechanical approach will never match the effect of a heartfelt passion and concern for others.

SERMON NO. 867

The light of the world

'Ye are the light of the world.' Matthew 5:14
SUGGESTED FURTHER READING: Philippians 2:12–16

The believer is appointed to be a lighthouse to others, a cheering lamp, a guiding star. It is true that his light will be increased as he learns more of Christ; he will be able to impart more instruction to others when he has received more, but even while he is yet a beginner, his faith in Jesus is in itself a light; men see his good works even before they discover his knowledge. The man of faith who aims at holiness is a light of the world, even though his knowledge may be very limited and his experience that of a babe. Every Christian should see the application of the text to himself. It is not spoken to the apostles or to ministers exclusively, but to the entire body of the faithful—'Ye are the light of the world.' You humble men and women whose usefulness will be confined to your houses or to your workplaces, whose voices will never be heard in the streets, whose speech will only be eloquent in the ears of those who gather by your firesides, noiseless and unobserved as your lives will be, you are the true light of the world. Not alone the men whose learned volumes load our shelves, not alone the men whose thundering tones startle the nations, or who with busy care for God's glory compass sea and land to find subjects for the kingdom of Jesus, but you, each one of you, who are humbly resting upon the Saviour and lovingly carrying out your high vocation as the children of God and followers of his dear Son. Let us never forget that light must first be imparted to us, or it can never go forth from us. We are not lights of the world by nature; at best we are but lamps unlit until the Spirit of God comes. Ask yourself whether God has ever kindled you by the flame of his Spirit. Have you been delivered from the power of darkness and translated into light?

FOR MEDITATION: To help others the light in a lighthouse must be lifted up and lit up (Matthew 5:14–16). Even the Lord Jesus Christ, 'the light of the world', had to be lifted up on the cross (John 3:14,19; 8:12,28; 12:32,46). We must be lifted up from the darkness of sin and lit up by 'the light of the world' (John 8:12; 12:36,46; Ephesians 5:8,14) before we also can shine as 'the light of the world' (Philippians 2:15; 1 Peter 2:9). Are you opting to remain in darkness (John 3:19)?

SERMON NO. 1109

Make this valley full of ditches

'And he said, Thus saith the LORD, *Make this valley full of ditches. For thus saith the* LORD, *Ye shall not see wind, neither shall ye see rain; yet that valley shall be filled with water, that ye may drink, both ye, and your cattle, and your beasts.'* 2 Kings 3:16–17
SUGGESTED FURTHER READING: 2 Corinthians 3:1–6

Without the Spirit of God we are like a ship stranded on the beach; when the tide has receded, there is no moving her until the flood shall once again lift her from the sands. We are like the frozen ship, of which we read the other day, frostbound in the far-off Arctic Sea: until the Spirit of God shall thaw the chilly coldness of our natural estate and bid the lifebloods of our heart flow forth, there we must lie, cold, cheerless, lifeless and powerless. The Christian, like the mariner, depends upon the breath of heaven, or his vessel is without motion. We are like the plants of the field, and this genial season suggests the metaphor: all the winter through, vegetation sleeps wrapped up in her frost garments, but when the mysterious influence of spring is felt, she unbinds her cloak to put on her vest of many colours, while every bud begins to swell and each flower to open. And so a church lies asleep in a long and dreary winter until God the Holy Spirit looses the bands of lethargy, and hearts bud and blossom, and 'the time of the singing of birds is come'. This doctrine has been preached hundreds of times and we all know it, but for all that we all forget it; and especially when we are in earnest about our work and perceive our personal responsibility, there is no truth that needs to be insisted upon more thoroughly than this—'without me ye can do nothing.' Until we are utterly empty of self, we are not ready to be filled by God; until we are conscious of our own weakness, we are not fit platforms for the display of the divine omnipotence. Until the arm of flesh is paralysed and death is written upon the whole natural man, we are not ready to be endowed with the divine life and energy.

FOR MEDITATION: Without the working of the Holy Spirit it is impossible to be born into the kingdom of God (John 3:5), to belong to Christ (Romans 8:9), to receive spiritual truths (1 Corinthians 2:13–14), to submit to Christ's lordship (1 Corinthians 12:3) or to live in a godly manner (Jude 19). So why do we so often try to do God's work in our own strength and in our own ways?

The sin-offering for the common people

'If his sin, which he hath sinned, come to his knowledge: then he shall bring his offering, a kid of the goats, a female without blemish, for his sin which he hath sinned. And he shall lay his hand upon the head of the sin offering, and slay the sin offering.' Leviticus 4:28–29
SUGGESTED FURTHER READING (Spurgeon): 1 John 1:5–2:2

Lay your hands upon Christ Jesus, according to the verse of the poet—

'My faith would lay her hand on that dear head of thine,
While like a penitent I stand, and there confess my sin.'

Now that act of laying on the hand signified *confession*. It meant this: 'Here I stand as a sinner and confess that I deserve to die. This goat which is now to be slain represents in its sufferings what I deserve of God.' Sinner, confess your sin now unto your great God; acknowledge that he would be just if he condemned you. Confession of sin is a part of the meaning of laying on of the hand. The next meaning was *acceptance*. The person laying his hand said, 'I accept this goat as standing for me. I agree that this victim shall stand instead of me.' That is what faith does with Christ; it puts its hand upon the ever-blessed Son of God and says, 'He stands for me; I take him as my substitute.' The next meaning of it was *transference*. The sinner standing there confessing, putting his hand on the victim and accepting it, did by that act say, 'I transfer, according to God's ordinance, all my sin which I here confess from myself to this victim.' By that act the transference was made. There is a blessed passage which says that 'the Lord hath laid on him the iniquity of us all.' From this expression an objection has been raised to that blessed hymn *'I lay my sins on Jesus.'* Cannot both utterances be true? God did lay sin in bulk upon Christ, but by an act of faith every individual in another sense lays his sins on Jesus, and it is absolutely needful that each man should do so, if he would participate in the substitution.

FOR MEDITATION: Men could not lay hands on the Lord Jesus Christ to make him king (John 6:15) or harm him (Matthew 21:46; Luke 4:29–30; 20:19; John 7:30,44; 8:20). But because he let wicked men lay hands upon him and crucify him (Matthew 26:50; Mark 14:46; Acts 2:23), we can all now lay our hands on him by faith and so lay hold on eternal life.

SERMON NO. 1048

The fourfold treasure

'But of him are ye in Christ Jesus, who of God is made unto us wisdom, and righteousness, and sanctification, and redemption: that, according as it is written, He that glorieth, let him glory in the Lord.' 1 Corinthians 1:30–31
SUGGESTED FURTHER READING: Ephesians 1:1–10

Different translators have read this passage in various ways; 'of him' they think should properly be 'through him': through God are we in Christ Jesus. Are you this day united to Christ, a stone in that building of which he is both foundation and topstone, a limb of that mystical body of which he is the head? Then you did not get there of yourself. No stone in that wall leaped into its place; no member of that body was its own creator. You came to be in union with Christ through God the Father. You were ordained unto this grace by his own purpose, the purpose of the infinite Jehovah, who chose you before the world was. 'Ye have not chosen me, but I have chosen you'. The first cause of your union with Christ lies in the purpose of God who gave you grace in Christ Jesus from before the foundation of the world. And as to the purpose, so to the power of God is your union with Christ to be attributed. He brought you into Christ. You were a stranger; he brought you near. You were an enemy; he reconciled you. You would never have come to Christ to seek for mercy if first of all the Spirit of God had not appeared to you to show you your need and to lead you to cry for the mercy that you needed. Through God's operation as well as through God's decree you are this day in Christ Jesus. It will do your souls good, my brethren, to think of this very commonplace truth. Many days have passed since your conversion, it may be, but do not forget what a high day the day of your new birth was; and do not cease to give glory to that mighty power which brought you 'out of darkness into his marvellous light'. You did not convert yourself; if you did, you still need to be converted again. Your regeneration was not of the will of man, nor of blood, nor of birth; if it were so, let me tell you the sooner you are rid of it the better. The only true regeneration is of the will of God and by the operation of the Holy Spirit; 'by the grace of God I am what I am'.

FOR MEDITATION: 'Salvation is of the Lord' (Jonah 2:9), whether we focus on him choosing (2 Thessalonians 2:13), calling (2 Timothy 1:9) or cleansing us (Titus 3:5); 'to you is the word of this salvation sent' (Acts 13:26).

A new song for new hearts

'And in that day thou shalt say, O LORD, *I will praise thee: though thou wast angry with me, thine anger is turned away, and thou comfortedst me.' Isaiah 12:1*
SUGGESTED FURTHER READING: 1 Timothy 1:12–17

This is a song which is peculiar in its character and appropriate only to the people of God. I may say of it, 'no man could learn that song but the redeemed'. Only he who has felt his vileness and has had it washed away in the 'fountain filled with blood' can know its sweetness. It is not a Pharisee's song; it has no likeness to 'God, I thank thee, that I am not as other men are'; it confesses, 'thou wast angry with me,' and therein owns that the singer was even as others; but it glories that through infinite mercy the divine 'anger is turned away,' and herein it leans upon the appointed Saviour. It is not a Sadducean song; no doubt mingles with the strain. It is not the philosopher's query, 'There may be a God, or there may not be'; it is the voice of a believing worshipper. It is not, 'I may be guilty, or I may not be.' It is all positive, every note of it; 'thou wast angry with me,'—I know it, I feel it, yet 'thine anger is turned away'; of this too I am sure. I believe it upon the witness of God and I cannot doubt his word. It is a song of strong faith and yet of humility. Its spirit is a precious incense made up of many costly ingredients. We have here not one virtue alone but many rare excellences. Humility confesses, 'thou wast angry with me'. Gratitude sings, 'thine anger is turned away'. Patience cries 'thou comfortedst me.' Holy joy springs up and says, 'I will praise thee'. Faith, hope and love all have their notes here, from the bass of humility up to the highest alto of glorious communion; all the different parts are represented. It is a full song, the swell of the diapason of the heart.

FOR MEDITATION: Do you accept that God has every right to be angry with you? The Lord Jesus Christ can save you from God's anger (1 Thessalonians 1:10) because he endured it himself when he died on the cross in the place of sinners (Romans 5:8–9); those who fail to trust in him are warned that God's anger has not been turned away but remains upon them (John 3:36).

SERMON NO. 928

The gospel of Abraham's sacrifice of Isaac

'He that spared not his own Son, but delivered him up for us all.'
Romans 8:32
SUGGESTED FURTHER READING: 1 John 4:9–14

If Isaac had died, he could not have died for us. He might have died for us as an example of how we should resign life, but that would have been a small boon; it would have been no greater blessing than the Unitarian gospel offers when it sets forth Christ as dying for our exemption. But, beloved, the death of Christ stands altogether alone and apart, because it is a death altogether for others, endured solely and only from selfless affection to the fallen. There is not a pang that rends the Saviour's heart that needed to have been there if not for love to us, not a drop of blood that trickled from that thorn-crowned head or from those pierced hands that needed to be spilled if it were not for affection to such undeserving ones as us. And see what he has done for us! He has procured our pardon; we who have believed in him are forgiven. He has procured our adoption; we are sons of God in Christ Jesus. He has shut the gates of hell for us; we cannot perish, nor can any pluck us out of his hands. He has opened the gates of heaven for us; we shall be with him where he is. Our very bodies shall feel the power of his death, for they shall rise again at the sound of the trumpet at the last day. He was delivered for us his people, 'for us all'; he endured all for all his people, for all who trust him, for every son of Adam that casts himself upon him, for every son and daughter of man that will rely upon him alone for salvation. Was he delivered for you, dear friend? Have you a part in his death?

FOR MEDITATION: Consider the uniqueness of God's 'great love wherewith he loved us, even when we were dead in sins' (Ephesians 2:4–5). 'God so loved the world that he gave his only begotten son' (John 3:16). 'Greater love hath no man than this, that a man lay down his life for his friends' (John 15:13). 'If God so loved us' (1 John 4:11), are you responding to him in the way that you should?

SERMON NO. 869

The approachableness of Jesus

'Then drew near unto him all the publicans and sinners for to hear him.'
Luke 15:1
SUGGESTED FURTHER READING: Matthew 11:25–30

What is the way for a sinner to come to Christ? It is simply this; the sinner, feeling his need of a Saviour, trusts himself to the Lord Jesus Christ. This was the perplexity of my boyhood, but it is so simple now. When I was told to go to Christ, I thought, 'Yes, if I knew where he was, I would go to him; no matter how I wearied myself, I would trudge on till I found him.' I never could understand how I could get to Christ till I understood that it is a mental coming, a spiritual coming, a coming with the mind. The coming to Jesus which saves the soul is a simple reliance upon him, and if, today, being aware of your guilt, you will rely upon the atoning blood of Jesus, you have come to him, and you are saved. Is he not, then, approachable indeed, if there is so simple a way of coming? No good works, ceremonies or experiences are demanded; a childlike faith is the royal road to Jesus. This truth is further illustrated by the help which he gives to coming sinners in order to bring them near to himself. He it is who first makes them coming sinners. It is his eternal Spirit who draws them unto himself. They would not come to him of themselves; they are without desires towards him, but it is his work to cast secret silken cords around their hearts, which he draws with his strong hand and brings them near to himself. Depend upon it, he will never refuse those whom he himself draws by his Spirit. Rest assured he will never shut the door in the face of any soul that comes to feed at the gospel banquet, moved to approach by the power of his love. He once said, 'compel them to come in,' but he never said, 'shut the door in their faces and bolt them out.'

FOR MEDITATION: Christ's invitation to come to him could not be wider (Matthew 11:28; John 7:37). His reception of all who come to him could not be kinder (John 6:37). But the refusal of so many to come to him could not be more obstinate, foolish and insulting to him (John 5:40).

SERMON NO. 809

Miracles of love

'Thou hast loved my soul out of the pit of corruption.' Isaiah 38:17
(marginal reading)
SUGGESTED FURTHER READING: John 14:18–24

Lose your sense of Jesus' love and the power of your religion is gone. You have stolen the life if you have taken away the love. Believe it, know it, pray for it. Spirit of God, make them feel it, and anything shall be possible, whether of sin slain or duty wrought. I have often felt myself to be a mere expanse of foulness, like the mudflats by the seashore when the tide is out. As far as the eye can carry, you see a continent of mud with black rocks, rotting seaweed, pieces of wreck, creeping things innumerable and such foul matters as the eye might never wish to see again. What is to be done with this dismal region? Here lie the fisher boats embedded in the mud; what shall float them? It would be impossible to drag them down to the sea; must they lie there and decay? What is to be done with this mud and weed? Wait; and lo, at the appointed time the sea advances from its bed; ripple by ripple and wave by wave it rises, spreading out itself like a molten looking-glass, where just now all was foul; and lo, the boats are lifted; they walk the waters like things of life, while all that rotted in the noon-day sun is forgotten, and the waves follow each other with continuous flashes of silver sheen. O Lord, thou art that sea of love; thy mercies are thy waves of lovingkindness; let them come up and flood my soul; with infinite power of love, rise and cover all my nature. I hope the Lord will deal so with all of you. Never rest until you enjoy this love and, when you do enjoy it, keep it. If you find my Beloved, hold him and do not let him go.

FOR MEDITATION: God loves his people with an everlasting love (Jeremiah 31:3). Have you lost your sense of it? Better to cry 'Lord, where are thy former lovingkindnesses?' (Psalm 89:49) than to complain 'Wherein hast thou loved us?' (Malachi 1:2).

Intercessory prayer

'For yet my prayer also shall be in their calamities.' Psalm 141:5
SUGGESTED FURTHER READING: James 5:9–16

Earnest intercession will be sure to bring love with it. I do not believe you can hate a man for whom you habitually pray. If you dislike any brother Christian, pray for him doubly, not only for his sake, but for your own, that you may be cured of prejudice and saved from all unkind feeling. Remember the old story of the man who waited on his pastor to tell him that he could not enjoy his preaching. The minister wisely said, 'My dear brother, before we talk that matter over, let us pray together.' After they had both prayed, the complainant found he had nothing to say except to confess that he himself had been very negligent in prayer for his pastor, and he laid his not profiting to that account. I ascribe lack of brotherly love to the decline of intercessory prayer. Pray for one another earnestly, habitually, fervently, and you will knit your hearts together in love as the heart of one man. This is the cement of fair colours in which the stones of the church should be laid if they are to be compact together. Dear brethren, when you pray for one another, not only will your sympathy and love grow, but you will have kinder judgments concerning one another. We always judge leniently those for whom we intercede. If a talebearer represents my brother in a very black light, my love makes me feel sure that he is mistaken. Did I not pray for him this morning, and how can I hear him condemned? If I am compelled to believe that he is guilty, I am very sorry, but I will not be angry with him, but will pray the Lord to forgive and restore him, remembering myself also lest I be tempted.

FOR MEDITATION: Love and forgiveness are the proper companions of prayer (Matthew 5:44; Mark 11:25). If we are to pray like this for our foes (Luke 6:27–28), it should be even more natural to do so for our families and friends, as did Moses (Numbers 12:1,11–13) and Job (Job 32:3; 42:7–10) after facing criticism from them.

SERMON NO. 1049

Self-humbling

'Because thine heart was tender, and thou didst humble thyself before God, when thou heardest his words against this place, and against the inhabitants thereof, and humbledst thyself before me, and didst rend thy clothes, and weep before me; I have even heard thee also, saith the LORD.*'*
2 *Chronicles 34:27*
SUGGESTED FURTHER READING: Colossians 2:18–23

Do not mistake sham humility for real humility. There is a cant of humility which is infamous. People will say in prayer, 'Thy poor dust,' and use all sorts of depreciating expressions, when they are as proud as Lucifer; they will say before the Lord things concerning themselves which they are very far from believing, for from their manner and bearing it is clear that their estimate of themselves is far from being too low. There are others who think that laziness is humility; they cry, 'Oh, I could not do this! I could not do the other!' when they might do it, should do it, ought to do it and could do it, God the Holy Spirit helping them; but they shirk every duty because they have a sense of inability and they cover their idleness with the cloak of supposed humility. Moses was rebuked by God very strongly when he made excuses and would gladly have avoided going into the great work to which the Lord had called him. Let us not raise questions with our God when he calls us to labour but let us say, 'Here am I; send me.' Do not fall into that miserable counterfeit humility, but like men use all your strength for Jesus. Again, do not mistake unbelief for humility. 'I hope I am,' 'I trust I am,' and expressions of that kind savour far more of distrust of God than of humility of spirit, for the best form of humility is compatible with the highest degree of faith. In fact faith which is not humble is not true but spurious; and that is not genuine humility of the loveliest type which is not confident in God. Faith and humility should always walk together. Let the grace in you be real grace, and to that end ask the Spirit of God to work it in you.

FOR MEDITATION: We should be wary of those who practice pretence in their prayers (Luke 20:46–47) and in their preaching (Philippians 1:15–18); the practice of false humility can be just as misleading and futile (Colossians 2:8,18,23). Above all we should avoid doing these things ourselves.

SERMON NO. 748

How God condemned sin

'For what the law could not do, in that it was weak through the flesh, God sending his own Son in the likeness of sinful flesh, and for sin, condemned sin in the flesh.' Romans 8:3
SUGGESTED FURTHER READING (Spurgeon): Isaiah 53:1–12

God sent his Son. He is called in the text 'his own Son' to distinguish him from us who are only his sons by creation, or his sons by regeneration and adoption. He sent his own Son and he sent him in the flesh. Jesus Christ, the Son of God, was born into this world; he took upon himself our manhood: 'the Word was made flesh, and dwelt among us', and the apostles declare that they 'beheld his glory, the glory as of the only begotten of the Father, full of grace and truth.' The text uses very important words. It says that God sent his Son 'in the likeness of sinful flesh,' not in the likeness of flesh, for that would not be true, but in the same likeness as our sinful flesh. He was to all intents and purposes like ourselves, 'in all points tempted like as we are, yet without sin', with all our sinless infirmities, with all our tendencies to suffer, with everything human in him except that which comes to be human through human nature having fallen. He was perfectly man; he was like ourselves; and God sent him 'in the likeness of sinful flesh'. The joy of his coming is still in our hearts. He lived here his thirty two or thirty three years, but he was sent, the text tells us, for a reason which caused him to die. He was sent 'for sin'. This may mean that he was sent to do battle with sin, or that he was sent because sin was in the world, or, best of all, that he was sent to be a sin-offering. He was sent that he might be the substitute for sinners. God's great plan was this, that inasmuch as his justice could not overlook sin, and sin must be punished, Jesus Christ should come and take the sin of his people upon himself, and upon the accursed tree, the cross of ignominious note, should suffer what was due on our behalf, and that then through his sufferings the infinite love of God should stream forth without any contravention of his infinite justice. This is what God did.

FOR MEDITATION: Death came into the world because of sin (Romans 5:12). 'Christ Jesus came into the world to save sinners' (1 Timothy 1:15). 'Believe on the Lord Jesus Christ, and thou shalt be saved' (Acts 16:31).

Three precious things

'He is precious.' 1 Peter 2:7
'Precious promises.' 2 Peter 1:4
'Precious faith.' 2 Peter 1:1
SUGGESTED FURTHER READING: Joshua 23:1–14

His promises are precious because they tell of exceeding great and precious things. We have promises in the Bible which time would fail us to repeat, which for breadth and length are immeasurable; they deal with every great thing which the soul can want, promises of pardoned sin, sanctification, teaching, guidance, upholding, ennobling, progress, consolation and perfection. In this blessed book you have promises of the daily bread of earth and of the bread of life from heaven, promises for time and for eternity, for yourselves and for your children; all these are like the leaves of the tree, and Jesus is the apple of gold hidden among the foliage of promise. You have so many promises that all the conditions and positions of the believer are met. I liken the promises to the smith's great bunch of keys, which he brings when you have lost the key of your chest and cannot unlock it. He feels pretty sure that some one or other will fit and he tries them with patient industry. At last, yes, that is it; he has started the bolt and you can get at your treasures. There is always a promise in the volume of inspiration suitable to your present case. Make the Lord's testimonies your delight and counsellors, and they will befriend you at every turn. Search the Scriptures and you shall meet with a passage which will be so applicable to you as to appear even to have been written after your trouble had occurred; you will marvel at the wonderful tenderness and suitableness of it. As if the armourer had measured you from head to foot, so exactly shall the armour of the promise fit you. The promises are precious in themselves as being suitable to us, as coming from God, as being immutable, as being sure of performance, and as containing wrapped up within themselves all that the children of God can ever need.

FOR MEDITATION: God's promises are not only 'exceeding great and precious' (2 Peter 1:4), but also good (1 Kings 8:56), holy (Psalm 105:42) and better (Hebrews 8:6), because 'he is faithful that promised' (Hebrews 10:23). Do you trust him and take him at his word?

Things present

'Things present ... all are yours.' 1 *Corinthians* 3:22
SUGGESTED FURTHER READING: Ephesians 3:7–21

The favour of God is not for heaven only; it is ours today. Adoption into his family is not for eternity only; it is for this present time. We are today 'heirs of God, and joint-heirs with Christ', today to be instructed, to be fed, to be clothed, to be housed, to have the Father's kiss and live in the Father's heart. All things are ours. God himself is ours, our eternal inheritance. Lift up your eyes, heir of grace, and see what a treasure is opened up to you! Again, Christ is present and he is ours. There is today a 'fountain filled with blood', which puts away all sin; it is ours. There is a mercy-seat where all prayer is prevalent; it is open today. It is ours; come boldly. There is an Intercessor who takes our prayers and offers them. He is ours; and all his mighty pleas and divine authorities, which make him so successful an advocate, are all at our service today, not ours yesterday, nor ours in some happier hour, but ours now. Are any of you depressed? Do you feel yourselves great sinners? Then the fountain is yours as sinners; the Intercessor is yours while you are yet guilty, for it is written, 'if any man sin, we have an advocate with the Father'. Lay hold upon these present things and rejoice. The Holy Spirit too is a present blessing to you. The Comforter comes to you as a present boon from Christ and he brings you present enlightenment, present guidance, present strength and present consolation. All these are yours, all beams of the seven-branched golden candlestick, and all the oil that is treasured up for the lamps. The light and the source of the light are alike yours, and yours now. And if, beloved, there is any promise today written in the word of God, if there is any blessing today guaranteed to the elect family, if there is any mindfulness of providence or any abundance of grace, all these are yours and yours now.

FOR MEDITATION: Full salvation is yet to come, but Christians already *now* enjoy justification (Romans 5:9), atonement (Romans 5:11), freedom from condemnation (Romans 8:1) and God's mercy (Romans 11:30); 'now are we the sons of God' (1 John 3:2) who can pray to our Father in heaven 'Give us this day our daily bread' (Matthew 6:9,11). Do you possess present salvation?

SERMON NO. 870

The faithfulness of Jesus

'Having loved his own which were in the world, he loved them unto the end.' John 13:1
SUGGESTED FURTHER READING: Deuteronomy 7:6–11

'Having loved his own'; these four words are a brief but complete summary of the Saviour's conduct towards his disciples. He always loved them. There was never a single action or word which was contrary to the rule of love. He loved them with a love of pity when he saw them in their lost estate, and he called them out of it to be his disciples; touched with a feeling of their infirmities he loved them with a tender and prudent affection, and sought to train and educate them, that after his departure they might be good soldiers of his cross; he loved them with a love of contentment as he walked and talked with them and found solace in their company. Even when he rebuked them he loved them. He subjected them to many trials: for his sake they renounced all that they had; they shared his daily cross-bearing and hourly persecution, but love reigned supreme and undiminished amid it all. On Tabor or in Gethsemane he loved his own; alone or in the crowd his heart was true to them; in life and in death his affection failed not. He 'loved his own which were in the world'. It is a condensed life of Christ, a miniature of Jesus the Lover of souls. As you read the wonderful story of the four evangelists you see how true it is that Jesus loved his own: let me cast in by way of interjection this sentence, that when you come to read your own life's story in the light of the New Jerusalem, you will find it to be true also concerning your Lord and yourself. If you are indeed the Lord's own, he at all times deals lovingly with you and never acts in unkindness or wrath.

'He may chasten and correct, but he never can neglect;
May in faithfulness reprove, but he ne'er can cease to love.'

FOR MEDITATION: The Lord Jesus Christ could rightly claim to love his disciples (John 13:34; 14:21; 15:9,12). The apostle John in particular could testify to this fact on behalf of others (John 11:3,5) and on his own behalf (John 13:23; 19:26; 20:2; 21:7,20). Are you able to join the apostle Paul in saying 'the Son of God ... loved me, and gave himself for me' (Galatians 2:20)?

SERMON NO. 810

A bright light in deep shades

'Hearken to me, ye that follow after righteousness, ye that seek the LORD: *look unto the rock whence ye are hewn, and to the hole of the pit whence ye are digged.' Isaiah 51:1*
SUGGESTED FURTHER READING: Psalm 85:1–13

This is a lukewarm age. 'I would thou wert cold or hot' might be addressed to the churches of this day as justly as to the church of Laodicea. We will neither insist upon it, nor bring proofs about it, nor will we argue about it, but we will admit the charge just as the accuser brings it; and what then? Though I see much cause for our feeling grieved, still I see no cause for our being dispirited. The church has been in a like listless state before, and out of that languid condition God has roused her up and brought her forth. I am sure I need not unroll a page of history and ask you to glance your eye down it except for a second; for again and again you will see it has occurred that the church has fallen asleep, and her ministers have become as mute inglorious neuters, destitute of zeal, having no ardent passion and giving themselves up to no arduous enterprise. But it is only needed once more for God to make bare his arm and his church has been full of life and of power, renewing the vigour of youth, abounding in hope and intrepid in courage. Must you have a modern instance? Think of the days of Wesley and Whitefield. When they began to preach, gross darkness had covered this land. They did not appear to be the men who were likely to remove the veil that covered the nation, yet God used their very feebleness and eccentricity; he used everything about the men to be the means of restoring the church, reinforcing her ranks and augmenting her energies. Therefore, be of good cheer; though the church should slip and slide again, and disgrace herself by her lack of zeal, yet she is the spouse of Christ and he will not divorce her; he will turn to her in mercy yet again.

FOR MEDITATION: Has the church lost its first love (Revelation 2:4), adopted false teaching and condoned immorality (Revelation 2:14,20), become dead (Revelation 3:1–2) and lapsed into lukewarm self-satisfaction (Revelation 3:16–17)? The prospect of conquering is still held out even when the church is in such a state (Revelation 2:7,17,26; 3:5,21), but there will never be any restoration without repentance from these sins (Revelation 2:5,16,21; 3:3,19).

SERMON NO. 1050

The righteous holding on his way

'The righteous also shall hold on his way.' Job 17:9
SUGGESTED FURTHER READING: Hebrews 10:26–39

What a dreadful thing, not to persevere and yet to have had the name of a Christian! When a man goes up a ladder, if he falls at the first step, that is bad; but if he falls when he has nearly reached the top, what a falling there is! God save us from it! Let us not fall, for to fall backward into perdition is the worst way of falling into hell! Christian, it is not that you *may* persevere or not—it is not an optional blessing—you *must* persevere, or else all you have ever known and felt will be good for nothing to you. You *must* hold on your way if you are ultimately to be saved. Let me here say that I do not assert that a Christian must daily make progress in grace; he ought to do so and should do so; but even if he should not do so, he will not be cast away for that. Neither do I assert that a Christian should always be conscious that he is in the way, for many of the best of God's saints are tormented with many doubts and fears. Nor do I say that every departure from the way of God is inevitably fatal: far from it, for many have departed for a season and have been brought back and restored as penitent backsliders. Christian went down By-path meadow and yet returned to the right road: that is a very different case from Demas, who forsook the way to dig in the silver mine and perished in it. The general current of the soul, however, must be onward: the general current and tendency of the believer must be in the way of truth, both as to his heart and his life; and if it be not so, whatever boastings he may make about his faith, whatever experiences he may think he has had, if he does not hold out to the end, there is no salvation, no heaven, no bliss for him.

FOR MEDITATION: Yesterday's text reminded us to take note of our lowly origins; that should keep us humble and thankful. But the best way to avoid a fall and reach the summit is to continue climbing and not to keep looking down (Philippians 3:13–14; 2 Peter 1:5–11; 3:17–18).

Unto you, young men

'I have written unto you, young men, because ye are strong, and the word of God abideth in you, and ye have overcome the wicked one.' 1 John 2:14

SUGGESTED FURTHER READING: Proverbs 23:15–35

A form of the wicked one we must speak of but softly, but how hard to be overcome by the young man, I mean Madam Wanton, that fair but foul, that smiling but murderous fiend of hell, by whom so many are deluded. Solomon spoke of 'the strange woman', but the strong Christian, in whom the word of God abides, passes by her door and shuts his ear to her siren song. He flees 'youthful lusts', 'which war against the soul; he reserves both his body and his soul for his Lord who has redeemed him by his precious blood. Young man, if you are strong and 'have overcome the wicked one', you have overcome, I trust, that Lucifer of *pride*, and it is your endeavour to walk humbly with your God! You have given up all idea of merit. You cannot boast nor exalt yourself, but you bow humbly at the foot of the cross, adoring him who has saved you from the wrath to come. You have given up also, I trust, all subjection to the great red dragon of *fashion*, who draws with his tail even the very stars of heaven. There are some who would think it far worse to be considered unfashionable than to be thought unchristian. To be unchristian would be such a common accusation that they might submit to it, but to be unfashionable would be horrible indeed! Young men in London get to be affected by this. If the young men in the house are going to such-and-such an entertainment, if they all read a certain class of books, if they are dissipated and sceptical, then the temptation is to chime in with them, and only the man who is strong and has the word of God abiding in him, will overcome the wicked one by doing the right alone— *'Faithful among the faithless found'*.

FOR MEDITATION: Satan will ensure that the young man is assailed by youthful passions (2 Timothy 2:22), but purification and escape from Satan's snares is not only desirable (2 Timothy 2:21,25–26), but made possible by the power of God's word (Psalm 119:9). A young man can be a wonderful example to other believers (1 Timothy 4:12).

SERMON NO. 811

Prosperity under persecution

'*But the more they afflicted them, the more they multiplied and grew.*'
Exodus 1:12
SUGGESTED FURTHER READING: 2 Corinthians 11:2–15

Always take revenge on Satan if he defeats you, by trying to do ten times more good than you did before. It is in some such way that a dear brother now preaching the gospel, whom God has blessed with a very considerable measure of success, may trace the opening of his career to a circumstance that occurred to myself. Sitting in my pulpit one evening in a country village, where I had to preach, my text slipped from my memory, and with the text seemed to go all that I had thought to speak upon it. This was a rare thing to happen to me, but I sat utterly confounded. I could find nothing to say. With strong crying I lifted up my soul to God to pour out again within my soul the living water that it might gush forth from me for others; and I accompanied my prayer with a vow that if Satan's enmity thus had brought me low, I would take so many fresh men whom I might meet with during the week and train them for the ministry, so that with their hands and tongues I would avenge myself on the Philistines. The brother I have alluded to came to me the next morning. I accepted him at once as one whom God had sent, and I helped him and others after him to prepare for the ministry and to go forth in the Saviour's name to preach the gospel of the grace of God. Often when we fear we are defeated we ought to say, 'I will do all the more. Instead of dropping from this work, now will I make a general levy and a sacred conscription upon all the powers of my soul, and I will gather up all the strength I ever had in reserve and make from this moment a tremendous lifelong effort to overcome the powers of darkness and win for Christ fresh trophies of victory.'

FOR MEDITATION: When Satan first tempted Adam and Eve, God at once claimed future victory (Genesis 3:15). By his grace we can bounce back from spiritual defeat and engage wholeheartedly in his service. Consider the experiences of king Jehoshaphat (2 Chronicles 19:1–11) and the apostle Peter (Luke 22:31–34).

SERMON NO. 997

Angelic studies

'To the intent that now unto the principalities and powers in heavenly places might be known by the church the manifold wisdom of God.'
Ephesians 3:10
SUGGESTED FURTHER READING: 1 Peter 1:10–13

The 'principalities and powers in heavenly places' to whom the apostle here refers are, no doubt, the angels. These bright and glorious spirits, never having fallen into sin, did not need to be redeemed, and, therefore, in the sense of being cleansed from guilt, they have no share in the atoning sacrifice of Christ. Yet it is interesting to notice how our Lord did as it were pass and repass their shining ranks, when he sped his way down to the regions of death and when he came back triumphant to the realms of glory. Thus in one place 'we see Jesus, who was made a little lower than the angels for the suffering of death,' and in another place we learn that the Father 'raised him from the dead, and set him at his own right hand in the heavenly places, far above all principality, and power, and might, and dominion'. It is possible that the mediation of Christ has a bearing upon them and has henceforth confirmed them in their holiness, so that by no means shall they ever be tempted or led into sin in the future. It may be so, but this much seems to be evident that, though they had no direct share in redemption, they feel nevertheless an interest in it and are to be instructed by its results. The sublime plan of the gospel of the grace of God, which is so entirely beyond the compass of our natural faculties that we could never by searching have found it out, appears to have been equally beyond the grasp of angelic intelligence, a mystery that excited their wistful enquiry, until by the church (that is to say, by the divine counsel and conduct in forming and perfecting the church) there is made known unto them the manifold wisdom of God as they have never learned it before.

FOR MEDITATION: The eyes of angels are upon us not only when we repent (Luke 15:10), but also afterwards as we continue to live the Christian life (1 Corinthians 4:9; Hebrews 1:14). If we are going to be proper witnesses to them, their interest in us should have some impact on the way we behave (1 Corinthians 11:10; 1 Timothy 5:21; Hebrews 13:2).

SERMON NO. 933

To those who are 'almost persuaded'

'Then Agrippa said unto Paul, Almost thou persuadest me to be a Christian.' Acts 26:28
SUGGESTED FURTHER READING: Exodus 9:27–35

If a man is only almost convinced, he misses altogether the blessing, which being fully persuaded to be a Christian would have brought him. A leaky ship went out to sea and a passenger was almost persuaded not to trust his life in it, but he did so and perished. A bubble speculation was started in the city and a merchant was almost persuaded not to have shares in it, but he bought the scrip and his estate went down in the general shipwreck. A person exceedingly ill heard of a remedy reputed to be most effectual and was almost persuaded to take it, but he did not and therefore the disease grew worse and worse. A man who proposed to go into a subterranean vault in the dark was almost persuaded to take a lamp, but he did not and therefore he stumbled and fell. You cannot have the blessing by being almost persuaded to have it. Your hunger cannot be appeased by almost eating, nor your thirst quenched by almost drinking. A culprit was almost saved from being hanged, for a reprieve came five minutes after he was dropped, but he was altogether dead, despite almost escaping. A man who has been almost persuaded to be saved will at the last be altogether damned; his being almost convinced will be of no conceivable service to him. This seems so grievous, that the life of God, the light of God and the heaven of God should glide by some of you, and you should be almost persuaded and yet should miss them through not becoming Christians. Worse still, in addition to the loss of the blessing, there certainly comes an additional guilt to the man who, being almost persuaded, yet continues in his sin.

FOR MEDITATION: A miss is as good as a mile. In spiritual matters it is far better to be fully persuaded (Romans 4:21; 14:5). Are you persuaded that nothing can separate you from God's love in Christ Jesus (Romans 8:38–39) and that he is able to keep what you've committed to him against the Day of Judgment (2 Timothy 1:12)? Or are you just vaguely hoping for the best?

The deep-seated character of sin

'The sin of Judah is written with a pen of iron, and with the point of a diamond: it is graven upon the table of their heart, and upon the horns of your altars.' Jeremiah 17:1
SUGGESTED FURTHER READING: Romans 3:21–26

Jesus Christ is able to take our guilt away. His dying upon the cross is the means by which the foulest sinner out of hell can be made white as the angels of God, and that in a single instant. Do you understand the doctrine of the atonement? Let me sound it in your ears again. Sin is a thing which God must punish; the eternal laws of the universe demand that there shall never be an offence committed against the rules of God which shall escape without a penalty. The penalty of sin is death and God has never seen fit to mitigate this; its justice makes it perpetual. The Lord has been pleased to open a way of mercy by sending his only begotten Son into this world as our substitute. He became a man and he suffered for his people what they ought to have suffered. He endured at the hand of God what all the redeemed ought to have endured. Now, God, at this day, never pardons a sin without having first punished it; he punished it on Christ for us. God never punishes the man for whom Christ died, but all others must bear their iniquity. If you believe in Jesus Christ, then Jesus Christ died for you and God cannot put two to death for one offence, nor can he ask for payment twice for one debt; you are therefore free. Christ paid the debts of all his people and obtained their full discharge when he rose again from the dead; now every soul that believes in him is clear at the bar of divine justice, because it is written that, 'the blood of Jesus Christ his Son cleanseth us from all sin.'

FOR MEDITATION: The great Biblical doctrines of justification, redemption, propitiation (Romans 3:23–25), reconciliation and atonement (Romans 5:10–11) all boil down to the wonderful fact that Christ died for ungodly sinners (Romans 5:6–8). But they have no relevance to us unless we trust in him alone for forgiveness (Romans 3:22,26).

Golden vials full of odours

'Golden vials full of odours, which are the prayers of saints.' Revelation
5:8
SUGGESTED FURTHER READING: Daniel 9:3–19

In prayer the people of God declare better than they could by any other
means their sure belief that God is, for should we pray to One who has
no existence? Our prayer to God is, therefore, our continual assertion
that 'The Lord, he is the God; the Lord, he is the God.' Our asking for
special and particular mercies, and expecting them, is a declaration of
our belief in a living God, a conscious God, an acting God, a God who is
not asleep and far away, but who is near at hand listening to human
voices and able to fulfil human desires. This, then, is very agreeable to
God that we should believe and testify 'that he is, and that he is a
rewarder of them that diligently seek him.' What if I were to say that
prayer is in itself essentially a doxology? It is an utterance of glory to
God in his attributes. Do I ask him to bless me? Then I adore his power,
for I believe he can. Do I ask him to bless me? Then I adore his mercy, for
I trust and hope he will. Do I ask him to bless me because of such and
such a promise? Then I adore his faithfulness, for I evidently believe that
he is truthful and will do as he has said. Do I ask him to bless me not
according to my request, but according to his own wisdom? Then I adore
his wisdom; I am evidently believing in his prudence and judgment.
When I say to him, 'not my will, but thine, be done', I am adoring his
sovereignty. When I confess that I deserve to suffer beneath his hand, I
reverence his justice. When I acknowledge that he does right evermore, I
adore his holiness; and when I humbly say, 'Nevertheless, deal graciously
with thy servant and blot out my transgressions,' I am reverencing his
grace. We do not wonder, therefore, that through Jesus Christ the prayers
of the saints should be precious to God.

FOR MEDITATION: What would the content of your prayers tell others
about your conception of God's character? In the Lord's Prayer the Lord
Jesus Christ taught us to pray to God as Father, King, Sovereign,
Sustainer, Saviour and Protector (Matthew 6:9–13). 'After this manner
therefore pray ye' (Matthew 6:9).

More than conquerors

'Nay, in all these things we are more than conquerors through him that loved us.' Romans 8:37

SUGGESTED FURTHER READING (Spurgeon): Hebrews 11:32–40

The men who conquered in the fight up till now have been known only by these two things—they believed in Christ's love to them and were possessed with love to Christ; for there has been no other distinction than this. They have been rich; Caesar's household yielded martyrs. They have been poor; few of the inscriptions on the tombs of the catacombs are spelt correctly; they must have been very poor and illiterate persons who constituted the majority of the first Christian churches, yet all classes have conquered. At the stake bishops have burned and princes have died, but more numerous still have been the weavers, tailors and seamstresses. The poorest of the poor have been as brave as the wealthy; the learned have died gloriously, but the unlearned have almost stolen the palm. Little children have suffered for Christ; their little souls, washed in the blood of Jesus, have also been encrimsoned with their own; meanwhile the aged have not been behindhand. It must have been a sad but glorious sight to see old Latimer, when past seventy, putting off all his garments but his shirt, and then standing up and saying, as he turned round to Mr Ridley, 'Courage, brother! We shall this day light such a candle in England as, by the grace of God, shall never be put out.' If you wish to serve my master, old men, you have not passed the prime of your days for that. Young men, if you would be heroes, now is the opportunity. You who are poor, you may glow with as great a glory as the rich; and you who have substance, you may count it your joy if you are called in the high places of the field to do battle for your Lord. In this fight there is room for all who love the Lord, and there are crowns for each.

FOR MEDITATION: The Lord Jesus Christ has overcome both the world (John 16:33) and the devil (Luke 11:17–22). Because of his victory those who follow him are also able to overcome both the world (1 John 5:4–5) and the devil (Revelation 12:9–11) whatever their age (1 John 2:12–17).

A sermon to open neglecters and nominal followers of religion

'Jesus saith unto them, Verily I say unto you, That the publicans and the harlots go into the kingdom of God before you. For John came unto you in the way of righteousness, and ye believed him not: but the publicans and harlots believed him.' Matthew 21:31–32
SUGGESTED FURTHER READING: 1 Timothy 2:1–7

There is, my dear friends, the same gospel to be preached to one class of men as to every other class. I pray God the day may never come when we shall be found in our preaching talking about working classes, middle classes and upper classes. I know no difference between you; you are the same to me when I preach the gospel, whether you are kings and queens, or crossing sweepers; satin and cotton, broadcloth and fustian are alike to the gospel. If you are peers of the realm, we trim not our gospel to suit you, and if you are the basest of thieves, we do not exclude you from the voice of mercy. The gospel comes to men as sinners, all equally fallen in Adam, equally lost and ruined by sin. I have not one gospel for Her Majesty the Queen and another gospel for the beggar-woman. No, there is only one way of salvation, only one foundation, only one propitiation, only one gospel. Look to the cross of Christ and live. High was the brazen serpent lifted, and all that Moses said was, 'Look.' If a prince of the house of Judah was bitten, he was told to look; without looking his lion standard of costly emblazonry could not avail him; if some wretch in the camp was bitten, he must look, and the efficacy was the same for him as for the greatest of the host. Look! Look to Jesus. Believe in the Son of God and live! One brazen serpent for all the camp; one Christ for all ranks and conditions of men. What a blessing it would be if we were all enabled to trust Christ! My brethren, why not? He is worthy of the confidence of all. The Spirit of God is able to work faith in all. O poor sinner, look to him!

FOR MEDITATION: Whosoever trusts in the Lord Jesus Christ shall never die spiritually (John 11:26); 'whosoever shall call on the name of the Lord shall be saved' (Acts 2:21). Remember that there is an alternative for whosoever rejects the Saviour and his blessings (Revelation 20:15).

SERMON NO. 742 (1ST SERMON AT THE AGRICULTURAL HALL, ISLINGTON)

Ephraim bemoaning himself

'I have surely heard Ephraim bemoaning himself thus; Thou hast chastised me, and I was chastised, as a bullock unaccustomed to the yoke: turn thou me, and I shall be turned; for thou art the LORD my God.' Jeremiah 31:18

SUGGESTED FURTHER READING (Spurgeon): Luke 15:11–24

Broken prayers are the best prayers. Do not suppose that you require fine words and elegant phrases in order to affect the Lord. Your tearful eye shall be more mighty a metaphor, and your heavy sigh shall be more eloquent than the polished period and lofty climax of the orator. Only prostrate your soul before God with humble heart and downcast eye, and your Father will accept you. What man among you can stand against his children's tears? When King Henry II, in days past, was provoked to take up arms against his ungrateful and rebellious son, he besieged him in one of the French towns, and the son, being near to death, desired to see his father and confess his wrongdoing; but the stern old sire refused to look the rebel in the face. The young man, being sorely troubled in his conscience, said to those about him, 'I am dying; take me from my bed, and let me lie in sackcloth and ashes, in token of my sorrow for my ingratitude to my father.' Thus he died, and when the tidings came to the old man outside the walls that his boy had died in ashes, repentant for his rebellion, he threw himself upon the earth like king David and said, 'would God I had died for thee'. The thought of the boy's broken heart touched the heart of the father. If you, being evil, are overcome by your children's tears, how much more shall your Father who is in heaven find in your bemoanings and confessions an argument for the display of his pardoning love through Christ Jesus our Lord. This is the eloquence which God delights in—the broken heart and the contrite spirit. He heard and he understood all that Ephraim said, and he was moved by it. Note the word 'surely'—'I have surely heard Ephraim bemoaning himself'.

FOR MEDITATION: God is far more likely to listen to the broken prayers of those who cannot look up (Luke 18:13–14) and who may totally dry up (Romans 8:26–27) than to the long-winded oratorical displays of those who do not know when to shut up (Matthew 6:5–7).

SERMON NO. 743 (2ND SERMON AT THE AGRICULTURAL HALL, ISLINGTON)

Jesus at Bethesda; or, waiting changed for believing

'And a certain man was there, which had an infirmity thirty and eight years.
… Jesus saith unto him, Rise, take up thy bed, and walk. And immediately
the man was made whole, and took up his bed, and walked.' John 5:5–9
SUGGESTED FURTHER READING: Acts 16:16–34

As soon as your eye meets Christ, you are saved. Though yesterday you
were up to your neck in sin, yet if this morning you look to my once slain
but now exalted Master, you shall find eternal life. Take biblical
instances. Did the dying thief wait at the pool of ordinances? You know
how soon his believing prayer was heard, and Jesus said, 'To day shalt
thou be with me in paradise.' The three thousand at Pentecost, did they
wait for some great thing? No, they believed and were baptized. Look at
the jailer of Philippi. It was the dead of the night, the prison was shaken;
the jailer was alarmed and said, 'Sirs, what must I do to be saved?' Did
Paul and Silas say, 'Well, you must use the means and look for a blessing
upon the ordinances'? No, they said, 'Believe on the Lord Jesus Christ,
and thou shalt be saved, and thy house.' And that very night he was
baptized. Paul did not take the time about it that some think so
exceedingly necessary. He believed as I do, that there is life in a look at
Jesus; he bade men look, and looking they lived. Possibly you will see this
still more clearly if I remind you that the work of salvation is all done.
There is nothing for a sinner to do in order to be saved; it is all done for
him. You want washing; the bath does not need filling—'There is a
fountain filled with blood.' You want clothing. You do not have to make
the garment; the robe is ready. The garment of Christ's righteousness is
woven from the top throughout; all that is needed is to have it put on. If
some work remained for you to do, it might be a lengthened process, but
all the doing is accomplished by Christ. Salvation is not of works but of
grace, and to accept what Christ presents you is not a work of time.

FOR MEDITATION: While it is important to guard against the dangers of
easy-believism, it is possible to go to the opposite extreme and be too
reticent to urge unbelievers to respond to the gospel; 'now is the accepted
time; behold, now is the day of salvation' wrote the apostle Paul
(2 Corinthians 6:2), but even he had needed prompting not to delay
calling on the name of the Lord (Acts 22:16).

SERMON NO. 744 (3RD SERMON AT THE AGRICULTURAL HALL, ISLINGTON)

The unsearchable riches of Christ

'Unto me, who am less than the least of all saints, is this grace given, that I should preach among the Gentiles the unsearchable riches of Christ.'
Ephesians 3:8
SUGGESTED FURTHER READING: 1 Corinthians 2:1–5

Many preachers make a great mistake by preaching doctrine instead of preaching the Saviour. Certainly the doctrines are to be preached, but they ought to be looked upon as the robes and vestments of the man Christ Jesus, and not as complete in themselves. I love justification by faith—I hope I shall never have a doubt about that grand truth; but the cleansing efficacy of the precious blood appears to me to be the best way of putting it. I delight in sanctification by the Spirit; but to be conformed to the image of Jesus is a still sweeter and more forcible way of viewing it. The doctrines of the gospel are a golden throne upon which Jesus sits as king, not a hard, cold stone rolled at the door of the sepulchre in which Christ is hidden. Brethren, I believe this to be the mark of God's true minister, that he preaches Christ as his one choice and delightful theme. In an old romance they tell us that at the gate of a certain noble hall there hung a horn, and none could blow that horn but the true heir to the castle and its wide domains. Many tried it. They could make sweet music on other instruments; they could wake the echoes by other bugles; but that horn was mute, let them blow as they might. At last the true heir came, and when he set his lips to the horn, shrill was the sound and indisputable his claim. He who can preach Christ is the true minister. Let him preach anything else in the world, he has not proved his calling, but if he shall preach Jesus and the resurrection, he is in the apostolical succession. If Christ crucified is the great delight of his soul, the very marrow of his teaching and the fatness of his ministry, he has proved his calling as an ambassador of Christ.

FOR MEDITATION: Some get taken up with the personality of the preacher, others with ordinances; some thrive on signs and wonders, others on academic wisdom (1 Corinthians 1:12,17,22). If we want any of these to be the focal point, we are sadly in error. The Christian faith has its centre only in the person and work of the Lord Jesus Christ (1 Corinthians 1:23).

SERMON NO. 745 (4TH SERMON AT THE AGRICULTURAL HALL, ISLINGTON)

The end of the righteous desired

'Let me die the death of the righteous, and let my last end be like his!'
Numbers 23:10
SUGGESTED FURTHER READING: 2 Chronicles 21:5–6,18–20; 35:23–27

When the good man dies, he dies with honour. Who cares for the death of the wicked? A few mourning friends lament for a little while, but they almost feel it a relief within a day or two that such a one is gone. As for the righteous, when he dies there is weeping and mourning for him. Like Stephen, devout men carry him to the sepulchre and make great lamentation over him. Do you see the funeral of the weeds? They are hurried up in heaps, they are thrown over the garden wall, they are burned forthwith, and no one regrets them; they were no blessing in living; they are no lamentation in dying. Did you ever see the funeral of the wheat, if such I may call it? Here come the golden sheaves. The wagon is heavy with the precious freight: on the top stands one who gives a cheery note; and all around the harvest men and village maidens dance or shout for joy as they bring home the shocks of golden corn to the storehouse. Let me be gathered home with the triumphant funeral of the wheat which man values, garnered by angels and housed with songs of saintly spirits, rather than cast away as a reprobate and worthless thing, like the weeds of which men are thankful to be rid. May it be yours and mine, when we depart, to be remembered by those whom we have succoured in their need, whom we instructed in their ignorance, whom we comforted in their distress! May we not depart from this world shaken off from it, as Paul shook the viper from his hand, but may our ashes be gathered up as sacred dust, precious in the sight of the Lord. 'Let me' in that sense and every other 'die the death of the righteous'.

FOR MEDITATION: The death of the wicked is their entrance to a hopeless eternity (Proverbs 11:7). 'But the righteous hath hope in his death' (Proverbs 14:32). Those who die in the Lord are blessed (Revelation 14:13) and their death is precious in his sight (Psalm 116:15). What will others say after your death? And what will God himself say to you?

The perseverance of the saints

'Being confident of this very thing, that he which hath begun a good work in you will perform it until the day of Jesus Christ.' Philippians 1:6
SUGGESTED FURTHER READING: Isaiah 46:3–13

Paul was fully assured 'that he which hath begun a good work in' his people will surely finish it in due season. Indeed, dear friends, in the apostle's words there is good argument. If the Lord began the good work, why should he not carry it on and finish it? If he stays his hand, what can be the motive? When a man commences a work and leaves it half complete, it is often from lack of power; men say of the unfinished tower, 'This man began to build, and was not able to finish.' Lack of forethought or lack of ability must have stopped the work; but can you suppose Jehovah, the Omnipotent, ceasing from a work because of unforeseen difficulty which he is not able to overcome? He sees the end from the beginning; he is almighty; his arm is not shortened; nothing is too hard for him. It would be a base reflection upon the wisdom and power of God to believe that he has entered upon a work which he will not in due time conduct to a happy conclusion. God did not begin the work in any man's soul without due deliberation and counsel. From all eternity he knew the circumstances in which that man would be placed, though he foresaw the hardness of the human heart and the fickleness of human love. If then he deemed it wise to begin, how can it be supposed that he shall change and amend his resolve? There can be no conceivable reason with God for leaving off such a work; the same motive which dictated the commencement must be still in operation, and he is the same God; therefore, there must be the same result, namely, his continuing to do what he has done. Where is there an instance of God's beginning any work and leaving it incomplete?

FOR MEDITATION: Whereas God's work of creation took only a week (Genesis 2:1–3) and his work on the cross took only a day (Zechariah 12:10–13:1; John 19:28–30), his work in the Christian takes the rest of our lives. The Christian life is a marathon (Matthew 10:22), but we are assured that our Saviour is not only the author but also the finisher of our faith (Hebrews 12:2).

The king in his beauty

'Thine eyes shall see the king in his beauty: they shall behold the land that is very far off.' Isaiah 33:17
SUGGESTED FURTHER READING: John 12:12–19

Some of the worst of tyrants have delighted to call themselves kings by divine right, emperors by the will of God, monarchs by the grace of God, and the like. It may be so; I doubt not that many of earth's tyrants require much grace, lest their crimes should bring them to speedy ruin; and doubtless it is sometimes the will of God to inflict great scourges upon guilty nations; but, my brethren, Jesus Christ is no despotic claimant of divine right, but he is really and truly the Lord's Anointed! 'For it pleased the Father that in him should all fulness dwell'. God has given to him all power and authority. As the Son of man, he is now head over all things to his church, and he reigns over heaven, earth and hell with the keys of life and death at his girdle; 'and the government shall be upon his shoulder: and his name shall be called Wonderful, Counsellor, The mighty God, The everlasting Father, The Prince of Peace.' We recognise him as King by divine right. We see in him most clearly that true deity which 'doth hedge a king,' and meekly we bow before him whom God has appointed 'to be a Prince and a Saviour' to give repentance and forgiveness of sins. Certain princes have delighted to call themselves kings by the popular will, and certainly our Lord Jesus Christ is such in his church. If it could be put to the vote whether he should be King in the church, every believing heart would crown him. O that we could crown him more gloriously than we do! We should count no expense to be wasted that could glorify Christ. Suffering should be pleasure, and loss should be gain, if thereby we could surround his brow with brighter crowns and make him more glorious in the eyes of men and angels. Yes, he shall reign. Long live the King! All hail to thee, King Jesus!

FOR MEDITATION: The eternal kingship of Christ is his by God's appointment and was announced before his birth (Luke 1:32–33). Though his enemies regarded him as a usurper (Luke 23:2: John 19:12,15; Acts 17:7), he was born to be king (John 18:37) and is in fact the King of kings (Revelation 17:14; 19:16). Should that encourage or terrify you?

The sphere of instrumentality

'Jesus said, Take ye away the stone ... Jesus saith unto them, Loose him, and let him go.' John 11:39,44
SUGGESTED FURTHER READING: Matthew 15:1–20

The manufacture of new commandments is a very fascinating occupation for some people. You must not do this or that or the other, till one feels like a baby in reins. I find that ten commandments are more than I can keep without a deal of grace, and I do not mean to pay the slightest regard to any beyond. Liberty is the genius of our faith, nor do we mean to barter it away for the esteem of modern Pharisees. They say to us, 'Thou shalt not laugh on a Sunday. Thou shalt never create a smile in the House of God. Thou shalt walk to public services as though thou wert going to the whipping post, and thou shalt take care when thou preachest that thou dost always make thy discourse as dull as it can possibly be.' We do not reverence these precepts. Anything which is of God we honour, but not the sickening decrees of cant. We are men, not slaves. Our manhood is not annihilated by grace. We think, speak and act for ourselves, and are not the serfs of custom and fashion. We speak out our minds even when propriety is shocked and respectability is enraged. I would always give to young men this piece of advice: 'quit yourselves like men'; let nobody have to say that your religion is mamby-pamby and your conversation affected. Do not be always sugaring every person you speak of as 'Dear this' and 'Dear that,' for this savours of nauseous hypocrisy. Do not whine or turn up your eyes or affect to be very devout. Be holy, but not showy, true, but not obtrusive. Be men, be manly, be Christians, be like Christ. He was the very highest type of man; you never see anything stilted or unnatural in him; he is always himself, transparent, outspoken, brave, honest, true and manly.

FOR MEDITATION: Manliness is required not only in physical battles (1 Samuel 4:9; 2 Samuel 10:12), but also in spiritual warfare (1 Timothy 6:12); 'in understanding be men' (1 Corinthians 14:20). 'Watch ye, stand fast in the faith, quit you like men, be strong' (1 Corinthians 16:13).

Mature faith—illustrated by Abraham's offering up Isaac

'And he said, Take now thy son, thine only son Isaac, whom thou lovest, and get thee into the land of Moriah; and offer him there for a burnt offering upon one of the mountains which I will tell thee of.' Genesis 22:2
SUGGESTED FURTHER READING: Hebrews 11:17–22

Abraham was sustained under the trial by the conviction that it was possible for God to raise his son from the dead, and so to fulfil his promise. But under that and lower down, there was in Abraham's heart the conviction that by some means, if not by that means, God would justify him in doing what he was to do, that it could never be wrong to do what God commanded him, that God could not command him to do a wrong thing, and, therefore, that doing it he could not possibly suffer the loss of the promise made in regard to Isaac. In some way or other God would take care of him if he did but faithfully keep to God. And I think the more indistinct Abraham's idea may have been of the way in which God could carry out the promise, the more glorious was the faith which still held to it that nothing could frustrate the promise, and that he would do his duty, come what may. Brethren beloved in the Lord, believe that all things work together for your good, and that if you are commanded by conscience and God's word to do that which would beggar you or cast you into disrepute, it cannot be a real hurt to you; it must be all right. I have seen men cast out of work owing to their keeping the Lord's Day, or they have been for a little time out of a situation because they could not fall into the tricks of trade, and they have suffered awhile; but, alas, some of them have lost heart after a time and yielded to the evil. O for the faith which never will fly from the field under any persuasion or compulsion. If men had strength enough to say, 'If I die and rot, I will not sin; if they cast me out, yet nothing shall make me violate my conscience, or do what God commands me not to do, or fail to do what God commands me to perform!' Such was the faith of Abraham.

FOR MEDITATION: The sacrifices we make in order to trust and follow Christ are no great loss (Mark 10:28–30; Philippians 3:8–9; Hebrews 10:32–34); but to abandon conscience (1 Timothy 1:19) and faith in an attempt to recover what we have sacrificed is a great tragedy (1 Timothy 6:10; Hebrews 10:38–39).

SERMON NO. 868

The privileged man

'Then washed I thee with water; ... I anointed thee with oil. I clothed thee also with broidered work and shod thee with badgers' skin, and I girded thee about with fine linen and I covered thee with silk. I decked thee also with ornaments.' Ezekiel 16:9–11

SUGGESTED FURTHER READING: Matthew 26:47–56

How base does our sin appear in the light of this amazing mercy! I have read of one who was extremely poor, and who was helped again and again by a Christian man, and yet when the officers were out searching for the Protestant Christian, the man to betray him for the sake of the reward was the neighbour who had constantly eaten at his table, and who had been helped by his charity. This was brutal, that he who was so much under obligation should yet become a traitor. And yet it was only a neighbour. Your case is worse, believer, for you are a friend, and more, you profess to be a child of God, to be in union with Christ, and yet you have been a traitor to Jesus! O sweet Lord of my heart and monarch of my soul, with precious blood has thou sealed me as thine own, and fool that I am that I should cast my eyes on other beauties, or rather other shams, other painted Jezebels! Wretch that I am to wander thus in search of vain delights, to seek after earthly joys, to set my soul on earthly loves, and to let my Lord and Saviour go. O virgin souls who 'follow the Lamb whithersoever he goeth', may you never wander from your spiritual chastity as some of us have done. O you whose delights are with him still, who in 'the garden of nuts' and amongst 'the beds of spices' have beheld his face and seen those eyes which are 'like the fishponds in Heshbon, by the gate of Bath-rabbim', you that have been enchanted with his presence, cling you yet to his skirts, keep you ever to his company, and let no enchantment of the world induce you to desert him.

FOR MEDITATION: God does not mince his words when the members of Christ's church (his bride—2 Corinthians 11:2) forsake him and fall in love with the world again (2 Timothy 4:10). This act amounts to no less than spiritual adultery and smacks of hatred for God (James 4:4) rather than love for him (1 John 2:15). If you have abandoned your first love for him, God calls you to repent (Revelation 2:4–5).

SERMON NO. 813

Christ made a curse for us

'Christ hath redeemed us from the curse of the law, being made a curse for us: for it is written, Cursed is every one that hangeth on a tree.'
Galatians 3:13
SUGGESTED FURTHER READING: 2 Timothy 1:8–14

Sinners, you must either be cursed of God, or else you must accept Christ as bearing the curse instead of you. I beseech you, as you love your souls, if you have any sanity left, accept this blessed and divinely-appointed way of salvation. This is the truth which the apostles preached, and suffered and died to maintain; it was for this that the Reformers struggled; it was for this that the martyrs burned at Smithfield; it is the grand basic doctrine of the Reformation and the very truth of God. Down with your crosses and rituals, down with your pretensions to good works and your crouchings at the feet of priests to ask absolution from them! Away with your accursed and idolatrous dependence upon yourself; Christ has altogether finished salvation-work. Do not hold up your rags in competition with his fair white linen. Christ has borne the curse; do not bring your pitiful penances and your tears all full of filth to mingle with the precious fountain flowing with his blood. Lay down what is your own; come and take what is Christ's. Put away now everything that you have thought of being or doing to win acceptance with God; humble yourselves and take Christ Jesus to be the Alpha and Omega, the first and last, the beginning and end of your salvation. If you do this, not only shall you be saved, but you are saved: rest, weary one, for your sins are forgiven; rise, you who are lame through want of faith, for your transgression is covered; rise from the dead, corrupt one, like Lazarus from the tomb, for Jesus calls you! Believe and live. The words in themselves, by the Holy Spirit, are soul-quickening. Have done with your tears of repentance and vows of good living, until you have come to Christ; then take them up as you will. Your first lesson should be none but Jesus. O come to him!

FOR MEDITATION: The Bible teaches that those who preach a false gospel and those who rely on their own good deeds remain under God's curse (Galatians 1:8–9; 3:10). Jesus described their final destiny as the eternal fire (Matthew 25:41). A totally different destiny (Revelation 22:3) awaits all who have trusted in Christ to redeem them from the curse.

SERMON NO. 873

The wall daubed with untempered mortar

'One built up a wall, and, lo, others daubed it with untempered mortar: say unto them which daub it with untempered mortar, that it shall fall: ... Lo, when the wall is fallen, shall it not be said unto you, Where is the daubing wherewith ye have daubed it?' Ezekiel 13:10–12
SUGGESTED FURTHER READING: Acts 17:16–34

The mass of mankind, though they will put up with religion and will even show some sort of interest in it and some decent respect to it, yet have no more sense of its reality or its power than the swine that feed at a trough. Look at the dense masses thronging the thoroughfares of this huge city, and answer me. Are not most of them like the stones on the bed of the Jordan, dead and lifeless as to spiritual things? What do they care for heaven or hell? What do they care about the precious blood of Jesus or about the power of the Holy Spirit? It is a great deal more important to them to know what horse won the Derby, or what turf speculator gained thereby, than to ask who is going down to hell or who has an interest in the precious blood of Christ. Some silly dancer at the opera, some new invention, some novel trick of conjuring, some fresh anything or nothing, and the world is all agog; but as to things which will outlast sun and moon, and stand fast when the blue heaven, like a scroll, has been rolled up and put away, these all-important things our wiseacres consider trifles; they continue trampling God's eternal truth beneath their feet, as swine trample pearls, and rushing madly after the bubbles of this world, as if they were all that men were made to hunt after. This is the wall behind which many men hide. 'It really does not matter; it will be all right in the end; why make so much ado about it? Let a man mind his business and take what comes.' Alas, for an age given up to eating, drinking, marrying and giving in marriage; has it never heard of Noah's flood or of that greater deluge which so soon will sweep them all away?

FOR MEDITATION: Ignorance of spiritual priorities, whether natural or deliberate, has terrible consequences (Ephesians 4:17–19; 2 Peter 3:3–7). But ignorance is not the unforgiveable sin. Repentance from things done in ignorance plus faith in Christ results in forgiveness (Acts 3:17–19; 17:30; 1 Timothy 1:12–14).

SERMON NO. 816

Nazareth; or, Jesus rejected by his friends

'And all they in the synagogue, when they heard these things, were filled with wrath, and rose up, and thrust him out of the city, and led him unto the brow of the hill whereon their city was built, that they might cast him down headlong. But he passing through the midst of them went his way.' Luke 4:28–30
SUGGESTED FURTHER READING: Hebrews 3:7–4:2

How strangely sad it is that some, knowing so much, practise so little. I am afraid that some of you know the gospel so well that for this very reason it has lost much of its power with you, for it is as well-known as a thrice-told tale. If you heard it for the first time, its very novelty would strike you, but such interest you cannot now feel. It is said of Whitefield's preaching that one reason for its great success was that he preached the gospel to people who had never heard it before. The gospel was to the masses of England in Whitefield's day very much a new thing. The gospel had been either expunged from the church of England and from Dissenters' pulpits, or, where it remained, it was with the few within the church and was unknown to the masses outside. The simple gospel of 'believe and live' was so great a novelty, that when Whitefield stood up in the fields to preach to his tens of thousands, they heard the gospel as if it were a new revelation fresh from the skies. But some of you have become gospel-hardened. It would be impossible to put it into a new shape for your ears. The angles, the corners of truth, have become worn off to you. Sundays follow Sundays, and you come up to the Tabernacle; you take your seats and go through the service, and it has become as mere a routine with you as getting up and dressing yourselves in the morning. The Lord knows that I dread the influence of routine upon myself; I fear lest it should get to be a mere form with me to deal with your souls, and I pray God to deliver you and me from the deadly effect of religious routine. It would be better if some of you would change your place of worship, rather than sleep in the old one.

FOR MEDITATION: The symptoms of a hard heart include lack of understanding, blind eyes, deaf ears and memory loss (Mark 8:17–18). This spiritual disease is also known as unbelief (Mark 16:14; Acts 19:9; Hebrews 3:12–13). The prognosis is very bad (Proverbs 28:14; Romans 2:5) unless there is a complete change of heart.

SERMON NO. 753

Testimony and experience

'And many more believed because of his own word; and said unto the woman, Now we believe, not because of thy saying: for we have heard him ourselves, and know that this is indeed the Christ, the Saviour of the world.' John 4:41–42
SUGGESTED FURTHER READING: John 10:31–42

Sometimes this offer is made concerning an article of commerce—'This is an excellent production and here are recommendations given by people able to judge; but, moreover, you can take it home with you and try it for a month, and if it does not answer your purpose, it will be taken back.' That is always considered to be an honest system of trade. Now, we say concerning the things of God, if you do not care to take our testimony, do not take it; but do another thing—try the Lord Jesus for yourself. God does hear prayer: go and see if he does. God does accept penitent hearts, and he has regard to contrite spirits: come and see for yourself. *'There is life for a look at the Crucified One.'* Go and try it. If you can prove Jesus Christ to be false, if after having tried him he rejects you, very well; then it must be so; but there has never been anything of the kind yet; 'him that cometh to me I will in no wise cast out.' Did he ever cast out one of you? If so, he has broken his word, and that shall never be. 'Heaven and earth shall pass away,' but none of his words shall ever fail. He declares that 'he is able also to save them to the uttermost that come unto God by him'. Go to God by him and see. If he does not save you, if it turns out that you are beyond his power and that he cannot save to the uttermost, then tell it, preach the devil's gospel all the world over, and speak the truth however horrible it may be. We challenge you to the test. If God be God, serve him. If the gospel be true, believe it.

FOR MEDITATION: During the earthly ministry of the Lord Jesus Christ various invitations to test his claims were issued—'Come and see' (John 1:39,46; Matthew 28:6), 'go ... and ... see' (Matthew 28:10), 'handle me, and see' (Luke 24:39). Although unable to respond in the same physical sense, we cannot excuse ourselves from the command to 'taste and see that the Lord is good' (Psalm 34:8).

SERMON NO. 1053

Victor Emmanuel, emancipator

'To open the blind eyes, to bring out the prisoners from the prison, and them that sit in darkness out of the prison house.' Isaiah 42:7
SUGGESTED FURTHER READING: Romans 8:1–8

Habits of sin, like iron nets, surround the sinner, and he cannot escape their meshes. He imagines that he cannot help sinning. How often do the ungodly tell us that they cannot renounce the world, break off their sins by righteousness or believe in Jesus? Let all know that the Saviour has come to remove every bond of sin from the captive and to set him free from every chain of evil. I have known men strive against blasphemy, others against unchaste passions, and many more against a haughty spirit or an angry temper; when they have striven manfully but unsuccessfully in their own strength, they have been filled with bitter chagrin that they should have been so betrayed by themselves. When a man believes in Jesus his resolve to become a freeman is to a great extent accomplished at once. Some sins die the moment we believe in Jesus, and trouble us no more; others hang on to us and die by slow degrees, but they are overcome so as never again to get the mastery over us. O struggler after mental, moral, spiritual liberty, if you would be free, your only possible freedom is in Christ. If you would shake off evil habits or any other mental bondage, commit yourself to Christ the Liberator. Love him and you will hate sin. Trust him and you will no more trust yourself. Submit yourself to the sway of the incarnate God, and he will break the dragon's head within you and hurl Satan beneath your feet. Nothing else can do it. Christ must have the glory of your conquest of self. He can set you free from sin's iron yoke. He never failed yet. I earnestly entreat any man who desires to break off his sins (and we must break them off or perish by them) to try this divine remedy.

FOR MEDITATION: As slaves to sin (John 8:34), we cannot escape sinful desires (Romans 7:23–24), the judgment of God (Romans 2:2–3), death (Romans 6:20–21) and the damnation of Hell (Matthew 23:33). Only the truth of God, encountered in his Son, can free us (John 8:31–32,36).

N.B. Spurgeon began by referring to no. 915 in which he mentioned 'Italy's liberator' (see 13 February), assumed to mean Victor Emmanuel II (1820–1878), who in 1861 became the first king of united Italy.

Plenary absolution

'As far as the east is from the west, so far hath he removed our transgressions from us.' Psalm 103:12
SUGGESTED FURTHER READING: Psalm 32:1–11

I remember a lawyer making this remark about a man's will, that if he were about to leave all his property to some one person, it would be better not to make a recapitulation of all that he had, but merely to state that he bequeathed all to his legatee, without giving a list of the goods and chattels, because in making out the catalogue he would be pretty sure to leave out something, and that which he left out might be claimed by some one else. Indeed he gave us an instance of a farmer, who, in recounting the property he devised to his wife, intending her to have had all, actually omitted to mention his largest farm and the very house in which they lived. Thus his attempt to be very particular failed and his wife lost a large part of the property. We do not want too many particulars, and I am thankful that in this text there is a broad way of speaking which takes in the whole compass of enumeration; God has 'removed our transgressions'. That sweeps all 'our transgressions' away at once. If it had said 'our great transgressions', we should have been crying out, 'How about the little ones?' We should have been afraid of perishing by our lesser faults even if the huge crimes were pardoned. If it had said 'our transgressions against the law', we should have asked, 'What shall we do with our transgressions against the gospel?' If it had said 'our wilful transgressions,' that would have been very gracious, but we should have said, 'But what will become of our sins of ignorance?' If it had said 'our transgressions before we were converted,' then we should have exclaimed, 'But how shall we escape from our sins since conversion?' But here it is—'our transgressions'—God has removed them all. They are all gone—from the cradle to the tomb, sins in private, sins in public, sins of thought, word and deed—they are all removed. The moment you believe in Jesus, they are all gone!

FOR MEDITATION: To all who trust in Christ, God provides justification from all things (Acts 13:39), forgiveness for all trespasses (Colossians 2:13), redemption from all iniquity (Titus 2:14) and cleansing from all sin and unrighteousness (1 John 1:7,9). Salvation from sin covers everything, but, for unbelievers, nothing.

SERMON NO. 1108

Bands of love

'I drew them with cords of a man, with bands of love: and I was to them as they that take off the yoke on their jaws.' Hosea 11:4
SUGGESTED FURTHER READING: Galatians 3:23–4:7

When Xerxes led his army into Greece, there was a remarkable contrast between the way in which the Persian soldiers and the Grecian warriors were urged to combat. The unwilling hosts of Persia were driven to the conflict by blows and stripes from their officers; they were either mercenaries or cowards, and feared close contact with their opponents. They were driven to their duty as beasts are, with rods and goads. The armies of Greece were small, but each man was a patriot and a hero, and they marched to the conflict with quick and joyous step, with a martial song upon their lips. When they neared the foe, they rushed upon his ranks with an enthusiasm and a fury which nothing could withstand. No whips were needed for the Spartan men-at-arms; like high-mettled chargers they would have resented the touch; they were drawn to battle by the 'cords of a man,' and by the bands of patriotic love they were bound to hold their posts at all hazards. 'Spartans' would their leaders say, 'your fathers disdained to number the Persians with the dogs of their flock, and will you be their slaves? Is it not better to die as freemen than to live as slaves? What if your foes be many, yet one lion can tear in pieces a far-reaching flock of sheep. Use well your weapons this day! Avenge your slaughtered sires and fill the courts of Shushan with confusion and lamentation!' Such were the manly arguments which drew the Spartans and Athenians to the fight, not the whips so fit for beasts nor the cords so suitable for cattle. This illustration may set forth the difference between the world's service of bondage and the Christian's religion of love: the worldling is flogged to his duty under fear, terror and dread, but the Christian man is touched by motives which appeal to his highest nature, motives so dignified as to be worthy of the sons of God; he is not driven as a beast but moved as a man.

FOR MEDITATION: Serving God because we feel we have to is no credit to us. What a difference it makes when we serve him cheerfully and eagerly, simply because we want to. Which attitude motivates your giving (2 Corinthians 9:7), your good deeds (Philemon 14) and your care for others (1 Peter 5:2)?

SERMON NO. 934

The overflowing cup

'My cup runneth over.' Psalm 23:5
SUGGESTED FURTHER READING: Luke 18:18–30

It is impossible for a rich man to enter into the kingdom of heaven unless something more than ordinary is done. Our Lord has told us, however, that while it is impossible with man, it is possible with God; and we rejoice to find constantly a slender line of these 'camels' going 'through a needle's eye'. Rich men are led into the kingdom of heaven; the human impossibility becomes divine fact. Still, riches are no small hindrance to those who would run in the ways of truth. The danger is that these worldly goods should become our gods and that we should set too great store by them. One day Andrew Fuller went into a bullion merchant's and was shown a mass of gold. Taking it into his hand, he very suggestively remarked, 'How much better it is to hold it in your hand than to have it in your heart!' Goods in the hand will not hurt you, but goods in the heart will destroy you. Not long ago a burglar, escaping from a policeman, leaped into the Regent's Canal and was drowned by the weight of the silver which he had stolen. How many there are who have made a god of their wealth and who, in hasting after riches, have been drowned by the weight of their worldly substance! Notice a fly when it alights upon a dish of honey. If it just sips a little and flies away, it is fed and is the better for its meal; but if it lingers to eat again and again, it slides into the honey, it is bedaubed, it cannot fly and it rolls in the mass of the honey to its own destruction. If God makes your cup run over, beware lest you perish, as too many have done, through turning your blessing into a curse. If your cups runs over, take care to use what God has given you for his glory.

FOR MEDITATION: Wealth does not have to be a snare, as long as those who possess it remember that they did not acquire it independently of God (Deuteronomy 8:17–18). The rich need to glory in knowing God and to trust in him instead of glorying and trusting in their riches (Jeremiah 9:23–24; 1 Timothy 6:17).

Life by faith

'The just shall live by faith.' Galatians 3:11
SUGGESTED FURTHER READING: Mark 4:26–34

A few weeks ago we saw the hawthorn covered with a delicious luxuriance of snow-white flowers, loading the air with fragrance; no one among the admiring gazers supposed that those sweet May blossoms caused the hawthorn to live. After a while we noticed the horse chestnut adorned with its enchanting pyramid of flowers, but no one foolishly supposed that the horse chestnut was sustained and created by its bloom: we rightly conceived these forms of beauty to be the products of life and not the cause of it. You have here, in nature's emblems, the true doctrine of the inner life. Holiness is the flower of the new nature. It is inexpressibly lovely and infinitely desirable; it must be produced in its season, or we may justly doubt the genuineness of a man's profession; but the fair graces of holiness do not save, or give spiritual life, or maintain it—these are streams from the fount, not the fountain itself. The most athletic man in the world does not live by being athletic, but is athletic because he lives and has been trained to a perfection of physical vigour. The most enterprising merchant holds his personal property not on account of his character or deservings, but because of his civil rights as a citizen. A man may cultivate his land up to the highest point of production, but his right to his land does not depend upon the mode of culture, but upon his title deeds. So the Christian should aim after the highest degree of spiritual culture and heavenly perfection, and yet his salvation, as to its justness and security, depends not on his attainments, but rests upon his faith in a crucified Redeemer, as it is written in the text, 'The just shall live by faith.' Faith is the fruitful root, the inward channel of sap, the great life-grace in every branch of the vine.

FOR MEDITATION: Faith needs to be shown by works, otherwise it is dead (James 2:17–18), but relying on works without faith would just be a case of showing off (Ephesians 2:8–9). Contrast the unattractiveness of both of these with the beauty of genuine faith working properly by love (Galatians 5:6).

Ingratitude of man

'He came unto his own, and his own received him not.' John 1:11
SUGGESTED FURTHER READING: Luke 17:11–19

To bring a charge of ingratitude against a man is a very strong thing to do. I would not like to be called untruthful—I should grievously feel it—but to be called ungrateful is equally as degrading. Can any accusation be more dishonouring? Ingratitude is a mean and despicable vice; he who is guilty of it is unworthy of the name of man. A soldier, who had been kindly rescued from shipwreck and hospitably entertained, was mean enough to endeavour to obtain from Philip of Macedon the house and farm of his generous host. Philip, in just anger, commanded that his forehead should be branded with the words 'The ungrateful guest.' That man must have felt like Cain when the mark of God was upon him; he must have wanted to hide himself for ever from the gaze of man. Prove a man ungrateful and you have placed him below the beasts, for even the brutes frequently exhibit the most touching gratitude to their benefactors. The old classic story of Androcles and the lion rises before us; the man healed the lion, and years later the lion, being let loose upon him, crouched at his feet and acknowledged him as a friend. Only the most despised creatures are used as metaphors of ingratitude; for instance, we speak of the ass which drinks, and then kicks the bucket it has emptied; but we never speak thus of nobler animals. An ungrateful man is thus lower than the animals; inasmuch as he returns evil for good, he is worse than bestial; he is devilish. Ingratitude is essentially infernal. Ingratitude to friends is vile, to parents it is worse, and to the Saviour it is worst of all. It is a very serious matter that we should be open to an indictment for ingratitude towards the Lord Jesus Christ.

FOR MEDITATION: When good is repaid with evil, it is not only a distressing experience for the undeserving sufferer (Psalm 35:12; 109:5), but also far from being in the best interests of the guilty party (Proverbs 17:13). David acknowledged that he would deserve severe punishment if guilty of such behaviour himself (Psalm 7:4–5).

SERMON NO. 1055

The saint and the Spirit

'But ye know him; for he dwelleth with you, and shall be in you.' John
14:17
SUGGESTED FURTHER READING: 1 Corinthians 3:16–17

Jesus Christ gave us his righteousness and his blood, but he did a great
deal more; he gave us *himself*: he 'loved me, and gave himself for me.'
You have learned to distinguish between the gifts of Christ, and Christ
himself. Now, the Holy Spirit gives us his operations and his influences,
for which we should be very grateful, but the greatest gift is not the
operation nor the influence, but *himself*: 'he dwelleth with you, and shall
be in you.' The great covenant gift is the Holy Spirit himself. Do you
understand that truth? It is asserted many times in Scripture that the
bodies of the saints are the temples of the Holy Spirit. God dwells in you;
you are the temples of God. Now, do not cut that down and say that it
means that he influences us and operates upon us. It does mean that, but
it means a great deal more; it means literally this, that the Holy Spirit,
the third Person of the sacred Trinity, actually dwells in every regenerate
man and woman, that he has made our bodies to be his shrine, and that
he is the indwelling Lord. Do you perceive this grand doctrine? It involves
not merely the graces of God, nor the operations of the Spirit, but the
Spirit himself dwelling in us. He is everywhere, he fills all in all, but still
he has a special residence; and though we are told in John 14:23 that the
Father and the Son take up their abode with us, yet this is not in the same
sense in which the Holy Spirit does. He *personally* dwells in the church
and in each believer. God the Holy Spirit is pleased to dwell in our
bodies, not so as to deify our humanity, or to take us into connection
with Deity in the same way as the humanity of Jesus was exalted, but still
so as truly to dwell in us and abide in us. Brethren, gather up this manna;
it is better than angels' food.

FOR MEDITATION: Sometimes obsession with a gift can blind us as to the
bigger picture (Matthew 23:18–19). Repentance is required if we make
more of the gifts of the Holy Spirit than we do of the Holy Spirit himself
(Acts 8:18–22). He himself is the far more important spiritual gift (Luke
11:13; Acts 2:38; 5:32; 15:8; Romans 5:5; 1 Thessalonians 4:8).

Wrecked, but not reckless

'All hope that we should be saved was then taken away.' Acts 27:20
SUGGESTED FURTHER READING: Luke 22:28–34

The strongest faith that ever was in this world has sometimes faltered. Even Abraham had times when his faith was exceeding weak, though, indeed, at other times 'he staggered not at the promise of God through unbelief'. David was a great man in battle, but 'David waxed faint' and was in danger of being slain. So you will find that the bravest of God's servants have times when it is hard to hold their own, when they would be glad to creep into a mouse-hole, if they could there find themselves a shelter. But this is the point—no soul that rests in Jesus will ever be wrecked. You may have tempests and tossings, but you will come to land; be sure of that. The old story tells us of Caesar in the storm, when he said to the trembling captain, 'Fear not! Thou carriest Caesar and all his fortunes!' Now, Christ is in the same boat with all his people. If one of his members can perish, he must perish too. 'Strong language!' you say. Well, it is all in that verse 'because I live, ye shall live also.' If you have got a man and you put him in the water, as long as his head is above the water, you cannot drown him. His feet are down in the mud; they will not drown, and he cannot drown. His hands are in the cold stream; they are not drowned and cannot be, because his head is all safe. Now, look at our glorious Head. See where he is exalted in the highest heavens at the right hand of the Father. The devil cannot drown me, and he cannot drown you if you are a member of Christ's body, because your Head is safe. Your Head is safe and you are safe too. Rest in this; your faith may be shaken, but it cannot be destroyed if you are resting upon Christ. Your little temporary foundations that may have overlain Christ may move, but the rock of Christ Jesus never can.

FOR MEDITATION: As the Head of his church the Lord Jesus Christ is concerned for the growth and welfare of the whole body (Ephesians 4:15–16; 5:23,29–30; Colossians 2:19). It would be totally out of character for him as the Head to abandon any member of his body and say 'I have no need of you' (1 Corinthians 12:21).

SERMON NO. 1070

The sad wonder

'And he marvelled because of their unbelief.' Mark 6:6
SUGGESTED FURTHER READING: Luke 7:1–10

There were but two occasions when our Lord Jesus is recorded to have marvelled at all; both of these were concerning faith. First he marvelled at the centurion: 'I have not found so great faith, no, not in Israel.' The centurion had said that he was not worthy that the Lord should come under his roof, but relied upon the potency of the Master's word spoken at any distance to chase out the fever, on the ground that a word from himself was sufficient to command a soldier to obedience, and therefore a command from Christ would call diseases to obedience too. On the slenderest ground comparatively this Roman Gentile believed in Christ to a very high degree, ascribing to Christ the full power of the omnipotent God, who says to the forces of nature, 'Do this' and it is done. Jesus therefore marvelled that not in all Israel had he found the faith which he had discovered in this Gentile, who had comparatively slender opportunity of knowing him, of hearing his teaching, or of searching into the evidences of his mission as they were contained in the sacred books. On the second occasion he marvelled at the absence of faith where it might have been expected to be found, namely in his own fellow townsmen: 'he marvelled because of their unbelief.' So you see that in both instances it was faith, or the absence of it, that caused Christ to wonder. See the importance of faith! Never place that precious grace in a secondary position. That which can make Jesus marvel, that which seems to him to be both in its presence and in its absence a thing to be marvelled at, ought to be a very great point of consideration with us; it should be frequently thought upon and always estimated at the highest rate. Have you believed? No man ever asked you a weightier question. Are you still in unbelief? No tongue can ever suggest a more solemn enquiry. Do you believe on the Son of God, or are you yet 'in the gall of bitterness, and in the bond of iniquity', wrapped up in your unbelief?

FOR MEDITATION: Jesus marvelled at both faith and unbelief. Contemplating him should make us marvel, but that exercise can either challenge unbelief (Matthew 8:26–27; 21:19–21) or confirm it (Matthew 22:22; Luke 20:26; John 9:30). What effect does marvelling at Jesus have upon you?

A blessed wonder

'When Jesus heard it, he marvelled, and said to them that followed, Verily I say unto you, I have not found so great faith, no, not in Israel.'
Matthew 8:10
SUGGESTED FURTHER READING: Mark 5:25–34

Reason thus with yourself; may the Holy Spirit help you to do so. Let this be the subject of your soliloquy: 'If I were omnipotent, as Christ is, it would be as easy for me to move a mountain as a molehill; therefore it is as easy for him to take away my great sins as another's little sins; if there be a universal cleansing fluid, it will take out great spots as well as little spots, and therefore the blood of Christ can wash out my great sins as well as the lesser sins of other people. One stroke of the hand and the bill is receipted; it is as easy to write a receipt for a bill of fifty thousand pounds as for a bill for ten pence; so if Jesus Christ, who has already paid believers' debts, calls me pardoned and absolved, it is done; he has the power to do it, and I rely upon the merit of his atoning blood.' O that you would do so now! These Sabbath days, how they are flying! Your time, how it is passing away, and with it your opportunities for finding mercy! It does not seem long ago since we were in the depth of winter, and now we are getting near the longest day in summer, and anon the wings of time will soon carry us again into months of frost and snow. 'How long halt ye between two opinions?' Are these delays to continue for ever? Will you always go on hearing about these things, but never attending to them? I pray you by the flight of time, by the certainty of death to each one of you and your ignorance of its appointed hour, 'Seek ye the Lord while he may be found, call ye upon him while he is near'; 'lay hold on eternal life.' Like the centurion, come and put your faith in Jesus to save you; and though your faith will be marvellous, yet the honour shall be all to him and the glory to his blessed name.

FOR MEDITATION: Mere interest in spiritual concerns is likely to be interrupted and curtailed unexpectedly (Mark 6:20–21,27) either sooner (Acts 17:32–18:1) or later (Acts 24:24–27). The only safe course is to trust in Christ now while we know we still have the opportunity (John 12:35–36).

SERMON NO. 936

Things to come

'Things to come; all are your's.' 1 Corinthians 3:22
SUGGESTED FURTHER READING (Spurgeon): Revelation 21:1–27

You are on your way to the mansions of the blessed; rejoice as you make the pilgrimage. If you have no present reason for thankfulness, yet the future may yield you much. Break forth, therefore, into joy and singing, and with songs and everlasting joy upon your head make your way towards Zion. If it be so, that all the future is yours, meditate much upon it; make heaven the subject of your daily thoughts; live not on this present, which is but food for swine, but live on the future, which is meat for angels. How refined will be your communications if your meditations are sublime! Your life will be heavenly if your musings are heavenly. Take wings to your spirit and dwell amongst the angels. All these things are yours; then prepare for them. Day by day wash your souls in the all-cleansing blood of Jesus, which is the path of purity. By repentance cast off every sin; by a renewed application to Jesus and his Spirit, obtain fresh power against every evil. Stand ready for heaven with 'your loins girt about' and your lamp trimmed; be waiting for the midnight cry, 'Behold, the bridegroom cometh'. Let your life be spent in the suburbs of the celestial city in a devout sanctity of thought and act. Live upon the doorstep of the pearly gate, always waiting for the time when the angelic messenger shall say, 'Come up hither.' If indeed all things are yours day by day, gratefully bless God that, though you deserve to descend into hell, you have such a place reserved for you as heaven. You might have been cast away; the damnation of hell might have been your only outlook; it is grace alone that has made you to differ and given you a portion among those who are sanctified. Therefore bless God as long as you have any being, and let none hinder you in your sacred joy. Praise him night and day for what he has done for you.

FOR MEDITATION: Things to come pose no threat to those who trust in the Lord Jesus Christ (Romans 8:38–39). Meditate upon the return of the Saviour (James 5:7–8), the redemption of the believer (Luke 21:28) and the resurrection of the body (John 5:25,28–29). But the resurrection of judgment is a fearful prospect for unbelievers on whom the wrath of God is coming (Ephesians 5:6).

SERMON NO. 875

Daniel's undaunted courage

'Now when Daniel knew that the writing was signed, he went into his house; and his windows being open in his chamber towards Jerusalem, he kneeled upon his knees three times a day, and prayed, and gave thanks before his God, as he did aforetime.' Daniel 6:10
SUGGESTED FURTHER READING: Psalm 55:16–22

Daniel prayed 'three times a day'. That does not tell you how often he prayed, but how often he was in the posture of prayer. Doubtless he prayed three hundred times a day if necessary; his heart was always having commerce with the skies. But 'three times a day' he prayed formally. We usually take three meals in the day and it is well to give the soul as many meals as the body. We want the morning's guidance and the evening's forgiveness. but do we not also require the noontide's refreshment? Might we not well say at noontide, 'Tell me, O thou whom my soul loveth, where thou feedest, where thou makest thy flock to rest at noon'. It is well to keep in the spirit of Keble's hymn—*'Abide with me from morn till eve.'* If you find from morn till eve too long an interval between prayer, put in another golden link at midday. There is no rule in Scripture as to how often and when you should pray; it is left to the man's own gracious spirit. We need not come back to the bondage of the Mosaic covenant, to be under rule and rubric; we are left to that free Spirit who leads his saints aright. Yet 'three times a day' is a commendable number. Notice secondly the posture. That also is of little consequence, since we read in Scripture of men who prayed on the bed with their face to the wall. We read of David sitting before the Lord. How very common and acceptable a posture was that of standing before God in prayer! Yet there is a peculiar appropriateness, especially in private prayer, in the posture of kneeling. It seems to say, 'I cannot stand upright before thy majesty; I am a beggar and I put myself in the position of a beggar; I sue of thee, great God, on bended knee, in the posture of one who owns that he deserves nothing, but humbles himself before thy gracious majesty.'

FOR MEDITATION: See David's prayer-timetable in Psalm 55:16–17. Do you live that closely to God or is once a day too much effort? The Lord Jesus Christ taught his disciples to pray always (Luke 18:1) and the apostle Paul emphasised this to the early church (Ephesians 6:18; 1 Thessalonians 5:17).

SERMON NO. 815

The prayer of Jabez

'Oh that thou wouldest bless me indeed!' 1 Chronicles 4:10
SUGGESTED FURTHER READING: 2 Kings 20:1–6,21; 21:1–12

Learn to make a distinction between some things which you think to be spiritual blessings and others which are blessings indeed. Let me show you what I mean. Is it certainly a blessing to get an answer to your prayer after your own mind? I always like to qualify my most earnest prayer with 'not as I will, but as thou wilt.' Not only ought I to do it, but I would like to do it, because otherwise I might ask for something which it would be dangerous for me to receive. God might give it to me in anger, and I might find little sweetness in the grant, but much soreness in the grief it caused me. You remember how Israel of old asked for flesh and God gave them quails; but while the meat was yet in their mouths the wrath of God came upon them. Ask for the meat, if you like, but always put in this: 'Lord, if this is not a real blessing, do not give it to me;' 'bless me indeed!' I hardly like to repeat the old story of the good woman whose son was ill, a little child near death's door; she begged the Puritan minister to pray for his life. He did pray very earnestly, but put in, 'If it be thy will, save this child.' The woman said, 'I cannot bear that: I must have you pray that the child shall live. Do not put in any ifs or buts.' 'Woman,' said the minister, 'it may be you will live to rue the day that ever you wished to set your will up against God's will.' Twenty years afterwards she was carried away in a fainting fit from under Tyburn gallows-tree, where that son was put to death as a criminal. Although she had lived to see her child grow up to be a man, it would have been infinitely better for her had the child died, and infinitely wiser had she left it to God's will. Do not be quite so sure that what you think an answer to prayer is any proof of divine love.

FOR MEDITATION: God's answer to Hezekiah's prayer (2 Kings 20:5–6) pleased him, but the extra 15 years of life were the most spiritually barren of his reign—note his pride (2 Chronicles 32:24–25) and his 'I'm all right, Jack' attitude (2 Kings 20:16–19). The wickedness of his son Manasseh, despite his later repentance, sealed Judah's fate (2 Kings 21:10–15); Manasseh was born three years into Hezekiah's 15 year extension of life and grew up when his father was far from his best (2 Kings 21:1)! This should make us want to pray 'not my will, but thine be done' (Luke 22:42).

Alive or dead—which?

'He that hath the Son hath life; and he that hath not the Son of God hath not life.' 1 John 5:12
SUGGESTED FURTHER READING: John 6:35–59

Having the Son is good evidence of eternal life, from the fact that faith by which a man receives Christ is in itself a living act. Faith is *the hand of the soul*, but a dead man cannot stretch out his icy limbs to take of that which is presented to him. If I, as a guilty, needy sinner, with my empty hand receive the fulness of Christ, I have performed a living act; the hand may quiver with weakness, but life is there. Faith is *the eye of the soul*, by which the sin-bitten sinner looks to Christ, lifted up as Moses lifted up the serpent in the wilderness; but from the stony eyes of death no glance of faith can dart. There may be all the organisation by which it should look, but if life be absent the eye cannot see. If, therefore, my eye of faith has looked alone to Jesus, and I depend upon him, I must be a living soul; that act has proved me to be alive unto God. Looking to Jesus is a very simple act; indeed it is a childlike act, but still it is a living one: no sight gleams from the eyeballs of death. Faith, again, is *the mouth of the soul*; by faith we feed upon Christ. Jesus Christ is digested and inwardly assimilated, so that our soul lives upon him; but a dead man cannot eat. Whoever heard of corpses gathering to a banquet? There may be the mouth, the teeth, the palate and so forth; the organisation may be perfect, but the dead man neither tastes the sweet nor relishes the delicious. If, then, I have received Christ Jesus as the bread which came down from heaven, as the spiritual drink from the rock, I have performed an action which is in itself a clear evidence that I belong to the living in Zion.

FOR MEDITATION: Have you experienced the spiritual blessings promised to those who touch Christ with the hand of faith (John 20:27), who see Christ with the eye of faith (John 9:35–39; 20:29) and who call upon Christ with the mouth of faith (Romans 10:8–13)?

SERMON NO. 755

Safe shelter

'He shall cover thee with his feathers, and under his wings shalt thou trust.' Psalm 91:4

SUGGESTED FURTHER READING: Jeremiah 45:1–5

We all know how singularly the Lord has shielded those who trusted in him in times of pestilence. God's Providence House, still standing in Watergate Street at Chester, is a lasting proof of the power of faith, with its old letters cut in the black wood 'God's Providence is Mine Inheritance.' When everybody else was flying out of Chester into the countryside, the man who lived in that house just wrote that inscription up over the door and stopped in the town, depending on God that he should be preserved, and none in his house fell a victim to that black death which was slaying its thousands on all sides. Strong faith has always a particular immunity in times of trouble. When a man has really, under a sense of duty, under a conscientious conviction, rested alone in God, he has been enabled to walk where the thickest dangers were flying, all unharmed. He has put his foot upon the adder, and the young lion and the dragon he has trampled under his feet (see Psalm 91:13). God has verified and vindicated his promise, and the child of God that could so trust him has never been put to confusion. However, there are some dangers from which the Providence of God does not preserve the Lord's people, but still he covers them with his feathers in another sense, by giving them grace to bear up under their troubles. It little matters whether a man has no burden and no strength, or a heavy burden and great strength. Probably of the two, if it were put to most of us, we should prefer to have the burden and the strength. It is generally the case that if you have little trouble, you will have little faith; but if you have great faith, you must expect to have great trouble. A manly spirit would choose to take the trouble and take the faith too. Well then, God will give you this covert with his feathers; though you have to carry the load, you shall have strength enough to carry it.

FOR MEDITATION: Read the whole of Psalm 91. At times the believer enjoys the successes of faith (Hebrews 11:32–34), but never take these for granted; at other times God will allow the believer to experience the sufferings of faith (Hebrews 11:35–38). Faith in the living God is valid regardless of the circumstances or outcome (Hebrews 11:39).

The profit of godliness in this life

'Bodily exercise profiteth little: but godliness is profitable unto all things, having promise of the life that now is, and of that which is to come. This is a faithful saying and worthy of all acceptation.' 1 Timothy 4:8–9
SUGGESTED FURTHER READING (Spurgeon): 1 Timothy 6:6–19

You who have godliness and live in the fear of God, believe that in godliness there is provided for you comfort, joy and delight for 'the life that now is'. Do not postpone your feasting upon Christ till you see him face to face. Feed on him this day. Do not wait for the joys of the Holy Spirit till you have shaken off this cumbrous clay; the joy of the Lord is your strength today. Do not think that your peace and rest remain as yet in the future, hidden from you; eternal life with its present blessings is a present possession. 'We which have believed do enter into rest', and may enter now.

'The men of grace have found glory begun below,
Celestial fruits on earthly ground from faith and hope do grow.'

We do not say that godliness has made all believers rich, for some here will be content always to be poor. All the faithful cannot claim that godliness has brought them earthly treasure, for some of the greatest of them have confessed that 'if in this life only we have hope in Christ, we are of all men most miserable.' But all of us can declare that we have found in godliness the highest happiness, the supremest delight and the richest consolation. You who profess godliness, do not be content unless you have the 'promise of the life that now is'. Believe that you can now be raised up together and made to 'sit together in heavenly places in Christ Jesus'. You cannot find a heaven in things below 'where moth and rust doth corrupt,' but you can, while here, if you 'set your affection on things above, not on things on the earth', find glory begun within you and a young heaven already shining about your path.

FOR MEDITATION: God has given us all that relates to godliness (2 Peter 1:3), which is associated with sincerity (2 Corinthians 1:12), honesty (1 Timothy 2:2), contentment (1 Timothy 6:6), deliverance from temptation (2 Peter 2:9), and persecution (2 Timothy 3:12). Read Mark 10:29–30 for promises relating to 'this time' and 'the world to come'.

SERMON NO. 937

The profit of godliness in the life to come

'Godliness is profitable unto all things, having promise of the life that now is, and of that which is to come.' 1 Timothy 4:8
SUGGESTED FURTHER READING: 2 Corinthians 4:13–18

If you are godly, that is, if you have submitted to God's way of salvation, if you trust God, love God and serve God, if you are in fact a converted man, you have now the promise of the life 'which is to come.' When we get a promise from a man whom we trust, we feel quite easy about the matter under concern. A note of hand from many a firm in the city of London would pass current for gold any day in the week; and surely when God gives the promise, it is safe and right for us to accept it as if it were the fulfilment itself, for it is quite as sure. We have the promise; let us begin to sing about it; what is more, we have a part in the fulfilment of it, for Christ gives unto his sheep eternal life: shall we not sing concerning that? Believe in Jesus; you have eternal life now. There will be no new life given to you after death. Christian, you have even now within you the germ which will develop into the glory-life above. Grace is glory in the bud. You have the earnest of the Spirit; you have already a portion of the promise which is given to godliness. What you should do is to live now in the enjoyment of the promise. You cannot enjoy heaven, for you are not there, but you can enjoy the promise of it. Many a dear child, if it has a promise of a treat in a week's time, will go skipping among its little companions merry as a lark about it. It has not the treat yet, but it expects it; I have known in our Sunday-schools our little boys and girls months before the time came for them to go into the country, as happy as the days were long, in prospect of that little pleasure. Surely you and I ought to be childlike enough to begin to rejoice in the heaven that is so soon to be ours.

FOR MEDITATION: What are your expectations of heaven? The Christian can look forward now to a heavenly home (2 Corinthians 5:1–2), to a heavenly Saviour (Philippians 3:20–21; 1 Thessalonians 1:10), to a heavenly hope (Colossians 1:5), to a heavenly kingdom (2 Timothy 4:18), to a heavenly country (Hebrews 11:16) and to a heavenly inheritance (1 Peter 1:4).

SERMON NO. 946

Leaning on our beloved

'Who is this that cometh up from the wilderness, leaning upon her beloved?' Song of Solomon 8:5
SUGGESTED FURTHER READING (Spurgeon): Psalm 63:1–11

We lean upon our beloved as God and man. I have known times when I have felt that none but God could bear me up; there are other seasons when, under a sense of sin, I have started back from God and felt that none but the Man Christ Jesus could minister peace to my anguished heart. Taking Christ in the double nature as God and man, he becomes thus a suitable leaning place for our spirit, whatever may happen to be the state in which our mind is found. Beloved, we lean upon Christ in all his offices. We lean upon him as priest; we expect our offerings, our praises and our prayers to be received, because they are presented through him. Our leaning for acceptance is on him. We lean upon him as our prophet. We do not profess to know or to be able to discover truth of ourselves, but we sit at his feet, and what he teaches we receive as certainty. We lean upon him as our King. He shall fight our battles for us and manage all the affairs of our heavenly citizenship. We have no hope of victory but in the strength of him who is the Son of David and the King of kings. We lean upon Christ in all his attributes. Sometimes it is his wisdom—in our dilemmas he directs us; at other times it is his faithfulness—in our strong temptations he abides the same. At one time his power gleams out like a golden pillar and we rest on it, and at another moment his tenderness becomes conspicuous and we lean on that. There is not a trait of his character, not a mark of his person, whether human or divine, upon which we do not feel it safe to lean, because he is as a whole Christ, perfection's own self, lovely and excellent beyond all description. We lean our entire weight upon him.

FOR MEDITATION: We need to trust in the Lord with all our heart and to acknowledge him in all our ways (Proverbs 3:5–6). There is no value in leaning upon our own understanding (Proverbs 3:5) nor in professing to lean upon the Lord while actually going our own ways (Micah 3:11).

The widow of Sarepta

'And the word of the LORD *came unto him, saying, Arise, get thee to Zarephath, which belongeth to Zidon, and dwell there: behold, I have commanded a widow woman there to sustain thee.'* 1 Kings 17:8–9
SUGGESTED FURTHER READING: Jonah 3:1–10

There are some who say, 'If I am to be saved I shall be saved.' Did they ever hear of a certain Ludovic, an Italian philosopher, who had imbibed the idea of predestination to the exclusion of every other truth? He could see nothing but fate and thought religious activity useless. A physician, a godly man, who attended him during his sickness, desiring to convince him of his error, said to him as he stood by his bedside, 'I shall not send you any medicine; I shall not attend to you; in fact, I shall not call any more, because if you are to live you will live, and if you are to die you will die; therefore, it is of no use my attending to you.' He went his way, but in the watches of the night Ludovic, who had been the slave of a notion, turned it over and saw the folly of it; he saw that there were other truths besides predestination and he acted like a sane man. As God accomplishes the healing of the sick by the use of medicines, he usually accomplishes also the saving of souls by the means of grace; and as I, not knowing whether I am elected to be healed or not, yet go to the physician, so I, not knowing whether I am elect to be saved or not, yet will go to Jesus as he bids me go, and put my trust in him, and I hope I shall be accepted in him. Dear hearer, do not trifle away your soul by thrusting your head into doctrinal difficulties. Do not be a fool any more, but go to Jesus as you are and put your trust in him, and you will not find this knotty point a terror to you; it will indeed become like butter in a lordly dish to you; it will be to you savoury meat.

FOR MEDITATION: While it is true that believers are chosen by God to be saved (2 Thessalonians 2:13), the response commanded by God is not passive but active; we are never told to be chosen and be saved, but to believe and be saved (Mark 16:16; Acts 16:31; Romans 10:9) and to call upon the name of the Lord and be saved (Acts 2:21; Romans 10:13).

In the hay-field

'He causeth the grass to grow for the cattle.' Psalm 104:14
SUGGESTED FURTHER READING: Joel 2:21–32

Why is it that God gives the cattle the grass? You will perhaps be surprised when I say to you that the reason is because they belong to him. Here is a text to prove it—'every beast of the forest is mine, and the cattle upon a thousand hills.' That is why he provides grass for them, because they are his own property. How is it that Christ is provided for God's people? Because 'the Lord's portion is his people; Jacob is the lot of his inheritance.' Of every herd of cattle in the world God could say, 'They are mine.' Long before the farmer put his brand, God had set his creating mark upon it. They are God's making, preserving and feeding altogether. So, before the stamp of Adam's fall was set upon our brow, the stamp of electing love was set there; 'in thy book all my members were written, which in continuance were fashioned, when as yet there was none of them.' Another thing may perhaps surprise you still more; God feeds the cattle because he has entered into a covenant with them to do so. 'What! A covenant with the cattle!' says somebody. Yes, truly so, for when God spoke to his servant Noah in that day when all the cattle came out of the ark, we find him saying, 'I establish my covenant with you, and with your seed after you; and with every living creature that is with you, of the fowl, of the cattle, and of every beast of the earth with you'. So there was a covenant made with the cattle, and that covenant was that seedtime and harvest should not fail; therefore the earth brings forth for them and the Lord causes the grass to grow. Does Jehovah keep his covenant with cattle and will he not keep his covenant with his own beloved? It is because his chosen people are his covenanted ones in the person of the Lord Jesus that he provides for them all that they shall need in time and in eternity.

FOR MEDITATION: 'But ask now the beasts, and they shall teach thee' (Job 12:7). God's care for birds (Matthew 6:26; 10:29) and for cattle (Exodus 9:18–20; 2 Kings 3:17; Jonah 4:11) is a powerful reminder to us that he cares for people even more (Jonah 4:11; Luke 12:6–7,24).

'By him the birds are fed; Much more to us, his children, He gives our daily bread.'

SERMON NO. 757

Untrodden ways

'For ye have not passed this way heretofore.' Joshua 3:4
SUGGESTED FURTHER READING: 1 Samuel 13:5–14

If you are now about to enter into a great trouble, *do not hurry*; make no rash haste. Often, when we are afraid of a thing, we dash into it like a moth dazzled by the candle's flame. We become so disturbed in our minds that we do not act wisely and prudently, but fall into that haste which brings no good speed. The children of Israel did not rush pell-mell to Jordan to swim across, but waited while the priests went on before and tarried till the ark stood in the midst of Jordan. Everything was done deliberately. Ask grace to do the same. Be calm. If the grace of God does not make us calm in the time of peril and suffering, we have some reason to question whether it is healthily operating upon our spirits at all. But next, while you do not hurry, *do not hesitate*. Not one man of all the tribes said, 'I must wait and see others cross, and know whether the road really is open.' At the moment the trumpets sounded the advance they all went on, asking no questions. A brave man must have been that first priest who went right up to the brink of Jordan and put down his foot. It must have been a noble sight to see the water suddenly roll right away in curling waves till it made a great wall of sparkling crystal up towards the right. He was a brave man who stepped there first and passed along the novel way which God had newly fashioned. His was the first foot which had trodden the bottom of that ancient river, the river Jordan. Be brave also, my dear brother, and go straight on, though it were a river of fire instead of water. If Jehovah bids you the way is right, hesitate not.

FOR MEDITATION: When we know what God commands us to do, we should make haste to obey him (Psalm 119:60), but we need to have waited upon him in the first place (Psalm 37:7,34; Habakkuk 2:1–3). Even the apostles had to wait a little before it was God's time for them to start carrying out the Great Commission (Acts 1:4,8).

Delay is dangerous

'And her brother and her mother said, Let the damsel abide with us a few days, at the least ten; after that she shall go.' Genesis 24:55
SUGGESTED FURTHER READING: Acts 24:22–27

A number of men are upstairs in a house, amusing themselves with a game of cards. What is that? The window is red! What is that cry in the street? 'The house is on fire!' says one. 'Oh!' answers another, 'Shuffle the cards again; let us finish the game; we have plenty of time.' 'Fire! Fire!' The cry rises more sharply from the street, but they keep on. One of them says, 'It is all right; I have the key of the door on the roof, and we can get out at the last minute; I know the way over the roofs—it is all right.' Presently one of them says, 'Are you sure we can get through that door?' and he goes and tries, but finds it locked. 'Never mind,' is the answer, 'I have the key.' 'But are you sure you have the key?' 'Oh, yes! I am sure I have; here it is; try it for yourself, and do not be such a coward, man; try it.' The man tries the key. 'It will not turn!' says he. 'Let me try,' says his friend. He comes, puts it in the lock and tries it. 'Oh no!' he shrieks, 'It is the wrong key!' Now, sirs, will you go back to your game again? No, now they will strain every nerve and labour to open the door, only to find, possibly, that it is all too late for them to escape. So, some of you are saying, 'Oh, yes! What the preacher says is well enough, but, you know, we can repent whenever we like; we have a key that can turn the grace of God whenever we please; we know the way—it is just to trust Christ, and we can do that whenever we please; we shall get out.' But suppose you cannot do that whenever you please! Suppose the day is come when you shall call, and he will not answer, when you shall stretch out your hand, but no man shall regard. Suppose you should cry, 'Lord, Lord, open to us', and the answer should be, 'I never knew you: depart from me, ye that work iniquity.' Besides, if you think that that key will open the door, and you can repent now, why do you not repent now?

FOR MEDITATION: In times of physical danger the most sensible course of action is a hasty departure (Genesis 19:15–22; 1 Samuel 23:26; Acts 22:18). How much more important it is to flee to Christ for refuge (Hebrews 6:18) from the wrath to come (Luke 3:7) before it is too late.

Sleep not

'Let us not sleep, as do others.' 1 Thessalonians 5:6
SUGGESTED FURTHER READING: Mark 13:32–37

The Lord Jesus may come in the night. He may come in the heavens with exceeding great power and glory before the rising of another sun; or he may tarry awhile and yet, though it should seem to us to be long, he will come quickly, for 'one day is with the Lord as a thousand years, and a thousand years as one day.' Suppose, however, he were to come tonight; if now, instead of going along to your homes and seeing once more the streets busy with traffic, the sign of the Son of Man should be revealed in the air, because the King had come in his glory and his holy angels with him, would you be ready? I press home the question. The Lord may suddenly come; are you ready? You who profess to be his saints—are your loins girt up, and your lamps trimmed? Could you go in with him to the supper, as guests who have long expected him, and say, 'Welcome, Son of God'? Have you not much to set in order? Are there not still many things undone? Would you not be afraid to hear the midnight cry? Happy are those souls who live habitually with Jesus, who have given themselves up completely to the power of his indwelling Spirit and who 'follow the Lamb whithersoever he goeth.'; 'they shall walk with me in white: for they are worthy.' Wise are they who live habitually beneath the influence of the Second Advent, 'looking for and hasting unto the coming of the day of God'. We would have our window opened towards Jerusalem; we would sit as upon our watch-tower whole nights; we would be ready girt to go out of this Egypt at a moment's warning. We would be of that host of God who shall go out harnessed, in the time appointed, when the signal is given. God grant us grace to be found in that number in the day of his appearing, but, 'let us not sleep, as do others'.

FOR MEDITATION: In his sermon Spurgeon gave many examples of people who had slept to their cost—Sisera (Judges 4:21), Samson (Judges 16:19–20), Saul (1 Samuel 26:7–12), the sluggard (Proverbs 24:30–34), Jonah (Jonah 1:5–6), the wise as well as the foolish virgins (Matthew 25:5), the apostles (Matthew 26:40–45) and Eutychus (Acts 20:9). God is ready for the judgment (1 Peter 4:5) and we must be ready too (Matthew 24:44) to avoid disaster (1 Thessalonians 5:2–3).

A good soldier of Jesus Christ

'A good soldier of Jesus Christ.' 2 Timothy 2:3
SUGGESTED FURTHER READING: Ephesians 6:10–18

The Christian is *a self-sacrificing man* as the soldier must be. To protect his own country the soldier must expose his own self; to serve his king he must be ready to lay down his life. Surely he is no Christian who never felt the spirit of self-sacrifice. If I live unto myself, I am living unto the flesh, and of the flesh I shall reap corruption. Only he who lives to his God, to Christ, to the truth, to the church and to the good old cause, only he is the man who can reckon himself at all to be a soldier of Jesus Christ. A soldier is *a serving man*. He does not follow his own pleasure; he is under law and rule; each hour of the day has its prescribed duty; he must be obedient to the word of another and not to his own will and whim. Such is the Christian. We serve the Lord Jesus Christ. Though no longer the slaves of man so as to dread his frown, we are servants of Christ who has loosed our bonds. The soldier is often *a suffering man*. There are wounds, toils and frequent lyings in the hospitals; there may be ghastly cuts which let the soul out with the blood. Such the Christian soldier must be, ready to suffer, enduring hardness, not looking for pleasure of a worldly kind in this life, but counting it his pleasure to renounce his pleasure for Christ's sake. Once again, the true soldier is *an ambitious man*. He pants for honour and seeks for glory. On the field of strife he gathers his laurels, and amidst a thousand dangers he reaps renown. The Christian is fired by higher ambitions than earthly warriors ever knew. He sees a crown that can never fade; he loves a King who best of all is worthy to be served; he has a motive within him which moves him to the noblest deeds, a divine spirit impelling him to the most self-sacrificing actions. Thus you see that the Christian is a soldier, and it is one of the main things in the Christian life to 'earnestly contend for the faith' and to fight with valour against sin.

FOR MEDITATION: As a fellow soldier (Philippians 2:25; Philemon 2), the Christian worker also has to be prepared to play his part as a fellow son, a fellow supporter, a fellow servant and a fellow sufferer (Philippians 2:25–26,30); Epaphroditus clearly set out to please God who had 'chosen him to be a soldier' (2 Timothy 2:4).

SERMON NO. 938

A well-ordered life

'Order my steps in thy word: and let not any iniquity have dominion over me.' Psalm 119:133
SUGGESTED FURTHER READING: 2 Peter 1:1–11

All Christians should endeavour so to balance their lives that there should not be an excess of one virtue and a deficiency of another. Alas! Have we not known professors whose graces in one department have been so apparent as to become glaring, while the absence of other graces has been lamentably manifest. Courage some will have till they become rude, coarse and intrusive; modesty will rule in others till they are cowardly and pliable. Not a few are so full of love that their talk is sickening with cant expressions, disgusting to honest minds; others are so faithful that they see faults which do not exist, while a third class are so tender that for the most glaring vice they make apologies, and sin goes unrebuked in their presence. The character of our Lord was such that no one virtue has undue preponderance. Take Peter, and there is a prominent feature peculiar to himself; one quality attracts you. Take John, and there is a lovely trait in his character which at once chains you, and his other graces are unobserved. But take the life of the blessed Jesus, and it shall perplex you to discover what virtue shines with purest radiance. His character is like the lovely countenance of a classic beauty, in which every single feature is so in exact harmony with all the rest, that you are struck with a sense of general beauty, but do not remark upon the flashing eye, or chiselled nose, or the coral lips: an undivided impression of harmony remains upon your mind. Such a character should each of us strive after, a mingling of all perfections to make up one perfection, a combining of all the sweet spices to make up a rare perfume, such as only God's Holy Spirit himself can make, but such as God accepts wherever he discovers it. May we have grace to keep the proportions of the virtues; but remember that this can only become ours by waiting upon God with daily prayer, crying, 'Order my steps in thy word'.

FOR MEDITATION: The Holy Spirit produces balanced 'fruit' in the life of the Christian, not a choice of selected 'fruits' (Galatians 5:22) such as 'faith without works' (James 2:20), zeal without knowledge (Romans 10:2), or knowledge and faith without love (1 Corinthians 8:1–3; 13:2).

SERMON NO. 878

The Pleiades and Orion

'Canst thou bind the sweet influences of Pleiades, or loose the bands of Orion?' Job 38:31
SUGGESTED FURTHER READING: Psalm 104:1–35

Most of you know that singularly beautiful cluster of stars called the Pleiades, very small, but intensely bright. These are most conspicuous about the time of spring, and hence, in poetry, the vernal influences which quicken the earth and clothe it with the green grass and the many-coloured flowers are connected with the Pleiades. By 'the sweet influences of Pleiades' we understand those benign influences which produce the spring and the summer; these no man can restrain. Orion, a very conspicuous constellation with its glittering belt, is best seen towards the close of autumn, just before winter; it is a southern and wintry sign, and hence, poetically, the winter is traced to 'the bands of Orion'; no man is able to loosen the bonds of frost, or check the incoming of the cold. The whole verse asserts that none can restrain the revolutions of the seasons: when God ordains the spring, the shining months come laughing on; when he calls for winter, snow and ice must rule the dreary hour. The farmer is entirely dependent upon God; he may plough with industry and cast in the good seed with hope, but unless the sweet influences of heaven be given, he can reap no harvest. If the drought be long and severe, he cannot cause the clouds to drench the thirsty furrows; if the rain descends in torrents, drowning the pastures, he cannot seal up the bottles of heaven. He is absolutely dependent upon God, who governs all things according to his will; and we, who know so little of agricultural operations, being so far removed from the country which *God* has made, living in the town which *man* has made, we also are as dependent as any, and follow what merchandise we will, it is from the field that our nourishment must come. All beasts, birds and creatures are entirely and absolutely dependent upon God, and unless he helps them, they cannot help themselves. This is the simple teaching of the verse.

FOR MEDITATION: God who created the stars (Genesis 1:14–16; Psalm 8:3) in recognisable constellations (Job 9:8–9; Isaiah 13:10; Amos 5:8), also exercises loving care towards mankind (Psalm 8:4–6). He has promised to maintain the seasons (Genesis 8:22). Do you depend upon him?

SERMON NO. 818

No quarter

'Elijah said unto them, Take the prophets of Baal; let not one of them escape.' 1 Kings 18:40
SUGGESTED FURTHER READING: Hebrews 12:1–4

Some will say that they have a constitutional tendency to a sin, and therefore they cannot overcome it; they take out a licence to sin and reckon themselves clear though they indulge their evil propensity. Brethren, this will never do. Indulgences for sin issued by the Pope are now rejected; shall we write them out for ourselves? Is Christ the messenger of sin? I know that some persons feel they are excused in the use of bitter language occasionally, because they are provoked, but I find no such excuses in the Word of God. In no one passage do I find a permit for any sin or a furlough from any duty. Sin is sin in any case and in any man, and we are not to apologise for it, but to condemn it. It is pleaded by some that their father was passionate and they are passionate, and therefore it runs in their blood, but let them remember that the Lord must cleanse their blood, or they will die in their sin. Others will say that their constant discontent, moroseness, murmuring and tendency to quarrel with everybody, must be set down to their infirmity of body. Well, I am not their judge; but the word of the Lord judges them and declares that sin shall not have dominion over the believer. Does a sin easily beset us? We are doubly warned to lay it aside. More grace is needed and more grace may be had. Never suppose that God has given to you a licence for any sin, so that you may live in it as long as you please; no, believe that Jesus has come to save us from our sins. I have received no intimation from the Lord to deal delicately with any man's sins, or to become an apologist for transgression. My message is that of Elijah—'Take the prophets of Baal; let not one of them escape.'

FOR MEDITATION: Christ died to save us from all our sin, not from part of it (see meditation for 4 June). Relying on God's enabling, we should also take positive steps to rid ourselves of every known sin (2 Corinthians 7:1; Ephesians 4:31; 5:3; Colossians 3:8; 1 Thessalonians 5:22; Hebrews 12:1; James 1:21; 1 Peter 2:1). God has left no loophole for your favourite sin.

SERMON NO. 1058

The glorious gospel of the blessed God

'According to the glorious gospel of the blessed God, which was committed to my trust.' 1 Timothy 1:11
SUGGESTED FURTHER READING: Titus 2:1–10

We must believe the gospel and maintain it, for it is committed to our trust. It seems to me, however, that the most of us may best fulfil our responsibility to the gospel by adorning it in our lives. Men give jewels to those whom they love; and so, if we love the gospel, let our virtues be the jewels which shall display our love. A servant girl may adorn the gospel. She goes to a place of worship and perhaps her irreligious mistress may object to her going. I remember Mr Jay telling a story of such a case, where the master and mistress had forbidden the girl to attend a Dissenting place of worship. She pleaded very hard and at last determined to leave the house. The master said to his wife, 'Well, you see our servant is a very excellent servant; we never had such an industrious girl as she is. Everything in the house is kept so orderly and she is so obedient. Now, she does not interfere with our consciences; it is a pity we should interfere with hers. Wherever she goes, it certainly does her no hurt—why not let her go?' In the next conversation the wife said, 'I really think that our servant gets so much good where she goes, that we had better go and hear for ourselves.' They were soon members of the very same church of which they had thought so lightly at first. Each of us in our position can do this. We are not all called to preach in boxes called pulpits, but we may preach more conveniently and much more powerfully behind the counter or in the drawing-room or in the parlour or in the field or wherever else providence may have placed us. Let us endeavour to make men mark what kind of gospel we believe.

FOR MEDITATION: Christians are not to be taken up with outward adornments which show off self (1 Timothy 2:9; 1 Peter 3:3), but with the inward and outward adornments of godliness (1 Timothy 2:10; 1 Peter 3:4–5) which show off the Saviour (Titus 2:10).

SERMON NO. 758

Praises and vows accepted in Zion

'Praise waiteth for thee, O God, in Sion: and unto thee shall the vow be performed. O thou that hearest prayer, unto thee shall all flesh come.'
Psalm 65:1–2
SUGGESTED FURTHER READING: Psalm 47:1–9

Have I not gone into places called houses of God where the praise has waited for a woman—for the Virgin, where praise has waited for the saints, where incense has smoked to heaven, and songs and prayers have been sent up to deceased martyrs and confessors who are supposed to have power with God? In Rome it is so, but in Zion it is not so. Praise waiteth for thee, O Mary, in Babylon; but 'Praise waiteth for thee, O God, in Sion'. Unto God alone the praise of his true church must ascend. If Protestants are free from this deadly error, I fear they are guilty of another, for in our worship we too often minister unto our own selves. We do so when we make the tune and manner of the song more important than the matter of it. I am afraid that where organs, choirs and singers are left to do the praise of the congregation, minds are more occupied with the due performance of the music than with the Lord, who alone is to be praised. God's house is meant to be sacred unto himself, but too often it is made an opera-house and Christians form an audience, not an adoring assembly. The same thing may happen amid the simplest worship, even though everything which does not savour of gospel plainness is excluded, for in that case we may drowsily drawl out the words and notes with no heart whatever. To sing with the soul, this only is to offer acceptable song! We come together not to amuse ourselves, to display our powers of melody or our aptness in creating harmony; we come to pay our adoration at the footstool of the Great King, to whom alone be glory for ever and ever. True praise is for God alone.

FOR MEDITATION: Read Romans 11:36. As with everything else the object of our singing should be God and his glory. Both Old and New Testaments speak of singing to the Lord (Exodus 15:1; Colossians 3:16) and of singing a new song to the Lord (Psalm 33:3; 40:3; 96:1; 98:1; 144:9; 149:1; Isaiah 42:10; Revelation 5:9, 14:3). When you are 'speaking to yourselves in psalms and hymns and spiritual songs' in your church, are you also 'singing and making melody in your heart to the Lord' (Ephesians 5:19)?

SERMON NO. 1023

More and more

'But I will hope continually, and will yet praise thee more and more.'
Psalm 71:14
SUGGESTED FURTHER READING: Psalm 118:1–29

Can you count your great mercies? I cannot count mine. Perhaps you think the numeration easy. I find it endless. I was thinking the other day, and I will venture to confess it publicly, what a great mercy it was to be able to turn over in bed. I could almost clap my hands for joy when I found myself able to turn in bed without pain. This day it is to me a very great mercy to be able to stand upright before you. We carelessly imagine that there are only a score or two of great mercies, such as having our children about us, or enjoying health and so on; but in trying times we see that innumerable minor matters are also great gifts of divine love and entail great misery when withdrawn. Sing then as you draw water at the 'nether springs', and, as the brimming vessels overflow, praise the Lord yet 'more and more.' But ought we not to praise God 'more and more' when we think of our spiritual mercies? What favours have we received of this higher sort! Ten years ago you were bound to praise God for the covenant mercies you had even then enjoyed; but now, how many more have been bestowed upon you, how many cheerings amid darkness, answers to prayer, directions in dilemma, delights of fellowship, helps in service, successes in conflict, revelations of infinite love! To adoption there has been added all the blessings of heirship, to justification all the security of acceptance, to conversion all the energies of indwelling. As there was no silver cup in Benjamin's sack till Joseph put it there, so there was no spiritual good in you till the Lord of mercy gave it. Therefore, praise the Lord.

FOR MEDITATION: Great men of God rejoice in the greatness of God's mercy. Listen to Moses (Numbers 14:18–19), Solomon (2 Chronicles 1:8), Nehemiah (Nehemiah 13:22), David (Psalm 86:13; 103:11; 108:4; 145:8) and Paul (Ephesians 2:4). Doing this can be a great witness (Luke 1:58).

N.B. This sermon followed the longest gap in Spurgeon's ministry so far due to illness. He preached twice in April and not at all in May and June 1871, but updated his readers by appending letters to some of the sermons printed in his absence. His first four Sundays back he preached only in the morning.

SERMON NO. 998

The pilgrim's grateful recollections

'Therefore thou shalt keep the commandments of the LORD thy God, to walk in his ways, and to fear him.' Deuteronomy 8:6
SUGGESTED FURTHER READING: 1 Samuel 15:10–24

Let your obedience be *universal*; 'keep the commandments of the Lord' and 'walk in his ways'. Set your heart to the Scriptures to find out what the commandments are, and then, once knowing, perform at once. Settle it in your soul that you only want to know it is his will, and you will, by his grace, neither question nor delay, but 'Whatsoever he saith unto you, do it.' Shut not your eyes to any part of his teaching; be not wilfully blind where Christ would guide you with his word. Let your obedience be entire. In nothing be rebellious. Let that obedience be *careful*. Does not the text say 'keep the commandments' and Deuteronomy 8:1 'observe to do'? Keep it as though you kept a treasure, carefully putting your heart as a garrison around it. Observe it as they do who have some difficult art, and who watch each order of the teacher and trace each different part of the process with observant eye, lest they fail in their art by missing any one little thing. Keep and observe. Be careful in your life. Be scrupulous. You serve a jealous God; be jealous of yourself. Let your obedience be *practical*. The text says 'walk in his ways'. Carry your service of God into your daily life, into all the minutiae and details of it. Do not have an unholy room in your house. Let the bedroom, the banqueting-hall, the place of conversation, the place of business and every other place be holiness unto your God; 'walk in his ways'. Whereas others walk up and down in the name of their God, and boast themselves in the idols wherein they trust, walk in the name of Jehovah your God and glory always to confess that you are a disciple of Jesus, God's dear Son. And let your obedience *spring from principle*, for the text says, 'to walk in his ways, and to fear him.'

FOR MEDITATION: The Lord Jesus Christ has given us a perfect example of total obedience to God's will whatever the cost (Romans 5:19; Philippians 2:8; Hebrews 5:8). In his church the goal is for obedience to be shown by every Christian (2 Corinthians 7:15) in every thought (2 Corinthians 10:5), in every thing (2 Corinthians 2:9) and at every time (Philippians 2:12).

SERMON NO. 939

An assuredly good thing

'It is good for me to draw near to God.' Psalm 73:28
SUGGESTED FURTHER READING: Romans 8:18–27

Shall I tell you how I have sometimes drawn near to God? I have been worn and wearied with a heavy burden and have resorted to prayer. I have tried to pour out my soul's anguish in words, but there was not vent enough by way of speech, and therefore my soul has broken out into sighs, sobs and tears. Feeling that God was hearing my heart-talk, I have said to him, 'Lord, behold my affliction; thou knowest all about it; deliver me. If I cannot exactly tell thee, there is no need of my words, for thou dost see for thyself. Thou searcher of hearts, thou readest me as I read in a book; wilt thou be pleased to help thy poor servant? I scarce know what help it is I want, but thou dost know it. I cannot tell thee what I desire, but teach me to desire what thou wilt be sure to give. Conform my will to thine.' Perhaps at such a time there may be a peculiar bitterness about your trouble, a secret with which no stranger may interfere, but tell it all out to your God. With broken words, sighs, groans and tears lay bare the inmost secret of your soul. Taking off the doors of your heart from their hinges, bid the Lord come in to walk through every chamber and see the whole. I do not know how to tell you what drawing near to God is better than by this rambling talk. It is getting to feel that the Lord is close to you, and that you have no secret which you wish to keep back from him, but have unveiled your most private and sacred desires to him. This getting right up to Jesus, our Lord, the leaning of the head, when it aches with trouble, upon the heart that always beats with pity, the casting of all care upon him, believing that he cares for you, pities you and sympathises with you—this is drawing near unto God. 'It is good for me to draw near to God.'

FOR MEDITATION: Consider the experiences of some who have drawn near to God in their distress (Psalm 69:16–18; 107:17–20; Lamentations 3:55–57). Their confidence was in the fact that he draws near to those who draw near to him (James 4:8). So 'let us draw near with a true heart in full assurance of faith' (Hebrews 10:22).

SERMON NO. 879

The minstrelsy of hope

'God, even our own God, shall bless us. God shall bless us.' Psalm 67:6–7
SUGGESTED FURTHER READING: Romans 5:1–5

Once on a time certain strong labourers were sent forth by the great King to level a primaeval forest, to plough it, to sow it and to bring him back the harvest. They were stout-hearted, strong and willing enough for labour, and well they needed all their strength and more. One stalwart labourer was named Industry—consecrated work was his. His brother Patience, with muscles of steel, went with him and tired not in the longest days, under the heaviest labours. To help them they had Zeal, clothed with ardent and indomitable energy. Side by side there stood his kinsman Self-denial and his friend Importunity. These went forth to their labour and they took with them, to cheer their toils, their well-beloved sister Hope; and well it was they did, for the forest trees were huge and needed many sturdy blows of the axe before they would fall prone upon the ground. One by one they yielded, but the labour was immense and incessant. At night when they went to their rest, the day's work always seemed so light, for, as they crossed the threshold, Patience, wiping the sweat from his brow, would be encouraged, and Self-denial would be strengthened, for they heard a sweet voice within sing, 'God, even our own God, shall bless us. God shall bless us'. They felled the giant trees to the music of that strain; they cleared the acres one by one; they tore from their sockets the huge roots; they dug the soil; they sowed the corn and waited for the harvest, often much discouraged, but still in silver chains and golden fetters by the sweet sound of the voice which chanted so constantly, 'God, even our own God, shall bless us.' They never could refrain from service, for she could never refrain from song. They were ashamed to be discouraged, they were shocked to be despairing, for still the voice rang out clearly at morn and eventide—'God, even our own God, shall bless us. God shall bless us'. You know the parable; you recognise the voice: may you hear it in your souls today!

FOR MEDITATION: Think about the importance of hope's relationship to joy (Romans 5:2; 12:12; 15:13), patience (Romans 8:25; 15:4), peace (Romans 15:13), love (1 Corinthians 13:7) and faith (Hebrews 11:1). The Christian's hope is not only good (2 Thessalonians 2:16) but better (Hebrews 7:19); but to lack hope is a sad state to be in (Ephesians 2:12; 1 Thessalonians 4:13).

SERMON NO. 819

To the thoughtless

'The ox knoweth his owner, and the ass his master's crib: but Israel doth not know, my people doth not consider.' Isaiah 1:3
SUGGESTED FURTHER READING: Titus 3:3–8

If I consider awhile, I see that I have not lived as I ought to have lived; I have often done wrong. That is quite clear to me and it is equally clear that the ruler of the world ought to punish sin. The letting off of certain atrocious murderers of late and the easy way in which certain criminals have escaped makes us all demand a little more vigorous dispensation of justice, or else we should have our land made a pandemonium. Even so, if God did not punish sin, he would not be a wise and efficient moral governor for the world. Then if God must punish sin, he must punish me and I must expect to suffer. But when I turn to this Book I find he has devised a way by which to save me. He has laid sin upon Christ so that I may escape. If I am puzzled to see how the sin of one could be laid upon another, I find in the word of truth that Christ Jesus is one with his people, and it is right enough that he should take their sin and suffer in their stead. I find that Christ actually did take the sins of all those who trust him and really suffered in their stead. That seems to me to be a glorious truth. It meets the case of justice and leaves a door for mercy. How can I avail myself of what Christ has done? I find in the Word that I am commanded to trust him. Trust him! That does not seem to be a harsh demand. He is true, he is great, he is God. I will trust him. God help me to trust him. I learn that whoever trusts him is saved. That is a glorious truth. I am saved and pardoned now, for I believe in Jesus. Will not some of you turn these things over in your minds? I pray God the Holy Spirit to lead you to do so.

FOR MEDITATION: Do you rejoice in the God who is both 'a just God and a Saviour' (Isaiah 45:21)? One of the glories of the gospel is that God can both 'be just, and the justifier of him which believeth in Jesus' (Romans 3:26). 'If we confess our sins, he is faithful and just to forgive us our sins' (1 John 1:9).

Jesus putting away sin

'But now once in the end of the world hath he appeared to put away sin by the sacrifice of himself.' Hebrews 9:26
SUGGESTED FURTHER READING: Daniel 9:20–27

Christ not only came to put away some of the attributes of sin such as the filth of it, the guilt of it, the penalty of it and the degradation of it, but he came to put away sin itself, for sin, you see, is the fountain of all the mischief. He did not come to empty out the streams, but to clear away the fatal source of the pollution. He appeared to put away sin itself, sin in its essence and being. Do not forget that he did take away the filth of sin, the guilt of sin, the punishment of sin, the power of sin and the dominion of sin, and that one day he will kill in us the very being and existence of sin, but do recollect that he aimed his stroke at sin itself. My Master seemed to say, as the king of Syria did of old, 'Fight neither with small nor great, save only with the king'. He aimed his arrows at the monster's head, smote his vital parts and laid him low. He put hell itself to flight and captivity was led captive. What a glorious word—our Lord 'put away sin'! We read in the Word of God that he cast it 'into the depths of the sea'; that is glorious; nobody can ever find it again—in the shoreless depths of the sea Jesus drowned our sins. Again, we find he removed it 'as far as the east is from the west'. Who can measure that distance? Infinite leagues divide the utmost bounds of space; so far has he removed our transgressions from us. We read again that he has made 'an end of sins'. You know what we mean by making an end of a thing; it is done with, annihilated, utterly destroyed and abolished. Jesus, we here read, has 'put away sin'; he has divorced it from us. Sin and my soul are no more married. Christ has put sin away.

FOR MEDITATION: Christ came and died not only to save and cleanse us from the plurality of our sins (Matthew 1:21; 26:28; 1 Corinthians 15:3; Galatians 1:4; Hebrews 1:3; 9:28; 10:12; 1 Peter 2:24; 3:18; 1 John 2:2; 3:5; 4:10; Revelation 1:5), but also to deliver us from the underlying disease of sin itself (Isaiah 53:10; John 1:29; Romans 8:3; 2 Corinthians 5:21; Hebrews 9:26; 1 John 1:7). Have you trusted him to save you from your sin and your sins?

A safe prospective

'At the time appointed the end shall be.' Daniel 8:19
SUGGESTED FURTHER READING: James 5:7–11

There are certain 'ends' to which you and I are looking forward with great expectancy. There is *the end of the present trouble*—let us think of that. I do not know what your particular trouble may be, but this I know: as surely as you are in the furnace you will be anxious to be delivered out of it. Whatever submission we may have to the divine will, it is not natural for us to love affliction; we desire to reach the end and come forth from the trial; 'at the time appointed the end shall be.' *You have been slandered in your character*—a very frequent trial to God's servants—and you are irritated, vexed and in a great haste to answer it, to refute the slander and to vindicate your reputation. Be still. Be very quiet and patient. Bear it all; 'stand still, and see the salvation of the Lord,' for 'Light is sown for the righteous,' 'And he shall bring forth thy righteousness as the light, and thy judgment as the noonday'; 'at the time appointed the end shall be.' When the dogs are tired they will leave off barking, and when the Lord bids them be still, they shall not dare to move a tongue against you; 'at the time appointed the end shall be.' *You are in poverty.* It is some time since you had a situation in which you could earn your daily bread. You have been walking wearily up and down these hard London streets; you have been searching the advertisement sheet; you have looked everywhere for something to do; you gaze upon your dear wife and pitiful children with ever-increasing anxiety. Are you a child of God? Have you learned to cast your burden upon the Lord? Then, 'at the time appointed the end shall be.' There shall yet be deliverance for you. 'Trust in the Lord, and do good; so shalt thou dwell in the land, and verily thou shalt be fed.'

FOR MEDITATION: In times of trial there is often a temptation to envy the wicked and to forget that the godly have a bright future (Proverbs 23:17–18) which is in sharp contrast to the future awaiting the ungodly (Psalm 37:37–38). Take time to consider the end of the godly (Hebrews 13:7) and of the ungodly (Psalm 73:17–20).

The withering work of the Spirit

'The grass withereth, the flower fadeth: because the Spirit of the LORD *bloweth upon it: surely the people is grass.' Isaiah 40:7 (cf. 1 Peter 1:24)*
SUGGESTED FURTHER READING: John 16:5–15

It is the Spirit's work to wither. I rejoice in our translation, 'because the Spirit of the LORD bloweth upon it'. It is true the passage may be translated, 'The wind of the LORD bloweth upon it'. One word, as you know, is used in the Hebrew both for 'wind' and 'Spirit', and the same is true of the Greek; but let us retain the old translation here, for I conceive it to be the real meaning of the text. The Spirit of God it is that withers the flesh. It is not the devil that killed my self-righteousness. I might be afraid if it were: nor was it myself that humbled myself by a voluntary and needless self-degradation, but it was the Spirit of God. Better to be broken in pieces by the Spirit of God than to be made whole by the flesh! What does the Lord say? 'I kill'. But what next? 'I make alive'. He never makes any alive except those he kills. Blessed be the Holy Spirit when he kills me, when he drives the sword through the very bowels of my own merits and my self-confidence, for then he will make me alive. 'I wound, and I heal'. He never heals those whom he has not wounded. Then blessed be the hand that wounds; let it go on wounding; let it cut and tear; let it lay bare to me myself at my very worst, that I may be driven to self-despair and may fall back upon the free mercy of God and receive it as a poor, guilty, lost, helpless, undone sinner, who casts himself into the arms of sovereign grace, knowing that God must give all, that Christ must be all, that the Spirit must work all and that man must be as clay in the potter's hands, that the Lord may do with him as seems good. Rejoice, dear brother, however low you are brought, for if the Spirit humbles you, he means no evil, but he intends infinite good to your soul.

FOR MEDITATION: The work of the Holy Spirit should never be treated lightly and superficially. Although he is described as the Comforter (John 14:16,26; 15:26; 16:7), we as sinners first encounter him as one who rebukes and convicts us (John 16:8). Playing with fire is never advisable (Matthew 3:11–12).

The winnowing fan

'Follow peace with all men, and holiness, without which no man shall see the Lord: looking diligently lest any man fail of the grace of God; lest any root of bitterness springing up trouble you, and thereby many be defiled.' Hebrews 12:14–15
SUGGESTED FURTHER READING: James 3:13–18

There are in the text two things to be followed. The fourteenth verse tells us what they are. 'Follow peace with all men, and holiness, without which no man shall see the Lord'. We are to follow peace and holiness; the two are consistent with each other and may be followed together. Peace is to be studied, but not such a peace as would lead us to violate holiness by conforming to the ways of unregenerate and impure men. We are only so far to yield for peace sake as never to yield a principle; we are to be so far peaceful as never to be at peace with sin, peaceful with men, but contending earnestly against evil principles. 'Follow peace', but let the following of it be guarded by the other precept, 'holiness'. With equal ardour we are to follow holiness. Some who have aimed at holiness have made the great mistake of supposing it needful to be morose, contentious, faultfinding and censorious with everybody else. Their holiness has consisted of negatives, protests and oppositions for opposition's sake. Their religion lies mainly in contrariness and singularities; to them the text offers this wise counsel—follow holiness, but also follow peace. Courtesy is not inconsistent with faithfulness. It is not needful to be savage in order to be sanctified. A bitter spirit is a poor companion for a renewed heart. Let your determination for principle be sweetened by tenderness towards your fellow men. Be resolute for the right, be also gentle, pitiful and courteous. Consider the meekness as well as the boldness of Jesus. Follow peace, but not at the expense of holiness. Follow holiness, but do not needlessly endanger peace.

FOR MEDITATION: Christians are commanded to practice mutual submission (Ephesians 5:21) and courtesy (1 Peter 3:8–9), but should never become 'yes-men'. The apostle Paul tells us to live peaceably with all as far as it is possible (Romans 12:18), but did not shrink from opposing the compromising behaviour of the apostle Peter (Galatians 2:11–14).

SERMON NO. 940

The former and the latter rain

'Let us now fear the LORD *our God, that giveth rain, both the former and the latter, in his season: he reserveth unto us the appointed weeks of the harvest.' Jeremiah 5:24*
SUGGESTED FURTHER READING: Galatians 6:7–10

In commencing any Christian work novelty greatly assists enthusiasm, and it is very natural that under first impulses the beginner should achieve an easy success. The difficulty of the Christian is very seldom the commencement of the work; the true labour lies in the perseverance which alone can win the victory. I address some Christians who have now been for years occupied with a service which the Holy Spirit laid upon them; I would remind them of the early rain of their youthful labours, the moisture of which still lingers on their memories, although it has been succeeded by long years of drought. Brethren, be encouraged; a latter rain is yet possible. Seek it. That you need it so much is a cause for sorrow, but if you really feel your need of it, be glad that the Lord is working in you such sacred desires. If you did not feel a need for more grace, it would be a reason for alarm; but to be conscious that all that God did by you in the past has not qualified you to do anything without him now, to feel that you lean entirely upon his strength now as much as ever, is to be in a condition in which it shall be right and proper for God to bless you abundantly. Wait upon him, then, for the latter rain; if he has given you a little of blessing in past years, ask that he would return and give you ten times as much now, even now, so that, at the last, if you have sown in tears, you may 'come again with rejoicing,' bringing your sheaves with you. The danger of every Christian worker is that of falling into routine and self-sufficiency. We are most apt to do what we have been accustomed to do, and to do it half-asleep.

FOR MEDITATION: In God's eyes our previous work in his service is not gone and forgotten, but that gives us no excuse for resting on our laurels; we are to keep going (Hebrews 6:10–11). Even Timothy needed a prod from the apostle Paul to stir up the gift of ministry God had entrusted to him (2 Timothy 1:6).

SERMON NO. 880

Working out what is worked in

'Work out your own salvation with fear and trembling. For it is God which worketh in you both to will and to do of his good pleasure.'
Philippians 2:12–13
SUGGESTED FURTHER READING: Titus 2:11–15

The text says, 'your own salvation', and that is correct enough. Holiness is salvation. We are not to work out our salvation from the *guilt* of sin— that has been done by Christ; we have now to work out our salvation from the *power* of sin. God has in effect worked that in us; he has broken the yoke of sin in our hearts; it lives, struggles and contends, but it is dethroned and our life is to be the continual overthrow and dethronement of sin in our members. A man may be saved from the guilt of sin and yet at present he may not be altogether saved from the power of pride; for instance, a saved man may be defiled by being purse-proud, or proud of his position or of his talents; now the believer must with fear and trembling work out his salvation from that most intolerable evil. A man may be the subject of a quick and hasty disposition; he may be often angry without a cause. My brother, your salvation from sin is not complete until you are saved from a bad temper; day by day you should work out your salvation from that with solemn resolution. I might take any form of besetting sin, or any one of the temptations which come from the world, the flesh and the devil, and in each case bid you labour for salvation from this bondage. Our business is to be continually fighting for liberty from sin, contending earnestly that we may not wear the shackles of any infirmity, that we may not be the bondslaves in any shape or form of the works of the devil. Working out by vehement efforts after holiness our entire deliverance from sin that dwells in us and from sin that contends without us is, I believe, to be the great business of the Christian's life.

FOR MEDITATION: While we cannot make any contribution towards saving ourselves, we do after conversion have a part to play when it comes to being saved from ourselves; we are to cleanse and purify ourselves (2 Corinthians 7:1; 1 John 3:3). For lists of bad behaviour to discard see Ephesians 4:25–31 and Colossians 3:5–9.

SERMON NO. 820

Believing to see

'I had fainted, unless I had believed to see the goodness of the LORD in the land of the living.' Psalm 27:13
SUGGESTED FURTHER READING: Exodus 14:15–31

If we shall just trust God and believe that God never did leave a work that he put us upon and never sets us to do a thing without meaning to help us through with it, we shall soon see that the God of Israel lives and that his 'hand is not shortened, that it cannot save; neither his ear heavy, that it cannot hear'. Let us recollect Israel when they came to the Red Sea. There it was, a roaring, billowy sea; but they were bidden to march through it and they did march; and though the waters roared before them fiercely, yet when Moses stretched out his hand over the sea, the depths stood upright on a heap and the waters were congealed in the heart of the sea. And so shall it be with you, brethren, and with your faith. Believe in God and face your difficulties, and they shall fly before you. Then recollect the Egyptians. They attempted to do the same thing. They thought, 'That is all right; we will do as they have done before us.' But notice that they said all this because all the difficulties had been cleared away. There was the Red Sea all dry before them. Any fool could march through there! But, unfortunately, while faith can march through a sea dry-shod, unbelief only begins to march when it is all dry, and presently unbelief gets drowned. Unbelief wants to see and God strikes it blind. Faith does not want to see but God opens its eyes and it sees God, ever present to help and deliver it. Now, you who are working for Christ, you who are troubled in your business, you who are in any way exercised, remember the life of faith. Remember that you are not called to walk by sight, but by faith. David 'believed to see'; do likewise and great shall be your joy.

FOR MEDITATION: Those who trust in Christ without having seen him enjoy great blessings (John 20:29; 1 Peter 1:8–9). Faith in him leads to greater sight (John 1:49–51), but unbelief results in loss of sight (John 3:36: 9:39).

SERMON NO. 766

The sweet harp of consolation

'Fear thou not; for I am with thee.' Isaiah 41:10
SUGGESTED FURTHER READING: Matthew 14:22–33

As I thought of the life of faith, I saw before my eyes, as in a vision, a lofty staircase of light and, led by an invisible hand, I mounted step by step; when I had ascended long and far, it turned and turned again and again. I could see no supports to this elevated staircase, no pillars of iron, no props of stone—it seemed to hang in air. As I climbed, I looked up to see whither the staircase went, but I saw no further than the step on which I stood, except that now and then the clouds of light above me parted asunder, and I thought I saw the throne of the Eternal and the heaven of his glory. My next step seemed to be upon the air, and yet when I boldly put down my foot I found it firm as adamant beneath me. I looked back on the steps which I had trodden and was amazed, but I dared not tarry, for 'forward' was the voice which urged me on, and I knew, for faith had told me, that the winding stair would end at last beyond the sun, moon and stars in the excellent glory. As now and then I gazed down into the depths out of which the stair had lifted me, I shuddered at my fate should I slip from my standing, or should the next step plunge me into the abyss! Over the edge of that on which I stood I gazed with awe, for I saw nothing but a gaping void of black darkness and into this I must plunge my foot in the faith of finding another step beneath it. I should have been unable to advance and would have sat down in utter despair had I not heard the word from above of one in whom I trusted, saying, 'Fear thou not; for I am with thee'. I knew that my mysterious guide could not err. I felt that infinite faithfulness would not bid me take a step if it were not safe; and therefore mounting still, I stand at this hour happy and rejoicing, though my faith be all above my own comprehension.

FOR MEDITATION: Walking by faith and not by sight (2 Corinthians 5:7) is bound to involve taking steps into apparent uncertainty (Hebrews 11:8), but the goal is 'a city which hath foundations, whose builder and maker is God' (Hebrews 11:10).

SERMON NO. 760

Behold the Lamb

'Behold the Lamb of God!' John 1:36
SUGGESTED FURTHER READING: Ephesians 4:1–16

No subject so well balances the soul as Jesus, the Lamb of God. Other themes disturb the mental equilibrium and overload one faculty at the expense of others. I have noticed in theology that certain brethren meditate almost exclusively upon doctrine, and I think it is not too critical to say that they have a tendency to become hard, rigid and far too militant. It is to be feared that some doctrinalists miss the spirit of Christ in fighting for the words of Christ. God forbid I should speak against earnestly contending for the true faith, but still without fellowship with the living Saviour we may through controversy become ill-developed and onesided. I think I have noticed that brethren who give all their thoughts to experience are also somewhat out of square. Some of them dwell upon the experience of human corruption until they become melancholy, and are at the same time apt to censure those who enjoy the 'liberty of the children of God.' Other brethren turn all their attention to the brighter side of experience, and these are not always free from the spirit of carnal security which leads them to look down upon trembling and anxious hearts as though they could not possess true faith in God. I think also that I have noticed that those who pay all their homage at the shrine of practical theology have a tendency to become legal and to exchange the privileges of believers for the bondage of servants. This also is a grievous fault. But when a man takes Christ Jesus crucified to be his mind's main thought, he has all things in one, doctrine, experience and practice combined. As Canaan contained Carmel, Sharon, Eschol and Hermon, so Jesus comprehends all good things. If 'the Lamb of God, which taketh away the sin of the world' be the object of our thoughts, we have them all in one. 'A bundle of myrrh is my wellbeloved unto me', 'a cluster of camphire in the vineyards of En-gedi.'

FOR MEDITATION: As 'the Word' (John 1:1), the Lord Jesus Christ is full of the best doctrine (John 7:16–17); as 'a man of sorrows' (Isaiah 53:3) who 'rejoiced in spirit' (Luke 10:21) he is full of balanced experience; as 'the good shepherd' (John 10:11,14) 'who went about doing good' (Acts 10:38) he is full of bountiful practice. All things are ours, if we are Christ's (1 Corinthians 3:21–23).

SERMON NO. 1060

Number one thousand; or, 'Bread enough and to spare'

'And when he came to himself, he said, How many hired servants of my father's have bread enough and to spare, and I perish with hunger!' Luke 15:17
SUGGESTED FURTHER READING: Romans 6:12–19

Some years ago there was a crossing-sweeper in Dublin at the corner with his broom; in all probability his highest thoughts were to keep the crossing clean and look for pennies. One day a lawyer put his hand upon his shoulder and said to him, 'My good fellow, do you know that you are heir to a fortune of ten thousand pounds a year?' 'Do you mean it?' said he. 'I do,' he replied. 'I have just received the information; I am sure you are the man.' He walked away and he forgot his broom. Are you astonished? Why, who would not have forgotten a broom when suddenly made possessor of ten thousand pounds a year? So I pray that some poor sinners, who have been thinking of the pleasures of the world, when they hear that there is hope and that there is heaven to be had, will forget the deceitful pleasures of sin and follow after higher and better things. The prodigal, when he said, 'I will arise and go to my father,' became in a measure reformed from that very moment. How? Why, he left the swine-trough; more, he left the wine cup and he left the harlots. He did not go with the harlot on his arm and the wine cup in his hand, saying, 'I will take these with me and go to my father.' It could not be. These were all left and, though he had no goodness to bring, yet he did not try to keep his sins and come to Christ. Some of you, I fear, will make mischief even out of the gospel and will dare to take the cross and use it as a gallows for your souls. If God is so merciful, you will go therefore and sin the more; and because grace is freely given, therefore you will 'continue in sin, that grace may abound'. If you do this, I would solemnly remind you that I have no grace to preach to such as you. Your 'damnation is just.'

FOR MEDITATION: All who lay claim upon the name of Christ have a responsibility to depart from iniquity (2 Timothy 2:19). It is sheer hypocrisy for one who professes to be a Christian to associate the name of Christ with scandalous behaviour (1 Corinthians 6:15) and to cause Christ to be regarded as the promoter of sin (Galatians 2:17).

The tender pity of the Lord

'Like as a father pitieth his children, so the LORD *pitieth then that fear him. For he knoweth our frame; he remembereth that we are dust.' Psalm 103:13,14*
SUGGESTED FURTHER READING: Romans 14:1–13

Old John Berridge, as odd as he was good, had a number of pictures of different ministers round his room, and he had a looking glass in a frame to match. He would often take a friend into the room and say, 'That is Calvin, that is John Bunyan,' and when he took him up to the looking glass he would add, 'and that is the devil.' 'Why,' the friend would say, 'it is myself.' 'Ah,' said he, 'there is a devil in us all.' Being so imperfect we ought not to condemn. Remember also that if we are not patient and forbearing, there is clear proof that we are more imperfect than we thought we were. Those who grow in grace grow in forbearance. He is but a mere babe in grace who is always saying, 'I cannot put up with such conduct from my brother.' My dear brother, you are bound even to wash the disciples' feet. If you knew yourself and were like your Master, you would have the charity which 'hopeth all things, endureth all things.' Remember that your brothers and sisters in Christ, with whom you find so much fault, are God's elect for all that, and if *he* chose them, why do you reject them? They are bought with Christ's blood, and if he thought them worth so much, why do you think so little of them? Recollect, too, that with all their badness there are some good points in them in which they excel *you*. They do not know so much, but perhaps they act better. It may be that they are faulty in pride, but perhaps they excel you in generosity; or if perhaps one man is a little quick in temper, yet he is more zealous than you. Look at the bright side of your brother and the dark side of yourself instead of reversing the order as many do. Remember there are points about every Christian from which you may learn a lesson. Look to their excellences and imitate them.

FOR MEDITATION: The fruit of mutual forbearance is peaceful unity (Ephesians 4:2–3) and forgiveness (Colossians 3:13). Loving fellowship of this kind provokes love and good works (Hebrews 10:24), but the lack of forbearance provokes something completely different (Galatians 5:15,26).

SERMON NO. 941

The believer a new creature

'Therefore if any man be in Christ, he is a new creature.' 2 Corinthians 5:17
SUGGESTED FURTHER READING: 2 Corinthians 3:12–4:6

The mode of this great change is somewhat like this: at first the man is ignorant of his God; he does not know God to be so loving, kind and good as he is; then the Holy Spirit shows the man Christ, lets him see the love of God in the person of Christ, and thus illuminates the understanding. Whereas the sinner thought nothing of God before, or his few stray thoughts were all dark and terrible, now he learns the infinite love of God in the person of Christ, and his understanding gets clearer views of God than it ever had before. Then, in turn, the understanding acts upon the affections. Learning God to be good and kind, the heart, which was hard towards God, is softened, and the man loves the gracious Father who gave Jesus to redeem him from his sins. The affections being changed, the whole man is on the way towards a great and radical renewal, for now the emotions find another ruler. The passions, once rabid as vultures at the sight of the carrion of sin, now turn with loathing from iniquity, and are only stirred by holy principle. The convert grows vehement against evil, as vehement as he once was against the right. Now he longs and pines after communion with God as once he longed and pined after sin. The affections, like a rudder, have changed the direction of the emotions, and meanwhile the will, that stubbornest thing of all, that iron sinew, is led in a blessed captivity, wearing silken fetters. The heart wills to do what God wills; it wills to be perfect, 'for to will is present with me; but how to perform that which is good I find not.' See then how great is the change wrought in us by being in Christ! It is a thorough and entire change, affecting all the parts, powers and passions of our manhood. Grace does not reform us, but recreates us; it does not trim away here and there an evil outgrowth, but it implants a holy and divine principle which goes to instant war with all indwelling sin and continues to fight until corruption is subdued and holiness is enthroned.

FOR MEDITATION: This great change begins at the moment of conversion (Acts 3:19) and will be completed at the moment of glorification (1 Corinthians 15:51–52; Philippians 3:20–21), but involves a lot of ongoing sanctification in between (2 Corinthians 3:18).

SERMON NO. 881

Hope in hopeless cases

'Bring him hither to me.' Matthew 17:17
SUGGESTED FURTHER READING: Hebrews 2:14–18

How is it that Satan has the impudence to make men despair? Surely it is a piece of his infernal impertinence that he dares to do it. Despair, when you have an omnipotent God to deal with you? Despair, when the precious blood of the Son of God is given for sinners? Despair, when God delights in mercy? Despair, when the silver bell rings, 'Come unto me, all ye that labour and are heavy laden, and I will give you rest'? Despair, while life lasts, while mercy's gate stands wide open, while the heralds of mercy beckon you to come, while 'though your sins be as scarlet, they shall be as white as snow; though they be red like crimson, they shall be as wool'? I say again, it is infernal impertinence that has dared to suggest the idea of despair to a sinner. Christ unable to save? Never can it be. Christ outdone by Satan and by sin? Impossible. A sinner with diseases too many for the great Physician to heal? I tell you that if all the diseases of men were met in you, and all the sins of men were heaped on you, and if blasphemy, murder, fornication, adultery and every sin that is possible or imaginable had all been committed by you, yet the precious blood of Jesus Christ, God's dear Son, 'cleanseth us from all sin.' If you will but trust my Master, who is worthy to be trusted and deserves your confidence, he will save you even now. Why delay, why raise questions, why debate, why deliberate, mistrust and suspect? Fall into his arms; he cannot reject you, for he has himself said, 'him that cometh to me I will in no wise cast out.' Yet, I do despair of converting you unless the Master does it. It is mine to tell you this, but I know you will not hear it, or, hearing it, will reject it unless Christ shall come with power by his Spirit. O may he come today.

FOR MEDITATION: The hope of hypocrites, the wicked and unjust men will perish (Job 8:13–14; Proverbs 11:7), but there is hope even for them if they repent and turn back to God (Ezekiel 33:11,14–16). How wonderfully the repentant thief who was crucified with Christ proved it (Luke 23:39–43).

The shrill trumpet of admonition

'Moab hath been at ease from his youth, and he hath settled on his lees, and hath not been emptied from vessel to vessel.' Jeremiah 48:11
SUGGESTED FURTHER READING: Acts 8:9–24

There are many in the professing Christian church who are in the same state as Moab. They called to see the church officers and asked if they could be accepted into the church. No objection was raised; the pastor conversed with them; they talked very fairly and deceived him: they have been baptised. As often as the table of communion is spread, they sit with God's people and partake of the emblems of the Saviour's crucified body. But though their profession is a very comely one and their outward conduct exceedingly honourable, yet they lack the inward spiritual grace. They have the virgin's lamp, but they have no oil in the vessel with their lamps; and yet so comfortable are these professors that they slumber and sleep. I have known many a true believer much troubled for fear he should be a hypocrite, while many a hypocrite has never asked a question. Thousands who have gone safely to heaven have on the road stopped many times, put their fingers to their brow and said, 'Am I a true believer? What strange perplexities arise! Have I really passed from death to life, or is it a fancy and a dream?' And yet I say to you that the hypocrite has gone singing on his way, secure, as he thought, of passing through the gate of pearl, until he found himself at last dragged back to the hole in the side of the hill, which is the secret gate of hell. Many, who were fair to look upon, have been rotten at the core, such fruit as the King could not accept at his table. You who never ask whether you are Christians, begin to question yourselves. 'Examine yourselves, whether ye be in the faith;' let not presumption hold you in its deadly embrace. Remember, you may think yourself a believer, and everybody else may think so too, and you may fail to find out your error until it is too late to rectify it.

FOR MEDITATION: Confidence and boldness before God and in the things of God are not necessarily proofs of being right with God (Matthew 7:22–23; Luke 18:11–14). They may amount to sheer presumption and be accompanied by a whole host of sins (2 Peter 2:10,18–19).

Rahab

'By faith the harlot Rahab perished not with them that believed not, when she had received the spies in peace.' Hebrews 11:31
'Likewise also was not Rahab the harlot justified by works, when she had received the messengers, and had sent them out another way?' James 2:25
SUGGESTED FURTHER READING (Spurgeon): Joshua 2:1–14

I have often tried to put myself in Rahab's place and have said, 'Suppose I had been hiding two servants of God during the days of Claverhouse's dragoons; for instance, if I had Alexander Peden and Cameron in the back room, and two dragoons should ride up to my door and demand, "Are the ministers here?"' I have tried to imagine what I should say and I have never yet been able to make up my mind. I suppose I have more light than Rahab and certainly more leisure to consider the case, and yet I do not see my way. I do not wonder, therefore, that she blundered. I am not astonished that she said what she did, for it would readily suggest itself to her ignorant and anxious mind. I have turned over a great many schemes of what I would have said. I do not see how I could have said, 'Yes, they are indoors.' That would be to betray God's servants, and that I would not do. I have concocted a great many pretty-looking plans, but upon examination they appear to be more or less tinctured with the deceit which tries to justify or conceal deceit, and I have had to abandon them as being no better than falsehood and perhaps not quite so good. I am not sure whether Rahab's lie was not more honest and outspoken than many an evasion which has suggested itself to very clever people; as a rule things which are not obvious, and need cleverness to suggest them, are rather suspicious. If you strip these clever plans, they peel into falsehoods. I do not want to say a word of apology for the falsehood. It is altogether wrong; but before you condemn Rahab, be sure that you do not condemn yourself; ask yourself what you would have said, or done under the circumstances. To tell the truth is always right.

FOR MEDITATION: Rahab found herself unable to be true both to the people of God and to their enemies. While we cannot use her behaviour as an excuse for telling lies, she does provide us with a remarkable and unexpected example of kindness towards God's people (Joshua 2:12). Do you take every opportunity to do likewise (Galatians 6:10)?

SERMON NO. 1061

The best cloak

'And was clad with zeal as a cloke.' Isaiah 59:17
SUGGESTED FURTHER READING: Mark 6:30–56

In three years of Christ's life you behold epitomised three thousand years of ordinary existence. I do not know how it seems to you, but the life of Christ appears to me to be the longest life I ever read. It is such a condensed, massive, close-grained life! It is very short—in truth it consists of only three years of labour, as the former part of his life was spent in obscurity, and there we leave it as God has left it—but the three active years of his earthly sojourn are crowded with incident. Why, he is here, there and everywhere! All the day he is working and all the night he is praying: you read of the cold mountains and the midnight air as witnessing the fervour of his prayer; and then, at morning light, he is healing the sick or preaching the gospel, never pausing but constantly pressing on like a racer to the goal. We meet with incidents like 'they took him even as he was in the ship', implying that he could not walk down to the vessel because he was too faint, but they bore him away even as he was. On board the ship he was so weary, so utterly overcome, that when the storm came on, he slept, slept while the sea and the sky were mingled, and the ship was likely to go to pieces, slept from sheer weariness and lack of rest. Remember that all this was not merely work of the body, but (that which I dare say some of you think very easy, but which, if you were to try it, you would find to be the most laborious work in the world) brain-work; and in our Lord's case it was brain-work of the most intense kind, for Jesus never preached a careless sermon, never produced a single address before the people that was uninstructive or shallow, and never delivered a speech in an efficient manner, coldly and heartlessly. He was a man like ourselves, albeit he was God, and (I am speaking of his humanity now) that human soul of his achieved centuries of work in those three plenteous years.

FOR MEDITATION: Most of the things done by the Lord Jesus Christ were never recorded; the world itself would not be big enough for the biographies which would be written (John 20:30; 21:25). Make sure you have grasped the most important things that he did (1 Corinthians 15:3–4) and that you have obtained eternal life by trusting in him (John 20:31).

SERMON NO. 832

Altogether lovely

'Yea, he is altogether lovely.' Song of Solomon 5:16
SUGGESTED FURTHER READING: Colossians 1:28–2:3

When the old Puritan minister had delivered his discourse, and dwelt upon firstly, secondly, thirdly and perhaps upon twenty-fifthly, before he sat down he usually gave a comprehensive summary of all that he had spoken. Every one who carefully noted the summary would carry away the essence of the sermon. The summary was always looked upon by the Puritan hearer as one of the most valuable helps to memory and consequently a most important part of the discourse. In these five words the spouse here gives you her summary. She had delivered a tenfold discourse concerning her Lord; she had described in detail all his various beauties, and when she surveyed him from head to foot, she gathered up all her commendations in this sentence: 'yea, he is altogether lovely.' Remember these words and know their meaning, and you possess the quintessence of the spouse's portion of the Song of Songs. Now, as in this allegorical song, the bride sums up her witness in these words, so may I say that all the patriarchs, prophets, apostles, confessors and the entire body of the church have left us no other testimony. They all spoke of Christ and commended him. Whatever the type, symbol, obscure oracle or open word in which they bore witness, that witness all amounted to this: 'yea, he is altogether lovely'; and I will add that since the canon of inspiration has closed, the testimony of all saints, on earth and in heaven, has continued to confirm the declaration made of old. The verdict of each particular saint and of the whole elect host as a body is still this: 'yea, he is altogether lovely.' From the sighs and the songs which mingle on the dying beds of saints, I hear this note supreme above all others, 'he is altogether lovely'; and from the songs unmingled with groans, which perpetually peal forth from immortal tongues before the presence of the Most High, I hear this one master note, 'yea, he is altogether lovely.'

FOR MEDITATION: The apostle Paul instructed Christians to think about whatever is true, honest, just, pure, lovely, of good report, virtuous and praiseworthy (Philippians 4:8). There is surely no better way of covering all these than by remembering Jesus Christ (2 Timothy 2:8).

The way

'Jesus saith unto him, I am the way.' John 14:6
SUGGESTED FURTHER READING: John 8:25–47

We get our best apprehensions of the Father through the Son; 'he that hath seen me hath seen the Father'. It is only by Christ that we realise the Fatherhood of God. I do not believe any man has any idea of what the Fatherhood of God is till he knows Jesus Christ as 'the first-born among many brethren', and knows the power of his atonement to bring us near to God. The common fatherhood doctrine that God is the Father of us all, because he made us all, is not true in the most real and tender sense of Fatherhood. A potter makes ten thousand vessels, but he is not the father of one of them. It is not everything that a man makes that he is the father of, or, if he be so called, it is only in a modified sense. We are God's children when we are created anew in Christ Jesus, when regeneration has made us 'partakers of the divine nature'. Sonship is no ordinary privilege common to all mankind; it is the high prerogative of the chosen; for what says the Scripture? 'Behold, what manner of love the Father hath bestowed upon us, that we should be called the sons of God: therefore the world knoweth us not, because it knew him not.' When we are adopted into the divine family, then and not till then do we know God as the Father. As for unbelievers, they have not known the Father, for our Lord says, 'O righteous Father, the world hath not known thee'. He that has seen Christ has seen the Father, and only he; but the very essence of Christ is seen in his expiatory death, and therefore we can never grasp the Fatherhood of God till we have believed in the atonement of his Son. 'Whosoever denieth the Son, the same hath not the Father: but he that acknowledgeth the Son hath the Father also.' May we then realise the Father through knowing in very deed the Lord, for he is the only way to a knowledge of the Father.

FOR MEDITATION: Eternal life involves knowing God the Father and God the Son (John 17:3). Knowing and seeing God the Son enables us to know and see God the Father (John 8:19; 12:45; 14:7–9). God becomes our Father when we receive the Son (John 1:12). To reject God the Son is to reject God the Father as well (John 5:23; 8:42; 15:23–24; 1 John 2:23; 2 John 9). Jesus said 'no man cometh unto the Father, but by me' (John 14:6).

SERMON NO. 942

The echo

'When thou saidst, Seek ye my face; my heart said unto thee, Thy face,
LORD, *will I seek.' Psalm 27:8*
SUGGESTED FURTHER READING: Psalm 105:1–6

You who love the Lord, you are all day long hearing God say 'Seek ye my face'. When the morning light awakens you, it is God saying, 'Up, my child; the light natural streams from the sun: come and seek the light spiritual; seek my face.' If you wake to abundant mercies, why, all the provisions on the table ought to say to you, 'I am God's gift to you; seek the face of the Giver;' go to him with a note of praise; be not ungrateful and suppose that you are in want and have to say, 'What shall I eat and what shall I drink?' while all your wants say to you, 'Seek the Lord's face; he has provision; go to him.' Your abundance or your necessity may equally be a signpost to point you on the road to God. Suppose your child comes and asks you for something: it is God teaching you to do the same, to go like a child to your heavenly Father. If you are full of joy, should not your joy be like the chariots of Amminadib, to bear you to Jesus' feet? And if you are full of grief, should not your sorrow be as a swift ship that is blown by the winds? Should you not get nearer to God thereby? During the day you perhaps hear of the fall of some professor: what does that say to you? 'Seek God's face, that you may be held up.' Perhaps you hear a sinner swear: what does that say to you, but 'Pray for that sinner'? All the sins we see others commit ought to be so many jogs to our memory to pray for the coming of Christ and for the salvation of souls. In this way you may go through the world; and the very stones in the street will say to you, 'Seek the Lord's face.' If you meet a funeral, what does that say? 'You will soon be dying; seek the Lord's face now.' And when the Sabbath comes, what a call is that—'Seek ye my face'!

FOR MEDITATION: When do you seek God's face? This is something we each need to do individually in our own spiritual interests (Psalm 24:3–6) and which God's people as a body need to do in the spiritual interests of a wicked nation (2 Chronicles 7:14).

The panting hart

'As the hart panteth after the waterbrooks, so panteth my soul after thee, O God.' Psalm 42:1
SUGGESTED FURTHER READING: Song of Solomon 5:2–8

Why do we wander? Why do we grieve the Holy Spirit? Why do we turn aside from God, our exceeding joy? Why do we provoke him to jealousy and cause him to make us grope in darkness and sigh out of a lonely and desolate heart? There is much of an evil heart of unbelief in these departings from the living God; if, therefore, we can join in the language of the text, we must not too much congratulate ourselves, for though it be a sign of grace to pant after God as the hart pants for the waterbrooks, yet it is an equally certain sign of a want of more grace and the loss of a privilege which we should always strive to possess. We are yet but poor in spiritual things when we might be rich; we are thirsting when we might put cups to our lips. At the same time there is very much which is commendable in the desire expressed in the text; the insatiable desire which burned in the psalmist's heart is a heavenly flame kindled from above. If I have not my Lord in near and dear communion, it is at least the next best thing to be unutterably wretched until I find him. If I do not sit at his banquets, yet 'Blessed are they which do hunger and thirst after righteousness'. If my beloved be not in my embrace, yet so long as I am not contented without him, so long as I sigh, cry and follow hard after him, I may be assured that I am in the possession of his love and that before long I shall find him to the joy of my soul. Our text, then, has a warp and a weft of differing colours, mingling sin and grace: the wine is mixed with water, yet it is wine; there is some alloy in the silver, yet silver it assuredly is. The psalmist sighs as none but a saint can do, and yet if he had not been a sinner too, such sighs would not be necessary. Such good and such evil are in you; search and look, and pray the great Spirit to remove the ill and nourish the good.

FOR MEDITATION: We ought not to treat our spiritual backslidings and shortcomings lightly, but neither should we let them dampen or tarnish our desires to draw near to God. The apostle Paul did not regret causing grief to the unspiritual Corinthian church (2 Corinthians 7:8), but the reason for his rejoicing was not the grief he had to cause, but the wonderful repentance and turning back to God which followed (2 Corinthians 7:9–11).

SERMON NO. 822

Songs of deliverance

'They that are delivered from the noise of archers in the places of drawing water, there shall they rehearse the righteous acts of the LORD, even the righteous acts toward the inhabitants of his villages in Israel: then shall the people of the LORD go down to the gates.' Judges 5:11
SUGGESTED FURTHER READING: Psalm 126:1–6

In Deborah's day, when one friend came to the well and met another and half-a-dozen gathered together, one would say, 'Delightful change this! We could not come to the well a month ago without being afraid that an arrow would pierce our hearts.' 'Yes' said another, 'our family went without water for a long time. We were all bitten with thirst because we dare not come to the well.' Then another would say, 'But have you heard how it is? It was that woman Deborah, the wife of Lapidoth, who called out Barak and went with him to the battle. Have you not heard of the glorious fight they had and how the river Kishon swept Jabin away and Jael smote Sisera through the temples?' 'This is the Lord's doing; it is marvellous in our eyes' said another. And so, around the well's brink, when they were 'delivered from the noise of archers', they rehearsed the works of God; and before they wended their way to their several homes, they said to one another, 'Let us sing unto the praise of God who has set our country free;' and so, catching the tune, each woman went back to her village home, bearing the pitcher for her household and singing as she went. This is very much what we ought to do. When we come together, we ought to rehearse the work that Jesus Christ has done for us, the great work which he did on Calvary, and the great work which he is doing now before the Father's throne. We should talk experimentally, telling one another of what we have known, what Christ has done for us, through what troubles we have been sustained, in what perils we have been preserved, what blessings we have enjoyed and what ills, so well deserved, have been averted from us. We have not enough of this rehearsing the works of the LORD.

FOR MEDITATION: Spurgeon went on to quote Malachi 3:16—'Then they that feared the LORD spake often one to another: and the LORD hearkened, and heard it'. When we meet together, there should be mutual encouragement (Hebrews 10:25) as we address one another in songs of praise and thanksgiving to God (Ephesians 5:19–20; Colossians 3:16).

Moses' decision

'By faith Moses, when he was come to years, refused to be called the son of Pharaoh's daughter; choosing rather to suffer affliction with the people of God, than to enjoy the pleasures of sin for a season; esteeming the reproach of Christ greater riches than the treasures of Egypt: for he had respect unto the recompense of the reward.' Hebrews 11:24–26
SUGGESTED FURTHER READING: Luke 12:32–48

Oh that men would measure everything in the scales of eternity! We shall be before the bar of God, all of us, in a few months or years; how do you think we shall feel then? One will say, 'I never thought about religion at all,' and another, 'I thought about it, but I did not think enough to come to any decision about it. I went the way the current went.' Another will say, ' I knew the truth well enough, but I could not bear the shame of it; they would have thought me fanatical if I had gone through with it.' Another will say, 'I halted between two opinions; I hardly thought I was justified in sacrificing my children's position for the sake of being out and out a follower of the truth.' What wretched reflections will come over men who have sold the Saviour as Judas did! What wretched deathbeds must they have who have been unfaithful to their conscience and untrue to their God! But with what composure will the believer look forward to another world! He will say, 'By grace I am saved, and I bless God I could afford to be ridiculed and could bear to be laughed at. I could lose that situation, I could be turned out of that farm and could be called a fool, and yet it did not hurt me. I found solace in the society of Christ; I went to him about it all and I found that to be reproached for Christ was a sweeter thing than to possess all the treasures of Egypt. Blessed be his name! I missed the pleasures of the world, but they were no loss to me. I was glad to miss them, for I found sweeter pleasure in the company of my Lord, and now there are pleasures to come which shall never end.'

FOR MEDITATION: Like Moses 'let us lay aside ... the sin which doth so easily beset us ... looking unto Jesus' (Hebrews 12:1–2) in the confidence that we 'have in heaven a better and an enduring substance' (Hebrews 10:34–35) and that God 'is a rewarder of them that diligently seek him' (Hebrews 11:6).

SERMON NO. 1063

A serious remonstrance

'My father, if the prophet had bid thee do some great thing, wouldest thou not have done it? how much rather then, when he saith to thee, Wash and be clean?' 2 Kings 5:13

SUGGESTED FURTHER READING: Matthew 23:25–33

It is a sad discovery the unbeliever makes when he feels that his self-righteousness has vanished, and all his fair white linen is suddenly turned to masses of spiders' webs, to be swept away. But what must be the fate of such a man at the bar of God? I think I see the King coming in his glory, and the last tremendous morning dawn. When the King sits on his glory-throne, where are the self-righteous? Where are they? I cannot see them. Where are they? Come, Pharisee, come and tell the Lord that you did fast twice in the week, and then was not even as the Tax-collector! There sits the Tax-collector at the right hand of the judge! Come and say that you were cleaner and more holy than he! But where is the wretch? Where is he? Come here, you proud and ostentatious ones, who said you had no need to be washed in the blood; come and tell the Judge so; tell him he made a mistake; tell him that the Saviour was only needed to be a make-weight and assistant to those who could help themselves! But where are they? Why, they were dressed so finely; can those poor, naked, shivering wretches be the boasting professors we used to know? Yes. Hear them as they cry to the rocks to fall on them and the hills to cover them, to hide them from the presence of the great Judge whom in their lifetime they insulted by putting their poor merits in comparison with the boundless wealth and merit of Christ's blood. May it never be your lot nor mine to commit the blasphemy of preferring the labour of our hands to the handiwork of Christ.

FOR MEDITATION: Jesus rejected the self-washing on which the Pharisees prided themselves (Mark 7:1–7; Luke 11:37–40). He visually demonstrated to his disciples that we must allow him to wash us (John 13:8). Only his blood can wash away our sin and fit us for heaven (Revelation 1:5; 7:14).

'Have you been to Jesus for the cleansing power?
Are you washed in the blood of the Lamb?'

Your own salvation

'Your own salvation.' Philippians 2:12
SUGGESTED FURTHER READING: Luke 9:46–56

I know some who greatly need to look to their own salvation. I refer to those who are always criticising others. They can hardly go to a place of worship without observing their neighbour's dress or conduct. Nobody is safe from their remarks; they are such keen judges and make such shrewd observations. You faultfinders and talebearers, look to 'your own salvation'. You condemned a minister the other day for a supposed fault, and yet he is a dear servant of God who lives near his Master; who are you, sir, to use your tongue against such a one as he? The other day a poor humble Christian was the object of your gossip and your slander to the wounding of her heart. Oh, see to yourself. If those eyes which look outward so piercingly would sometimes look inward, they might see a sight which would blind them with horror. Blessed horror, if it led them to turn to the Saviour who would open those eyes afresh and grant them to see his salvation. I might also say that in this matter of looking to personal salvation, it is necessary to speak to some who have espoused great public designs. I trust I am as ardent a Protestant as any man living, but I know too many red-hot Protestants who are little better than Romanists, for though the Romanists of old might have burnt them, they would certainly withhold toleration from Romanists today, if they could; and therein I see not a pin to choose between the two bigots. Zealous Protestants, I agree with you, but yet I warn you that your zeal in this matter will not save you, or stand in the stead of personal godliness. Many an orthodox Protestant will be found at the left hand of the Great Judge.

FOR MEDITATION: When we judge others, we are usurping the position occupied by 'the Judge of all the earth' (Romans 14:4,10; James 4:11–12) and we are inviting his judgment upon ourselves (Matthew 7:1; Romans 2:1–3). The route to avoiding his judgment involves judging ourselves instead (1 Corinthians 11:31).

SERMON NO. 1003

The spur

'I must work the works of him that sent me, while it is day: the night cometh, when no man can work.' John 9:4
SUGGESTED FURTHER READING: Psalm 90:1–17

Jesus meant that he had an earthly lifetime in which to labour, and when that was over he would no more perform the kind of labour he was then doing. He called his lifetime a day to show us the shortness of it. We reckon life as a matter of years and we even think of the years as though they were of extreme length, though every year seems to spin round more swiftly than before; men who are growing grey will tell you that life seems to travel at a much faster rate than in their younger days. To a child a year appears a long period; to a man even ten years is a short time; to God the Eternal a thousand years are as one day. Our Lord here sets us an example of estimating our time at a high rate on account of its brevity. It is a day you have at the longest. How short is that day! Young man, is it your morning? Are you just converted? Is the dew of penitence still trembling upon the green blade? Have you just seen the first radiance which streams from the eyelids of the morning? Up, and serve your God with all your heart! Or have you known the Lord so long that it is noon with you, and the burden and heat of the day are on you? Use all diligence and make good speed, for your sun will soon decline. Or have you long been a Christian? Then the shadows lengthen and your sun is almost down. Quick, let both your hands be used. Strain every nerve; put every sinew to the stretch. Do all at all times and in all places that ingenuity can devise or that zeal can suggest to you, for 'the night cometh when no man can work.'

FOR MEDITATION: The shortness of time should affect our behaviour (Romans 13:11–13) and our attitudes towards each other (Hebrews 10:25) and outsiders (Colossians 4:5). Do you redeem the time? Your answer will show whether you are wise or not (Ephesians 5:15–16).

N.B. Spurgeon closed this sermon with a reference to the recently-declared Franco-Prussian war and to the night which could soon descend upon Europe. The war resulted in a new German empire in 1871 and seeds were sown for a future twentieth century conflict when it would be said that 'the lamps are going out all over Europe' (Sir Edward Grey, 1914).

SERMON NO. 943

Multitudinous thoughts and sacred comforts

'In the multitude of my thoughts within me thy comforts delight my soul.' Psalm 94:19
SUGGESTED FURTHER READING: Philippians 4:4–13

I may be addressing some of you today who are perplexed with a multitude of conflicting thoughts as to your course in life. You do not know what to do. A certain plan has suggested itself and for a time it has seemed the very best course for you; but just now your mind wavers, for another course presents itself and there is much to say in its favour. You are bewildered, you cannot see the clue of providence, and you are lost as in a maze. Indeed at this very moment you are much dispirited, for you have tried various ways and methods to escape from your present difficulty, but you have been disappointed where you expected relief, and probably that which you are about to attempt will end in disappointment too. Your thoughts compass you about like bees or as the flies of Egypt's plague; they worry, but do not help you. You are distracted and your thoughts have no order about them, for while they lean one way at this moment, they drag you in the opposite direction the next second. The currents meet and twist you as in a whirlpool. Now, my dear perplexed friend, at such a time your plight may remind you of the children of Israel at the Red Sea, with the sea before them, the rocks on either hand and the cruel Egyptians in the rear; you must imitate their action and 'stand still, and see the salvation of the Lord'. But you reply, 'I cannot be quiet; I am too agitated.' Brother, 'let patience have her perfect work'; 'in quietness … shall be your strength'. Yet you reply, 'My spirit is restless and impetuous; I wish I could be calm, for then I could better judge of my position and probably discover the way of escape; but I am perturbed, perplexed, tossed up and down, and distracted. Alas! What shall I do?' Listen then to the text—'In the multitude of my thoughts within me thy comforts delight my soul.' Turn your eye to those deep things of God, which have a divine power to allay the torment of your spirit.

FOR MEDITATION: When we do not know what to do, the best thing to do is to ensure that our eyes are upon God (2 Chronicles 20:12) whether we are concerned about our salvation (Luke 10:25; Acts 16:30–31), our supplication (Luke 11:1; Romans 8:26), our speaking (Luke 12:11–12; Mark 9:5–7) or our survival (Luke 12:17–18,22,29–31).

SERMON NO. 883

The way everlasting

'Lead me in the way everlasting.' Psalm 139:24
SUGGESTED FURTHER READING: Psalm 25:4–10

'Lord, lead *my understanding* and my intellect in the way of revelation; make me to know thy covenant truths and the great doctrines of grace. Let me not be satisfied to know half the truth and think I know it all, but lead me into all thy truth. Let there not be one doctrine that I would erase, nor one precept that I would forget, nor one single word in thy Book that I would blot out. Lord, lead me as to my understanding, knowledge and thoughts—"lead me in the way everlasting".' The Psalmist means *his emotions* too, as well as his intellectual part. 'Lord, lead me in thy way, for well I know that if my head should go without my heart, yet were I all undone. Lord, help me to love not the world nor the things that are of the world, but "lead me in the way everlasting". Let my best passions boil when Christ is the fire. Let my heart be in its best trim when Christ has come to see it, like a garden that is watered by his presence and whose fruits are ripened by the sunlight of his love.' He refers *his tongue* to the same leading. 'Lord, grant that my tongue may not be a slanderous tongue, or a trifling tongue, or a lascivious tongue or a tongue that talks for mere talk's sake; but, Lord, salt my tongue for me. Grant me grace so to speak that my conversation shall edify the hearer— "lead me in the way everlasting".' He means, indeed, himself as to *his actions.* 'I would keep thy way, O Lord, when I go to my chamber, not sinning there, when I come down to my meals, not getting out of thy way by wrong eating or drinking, when I go to my shop, or to my work, to the fields or to the market, to the streets and to the Exchange; let me not err in anything. Still, Lord, "lead me in the way everlasting" and may no path of business, recreation, society or solitude ever take me out of thy way.'

FOR MEDITATION: David prayed, 'lead me, and guide me' (Psalm 31:3). His experience of God's faithful leading (Psalm 23:2,3) gave him confidence that God would lead him wherever he was (Psalm 139:10). Hence his constant request 'lead me'—'in thy righteousness' (Psalm 5:8), 'in thy truth' (Psalm 25:5), 'in a plain path' (Psalm 27:11), 'to the rock that is higher than I' (Psalm 61:2), 'into the land of uprightness' (Psalm 143:10)—in short 'in the way everlasting' (Psalm 139:24).

SERMON NO. 903

The eye—a similitude

'Keep me as the apple of the eye.' Psalm 17:8
SUGGESTED FURTHER READING: Luke 11:33–36

Keep me as the eye ought to be kept. It should be *single*. 'The light of the body is the eye: therefore when thine eye is single, thy whole body also is full of light; but when thine eye is evil, thy body also is full of darkness.' Keep me single-minded, Lord, consecrated wholly and devoted alone to thee. The eye should be *clear*. Any speck on its retina would obscure our view of the landscape. With 'an inlet so small,' as one of the poets writes, 'that a grain might close it,' the eye needs to be cleansed. God has provided arrangements for this without disturbing the beautiful mechanism of the little orb. Take heed that the eye of faith is kept clear. We need to be sprinkled with the precious blood and washed with clean water often, that we may always be pure, consciously sanctified. The cleansing water came with the blood from the heart of Christ, 'who through the eternal Spirit offered himself without spot to God'; thereby the conscience is purged and the heart made clean, actively and passively sanctified unto God. The eye needs to be *far-seeing*. It is a great pity when the eye can only see a short distance. We strain to see some ship far out at sea, that looks like a speck on the horizon, or we want to stretch our vision far over mountain and valley, river and lake, from some lofty Alp, compassing the entire prospect at a glance. It is well when our soul can take a wide view and embrace the grand perspective which revelation unfolds, not pestered with the cares of the day so as to obscure the immortal joys that await our arrival at the city of the blessed, not earth-bound and absorbed by incidents that transpire within the tick of the clock, but prospecting the fields of light beyond, where moments, hours, days, years and centuries are unknown. Raise your eyes, Christians.

FOR MEDITATION: David not only prayed 'lead me' (see yesterday's reading), but also 'keep me'. Is the Lord your keeper (Psalm 121:3,5)? If so you too like David can pray, 'keep my soul, and deliver me' (Psalm 25:20), 'Keep me, O LORD, from the hands of the wicked' (Psalm 140:4), 'keep the door of my lips' (Psalm 141:3), and 'Keep me from the snares which they have laid for me' (Psalm 141:9). 'The LORD bless thee, and keep thee' (Numbers 6:24) and enlighten the eyes of your understanding (Ephesians 1:18).

Our life, our work, our change

'All the days of my appointed time will I wait, till my change come.' Job
14:14

SUGGESTED FURTHER READING: Matthew 6:25–34

Job very wisely speaks of 'the days' of our appointed time. It is a prudent
thing to forbear the burden of life as a whole, and learn to bear it in the
parcels into which providence has divided it. Let us live as life comes,
namely by the day. Our God does not trust us with so much life as a
month at once; we live as the clock ticks, a second at a time. Is not that a
wiser method of living rather than to perplex our heads by living by the
month or by the year? You have no promise for the year: the word of
mercy runs, 'as thy days, so shall thy strength be.' You are not
commanded to pray for supplies by the year, but 'Give us this day our
daily bread.' The other day a good man, who has had many troubles and
borne them manfully for some fifteen or twenty years, replied to me,
when I asked him how his patience has held out, 'I said to my afflicted
wife the other day, when the coals came in, it takes several big fellows to
bring in the sacks, but our little kitchen-maid Mary has brought the
whole ton up from the cellar into our parlour; but she has done it a
scuttle-full at a time. She has surely moved tons of coal as ever did the
wagons when they brought them in, but she has moved them little by
little and done it easily.' This is how to bear the troubles of life, a day's
portion at a time. Wave by wave our trials come; let us breast them one
by one and not attempt to buffet the whole ocean's billows at once. Let us
stand as the brave old Spartan did in the Thermopylae of the day, and
fight the Persians as they come on one by one; thus shall we keep our
adversities at bay and overcome them as they advance in single file.

FOR MEDITATION: 'Take therefore no thought for the morrow: for the
morrow shall take thought for the things of itself. Sufficient unto the day
is the evil thereof' (Matthew 6:34). Long-term arrangements are
particularly foolhardy if we fail to involve God at the planning stage
(Luke 12:19–21; James 4:13–15).

Salvation all of grace

'By grace are ye saved.' Ephesians 2:8
SUGGESTED FURTHER READING: Acts 15:1–11

Grace is the fountain-head of salvation and is most conspicuous throughout. Grace is to be seen in our election, for 'there is a remnant according to the election of grace. And if by grace, then is it no more of works'. Grace is manifestly revealed in our redemption, for you know therein the grace of our Lord Jesus Christ, and it is utterly inconceivable that any soul could have deserved to be redeemed with the precious blood of Christ. The mere thought is abhorrent to every holy mind. Our calling is also of grace, for God 'hath saved us, and called us with an holy calling, not according to our works, but according to his own purpose and grace, which was given us in Christ Jesus before the world began'. By grace also we are justified; for over and over again the apostle insists upon this grand and fundamental truth. We are not justified before God by works in any measure or in any degree, but by faith alone; and the apostle tells us 'it is of faith, that it might be by grace'. We see a golden thread of grace running through the whole of the Christian's history, from his election before all worlds even to his admission to the heaven of rest. All along does grace 'reign through righteousness unto eternal life', and 'where sin abounded, grace did much more abound'. There is no point in the history of a saved soul upon which you can put your finger and say, 'In this instance he is saved by his own deservings.' Every single blessing which we receive from God comes to us by the channel of free favour, revealed to us in Christ Jesus our Lord. Boasting is excluded because deservings are excluded. Merit is an unknown word in the Christian church; it is banished once for all; our only shoutings over foundation or topstone are, 'Grace, grace unto it.'

FOR MEDITATION: Salvation by God's grace is frequently contrasted with the impossibility of salvation by our own deeds (Romans 11:5–6; Galatians 5:4; Ephesians 2:8–9; 2 Timothy 1:9; Titus 3:5–7). No wonder 'grace' is one of the very first terms to be found in all the epistles of Paul and Peter! Have you received 'Grace, mercy, and peace' from God our Father and the Lord Jesus Christ?

Bought with a price

'Ye are not your own: for ye are bought with a price: therefore glorify God in your body, and in your spirit, which are God's.' 1 Corinthians 6:19–20
SUGGESTED FURTHER READING (Spurgeon): 1 Peter 1:14–25

If it be true that we are not our own, and I hope it is true of you, then the inference from it is, 'I have no right to injure myself in any way.' My body is not my own; I have no right then, as a Christian, to do anything with it that would defile it. The apostle is arguing mainly against sins of the flesh and he says, 'the body is not for fornication, but for the Lord; and the Lord for the body.' We have no right to commit uncleanness, because our bodies are the members of Christ and not our own. He would say the same of drunkenness, gluttony, idle sleep, and even of such excessive anxiety after wealth as injures health with burdensome care. We have no right to profane or injure the flesh and blood which are consecrated to God; every limb of our frame belongs to God; it is his property; he has bought it 'with a price'. Any honest man will be more concerned about an injury done to another's property placed under his care, than if it were his own. When a son of the prophets was hewing wood with Elisha and the axe head flew off into the water, you remember how he said, 'Alas, master! for it was borrowed.' It would be bad enough to lose my own axe but it is not my own; therefore I doubly deplore the accident. I know this would not operate upon thievish minds. There are some who would have no further care about it, if it was another man's and they had borrowed it: 'Let the lender get it back, if he can.' But we speak to honest men and with them it is always a strong argument. Your body is another's; do it no injury.

FOR MEDITATION: By their impure behaviour the ungodly dishonour their own bodies (Romans 1:24). Any Christian doing the same commits an even greater sin, that of defiling and desecrating the temple of the indwelling Holy Spirit (1 Corinthians 3:16–17; 6:18–19).

N.B. On his deathbed the late deacon Thomas Cook had left this text for his fellow church-members. For the text which he left for the pastors see 20 August.

SERMON NO. 1004

An encouraging lesson from Paul's conversion

'But the Lord said unto him, Go thy way: for he is a chosen vessel unto me, to bear my name before the Gentiles, and kings, and the children of Israel; for I will shew him how great things he must suffer.' Acts 9:15–16
SUGGESTED FURTHER READING: Acts 2:22–36

We too often forget the person of the Lord Jesus Christ, and yet the power of the church lies in 'Christ the power of God, and the wisdom of God.' Some may remember Jesus, but not in his present personal character. In the Romish church its power over devout minds lies in no small degree in the fact that the person of Christ is much spoken of, loved and reverenced; but you seldom see the Christ of the Romish church in any but two attitudes. As a rule, either he is a babe in his mother's arms, or dead; scarcely ever is he set forth by them as the living King, Head and Lord. In both of those first aspects let him be reverenced; let the incarnate God and the dying Saviour have your hearts; but there is another fact to be borne in mind: 'he ever liveth'. That church which, not forgetting his birth nor his sacrifice, yet most clearly recognises that he still lives, is the church that shall win the day. We must have a living Head to the church. Men will assuredly invent a living head if they overlook the living Christ. They will find some priest or other whom they would gladly gird with the attributes of Deity and set up as the Vicar of Christ. But we have a living Christ, and when he is pleased to appear to any man by his Spirit and reveal himself to man apart from instrumentality—I speak not of miraculous appearances, but of other direct operations of his Spirit upon the spirits of men—then the church discovers yet again that he is in her midst fulfilling his promise: 'lo, I am with you alway, even unto the end of the world.' Still the Lord Jesus exerts a living force in the hearts and consciences of men.

FOR MEDITATION: 'I am he that liveth, and was dead; and, behold, I am alive for evermore' (Revelation 1:18). Without the resurrection our doctrine would be incomplete (Romans 4:24–25), baptism would lack some of its significance (Romans 6:4–5; Colossians 2:12) and Christians would have a dead leader like other faiths (Romans 14:9). We would be wasting our time, misrepresenting God, and the most miserable of people (1 Corinthians 15:14–19). 'But now is Christ risen from the dead' (1 Corinthians 15:20).

SERMON NO. 944

Help for seekers of the light

'We wait for light, but behold obscurity; for brightness, but we walk in darkness.' Isaiah 59:9
SUGGESTED FURTHER READING: Luke 18:9–14

Some appear to deal with God as if he were bound to give salvation, as if salvation were the inevitable result of a round of performances, or the deserved reward of a certain amount of virtue. They refuse to see that salvation is a pure gift of God, not of works, not the result of merit, but of free favour only, not of man, neither by man, but of the Lord alone. Though the Lord has placed it on record in his word in the plainest language that 'it is not of him that willeth, nor of him that runneth, but of God that sheweth mercy', yet most men in their hearts imagine that everlasting life is tied to duties and earned by service. Dear friend, you must come down from such boastful notions; you must come before God as a humble petitioner, pleading the promises of mercy, abhorring all idea of merit, and confessing that if the Lord condemns you he has a right to do it, and that if he saves you, it will be an act of pure, gratuitous mercy, a deed of sovereign grace. Too many seekers hold their heads too high; to enter the lowly gate of light you must stoop. On the bended knee is the penitent's true place. 'God be merciful to me a sinner' is the penitent's true prayer. If God should damn you, you could never complain of injustice, for you have deserved it a thousand times; if those prayers of yours were never answered and if no mercy ever came, you could not accuse the Lord, for you have no right to be heard. He could righteously withhold an answer of peace if he so willed to do. Confess that you are an undeserving, ill-deserving, hell-deserving sinner, and begin to pray as you have never prayed before. Cry out of the depths of self-abasement if you would be heard. Come as a beggar, not as a creditor.

FOR MEDITATION: It would be very unwise to say to God 'Pay me that thou owest' (Matthew 18:28), because the only thing God could owe us is the wages of sin, which is death (Romans 6:23). In the circumstances the only sensible request we can make is 'forgive us our debts' (Matthew 6:12).

The heaven of heavens

'And they shall see his face.' Revelation 22:4
SUGGESTED FURTHER READING: 1 John 2:28–3:3

The Italians so much admire the city of Naples that their proverb is, 'See Naples and die', as if there remained nothing more to be seen after that fair bay and city had been gazed upon. To behold the far fairer sight mentioned in the text men might well be content to die a thousand times. If it shall please God that we shall depart this life before the Master's appearing, we may laugh at death and count it to be gain, seeing that it introduces us to the place where we shall see his face. 'Thou canst not see my face: for there shall no man see me, and live' said the Lord of old; but that was true of mortals only and refers not to immortals who have put on incorruption: in yonder glory-land they see the face of God and yet live; the sight is the essence and excellence of their life. Here that vision might be too overpowering for the soul and body, and might painfully separate them with excess of delight, and so cause us death, but up yonder the disembodied spirit is able to endure the blaze of splendour, and so will the body also when it shall have been refined and strengthened in its powers by resurrection from the dead. Then these eyes, which now would be smitten with blindness should they look upon the superlative glory, shall be strengthened to behold eternally the Lord of angels, who is 'the brightness of his glory, and the express image of his person'. Brothers and sisters, regard the object of our expectations! See the happiness which is promised us! Behold the heaven which awaits us! Forget for a while your present cares: let all your difficulties and sorrows vanish for a season; and live for a while in the future which is so certified by faithful promises that you may rejoice in it even now!

FOR MEDITATION: Though it is not yet possible to see the face of Jesus, it is possible to rejoice in him (1 Peter 1:8); 'now we see through a glass, darkly; but then face to face' (1 Corinthians 13:12). But only those whose hearts have been purified (Matthew 5:8) and who have pursued holiness (Hebrews 12:14) will see him gladly then. All others will be terrified to see his face (Revelation 6:15–16).

SERMON NO. 824

Now, and then

'For now we see through a glass, darkly; but then face to face.' 1
Corinthians 13:12
SUGGESTED FURTHER READING: Exodus 33:12–23

It would be an inconvenience for us to know here as much as we shall
know in heaven. No doubt we have sometimes thought that if we had
better ears, it would be a great blessing. We have wished we could hear
ten miles away; but probably we should be no better off; we might hear
too much and the sounds might drown each other. Probably our sight is
not as good as we wish it were, but a large increase of ocular power
might not be of any use to us. Our natural organs are fitted for our
present sphere of being, and our mental faculties are, in the case of most
of us, properly adapted to our moral requirements. If we knew more of
our own sinfulness, we might be driven to despair; if we knew more of
God's glory, we might die of terror; if we had more understanding, unless
we had equivalent capacity to employ it, we might be filled with conceit
and tormented with ambition. But up there we shall have our minds and
our systems strengthened to receive more, without the damage that
would come to us here from overleaping the boundaries of order,
supremely appointed and divinely regulated. We cannot here drink the
wine of the kingdom; it is too strong for us; but up there we shall drink it
new in our heavenly Father's kingdom, without fear of the intoxications
of pride or the staggerings of passions. We shall know even as we are
known. Besides, dear friends, the atmosphere of heaven is so much
clearer than this, that I do not wonder we can see better there. Here there
is the smoke of daily care, the constant dust of toil and the mist of
trouble perpetually rising. We cannot be expected to see much in such a
smoky atmosphere as this; but when we shall pass beyond, we shall find
that no clouds ever gather round the sun to hide his everlasting
brightness. There all is clear.

FOR MEDITATION: Consider some of the glories of heaven—the Saviour's
face will shine like the sun (Revelation 1:16); so will the righteous
(Matthew 13:43). Heaven itself will be perfectly light, clear, transparent
and pure (Revelation 21:11,18,21,23–24; 22:1,5). No wonder such sights
overwhelmed the apostle John during his vision (Revelation 1:17; 22:8).

The healing of one born blind

'Since the world began was it not heard that any man opened the eyes of one that was born blind.' John 9:32
SUGGESTED FURTHER READING: Psalm 146:1–10

The best declaration of truth will not of itself remove birth-blindness and enable men to look unto Jesus. Nor do I believe that even the most earnest gospel appeals, nor the most vehement testimonies to its truth will convince men's understandings. All these things have their place and their use, but they have no power in and of themselves to enlighten the understanding savingly. I bring a blind friend to an elevated spot and I bid him look upon the landscape. 'See how the silver river threads its way amid the emerald fields. See how yonder trees make up a shadowy wood, how wisely yonder garden, near at hand, is cultivated to perfection and how nobly yonder lordly castle rises on that hill of matchless beauty.' See, he shakes his head; he has no admiration for the scene. I borrow poetical expressions, but still he joins not in my delight. I try plain words and tell him, 'There is the garden, there is the castle, there is the wood and there is the river; do you not see them?' 'No'; he cannot see one of them and does not know what they are like. What ails the man? Have I not described the landscape well? Have I been faulty in my explanations? Have I not given him my own testimony that I have walked these glades and sailed along that stream? He shakes his head; my words are lost. His eyes alone are to blame. Let us come to this conviction about sinners; for, if not, we shall hammer away and do nothing: let us be assured that there is something the matter with the sinner himself which we cannot cure, whatever we may do with him, and yet we cannot get him saved unless it be cured. Let us feel this, because it will drive us away from ourselves; it will lead us to our God, drive us to the strong for strength and teach us to seek for power beyond our own.

FOR MEDITATION: The devil blinds the minds of unbelievers to the light of the glorious gospel of Christ (2 Corinthians 4:4). It requires God to shine in our hearts to give us the light of the knowledge of his glory in the face of Jesus Christ (2 Corinthians 4:6). We need to pray that God will open the eyes of those who cannot naturally see the truth (2 Kings 6:15–17).

SERMON NO. 1065

A visit to the tomb

'He is not here: for he is risen, as he said. Come, see the place where the Lord lay.' Matthew 28:6
SUGGESTED FURTHER READING: John 19:41–20:10

I felt this afternoon, while I stood by the open grave in Norwood Cemetery, as though I heard a voice saying, 'Come, see the place where the Lord lay.' It does not matter much to us now about the precise spot. He lay in the grave: that is a prominent fact that preaches to us a pithy sermon. Any grave may well suit our purpose. In the little town of Campodolcino I once realised the tomb of Christ very vividly, in an affair which had been built for Catholic pilgrims. I was up on the hillside, and I saw written upon a wall these words—'And there was a garden.' It was written in Latin. I pushed open the door of this garden. It was like any other garden, but the moment I entered there was a hand with the words, 'And in the garden there was a new tomb.' Then I saw a tomb which had been newly painted, and when I came up to it I read thereon, 'A new tomb wherein never man lay.' I then stooped down to look inside the tomb, and I read in Latin the inscription, 'Stooping down, he looked, yet went he not in.' But there were the words written, 'Come, see the place where the Lord lay.' I went in and I saw there, graven in stone, the napkin and the linen clothes laid by themselves. I was all alone and I read the words, 'He is not here, for he is risen,' graven on the floor of the tomb. Though I dread anything scenic, histrionic and popish, yet certainly I realised very much the reality of the scene, as I did this afternoon in standing before the open tomb. I felt that Jesus Christ was really buried, really laid in the earth, and has really gone out of it; it is good for us to come and see the place where Jesus lay.

FOR MEDITATION: While it is right to concentrate on the death and resurrection of the Lord Jesus Christ, we ought not to forget what happened to him in between (1 Corinthians 15:4). Meditate on his tomb as a place where he was identified with the wicked (Isaiah 53:9) and where repentant sinners can be identified with him (Romans 6:4; Colossians 2:12).

N.B. During the afternoon Spurgeon and others had attended the funeral of a deacon at Norwood Cemetery, where Spurgeon himself was to be buried in 1892.

Lessons from nature

'Where the birds make their nests: as for the stork, the fir trees are her house. The high hills are a refuge for the wild goats; and the rocks for the conies.' Psalm 104:17–18
SUGGESTED FURTHER READING: Psalm 8:1–9

This Psalm is all through a song of nature, the adoration of God in the great outward temple of the universe. Some in these modern times have thought it to be a mark of high spirituality never to observe nature; I remember sorrowfully reading the expressions of a godly person, who, in sailing down one of the most famous rivers in the world, closed his eyes, lest the picturesque beauties of the scene should divert his mind from scriptural topics. This may be regarded by some as profound spirituality; to me it seems to savour of absurdity. There may be persons who think they have grown in grace when they have attained to this; it seems to me that they are growing out of their senses. To despise the creating work of God, what is it but, in a measure, to despise God himself? 'Whoso mocketh the poor reproacheth his Maker'. To despise the Maker, then, is evidently a sin; to think little of God under the aspect of the Creator is a crime. None of us should think it a great honour to ourselves if our friends considered our productions to be unworthy of admiration and injurious rather than improving to their minds. If, when they passed our workmanship, they turned their eyes away, lest they should suffer injury by looking at it, we should not regard them as very respectful to ourselves; surely the despising of that which is made is somewhat akin to the despising of the Maker himself. The psalmist tells us that 'the Lord shall rejoice in his works.' If he rejoices in what he has made, shall not those who have communion with him rejoice in his works also? 'The works of the Lord are great, sought out of all them that have pleasure therein.' Despise not the work, lest you despise the worker.

FOR MEDITATION: To worship and serve the creature more than the Creator is wicked (Romans 1:25), but there is no need to go to the other extreme. The things God has created have valuable lessons to teach us about God (Job 12:7–9; Romans 1:20) and point us in the direction of praising him (Psalm 8:1; 19:1; 104:24).

Ripe fruit

'My soul desired the first ripe fruit.' Micah 7:1
SUGGESTED FURTHER READING: 1 Corinthians 13:1–13

We shall, as we ripen in grace, have greater sweetness towards our fellow Christians. Bitter-spirited Christians may know a great deal, but they are immature. Those who are quick to censure may be very acute in judgment, but they are as yet very immature in heart. He who grows in grace remembers that he is but dust, and he therefore does not expect his fellow Christians to be anything more; he overlooks ten thousand of their faults, because he knows that his God overlooks twenty thousand in his own case. He does not expect perfection in the creature, and, therefore, he is not disappointed when he does not find it. As he sometimes has to say of himself, 'This is my infirmity,' so he often says of his brethren, 'This is their infirmity,' and he does not judge them as he once did. I know we who are young beginners in grace think ourselves qualified to reform the whole Christian church. We drag her before us and condemn her straightway; but when our virtues become more mature, I trust we shall not be more tolerant of evil, but more tolerant of infirmity, more hopeful for the people of God and certainly less arrogant in our criticisms. Sweetness towards sinners is another sign of ripeness; when the Christian loves the souls of men, when he feels that there is nothing in the world which he cares for so much as endeavouring to bring others to a knowledge of the saving truth, when he can lay himself out for sinners, bear with their ill-manners, bear with anything, so that he might lead them to the Saviour, then is the man mature in grace. God grant this sweetness to us all. Put all these together—a holy calm, cheerfulness, patience, a walk with God, fellowship with Jesus, an anointing from the Holy One—and I call them sweetness, heavenly lusciousness, the full-flavouredness of Christ. May this be in you and abound.

FOR MEDITATION: If God can take our infirmities into account (Romans 8:26; Hebrews 4:15), we ought to be able to make some allowance for the infirmities of others with the aim of building them up (Romans 15:1–2). The apostle Paul's authority was for the purpose of edification, not for destruction (2 Corinthians 10:8; 13:10), but those who think they know it all puff up rather than build up (1 Corinthians 8:1–2).

SERMON NO. 945

Serving the Lord

'Serving the Lord.' Romans 12:11
SUGGESTED FURTHER READING: Philippians 2:19–30

It is vitally needful that in all our service we sincerely and simply render our obedience to the Lord himself. Much that is done religiously is not done unto God. A sermon may be preached and contain excellent truth, and the language in which the truth is stated may be everything that could be desired, yet the service rendered may be to the hearers or to the man's own self, and not to God at all. You may go to your Sunday-school class and with great perseverance you may instruct those little children, but yet you may have served your fellow teachers or the general community rather than serving your God. To whom do you look for a reward? Whose smile is it that gladdens you? Whose frown would depress you? Whose honour do you seek in all that you are doing? Remember that which is uppermost in your heart is your master. If your deepest motive is to seem to be active, to appear to be diligent and to win commendation for taking your share in the church's work, you have not served God; you have sacrificed unto others. This is a point which, though it is very simple to speak of, is very searching indeed if it be brought home to heart and conscience, for then much of that which glitters will be found not to be gold, and the glory of much apparently excellent serving will dissolve in smoke. The Lord must be the sole object of your labour; the pursuit of his glory must, like a clear crystal stream, run through the whole of your life, or you are not yet his servant. Sinister motives and selfish aims are the death of true godliness; search and look, lest these betray you unawares.

FOR MEDITATION: Those who set out to serve men and who employ flattery as a means to that end have their reward, but they are not servants of Christ (Romans 16:17–18; Galatians 1:10). The approach taken by the apostle Paul is the one to follow (1 Thessalonians 2:4–6).

The sieve

'For, lo, I will command, and I will sift the house of Israel among all nations, like as corn is sifted in a sieve, yet shall not the least grain fall upon the earth.' Amos 9:9
SUGGESTED FURTHER READING: Proverbs 3:9–12

The farmer does not sift his wheat because he dislikes it, but just the opposite; he sifts it because it is precious. Child of God, your trials, changes, constant catastrophes and afflictions are no proof of lack of affection on the part of the Most High, but the very contrary. 'As many as I love, I rebuke and chasten'. It is because you are gold that you are in the crucible, and because you are wheat you are put in the sieve. Another man might have been much happier and more peaceful than you as to outward circumstances; I say not that he could have had a real peace like yours, which you possess within your heart; that is a different matter. But he might have had eyes standing out with fatness, possessing more than heart could wish; he might have spread himself like a green bay tree, being prosperous in life and having no bands in death, whereas you, as one of God's people, are often chastened, afflicted, tried and troubled. But you must reflect that there is great wrath in God's apparent mercy to the wicked; God is but fattening them like bullocks for the slaughter; but as for you, there is no divine wrath in your tribulation; it is all sent in love; love is in every loss, every bereavement, every bodily pain, nothing but love, even when the cup is bitterest. There is another thought also that may cheer you, that it cannot be the purpose of the husbandman to destroy the grain when he puts it into the sieve. I never heard of any farmer so doing. If he meant to burn it or let it rot, he would not take the trouble to sift it; it cannot be his intention to destroy it if he sifts it. And so, poor, timid believer, the Lord does not intend to destroy you by these trials. 'A bruised reed shall he not break'; he may bruise it, but not break it; 'and the smoking flax shall he not quench'. He will chasten, but not destroy. He will bring you low, but he will yet appear for your deliverance.

FOR MEDITATION: Even when Satan demands that the sieve be placed into his destructive hands, the Lord remains in control and is more than able to preserve his precious wheat (Job 1:12; 2:6; Luke 22:31–32).

SERMON NO. 825

A visit to the harvest field

'Be patient therefore, brethren, unto the coming of the Lord. Behold, the husbandman waiteth for the precious fruit of the earth, and hath long patience for it, until he receive the early and latter rain. Be ye also patient; stablish your hearts: for the coming of the Lord draweth nigh.' James 5:7–8
SUGGESTED FURTHER READING: Psalm 37:1–9

There is a story told of Mr Hill being on board a vessel once. It is said he heard the mate swear and afterwards he heard the captain use a profane oath. I think Mr Hill interposed as the captain was about to swear again and said, 'No, let us be fair. Your mate has sworn and you have had an oath. Now it is my turn to swear.' The captain looked at him somewhat astonished, but had to admit that there was a degree of rightness and propriety in every man having his turn. However, Mr Hill did not swear and the captain said, 'I suppose, sir, you don't mean to take your turn; you don't mean to swear.' 'Oh yes,' said the good old man, 'I mean to swear as soon as ever I can see the good of it.' We might do the same with our impatience. Let us be impatient as soon as ever we can see the use it will serve. If the farmer should want rain just now, his impatience would not influence the clouds and make them pour out their torrents. If a child happened to be very petulant, and have a very noisy tongue and a mischievous disposition, the mother's impatience would not calm the child, control its temper, still its fitful passion or subdue its stubborn humour. Whatever happens to you, there is nothing can happen to you worse than your being impatient, for of all troubles in the world that one can be troubled with, an impatient spirit is about the worst. O that you would endeavour to conquer impatience. It cast Satan out of heaven, when he was impatient at the honour and dignity of the Son of God. He was impatient at being a servant to his Maker and was driven from his high estate. Let us be rid of impatience which made Cain kill his brother and which has done a thousand mischievous things since. May God grant us to watch and wait patiently like the husbandman.

FOR MEDITATION: Anxiety and impatience are powerless to promote physical growth (Luke 12:25–26), but they are without doubt able to stunt the spiritual growth which patience can produce (Romans 5:3–4; James 1:3–4; 2 Peter 1:6).

A call for revival

'Come my beloved, let us go forth into the field; let us lodge in the villages. Let us get up early to the vineyards; let us see if the vine flourish, whether the tender grape appear, and the pomegranates bud forth.' Song of Solomon 7:11–12
SUGGESTED FURTHER READING: John 4:31–42

Travelling along our island just now you see everywhere the sickle or the reaping machine in full work; harvest whitens the plains; everywhere the loaded wagons are bearing home the precious fruits of the earth. My spirit is stirred within me and my soul is on flame, for I see everywhere a harvest except in the church of Christ. Reapers are busy everywhere except in the fields of our divine Boaz. All fields are ripe, but those of Bethlehem; all barns are filling but those of the Great Husbandman; Christ Jesus has scarce a sheaf ingathered of late; we hear of very few results from the sacred sowing of the word. Here and there the church, like Ruth, gathers an ear, a very precious ear it is true, for who shall estimate the value of a single soul? But we have no wave-sheafs as in the days of Pentecost, or, if we have them, they are few and far between; and as for the harvest home which we have so long expected, our eyes fail in looking for it in vain. The time when our churches can operate extensively with the greatest convenience will soon be upon us. We do not usually look for any great things during the summer, when congregations are scattered at the seaside. The summer of nature is the winter of the Church and the earth's winter is our harvest. These warm days will soon be gone and the long evenings will come and with them abounding opportunities of doing good. I would urge you all to sharpen your sickles and to prepare for the appointed weeks of our harvest with good hope and prayerful confidence. May God, by his Holy Spirit, inspire you with zeal for the work which awaits you, and give you to walk in fellowship with Jesus in all that you do.

FOR MEDITATION: Are you looking forward to the spiritual opportunities of a new term or session following your summer break? At times of harvest the Lord Jesus Christ instructed his followers to pray, then to go (Luke 10:2–3). This was the pattern they followed before reaping three thousand souls on the Day of Pentecost (Acts 1:8,14).

SERMON NO. 1066

Helps

'And God hath set some in the church, first apostles, secondarily prophets, thirdly teachers, after that miracles, then gifts of healings, helps, governments, diversities of tongues.' 1 Corinthians 12:28
SUGGESTED FURTHER READING (Spurgeon): Romans 12:6–13

'God hath set some in the church, first apostles' to go from place to place founding churches and ordaining ministers. There were 'secondarily prophets,' some of whom uttered prophecies, while others were gifted in their explanation. Then came 'thirdly teachers,' probably either pastors settled in churches teaching the Word, or evangelists journeying about and proclaiming the truth. Then came 'after that miracles, then gifts of healings,' and the apostle mentions another class of persons, called 'helps'. I suppose it would be very difficult to tell who precisely these people were. Some have thought they were assistant-ministers, who occasionally aided settled pastors in the pastoral work of visiting and in preaching the Word. Others have thought that they were assistant-deacons and perhaps even deaconesses. Others have supposed these 'helps' to have been attendants in the sanctuary, who took care that strangers were properly accommodated, and who managed those details which must be superintended in connection with any public gathering of people. But whoever they were, they appear to have been a useful body of people, worthy to be mentioned in the same verse as apostles, teachers, miracle-workers and those with gifts of healings. It strikes me that they were not people who had any official standing, but that they were only moved by the natural impulse and the divine life within them to do anything which would assist teacher, pastor or deacon in the work of the Lord. They were the sort of brethren who are useful anywhere, who can always stop a gap, and who are only too glad when they find that they can make themselves serviceable to the church of God in any capacity whatever.

FOR MEDITATION: Paul commended those who helped him (Romans 16:1–4) and encouraged this ministry (Philippians 4:3), as did John (3 John 5–8). 'Deaconing' is a function of all the saints (Matthew 27:55–56; Luke 8:2–3; 2 Corinthians 8:1–4; Ephesians 4:12; Hebrews 6:10), not limited to those appointed to the office of deacon (1 Timothy 3:10,13). Whom do you help?

Christis all

'Christ is all, and in all.' Colossians 3:11
SUGGESTED FURTHER READING: 1 Corinthians 15:19–28

Christ is the channel of all, the pledge of all, the sum of all. The *channel* of all. All love and mercy flow from God through Christ the mediator. We get nothing apart from him: 'no man cometh unto the Father, but by me.' Other conduits are dry, but this channel is always full: 'he is able also to save them to the uttermost that come unto God by him, seeing he ever liveth to make intercession for them.' Christ is the *pledge* of all. When God gave us Christ, he did as much as say, 'I have given you all things.' 'He that spared not his own Son, but delivered him up for us all, how shall he not with him also freely give us all things?' He is a covenant to us, the title-deeds of the promised rest. And, indeed, Christ is not only the channel of all and the pledge of all, but the apostle says he 'is all'; so I take it he is the *sum* of all. If you are going to travel on the Continent, you need not carry a bed with you, nor a house, nor a table, nor medicine, nor food; if you only have money in your purse, you have these condensed. Money is the representation of everything it can buy; it is a kind of universal talisman, producing what its owner wishes for. I have never yet met with a person in any country who did not understand its meaning: 'money answereth all things', says the wise man (Ecclesiastes 10:19), and this is true in a limited sense; but he that has Christ has indeed all things: he has the essence, the substance of all good. I have only to plead the name of Jesus before the Father's throne, and nothing desirable shall be denied me. If Christ is yours, 'all things are your's'. God, who gave you Christ, has in that one gift summed up the total of all you will want for time and for eternity, to obliterate the sin of the past, to fulfil the needs of the present, and to perfect you for all the work and bliss of the future.

FOR MEDITATION: The Lord Jesus Christ is not only 'all, and in all', but 'before all' (Colossians 1:17), 'over all' (Romans 9:5) and 'above all' (Ephesians 1:21). All things are by him and for him (1 Corinthians 8:6; Colossians 1:16). Do you acknowledge him in your life as your 'all in all'?

N.B. This text was left by the late deacon Thomas Cook for the pastors—see also 6 August.

SERMON NO. 1006

Seeking for Jesus

'Seeking for Jesus.' John 6:24
SUGGESTED FURTHER READING: John 5:32–47

I have known people who have been content to remain seekers all their days. They have felt comforted by the thought that they are seekers. Now, such comfort is daubed with untempered mortar. A man out of employment has been walking up and down the London streets to find something to do. His family is in need and he must find a situation. He is quite right to seek, but he will not be satisfied with seeking; he wants to find. Tramping the street will not feed his children. He is not contented with having called at many shops; he will not rest till he finds what he is after—he would be very foolish if he did. So to be a seeker after Christ, walking up and down the streets as it were, will not fill your hungry soul; you must get Christ himself. If any unemployed father of a family were to say, 'Well, I walk about so many days in the week and so many hours in the day, and I am quite satisfied, though I do not find anything to do,' you would think him a great simpleton. And so with you. It is a good sign when there is an appetite, but a mere appetite does not satisfy a man; he must eat the food provided. Your seeking Christ will not save you, unless it leads you in very deed to believe in Jesus. It is an ill sign when a man says, 'Well, I am doing my best. I am always at a place of worship, I am a Bible reader, I practise prayer at home. I do my best.' My dear friend, if you settle down in that idea, you are self-righteous and are off the road altogether; besides, you are lying to your own heart, for after all you are at enmity with God and the sign of that enmity is this, that you refuse to believe on his dear Son. If you were reconciled to God, you would love Jesus Christ and trust in him.

FOR MEDITATION: Beware of being one of those who are 'ever learning, and never able to come to the knowledge of the truth' (2 Timothy 3:7), and who even search the Scriptures but refuse to come to Christ (John 5:39–40). It is a tragedy to fail to obtain what you are seeking (Romans 11:7), especially if an inadequate seeking of Jesus results in dying in your sins (John 8:21).

SERMON NO. 947

A door opened in heaven

'After this I looked, and, behold, a door was opened in heaven.'
Revelation 4:1
SUGGESTED FURTHER READING (Spurgeon): Revelation 5:6–14

I think I may say that a door has often been opened in heaven to us at the communion-table. Astronomers select the best spots for observatories; they like elevated places which are free from traffic, so that their instruments may not quiver with the rumbling of wheels; they prefer also to be away from the smoke of manufacturing towns, that they may discern the orbs of heaven more clearly. Surely, if any one place is fitter to be an observatory for a heaven-mind than another, it is the table of communion.

'I have been there, and still will go,
'Tis like a little heaven below.'

Christ may hide himself from his people in preaching, as he did from his disciples on the road to Emmaus, but he made himself known unto them in breaking of bread. Prize much the solemn breaking of bread. That ordinance has been perverted, travestied and profaned; and hence some tender Christians scarcely value it at its right account. To those who will use it rightly, examining themselves and so coming to that table, it is indeed a divine observatory, a place of calm retirement from the world. The elements of bread and wine become the lenses of a far-seeing telescope, through which we behold the Saviour; and I say again, if there be one spot of earth clear from the smoke of care, it is the table where saints have fellowship with their Lord. A door is often opened in heaven at this banquet, when his banner over us is love; but if it be so sweet to enjoy the emblem, what must it be to live with Christ himself and drink the wine new with him in the kingdom of our Father!

FOR MEDITATION: When the Lord Jesus Christ instituted the Lord's Supper, his mind soared heavenwards as he anticipated his Father's coming kingdom (Luke 22:16,18). At the communion table we can have something of the same experience (1 Corinthians 11:26) if we have the mind of Christ.

The faculty baffled—the Great Physician successful

'And a certain woman, which had an issue of blood twelve years, and had suffered many things of many physicians, and had spent all that she had, and was nothing bettered, but rather grew worse, when she had heard of Jesus, came in the press behind, and touched his garment. For she said, If I may touch but his clothes, I shall be whole.' Mark 5:25–28
SUGGESTED FURTHER READING: Mark 9:14–29

This woman said to herself, 'The way of cure is for me to get near to Jesus; I can see that doctors are of no good. I cannot help myself, neither can all the world besides assist me. I must press to get near to him. If I cannot put my arms around him, yet a little of him is enough. If I cannot press to him so as to lay hold of him with my hand, yet as much as I can touch with my finger will be enough. I know if I cannot touch him, if I can but get near the ravellings of his garment and touch one of them, it will do.' It is a sweet truth that the least of Christ will save. If your faith is such a poor trembling thing that it is hardly fit to be called faith, yet if it connects you with Christ, you shall have the virtue that goes out from him. For remember it was not this woman's finger that saved her, but it was Christ whom she touched. True, the healing came by the act of faith, but the act of faith is not the healing; the healing all lies in the person, so that you are not to be looking to your faith, but to Jesus the Lord. Has your faith a good object? Are you resting in Jesus, God's Son, God's appointed propitiation? If so, your faith will bring you to heaven; it is good enough. The strongest faith a man ever had damned him, if it did not rest on Christ; the weakest faith ever man or woman had would certainly save, if it did but terminate in the precious person and all-sufficient work of Jesus.

FOR MEDITATION: Our faith may be weak (Romans 14:1) and we may feel the need for it to be increased (Luke 17:5), but even 'little faith' will prove to be saving faith if its sole object is the Lord Jesus Christ (Matthew 8:25–26; 14:30–31).

SERMON NO. 827

The resurrection credible

'Why should it be thought a thing incredible with you, that God should raise the dead?' Acts 26:8
SUGGESTED FURTHER READING: 1 Corinthians 15:50–58

I am quite certain that there are many wonders in the world which we should not have believed by mere report, if we had not come across them by experience and observation. The electric telegraph, though it be but an invention of man, would have been as hard to believe in a thousand years ago as the resurrection of the dead is now. Who in the days of packhorses would have believed in flashing a message from England to America? When our missionaries in tropical countries have told the natives of the formation of ice, and that people could walk across frozen water, and of ships that have been surrounded by mountains of ice in the open sea, the water becoming solid and hard as a rock all around them, the natives have refused to believe such absurd reports. Everything is wonderful till we are used to it, and resurrection owes the incredible portion of its marvel to the fact of our never having come across it in our observation—that is all. After the resurrection we shall regard it as a divine display of power as familiar to us as creation and providence are now. I have no doubt we shall adore and bless God, and wonder at resurrection for ever, but it will be in the same sense in which every devout mind wonders at creation now. We shall grow accustomed to this new work of God when we have entered upon our longer life. We were only born but yesterday and have seen little as yet. God's works require far more than our few earthly years of observation, and when we have entered into eternity, are out of our minority and have come of age, that which astounds us now will have become a familiar theme for praise.

FOR MEDITATION: The fact that we cannot understand something perfectly now does not mean that this will remain the case for ever (1 Corinthians 13:12). Even those closest to the Lord Jesus Christ had to learn that some things could not be taken in at the time, but would be made clear to them later (John 13:7,36; 16:12–13).

N.B. The American inventor Thomas Alva Edison (1847–1931) introduced his telegraph in 1872, the year in which this sermon was preached.

SERMON NO. 1067

The great assize

'For we must all appear before the judgment seat of Christ; that everyone may receive the things done in his body, according to that he hath done, whether it be good or bad.' 2 Corinthians 5:10
SUGGESTED FURTHER READING (Spurgeon): Matthew 25:31–46

If your faith is in Jesus, if you love Jesus, if your heart goes out to Jesus, if your life is influenced by Jesus, if you make him your example as well as your Saviour, there will be evidence; you cannot see it, but there will be evidence in your favour. For notice those gracious things, when the evidence was brought, and Christ said, 'I was an hungred, and ye gave me meat: I was thirsty, and ye gave me drink:' they said, 'O Lord, we never knew this.' Should any man stand up and say, 'I have plenty of evidence to prove my faith,' I should reply, 'Hold your tongue, sir! I am afraid you have no faith at all, or you would not be talking about your evidence.' But if you are saying, 'I am afraid I have not the evidence that will stand me in good stead at the last,' yet, if all the while you have been feeding the hungry, clothing the naked and doing all you can for Christ, I would tell you not to be afraid. The master will find witnesses to say, 'That man relieved me when I was in poverty. He knew I was one of Christ's and he came and helped me.' And another will come and say (perhaps it will be an angel), ' I saw him when he was alone in his chamber and heard him pray for his enemies.' And the Lord will say, 'I read his heart when I saw how he put up with rebuke, slander and persecution, and would not make any answer for my sake. He did it all as evidence that my grace was in his heart.' You will not have to fetch up the witnesses: the judge will call them, for he knows all about your case; and as he calls up the witnesses, you will be surprised to find how even the ungodly will be obliged to consent to the just salvation of the righteous.

FOR MEDITATION: 'For not he that commendeth himself is approved, but whom the Lord commendeth' (2 Corinthians 10:18). This was so during our Lord's life on earth (Mark 12:41–44; 14:3–9; Luke 7:2–9), it is still so now (Matthew 6:2–6,16–18) and it will be so at the last judgment (Matthew 7:21–23). He takes notice of the evidence given by others (Matthew 18:23–35; Luke 7:3–6).

SERMON NO. 1076

A cheerful giver beloved of God

'God loveth a cheerful giver.' 2 Corinthians 9:7
SUGGESTED FURTHER READING: 1 Chronicles 29:6–18

What is meant by 'a cheerful giver'? The rest of the verse tells us what is not meant and so helps us to see what is intended: 'not grudgingly, or of necessity: for God loveth a cheerful giver.' Not grudgingly—not giving as though you wished you could avoid it, and therefore giving as little as possible, counting the pence and reckoning them to be as precious as drops of blood, but giving with an ease, a spontaneousness, a freeness, a pleasure; this is a cheerful giver. To be this one must give proportionately, for cheerful givers reckon how much they should give and how much as good stewards may be expected at their hands. He who has a large income gives grudgingly if he gives no more than one who has but a tenth as much. He who has few expenses and lives at a small cost cannot be said to give cheerfully, if he gives no more than another man who has a large family and large outgoings. He evidently gives grudgingly if he does not give in proportion. Much has been said about giving the tenth of one's income to the Lord. That seems to me to be a Christian duty which none should for a moment question. If it were a duty under the Jewish law, much more is it so now under the Christian dispensation. But it is a great mistake to suppose that the Jew only gave a tenth. He gave very much more than that. The tenth was the payment which he *must* make, but after that came all the freewill offerings and all the various gifts at different seasons of the year, so that, perhaps, he gave a third, certainly much nearer that than a tenth. I do not, however, like to lay down any rules for God's people, for the Lord's New Testament is not a great book of rules; it is not a book of the letter, 'for the letter killeth', but it is the book of the Spirit, teaching us rather the soul of liberality than the body of it; instead of writing laws upon stones or paper, it writes laws upon the heart. Give, dear friends, as you have purposed in your heart, and give proportionately, as the Lord has prospered you.

FOR MEDITATION: As far as possible our giving to God should be private (Matthew 6:3–4), but nowadays when many give by cheque or banker's order, a few may be in on the secret and see how much we give. But God alone measures how cheerfully we give in the light of his knowledge of how much we retain (Mark 12:41–44).

SERMON NO. 835

Love's logic

'We love him, because he first loved us.' 1 John 4:19
SUGGESTED FURTHER READING: Romans 8:31–39

God loves me—not merely bears with me, thinks of me and feeds me, but loves me. It is a very sweet thing to feel that we have the love of a dear wife or kind husband; and there is much sweetness in the love of a fond child or a tender mother; but to think that God loves me, this is infinitely better! Who is it that loves you? God, the Maker of heaven and earth, the Almighty, All in all, does he love me, even he? If all men, all angels and all the living creatures that are before the throne loved me, that would be nothing to this—the Infinite loves me! And who is it that he loves? Me. The text says 'us.' 'We love him, because he first loved us.' But this is the personal point—he loves me, an insignificant nobody, full of sin, who deserved to be in hell and who loves him so little in return—God loves me. Beloved believer, does this not melt you? Does this not fire your soul? I know it does if it is really believed. It must. And how did he love me? He loved me so that he gave up his only begotten Son for me, to be nailed to the tree and made to bleed and die. And what will come of it? Why, because he loved me and forgave me, I am on the way to heaven and within a few months, perhaps days, I shall see his face and sing his praises. He loved me before I was born; before a star began to shine he loved me and he has never ceased to do so all these years. When I have sinned he has loved me; when I have forgotten him he has loved me; and when in the days of my sin I cursed him, yet still he loved me; and he will love me when my knees tremble and my hair is grey with age; 'even to hoar hairs' he will bear and carry his servant; and he will love me when the world is on a blaze, and love me for ever and for ever.

FOR MEDITATION: Can you rejoice like this in God the Father who so loved us that he gave his only begotten Son (John 3:16; 1 John 4:10)? That will depend on whether you have obeyed God by trusting in his Son who so loved us that he gave himself for our sins upon the cross (Galatians 2:20; Ephesians 5:2; 1 John 3:16).

SERMON NO. 1008

A string of pearls

'Blessed be the God and Father of our Lord Jesus Christ, which according to his abundant mercy hath begotten us again unto a lively hope by the resurrection of Jesus Christ from the dead.' 1 Peter 1:3
SUGGESTED FURTHER READING: Psalm 145:1–21

Show your gratitude and joy by blessing God. Bless him with your voices. Singing is heaven's work; practise it here. At your work, if you can, quietly raise a hymn and bless the Lord. But keep the fire on the altar of your hearts always burning. Praise him; bless him; 'his mercy endureth for ever', so let your praises endure. Bless him also with your substance. Do not give him mere words; they are but air, and tongues but clay. Give him the best you have. In the old superstitious times the churches used to be adorned with the rarest pearls and jewels, with treasures of gold and silver, for men then gave mines of wealth to what they believed to be the service of God. Shall the true faith have less operative power upon us? Shall the 'lively hope' make us do less for God than the mere dead hope of the followers of Rome? No, let us be generous at all times and count it our joy to sacrifice unto our God. Let us give him our efforts, our time and our talents. Bless the Lord, you Sunday-school teachers. Teach those dear children under a sense of your own obligations to God. You who go from house to house, you who preach in the streets, preach as those who are begotten unto a lively hope by the abundant mercy of God. Preacher, live more intensely and ardently than you have ever done. Deacons, serve the church more thoroughly than you have done as yet. Elders, give your whole souls to the care of Christ's flock, which he has redeemed with his blood. Workers for Jesus Christ, work not for him in an ordinary way, as men do for a master whose pay is no larger than he can be compelled to make it, but work with heart, soul and strength for him who loved you to the death and poured out his soul to redeem you from going down into hell. Thus prove that the divine nature is truly in you and that you possess the 'lively hope' implanted 'by the resurrection of Jesus Christ from the dead'.

FOR MEDITATION: We bless him because he first blessed us. Blessing God should come naturally to us if we have an appreciation of all the blessings he has already given us (Ephesians 1:3) and an assurance that he has blessings to give us in the future (Psalm 115:12–15,18; 134:1–3).

SERMON NO. 948

The silken fetter

'Fear the LORD *and his goodness.'* Hosea 3:5
SUGGESTED FURTHER READING (Spurgeon): Psalm 103:13–22

Many a man has put his trust in his riches and has presumed against the Most High; because he has enjoyed long years of success, he believes that no evil can befall him, but his pride towers aloft even to the very heavens. Alas, even in those men who are right-hearted, in whom grace reigns, it has too often happened that the goodness of God has not wrought in them a corresponding gracious result. Hezekiah was endowed with riches and displayed them with ostentatious pride: instead of honouring his God in the presence of the ambassadors that came from far, he sought only to give them a high idea of himself, and thus by the pride of his heart he brought upon himself a stern rebuke from his Lord. Asa prospered, but when he was lifted up in outward circumstances, he became also lifted up in heart and departed from the Most High. Even good men cannot always carry a full cup without some spilling. Even those whose hearts are right have not always found their heads steady enough to stand with safety upon the pinnacles of prosperity and honour. Yet, my brethren, though these things do occur as the results of the goodness of God, on account of the evil of our hearts, yet the true and right effect of goodness upon us ought to be to make us fear God, not to lift us up but to keep us down, not to make our blood hot with presumption but to cool and calm it with a grateful jealousy, not to exhilarate us unduly until we become profanely defiant but to sober us with conscious responsibility till we humbly sit with gratitude at the feet of him from whom our good things have proceeded. This then is to be the right and proper result of the goodness of God upon our hearts.

FOR MEDITATION: God's goodness ought to result in our repentance (Romans 2:4). Does God's goodness lead you to fear him (Psalm 33:5,8), to bless him (Psalm 107:8–9; 144:1–2—see also 28 August) and to serve him (Nehemiah 9:35—see also 15 August)?

SERMON NO. 888

Dying daily

'I die daily.' 1 Corinthians 15:31
SUGGESTED FURTHER READING: 2 Corinthians 13:5–10

Alas for that evil habit of looking back a few years ago and believing that we were then converted, and reckoning that it must be all right now because of something that happened then! It is most mischievous to live in the past and to be afraid to try our faith by present tests. We may live on experience if we will use experience in its proper place, but any man who is afraid to search present evidences and to try the foundation of his faith before God today, is treating his soul most wretchedly. How would you like to die today with a hope too weak and tender to endure to be questioned? Can you enter into eternity with a hope that you dare not put into the crucible? No, you feel you want sure work when it comes to the last; you need a safe and stable foundation to build your soul upon in the trying moment. Well then, see that your hope is stable now. Each day examine yourself whether you be in the faith, whether you have really repented of sin, whether you have actually and truly laid hold of Jesus Christ; search; see whether the root of the matter is in you, whether the fruit of the Spirit proceeds from you, whether God dwells in you, whether you walk after the flesh or after the Spirit. I would not foment doubts and fears, but I would press professors to avoid presumption. The man who is in a sound business does not object to overhaul his stock and examine his books, but the man to whom bankruptcy is imminent generally seeks to shut his eyes to his actual position. If you are right with God, you will desire to be quite sure; you will not flinch at heart-searching preaching; you will be anxious to be put into the sieve and to be tried even as by fire; your prayer will be, 'Cleanse thou me from secret faults.' 'Search me, O God, and know my heart'.

FOR MEDITATION: Even David, a man after God's own heart (1 Samuel 13:14; Acts 13:22), submitted himself to God for examination (Psalm 26:2; 139:23–24). He told his son Solomon to serve God, who searches every heart, wholeheartedly (1 Chronicles 28:9), no doubt recalling how Saul had fallen away despite a youthful change of heart (1 Samuel 10:9) and the time when he himself had needed a clean heart (Psalm 51:10). Sadly Solomon's heart in later years also turned away from God (1 Kings 11:1–4). Be warned!

SERMON NO. 828

Grace—the one way of salvation

'But we believe that through the grace of the Lord Jesus Christ we shall be saved, even as they.' Acts 15:11
SUGGESTED FURTHER READING: Galatians 2:7–16

A company of Jews have assembled to discuss a certain matter; some of them look very wise and bring up certain suggestions that are rather significant. They say, 'Well, perhaps these Gentile dogs may be saved; yes, Jesus Christ told us to go and preach the gospel to every creature; therefore, no doubt, he must have included these Gentile dogs. We do not like them, though, and must keep them as much under our rules and regulations as we can; we must compel them to be circumcised; we must have them brought under the full rigour of the law; we cannot excuse them from wearing the yoke of bondage.' Presently the apostle Peter gets up to speak, and you expect to hear him say to these gentlemen, 'Why, these 'Gentile dogs', as you call them, can be saved, even as *you*.' No; he adopts quite a different tone; he turns the tables and he says to them, 'we believe that you may be saved, even as they.' It was just as if I should have a company of persons here now who had been very bad and wicked and who had plunged into the deepest sin, but God's grace has met with them and made them new creatures in Christ Jesus: there is a church-meeting, and when these persons are brought before the church, suppose there were some of the members who should say, 'Yes, we believe that a drunkard may be saved, and a person who has been a harlot may, *perhaps*, be saved too.' But imagine that I were to stand up and reply, 'Now, my dear brethren, I believe that *you* may be saved even as *these*'— what a rebuke it would be! This is precisely what Peter meant. 'Oh' he said, 'do not raise the question about whether *they* can be saved; the question is whether *you*, who have raised such a question, will be saved'; 'we believe that through the grace of the Lord Jesus Christ we shall be saved, even as they.'

FOR MEDITATION: There are occasions when we need to take our eyes off others and mind our own spiritual business. Peter had learned this by experience (John 21:20–22) and Paul knew the wisdom of it in his own walk with God (1 Corinthians 9:27).

A simple remedy

'With his stripes we are healed.' Isaiah 53:5
SUGGESTED FURTHER READING: 2 Kings 5:1–14

Gospel healing is so very simple; our text describes it—'with his stripes we are healed.' These six words contain the marrow of the gospel, and yet scarcely one of them contains a second syllable. They are words for plain people, and in them there is no affectation of mystery or straining after the profound. I looked the other day into old Culpepper's Herbal. It contains a marvellous collection of wonderful remedies. Had this old herbalist's prescriptions been universally followed, there would not long have been any left to prescribe for; the astrological herbalist would soon have exterminated both sickness and mankind. Many of his receipts contain from twelve to twenty different drugs, each one needing to be prepared in a peculiar manner; I think I once counted forty different ingredients in one single draught. Very different are these receipts, with their elaboration of preparation, from the Biblical prescriptions which effectually healed the sick, such as 'take a lump of figs, and lay it for a plaister upon the boil,' or that other one 'Go and wash in Jordan seven times,' or that other 'take up thy bed, and walk.' One cannot but admire the simplicity of truth, while falsehood conceals her deformities with a thousand trickeries. If you would see Culpepper's Herbal carried out in spiritual things, go and buy a Directory for the carrying on of Ritualistic church services. You shall find there innumerable rules as to when you shall bow and to what quarter of the heavens you shall look, when you shall stand up and when you shall kneel, when you shall dress in black, in white, in blue or in violet, how you shall pray and what you shall pray, a collect being appointed for today and another for tomorrow. On the other hand, if you would know the true way of having your souls healed, go to the Word of God and study such a text as this: 'with his stripes we are healed.'

FOR MEDITATION: One of the beauties of the Christian gospel is that all the regulations governing Old Testament worship and sacrifices (Hebrews 9:1,9–10) were only temporary and have now been fulfilled and replaced by the single sacrifice of Christ upon the cross (Ephesians 2:15; Colossians 2:14). The Christian has no need to return to such rules and regulations (Colossians 2:16–17,20–21).

SERMON NO. 1068

Preach, preach, preach everywhere

'And he said unto them, Go ye into all the world, and preach the gospel to every creature. He that believeth and is baptized shall be saved; but he that believeth not shall be damned.' Mark 16:15–16
SUGGESTED FURTHER READING (Spurgeon): Romans 10:5–13

If a man would participate in the bounteous salvation which Christ has wrought, he must believe in Christ, he must trust Christ, he must believe Christ to be God's appointed Saviour and able to save him. He must act on that belief and trust himself in the hands of Jesus; if he does that he shall be saved. Further, the text says he must be baptised. Not that there is any virtue whatsoever in baptism, but it is a small thing for Christ to expect that the man trusting to be saved by him should own and avow his attachment to him. He that wishes to have Christ as his Saviour should be prepared openly to acknowledge that he is on Christ's side. Baptism thus becomes the badge of discipleship, the outward token of inward faith, by which a man says to all who look on, 'I confess myself dead to the world; I confess myself buried with Christ; I declare myself risen to newness of life in him; make what you will of it and laugh at it as much as you like, yet in the faith of Jesus as my Lord, I have taken leave of all else to follow him.' It is a point of obedience. Sometimes one has said in his heart, 'What a pity it is that baptism should have been introduced into this place; it makes a baulk of wood into which men may drive their ritualistic hook.' But then the Son of God himself has put it here and we cannot alter it. If it were not here, I would not have put it here, but it is here, and being here, it is at your soul's hazard to leave it out. I believe with all my heart that if you believe in Jesus Christ you will be saved, whether you are baptised or not, but I would not like to run the risk, mark you, for I have not got that in my text. It is, 'He that believeth and is baptized shall be saved'.

FOR MEDITATION: There are only two Gospel commands to obey in order to receive the forgiveness of sins—repentance from sin and faith in the Lord Jesus Christ (Mark 1:15; Acts 20:21), but the command to be baptised is linked to both as a public profession of genuine repentance and faith (Mark 16:16; Acts 2:38).

SERMON NO. 900

Travailing for souls

'As soon as Zion travailed, she brought forth her children.' Isaiah 66:8
SUGGESTED FURTHER READING: Philippians 3:17–21

A young man who had grown up and left the parental roof had been enticed into holding sceptical views. His parents were both earnest Christians and it almost broke their hearts to see their son so opposed to the Redeemer. On one occasion they induced him to go with them to hear a celebrated minister. He accompanied them simply to please them, and for no higher motive. The sermon happened to be upon the glories of heaven. It was a very extraordinary sermon and calculated to make every Christian in the audience leap for joy. The young man was much gratified with the eloquence of the preacher, but nothing more; he gave him credit for superior oratorical ability and was interested in the sermon, but felt none of its power. He chanced to look at his parents during the discourse and was surprised to see them weeping. He could not imagine why they, being Christians, should sit and weep under a sermon which was most jubilant in its strain. When he reached home, he said, 'Father, we have had a capital sermon, but I could not understand what could make you sit there and cry, and my mother too.' His father said, 'My dear son, I certainly had no reason to weep concerning myself, nor your mother, but I could not help thinking all through the sermon about you, for alas, I have no hope that you will be a partaker in the bright joys which await the righteous. It breaks my heart to think that you will be shut out of heaven.' His mother said, ' The very same thoughts crossed my mind, and the more the preacher spoke of the joys of the saved, the more I sorrowed for my dear boy that he should never know what they were.' That touched the young man's heart and led him to seek his father's God; and before long he was at the same communion table, rejoicing in the God and Saviour whom his parents worshipped.

FOR MEDITATION: When the seed of the Gospel is sown on hard soil, it sometimes takes the tears of God's people before there is any response (Psalm 126:5–6). The grief expressed by Jesus concerning Jerusalem's hardness of heart (Luke 13:34–35; 19:41–44) did not prevent its destruction in A.D. 70, but bore fruit in the breaking of many hearts and the conversion of three thousand on the Day of Pentecost (Acts 2:37–41).

SERMON NO. 1009

The unconquerable king

'I Nebuchadnezzar ... blessed the most High, and I praised and honoured him that liveth for ever, whose dominion is an everlasting dominion ...: and all the inhabitants of earth are reputed as nothing: and he doeth according to his will ...: and none can stay his hand.' Daniel 4:34–35
SUGGESTED FURTHER READING: Luke 1:46–55

What is the right spirit in which to contemplate all this? The first is *humble adoration*. Even in our public gatherings we do not have enough worship. O worship the King! Bow your heads now—bow your spirits rather and adore 'him that liveth for ever'. Your thoughts and emotions are better than bullocks and he-goats to be offered on the altar: God will accept them. Worship him with lowliest reverence, for you are nothing and he is all in all. Next let the spirit of your hearts be that of *unquestioning acquiescence*. He wills it! I will do it or I will bear it. God help you to live in perfect resignation. Next to that exercise the spirit of *reverent love*. Do I tremble before this God? Then I must seek more grace that I may love him as he is, not love him when my thoughts have diminished him of his splendour and robbed him of his glory, but love him even as an absolute sovereign, for I see that sovereignty exercised through Jesus Christ, my shield and his Anointed. Let me love my God and King, and be a courtier, happy to be admitted near his throne to behold the light of the Infinite Majesty. Lastly let our spirit be that of *profound delight*. I believe that to the advanced Christian there is no doctrine which contains such a deep sea of delight as this. The Lord reigns! The Lord is King for ever and ever! Why, then all is well. When you get away from God, you get away from peace. When the soul dives into him and feels that all is in him, then she feels a calm delight, a peace like a river, a joy unspeakable. Strive after that delight.

FOR MEDITATION: Think on God's glory as summarised in some of the great doxologies in the New Testament epistles (Romans 11:33–36; Ephesians 3:20–21; Jude 24–25).
    N.B. Spurgeon's text was appropriate to the surrender of Napoleon III to the King of Prussia, as reported in the previous night's papers. However, any connection was to be ascribed to the leading of the Holy Spirit, since Spurgeon chose the text on the morning before the news broke!

SERMON NO. 949

Real grace for real need

'He healed them that had need of healing.' Luke 9:11
SUGGESTED FURTHER READING: 1 John 3:4–16

'Thou shalt love the Lord thy God with all thy heart, and with all thy soul, and with all thy mind, and with all thy strength'. Are you keeping that? Why, you live as if there were no God; you know you do; day after day and even month after month, you never do anything to manifest love towards God. You have some love towards your relatives, but no passion like that is kindled in your spirit towards your God; you have no love at all, and yet the precept is, 'thou shalt love the Lord thy God with all thy heart'. Why, that one command is lodging charges against you at the bar of God every day. Indeed all the ten commandments you are constantly breaking; there is not one that you keep. These sins of yours are speeding as messengers up to the record office in heaven, and there you shall find written down every idle word, every sinful thought and every guilty action of your whole life. How will you bear to hear of all these in the latter days, when your body shall have arisen from the grave at the archangel's trumpet? How will you bear to hear the book read out that shall rehearse your sins? At the very thought of it your bones may be dissolved within you: sins against a righteous God, sins against his people, sins against his day, sins against his book, sins against your bodies, sins against your souls, sins of every kind, sins unseen of human eye, sins unknown to any but yourself and your God, all read and all proclaimed with trumpet voice while men and angels hear. You have need of healing, for you are scarlet, you are crimson, you are double-dyed with your iniquities. O that you knew this! O that you felt this! You have need of healing, and yet dark as the thought is, it gives me comfort, and it ought to give you comfort, to remember the text—Jesus 'healed them that had need of healing'; and if you are such, why should he not heal you?

FOR MEDITATION: We are all sinners who need spiritual healing. In the sacrifice of the Lord Jesus Christ God has provided the means for us to be healed (1 Peter 2:24). By commanding us to return to him God has prescribed for us the route by which we can be healed (Jeremiah 3:22; Hosea 6:1; 14:1,4). We can either be healed of our sin by returning to God (1 Peter 2:25), or reject his offer of healing by resisting him in unbelief (John 12:37–40).

SERMON NO. 889

The perfuming of the heart

'And hope maketh not ashamed; because the love of God is shed abroad in our hearts by the Holy Ghost which is given unto us.' Romans 5:5
SUGGESTED FURTHER READING: Isaiah 63:7–9

The pity of God towards the suffering I can understand, because of the goodness of his nature. The kindness of God towards the needy I can comprehend, because of the liberality of his character. That he should have compassion upon such as are ignorant and out of the way, that he should look constantly with tenderness upon those that are sore broken and ready to perish is easy enough for me to believe; but this is not what is spoken of in the text. It is not compassion, nor tenderness, nor pity, but it is love, which is something more than all these. You pity the beggar whom you could not love; you have compassion upon the villain in whom you could have no complacency; you look with tenderness upon sufferers who have nothing in their character or in their persons to attract your affection. Men usually think that they have gone far enough when they have rendered kindness, even if the heart glow with no affection, and they, as a rule, take this to be the rendering of love towards their neighbour; when they have permitted their compassion and tenderness to exhibit themselves, they feel that all is done that is demanded of them. But the text speaks not of this, but of love, direct attachment and affection, and of the love of God. I beseech you, lift up your souls, bid your understandings stand on tiptoe, and endeavour fully to grasp the idea of divine love. If you are in Christ Jesus, this day God loves you, but to what shall I liken love as it streams from the heart of Jehovah? We try to guess at what God's love to one of his people may be by our love to our own children, to our spouse, to our friend. Now in a far higher degree and sublimer sense, and after a loftier sort, even so God loves the people of his choice. Consider this, believer, and be astonished that love should come from God to such a one as yourself. The Lord loves you.

FOR MEDITATION: God kept telling his people Israel that he loved them (Isaiah 43:4; Jeremiah 31:3) and sent his messengers to tell them (Deuteronomy 7:8; 23:5). Yet they doubted him to his face (Malachi 1:2). Jesus assured his disciples that he had loved and would love them (John 13:34; 15:9,12). Do you have this assurance? There is a condition (John 14:21,23).

SERMON NO. 829

Serving the Lord with gladness

'Serve the Lord with gladness.' Psalm 100:2
SUGGESTED FURTHER READING: Colossians 3:16–4:1

By serving God we do not mean merely when we come to a place of worship; for to us, in one sense, there are no places of worship. All places are places of worship to a Christian; wherever he is, he ought to be in a worshipping frame of mind. When we serve God at the family altar, let us try as parents to mix gladness with it. It is a great mistake when the Christian parent makes the reading and prayer in the family a dull monotonous work. Let us be cheerful and happy at family worship. In your private devotions you should also 'Serve the Lord with gladness'. When you get half an hour or more with the Most High, ask him to enable you to carry out that command of this one hundredth Psalm— 'Serve the Lord with gladness'. But then the Christian's service for God lasts all the day long! The genuine Christian knows that he can serve God as much in the shop as he can in the meeting-house, and that the service of God can be carried on in the farmyard and market, while he is buying and selling, quite as well as in singing and praying. Should we not do our business much better if we looked upon it in that light? Would it not be a happy thing if, regarding all our work as serving God, we went about it with gladness? Perhaps your work is very hard; well, be not an eye-servant or a man-pleaser, but with singleness of heart serve God in that work, and you will perform it with gladness. Perhaps your situation is one in which your toil is very arduous. Consider that God has put you there. If you cannot see a door of removal, accept what God has given, and, accepting it from a Father's hand, you will be able to serve him with gladness. That is a real religion which goes with us through all the acts of daily life.

FOR MEDITATION: Christian service covers every aspect of life. Serving God with gladness means that we will serve him wholeheartedly (Deuteronomy 10:12; 11:13), in sincerity and truth (Joshua 24:14), willingly (1 Chronicles 28:9), with fear (Psalm 2:11), continually (Daniel 6:16,20), solely (Matthew 4:10; 6:24) and humbly (Acts 20:19). Do you make his service your delight?

SERMON NO. 769

Labouring and not fainting

'And hast borne, and hast patience, and for my name's sake hast laboured, and hast not fainted.' Revelation 2:3
SUGGESTED FURTHER READING: 2 Corinthians 6:3–13

Friends were debating the other day concerning the work of the ministry, the ease or the labour of it, and I reminded one of them of that saying of Richard Baxter—'God have mercy upon the man who finds the ministry of the gospel to be easy work, for he will have need of all God's mercy indeed when he renders up his account at the last great day.' I cannot conceive of a more atrocious offender against humanity and against God than the man who, having souls committed to his trust, finds it an easy thing to take care of them and watch for their salvation. The ministry is a matter which wears the brain, strains the heart and drains out the life of a man if he attends to it as he should. If God were served by any of us as he should be, I question whether we should not grow old before our time through labour and anguish, even as did that great lover of souls, 'Jesus, that great shepherd of the sheep'. Soul-winning is a work that might fill an angel's heart; it did fill a Saviour's hands. Any service for God, if it be done at all, should be hard work. If you want to be feather-bed soldiers go and enlist somewhere else, but Christ's soldiers must fight and they will find the battle rough and stern. We, of the church militant, are engaged in no mimic manoeuvres and grand parades; our life is real and earnest; our battle, though not with flesh and blood, is with 'spiritual wickedness in high places', and it involves hard blows and keen anguish. You must look for real fighting if you become a soldier of Christ, and, if the excuse for fainting be that the work is toilsome and too much a drag upon you, why did you begin it? You ought to have known this at the first. You should have counted the cost.

FOR MEDITATION: The Christian ministry should never be regarded as an easy option. Pastors and teachers will have to give an account of their work before God (Hebrews 13:17; James 3:1). Those who serve well will be well rewarded (1 Peter 5:2–4) and should receive particular honour from us now (1 Timothy 5:17).

SERMON NO. 1069

North and south

'I will say to the north, Give up; and to the south, Keep not back.' Isaiah 43:6
SUGGESTED FURTHER READING: Acts 18:1–11

If there be a brother who could do more for Christ, let him 'Keep not back'. Could you preach? Well, there are plenty of places needing occasional ministry and others that are quite destitute. I do not know a nobler occupation for a man who is in business than for him to be maintaining himself by his shop or whatever else his calling may be, and going out to suburban villages on the Sabbath to preach. I often wonder why more do not imitate the example of some good brethren, who are diligent in their business and also fervent in spirit in their Master's work. What reason can there be that for every little church there should be a pastor specially set apart for the work? It is a very desirable thing wherever there are enough Christian people to be able to support the minister that there should be such; but I believe we very much hamper ourselves in our Christian work through always imagining that a paid person set apart to preach is necessary for every Christian church. There ought to be more farmers who educate themselves and preach in their own barns or on the village greens. There ought to be more men of business who seek to improve their minds, that they may preach acceptably anywhere the gospel of Jesus Christ; and I hope the time will come when members of churches will not be so backward but will come forward and speak to the honour of the Lord Jesus. If you cannot edify a thousand, perhaps you can influence ten; if you cannot with a regular congregation continue to find fresh matter year after year (and believe me that is a very difficult thing), yet you can preach a sermon here and a sermon there, and tell to different companies the same story of the Saviour's love. I do not know what special work you can do, but something is within your power, and from that 'Keep not back'.

FOR MEDITATION: God has ordained that those who preach the gospel should get their living by the gospel (1 Corinthians 9:14). However, Paul felt so compelled to preach that he did not insist on his rights (1 Corinthians 9:12,15–18), but supported himself to avoid burdening his hearers (Acts 20:33–35; 1 Thessalonians 2:9; 2 Thessalonians 3:7–9). Do you encourage the laymen you know who preach the gospel? Should you be one of them?

Light for those who sit in darkness

'The people which sat in darkness saw great light; and to them which sat in the region and shadow of death light is sprung up.' Matthew 4:16
SUGGESTED FURTHER READING: Isaiah 8:16–9:7

Matthew did not quote from Isaiah correctly; I think he purposely alters it. Isaiah speaks in his ninth chapter of a people that 'walked in darkness'; but here the evangelist speaks of a people who 'sat in darkness'. That is a state of less hopefulness. The man who walks is active; he has some energy left and may reach a brighter spot; but a man sitting down is inactive and will probably stay where he is. 'The people which sat in darkness'—as if they had been there a long while and would be there longer yet. They sat as though they had been turned to stone. They 'sat in darkness' probably through despair; they had, after a fashion, striven for the light, but had not found it and so they gave up all hope. Their disappointed hearts told them that they might as well spare those fruitless efforts, and therefore down they sat with the stolidity of hopelessness. Why should they make any more exertion? If God would not hear their prayers, why should they pray any longer? Being ignorant of his abounding grace and of the way of salvation by his Son, they considered themselves as consigned to perdition. They 'sat in darkness'. Perhaps they sat there so long that they reached a state of insensibility and indifference; this is a horrible condition of heart, but, alas, a very common one. They said, 'What does it matter, since there is no hope for us? Let it be as fate appoints; we will sit still; we will neither cry nor pray.' How many have I met who are not only thus in darkness, but who are half-content to dare the terrible future and to wait sullenly till the storm-cloud of wrath shall burst over them. It is a most sad and wretched condition, but what a blessing it is that this day we have a gospel to preach to such.

FOR MEDITATION: The Lord alone can give light to those who sit in darkness as the prisoners of sin (Psalm 107:10–14; Isaiah 42:6–7; Luke 1:79). He is also a light to his people when even they find themselves sitting through days of darkness (Micah 7:7–9).

Means for restoring the banished

'Neither doth God respect any person: yet doth he devise means, that his banished be not expelled from him.' 2 Samuel 14:14
SUGGESTED FURTHER READING: Acts 13:4–12

I believe God not only uses good things, but even evil things, to bring his banished home. Satan has sometimes outshot himself. Goliath has been slain by his own sword. I have seen self-righteous men, callous to the appeals of the gospel, at last fall into gross sin, and then they have shuddered at the depravity they have discovered in their hearts and, by the sight of the sin of which they did not beforehand believe themselves to have been capable, they have been driven to the Saviour. Sin may thus through God's grace undermine its own dominion. And so with error. It is a grand thing when error works out its own absurdity. I look with great thankfulness to God upon the condition of the Romish church now. That infallibility dogma I believe will be, under God, the means of bringing some of his banished ones to see the truth as it is in Jesus. Many credulous but sincere persons could go long and far and scarce know where they were, thinking that their deadly error was the truth of God, but this last stage in the blind man's progress has proved too much for them. The new dogma is too manifest a lie and smells too strongly of the bottomless pit. I have conversed with one upon whom it has had that effect, a thorough believer in all the doctrines of the church of Rome until it came to that, and now he sees his ground cut from under him and I hope to baptise him as a believer in Christ Jesus. Though otherwise he would have been a priest to preach falsehood, he will now, I trust, proclaim the gospel of Jesus Christ. You cannot tell what will happen; in the world of mind there are revolutions of the most marvellous kind. The God of miracles has not ceased to do great marvels. It is ours to work and wait, and we shall surely see the salvation of God.

FOR MEDITATION: God sovereignly used evil men to effect his plan of redemption (Acts 2:23; 4:27–28); he has overruled persecution (Acts 8:1–6) and rejection (Acts 13:45–49) to spread the gospel. This does not allow us to call evil good (Isaiah 5:20) or do evil to promote good (Romans 3:8).

N.B. The doctrine of Papal infallibility had been decreed by the Vatican Council earlier in 1870.

The bellows burned

'The bellows are burned.' Jeremiah 6:29
SUGGESTED FURTHER READING: Acts 20:17–38

In my short time I have known certain churches in the paroxysms of delirium, meeting houses crowded, aisles filled, preachers stamping and thundering, hearers intoxicated with excitement and persons converted by wholesale, even children converted by hundreds—they said thousands. But a month or two later where were the congregations? Where were the converts? Echo has answered, 'Where?' Why, the converts were worse sinners than before, or mere professors, puffed up into a superficial religion from which they soon fell into a hopeless coldness, which has rendered it difficult ever to stir them again. I love all genuine revivals with all my heart and I would aid and abet them; but I now speak of certain spurious things which are not uncommon, where there has not been God's Holy Spirit, but mere excitement, loud talk, big words, fanaticism, rant and nothing more. Now, in such cases, why was it the fire went out? Why, the man who blew the bellows went away to use his lungs elsewhere, and as soon as the good man, who by his remarkable manner and telling style had created this stir, was gone, the fire went out. I have known quiet churches in which the same thing has happened in a manner equally grievous. The people have been very earnest and much good work has been done, but the departure to heaven of their excellent minister has been to this people what the death of a judge was to the children of Israel. May God spare those valued lives, which in our churches promote the earnestness of God's people, and may it be long before the bellows are burned! But our zeal ought not so to be sustained. The fervour of the church ought never to be dependent upon the eloquence or the ministrations of any particular individual. Principle ought to sway us, not passion, and real fervour, not the excitement which may be gathered from vehement speech and crowded assemblies.

FOR MEDITATION: Misplaced reliance on a preacher instead of God may not survive his departure. Be warned by some who soon lost their devotion to the apostle Paul (Galatians 4:13–16) and accepted another gospel (Galatians 1:6), but be encouraged by others who stood fast in the Lord despite Paul's fears for them in his absence (1 Thessalonians 3:5–8).

SERMON NO. 890

Grey hairs

'Gray hairs are here and there upon him, yet he knoweth not.' Hosea 7:9
SUGGESTED FURTHER READING: Isaiah 64:5–9

Decays in grace and backsliding are usually very much like the fall of the autumn leaves. You are watching the trees, for even now they are beginning to indicate the coming fall. They evidently know that their verdant robes are to be stripped from them, for they are casting off their first loose vestments. How slowly the time of the brown leaf comes on! You notice here and there a tinge of the copper hue, and anon the gold leaf or the bronze is apparent. Week after week you observe that the general fall of the leaves is drawing nearer, but it is a matter that creeps slowly on. And so with backsliders. They are not put out of the visible church all at once; they do not become open offenders all at once. The heart by slow degrees turns aside from the living God, and then at last comes the outward sin and the outward shame. God save us from falling by little and little! The devil's little strokes have felled many great oaks. Constant droppings of temptation have worn away many stones. God save us from this. Some cities have been taken by storm. Brave soldiers have made the irons of the scaling ladder bite on the top of the wall, and up they have swarmed in defiance of death and taken the city by sudden force within a few hours. But many other cities have been taken by the slow process of the siege; the supplies have been cut off; warriors have been slain at the sally-ports slowly; entrenchments have been thrown up nearer and nearer to the wall, mines have been dug under the bastions, forts have been weakened, gates have been shaken, and at last the city has been subdued. Where Satan captures one man by force of strong temptation, he captures ten by the gradual process of sapping and undermining the principles which should rule within. May God preserve us from this!

FOR MEDITATION: Trace the sad decline of Demas. He was a fellow worker (Philemon 24), he faltered in the way (Colossians 4:14, where he is last and, alone lacking any commendation, apparently least in a long list of Paul's helpers), he followed the world and he forsook the work (2 Timothy 4:10). Are you doing a Demas?

Our gifts, and how to use them

'Wherefore I put thee in remembrance that thou stir up the gift of God, which is in thee by the putting on of my hands.' 2 Timothy 1:6
SUGGESTED FURTHER READING: Mark 10:32–45

What must Jesus think of us when he remembers his own love? Was there ever such a contrast between his furnace heated seven times hotter and our iceberg spirits? He spared not himself and we are always sparing ourselves. He gives us everything to the last rag and hangs naked on the cross: we keep almost all to ourselves and count self-sacrifice to be hard. He labours and is weary, yet ceases not: we are a little weary and immediately we faint. He continued to preach on, notwithstanding all the ill return men made, but we take offence and throw up our work because we are not appreciated as we should be. Oh the little things which put some workers out of temper and out of heart. Oh the looks or the not-looks, the words or the silence, that will make some spirits give up any place, any service and any work; 'forbearing one another' seems to have gone out of fashion with many people; 'forgiving one another, even as God for Christ's sake hath forgiven you' is forgotten. If being door mats for Christ for all the church to wipe their feet upon would honour him, we ought to think it a great glory to be so used. Among genuine Christians the contention is for the lowest place: among sham Christians the controversy is for the higher positions. Some will ask the question 'Which is the higher office, that of elder or deacon?' and so on. What triviality! When the Master was going up to Jerusalem to die, there was a contention among the disciples which of them should be the greatest; and so it is with us; at times when grace is low, our opinion of ourselves is very high, and then our love to God is little, so that we soon take affront and are quick to resent any little insults, as we think them to be, where perhaps nothing of the kind was meant. May we be saved from all this littleness of soul!

FOR MEDITATION: The disciples perversely seemed to reserve their private discussions about which of them was the greatest to those occasions when Jesus had just told them about his forthcoming death and resurrection (Mark 9:31–34). They were even at it after he had instituted the Lord's Supper (Luke 22:17–19,24)! May we all learn the lesson he kept teaching them (Mark 9:35; 10:43–44; Luke 22:26).

SERMON NO. 1080

The ministry of gratitude

'And immediately she arose and ministered unto them.' Luke 4:39
SUGGESTED FURTHER READING: Micah 6:6–8

Many persons who profess to be converted aspire at once to preaching; a pulpit is the main thing for them and a large congregation is their ambition. They must do some great thing and occupy the chief seat in the synagogue. But this good woman did not think of preaching; women are always best when they don't; but she thought of washing Christ's feet and preparing him necessary food, which was her proper business. To these kind but simple actions she devoted herself. Attention to humble duties is a better sign of grace than an ambition for lofty and elevated works. There is probably far more grace in the loving service of a mother towards Christ in bringing up her children in the fear of God, than there might be if she were well known as taking a leading part in great public movements; there may be more service for Christ done by a workman in discharging his duties as such and trying to do good to his fellow workmen, than if he aspired to become a great leader of the minds and thoughts of others. Of course there are exceptions, for glorious was Deborah and great shall be her name in Israel, and those who are sent by God to lead his church shall not be without their reward, but even then when they have to look for personal evidences of grace they never dare say, 'We know that we have passed from death unto life because we preach the gospel,' for they remember that Judas did the same; they never say, 'We are confident of salvation because God has wrought wonders by us,' for they remember that the son of perdition had the same distinction; but they fall back upon the same evidences which prove the truth of the religion of humbler people; they rejoice in testimonies common to all the elect. 'We know that we have passed from death unto life, because we love the brethren.' The humbler graces and duties are the best test.

FOR MEDITATION: In God's analysis many who appear to be first will end up being last and vice versa (Matthew 19:30; 20:16; Luke 13:30). Wanting the preeminence is not a wise attitude to adopt (3 John 9–10). Far better to be promoted than to be relegated (Luke 14:7–11).

Negotiations for peace

'Preaching peace by Jesus Christ: (he is Lord of all).' Acts 10:36
SUGGESTED FURTHER READING: Colossians 1:11–23

If you are anxious to have peace, God's terms are these—I call them terms for want of a better word, but I mean no legality thereby. He asks no price of you, he demands no millions of money—indeed he demands no pounds at your hands. If he were hungry, he would not tell you; if he were thirsty, he would not come to you for drink, for Lebanon would not be 'sufficient to burn, nor the beasts thereof sufficient for a burnt offering.' He asks no gold from you, he asks no suffering from you, no passing through dreary penance or horrible despairing. It would be no satisfaction for him to see you suffer. He delights in happiness and is pleased to see us happy when it is safe for others that we should be so. Neither does he ask you to achieve merits to bring to him. You could not if he should demand it. You have sinned before and will sin again. All hope for you to make up the faultiness of the past by the perfection of the future is gone. You have broken the law; you cannot keep it. If you shall labour after life under the covenant of works, you must perish. God, therefore, does not ask you to save yourself by your own works, but he graciously tells you that he is full of mercy, full of compassion, delighting to forgive, ready to pass by your sins, and that at once. Here is all that the Lord asks of you and this he will enable you to do—trust sincerely in his only-begotten Son. On the cross Jesus suffered; turn your eyes to that cross. He rose again and ascended to heaven—trust him to save your soul, because 'he ever liveth to make intercession for' you.

FOR MEDITATION: We are the ones who by our own wickedness alienated ourselves from God and became his enemies (Colossians 1:21). God is the only one in the position to make peace, bring hostilities to an end and declare peace to us (Ephesians 2:13–17; Colossians 1:20). Read Romans 5:1 and check whether you have accepted his terms of peace.

Job's regret and our own

'Oh that I were as in months past, as in the days when God preserved me; when his candle shined upon my head, and when by his light I walked through darkness; as I was in the days of my youth, when the secret of God was upon my tabernacle.' Job 29:2–4
SUGGESTED FURTHER READING (Spurgeon): Revelation 2:1–7

You will never have your graces revived unless you go to the cross. Begin life again. The best air for a man to breathe when he is sickly is said to be that of his birthplace: it was at Calvary we were born; it is only at Calvary we can be restored when we are declining; 'do the first works'. As a sinner, go to the Saviour and ask to be restored. Then, as a further means of health, search out the cause of your declension. Probably it was a neglect of private prayer. Where the disease began, there must the remedy be applied. Pray more earnestly, more frequently, more importunately. Or was it a neglect of hearing the word? Were you enticed by novelty or cleverness away from a really searching and instructive ministry? Go back and feed on wholesome food again: perhaps that may cure the disease. Or have you been too grasping after the world? Brother, you loved God when you had just one shop, but you have two now and are giving all your time and thoughts to business, and your soul is getting lean. Strike off some of that business, for it is a bad business that makes your soul poor. I would not restrain industry or enterprise for a single moment; let a man do all he can, but not at the expense of his soul. Push, but do not push down your soul. You may buy gold too dear and may attain a high position in this world at a cost which you may have to rue all your days. Where the mischief began, there apply the remedy. And I urge upon you, and most of all upon myself, do not make excuses for yourself; do not palliate your faults; do not say it must be so; do not compare yourself with others, or you will be unwise; but to the perfect image of Christ let your heart aspire, to the ardour of your divine Redeemer, who loved not himself, but loved you.

FOR MEDITATION: The steps to be taken by the returning backslider mirror those taken by the repenting sinner. Consider how closely Revelation 2:4,5 retraces the footsteps of the Prodigal Son. Having left his first love (Luke 15:13), he remembered from whence he had fallen, he repented and he returned (Luke 15:17–20). Is it time for you to go and do likewise?

SERMON NO. 1011

The unrivalled eloquence of Jesus

'The officers answered, Never man spake like this man.' John 7:46
SUGGESTED FURTHER READING: Matthew 7:24–29

The Spirit of God has made many an ancient saying a speech from the living Jesus to us. At those words of his when he said, 'Lo, I come (in the volume of the book it is written of me,) to do thy will, O God', our faith has stood at Bethlehem's manger and we have seen the body prepared for him and himself putting on the form of a servant. His coming 'to seek and to save that which was lost' has become a personal coming to us and we have rejoiced in it exceedingly. Has not the voice which came of old from the sea when he said, 'it is I; be not afraid', been a voice to you? And the voice from Jerusalem, 'how often would I have gathered thy children together,' has it never bewailed the perishing ones around you? The voice from Bethany, 'I am the resurrection, and the life', has it never been heard at the burial of your brother? The voice from the table when he washed his disciples' feet, and bade them wash one another's feet, has it not excited you to humble service of the brethren? Have we not again and again heard the cry of Gethsemane, 'not as I will, but as thou wilt'? I cannot convince myself that I did not actually hear the Redeemer say that; at any rate I have rejoiced when in the spirit of resignation the echo of it has been heard in my own spirit. Do I not this very day hear him saying, though long ago he spoke it, 'Father, forgive them; for they know not what they do'? His intercession for my guilty soul, what is it but the continuance of that gentle prayer? And for certain that last concluding sentence, 'It is finished'—my ears may not have heard it, but my soul hears it now and rejoices to repeat the word. Who shall lay anything to my charge since Christ has consummated my deliverance from death, hell and sin, and brought in a perfect righteousness for me? Yes, these old sayings of Christ heard years ago we have heard in spirit, and after hearing them all our witness is, 'Never man spake like this man.'

FOR MEDITATION: Memorable individual sayings of the Lord Jesus Christ became fixed in the minds of the early Christians (Luke 22:61; 24:8; John 2:19,22; Acts 11:16; 20:35), but he also promised that the Holy Spirit would bring to the remembrance of the apostles everything he had said to them (John 14:26)? Do you let the word of Christ in general dwell in you richly (Colossians 3:16)?

SERMON NO. 951

David's holy wonder at the Lord's great goodness

'Oh how great is thy goodness, which thou hast laid up for them that fear thee; which thou hast wrought for them that trust in thee before the sons of men.' Psalm 31:19
SUGGESTED FURTHER READING: Psalm 34:1–22

The phrase 'the fear of God' is used, especially in the Old Testament, for the whole of piety. It does not signify merely the one virtue of fear—it does not signify that feeling at all in the sense of slavish fear—but it takes a wide sweep. The man who had the fear of God before his eyes, was one who believed in God, worshipped God, loved God, was kept back from evil by the thought of God, and moved to good by the desire to please God. The ungodly were the wicked ones, those who had no God. Those who had a godly fear were found diligently walking in holiness. The fear of God, I say, was the expression used for the whole of religion. Still, fear itself is a very important element in the Christian's character, if it be the right kind of fear. We have nothing to do with the terror of the bond-slave, for we are free and 'have not received the spirit of bondage again to fear'. Blessed be God, we have no fear of hell. It is not possible for a believer to be there. Talk of casting a believer into hell! As well talk of casting the Redeemer himself there! It is impossible. We have no fear, even, of losing our standing before God, for we do not stand before him in ourselves, but in the person of our Lord Jesus Christ. We cannot fall finally and fatally unless Jesus can fall. He says, 'because I live, ye shall live also.' But this is our fear—the fear which a dear child has of a tender father. It is not afraid that its father will kill it, or cease to love it, or banish it and turn it out of his house. It knows better; it trusts its father too well to indulge in such mischievous suspicions; but because it loves him, it fears to offend him. This is the very atmosphere in which a Christian breathes. He fears God and consequently desires to keep his commandments.

FOR MEDITATION: The fear of the Lord ought to affect every aspect of our lives whether it involves ruling over men (2 Samuel 23:3), our daily walk (Nehemiah 5:9; Acts 9:31), serving the Lord (Psalm 2:11), worshipping him (Psalm 5:7), perfecting holiness (2 Corinthians 7:1), submitting to one another (Ephesians 5:21) or our daily employment (Colossians 3:22). In how much of your life do you fear the Lord?

SERMON NO. 773

The altar

'The altar that sanctifieth the gift.' Matthew 23:19
SUGGESTED FURTHER READING: Hebrews 13:10–16

Are there not some among you who have been offering to God without an altar at all? I mean this: you have been striving, you say, to do your duty; you are an honourable member of the state. You have sought to be religious too and you have come up with the assembly of God's people. You never forget the Sabbath nor the offering of your morning and evening prayer, and you believe yourself, therefore, to be among the good and the righteous and you hope to be accepted at the bar of God. Yes, I see your sacrifice, but where is your altar? For, be assured, God will not receive your sacrifice without an altar, and for altars there is only one. You have forgotten the one essential thing. According to our text the altar sanctifies the gift: your gift is not sanctified at all then; it is an unsanctified, unacceptable gift. The whole of your life, though commendable in itself and to be imitated by others in its outward development, is not accepted of God because you have never placed that life upon the appointed altar of Christ Jesus; you have not offered it to God, having first trusted in Christ and looked to his merit for its acceptance. You have been depending upon yourself, and therefore you are no more likely to be saved than Cain was when he went about to offer a sacrifice of his own and could not submit to bring the lamb according to divine appointment. I could weep over some of you, who have so much that is good about you, because you forget the Lord Jesus. Why, you have forgotten the one, the main, the essential thing. Those morning and evening prayers of yours, what are they? If you have not seen Jesus on the cross and if you have not looked to his wounds, you have not prayed at all.

FOR MEDITATION: We ought to be making spiritual sacrifices to God in our daily living (Romans 12:1; Philippians 4:18), but such sacrifices are acceptable to God only when they are offered through the Lord Jesus Christ (Hebrews 13:15–16) by those who have come to Christ (1 Peter 2:4–5).

Footsteps of mercy

'If there be a messenger with him, an interpreter, one among a thousand, to shew unto men his uprightness: then he is gracious unto him, and saith, Deliver him from going down to the pit: I have found a ransom.' Job 33:23–24

SUGGESTED FURTHER READING: Hebrews 4:14–5:10

Jesus Christ is indeed a blessed interpreter. An interpreter must understand two languages. Our Lord Jesus understands the language of God. Whatever are the great truths of divine intelligence and infinite wisdom, too high and mysterious for us to comprehend or even to discern, Christ fully understands them all. He knows how to speak with God as the fellow of God, co-equal and co-eternal with him. His prayers are in God's language. He speaks to God's heart. He can make out the sighs, cries and tears of a poor sinner, and he can take up the meaning and interpret them all to God. He understands the divine language and thus he can communicate with God. Moreover, Jesus understands our language, for he is a man like ourselves, 'touched with the feeling of our infirmities', and smarting under our sicknesses. He can read whatever is in the heart of man, and so he can tell to God the language of man and speak to man in the language of man what God would say to him. How happy we ought to be that there is so blessed a Daysman to put his hand upon us both, that he can be equal with God and yet can be brother with poor simple men! The best of it is that our Lord is such an interpreter that he can not only interpret to the ear but also to the heart, and this is a great point. I, perhaps, might be enabled to interpret a Scripture to your ears, but when you have heard the letter you may miss the right, heavenly and spiritual meaning. But our Lord can bring the word home to your soul. He can tell you of God's mercy not in words only, but with a sweet sense of mercy shed abroad in your heart. He can make the sinner feel the way of salvation as well as know it; he can make him rejoice in it as well as listen to it. Oh, blessed interpreter!

FOR MEDITATION: Glory in the one mediator between God and men, the man Christ Jesus (1 Timothy 2:5), who is perfectly qualified for this role by his unique dual knowledge of both God (Matthew 11:27; John 7:29; 8:55; 10:15; 17:25) and man (Matthew 9:4; 12:25; Mark 12:15; Luke 6:8; John 2:25; 21:17). In knowing him we know and see the Father (John 14:7).

SERMON NO. 905

My prayer

'Quicken thou me in thy way.' Psalm 119:37
SUGGESTED FURTHER READING: Psalm 143:7–12

What is the path in which we require to be quickened? First, it is in the way of *duty in common life*. Am I a father?—'quicken thou me' to bring up my children aright. Am I a housewife? Lord 'quicken thou me' that my duties at home may be discharged as in thy fear. Am I a servant or master? Lord 'quicken thou me'. I have my temptations in my daily calling; quicken me to stand against them; I have also my daily opportunities for serving thee; quicken me to make use of them. It means next, 'quicken thou me' in *sacred activity*. Am I a preacher? Lord help me to preach with all my might and with all thy might too. Am I a teacher in a school? Lord grant that I may not go to sleep over my children, but may win their souls, being blessed by thee with the earnestness which tells upon youthful minds. Have I any other work to do? Am I a deacon or elder of the church? Let me be so ardent in piety that my fellow members may be excited by my zeal. You all have some work to do for Christ—I hope you have. If you have not, go home and begin; but if you are doing your work, I know your prayer must be, 'quicken thou me in thy way.' And the same is true of *hallowed worship*. We want to be quickened there, quickened in private prayer, quickened in public prayer, quickened in our family devotion, quickened in our reading of the Scriptures, quickened in our contemplations of divine love, quickened in all forms of worship. We require to be quickened in our growth in grace, in humility, in patience, in hope, in faith, in love, in every good gift. Especially we need to be quickened in communion with our God. Then let us pray the prayer, 'quicken thou me in thy way.'

FOR MEDITATION: Spurgeon began this sermon by referring to the nine repetitions of this prayer and the two acknowledgements of it being answered all to be found in Psalm 119. Consider what it means to be quickened according to God's word (vv. 25,50,107,154), God's way (v. 37), God's righteousness (v. 40), God's loving kindness (vv. 88,159), God's precepts (v. 93) and God's judgment(s) (vv. 149,156).

SERMON NO. 1072

Dwell deep, O Dedan!

'Dwell deep, O inhabitants of Dedan.' Jeremiah 49:8
SUGGESTED FURTHER READING: Hebrews 5:11–6:3

Dwell deep in the matter of Christian study. He who knows himself a sinner and Christ a Saviour, is certainly justified; but we desire to be something more than saved. The babe in grace is the Lord's child: but we do not wish to be always infants; there is a time when we should be no more children. Christ's babes should grow up to be men in Christ Jesus; and my earnest entreaty to all professors, both young and old, is that we seek deeply to study the word of God, that by feeding upon it we may grow. An instructed Christian is a more useful vessel of honour for the Master than an ignorant believer. I do not say that instruction is all, far from it; there is much in zeal and, with only slender knowledge, a man full of zeal may do a great deal; but if the zealous man has knowledge in proportion, how much more will he achieve? Dig deep in your researches into the Scriptures. I am always afraid lest any of you should take your doctrinal views from me and believe doctrines merely because I have taught you to do so. I charge you, if I preach anything that is not according to the Lord's word, away with it! And 'though we, or an angel from heaven, preach any other gospel' than the gospel of Jesus Christ, away with it! Do not regard our persons for a moment, in comparison with divine authority. Study the character of Christ. Do not merely know that he is Christ, but *who* he is—whose Son he is, what he is, what he did, what was meant by what he did, what he is doing, what he will do, and all the glorious hopes which cluster around his first and second advents, all the precious truths of his covenant of grace and the glorious attributes of eternal love. Do not be afraid of what are called 'the deep things of God.'

FOR MEDITATION: God's judgments and thoughts are very deep (Psalm 36:6; 92:5). Are you exploring them? When God's word falls upon shallow soil, there is serious danger of falling away after initial interest (Matthew 13:5–6,20–21), but nothing can shake those who dig deep foundations by hearing God's word and continuing to obey it (Luke 6:47–48). Which of these describes your attitude to the Bible?

SERMON NO. 1085

The unbeliever's unhappy condition

'He that believeth on the Son hath everlasting life: and he that believeth not the Son shall not see life; but the wrath of God abideth on him.' John 3:36

SUGGESTED FURTHER READING: Matthew 3:1–12

This is a part of a discourse by John the Baptist. We have not many sermons by that mighty preacher, but we have just sufficient to prove that he knew how to lay the axe at the root of the tree by preaching the law of God most unflinchingly, and also that he knew how to declare the gospel, for no one could have uttered sentences which more clearly contain the way of salvation than those in the text before us. Indeed this third chapter of the gospel according to the evangelist John is notable among clear and plain Scriptures, notable for being yet clearer and plainer than almost any other. John the Baptist was evidently a preacher who knew how to discriminate, a point in which so many fail; he separated between the precious and the vile, and therefore he was as God's mouth to the people. He does not address them as all lost nor as all saved, but he shows the two classes and keeps up the line of demarcation between those who fear God and those who do not. He plainly declares the privileges of the believer— he says he even now has eternal life; and with equal decision he testifies to the sad state of the unbeliever—he 'shall not see life; but the wrath of God abideth on him.' John the Baptist might usefully instruct most professedly Christian preachers. Although 'he that is least in the kingdom of heaven is greater than' John the Baptist, and ought, therefore, to bear witness to the truth more clearly, yet there are many who muddle the gospel, who teach philosophy, who preach a mingle-mangle which is neither law nor gospel; and those might well go to school to this rough preacher of the wilderness, and learn from him how to cry, 'Behold the Lamb of God, which taketh away the sin of the world.'

FOR MEDITATION: Consider some other verses which highlight the stark contrast between those who trust in Christ and those who don't (Mark 16:16; John 3:18; 1 Peter 2:6–8; 1 John 5:10–12). You are either in one group or the other. If you are still in the wrong group, the opportunity to change sides by putting your faith in the Lord Jesus Christ is still open to you (John 5:24).

SERMON NO. 1012

Done in a day, but wondered at for ever

'I will remove the iniquity of that land in one day. In that day, saith the LORD *of hosts, shall ye call every man his neighbour under the vine and under the fig tree.' Zechariah 3:9–10*
SUGGESTED FURTHER READING (Spurgeon): Psalm 103:1–12

Tarry a moment over that word 'I'. Let me take it and translate it. The 'I' of Jehovah is one, but three. To begin then—'The grace of the Lord Jesus Christ ... be with you', for it is the *Son* who says 'I will remove the iniquity of that land'. He was laid as the one foundation stone of our hope, upon which seven eyes are fixed (see Zechariah 3:9); he who was graven with the graver's tool when he was fastened to the cross and his side was pierced, he it is that has removed the iniquity of his people in one day by bearing it and making a recompense to Almighty justice for it. See then the Crucified; he uplifts his pierced hand, he bares his open side and he says, 'Sinner, look to me; I will remove your iniquity in one day.' But, 'the love of God ... be with you', for it is the *Father* who says, 'I will remove the iniquity of that land in one day.' The returning prodigal said, 'Father, I have sinned', and it was the father, the same offended father, who bid them take off his rags and kill for him the fatted calf; it was the father who rejoiced that his son that was lost was found, and that he who was dead was alive again; the Father therefore removes the sins of his children. And 'the communion of the Holy Ghost, be with you', for it is the *Holy Spirit* also who says, 'I will remove the iniquity of that land in one day.' He brings the blood that Jesus shed, the Jesus that the Father gave; he applies it to the conscience, sprinkles it upon the heart, and makes those to be actually and experimentally cleansed who in God's sight were cleansed by the death of Christ. 'I will remove' it. Oh, did you ever feel within your heart the power of the Holy Spirit removing your iniquity in one day? I shall never forget when my iniquity was removed; it was indeed in one single moment.

FOR MEDITATION: Think about Zechariah's other prophetical references to that one day when people in Jerusalem would look upon and mourn for the one they had crucified (Zechariah 12:10–11; John 19:37) and when a fountain would be opened to cleanse them from their sin and uncleanness (Zechariah 13:1). Praise God for Good Friday.

SERMON NO. 953

Strong consolation

'Wherein God, willing more abundantly to shew unto the heirs of promise the immutability of his counsel, confirmed it by an oath; that by two immutable things, in which it was impossible for God to lie, we might have a strong consolation, who have fled for refuge to lay hold upon the hope set before us.' Hebrews 6:17–18
SUGGESTED FURTHER READING: Titus 1:1–4

God has with an oath sworn by himself that all the heirs of promise shall be blessed for ever, saying, 'Surely blessing I will bless thee'. Who among us dare doubt this? Where is the hardy sinner who dares come forward and say, 'I impugn the oath of God'? Let us blush the deepest scarlet, and scarlet is but white compared with the blush which ought to mantle the cheek of every child of God to think that even God's children should, in effect, accuse their heavenly Father of perjury. Shame upon us! Forgive us, great God, this deep atrocity; and from this hour may we hold it certain that as thou hast sworn that he that flees for refuge to Christ shall be safe, that as thou hast promised that 'He that believeth and is baptized shall be saved', we who have so believed are secure beyond all question. Let us no more doubt our salvation than our existence, and no more think ourselves in jeopardy in the darkest hour than we think God's throne in jeopardy, or God's truth itself in peril. O believer, stand to it that the Lord cannot lie. Those words have rung in my ears like a bell—'impossible for God to lie'; of course it is. Next, 'things, in which it was impossible for God to lie,' as if there were some things more impossible than others. Then, 'immutable things, in which it was impossible for God to lie,' and then the finale, 'two immutable things, in which it was impossible for God to lie'. Catch the accumulation of the meaning, the tidal wave of reassuring thought. There is a force about it which is rather excessive than deficient, as though a huge battering ram were brought to crush a fly, or ocean stirred to tempest to waft a feather. Surely we have too much instead of too little evidence for our faith.

FOR MEDITATION: The all-powerful God does whatever he pleases (Psalm 115:3; 135:6), but he does not change (Malachi 3:6; James 1:17), cannot deny himself (2 Timothy 2:13), cannot lie (Titus 1:2), never leaves nor forsakes his people (Hebrews 13:5) and cannot be tempted with evil (James 1:13).

SERMON NO. 893

The Lord's name and memorial

'Instead of the thorn shall come up the fir tree, and instead of the brier shall come up the myrtle tree: and it shall be to the LORD *for a name, for an everlasting sign that shall not be cut off.' Isaiah 55:13*
SUGGESTED FURTHER READING: Romans 10:14–17

It is a gospel of hearing and not of doing. Look at Isaiah 55. See the second verse—'hearken diligently'. Notice the third verse—'Incline your ear,' and yet again—'hear, and your soul shall live'. Death came to us first through the eye, but salvation comes through the ear. Our first parent, Eve, *looked* at the fruit; she 'saw that the tree was good for food,' and so she plucked and so we fell. But no man rises to eternal life by signs and symbols appealing to the eye; it is by the use of the ear that the joyful news is communicated. The soldiers of Emmanuel would gladly take Eye-gate by storm, but it is not to be done. Ear-gate is a far more accessible point of attack for the gospel warrior. There we must sound the silver trumpet, and there we must keep the battering rams of the gospel continually beating, for 'faith cometh' not by seeing, but 'by hearing, and hearing by the word of God.' If you desire eternal life, you have not now to perform a dreary penance, or to pass through tormenting horrors of mind, or to live for years a meritorious life; you have only to listen to the gospel with attention and faith; listen to it and receive it into your soul, and that gospel will do for you what you can never do for yourself—it will change your nature; and when your nature is changed, then good works will follow as a result. If you seek good works as a cause of salvation, you will make a gross mistake, but if you will take the gospel to be in you the cause and root of holiness, then all manner of good things shall spring up to your comfort and to God's praise. The first business of a sinner is to hear the gospel. Note how it is over and over again—'hearken ... Incline your ear ... hear, and your soul shall live'. I charge you, frequent a gospel ministry; I beseech you, search the Scriptures.

FOR MEDITATION: The Lord Jesus Christ repeatedly drew attention to the importance of hearing God's word and responding positively to it (Matthew 7:24; Luke 11:28; John 5:24). Merely hearing God's word and responding negatively is a worse than useless activity (Matthew 7:26–27; James 1:22–24).

SERMON NO. 833

The Lord blessing his saints

'Ye are blessed of the LORD *which made heaven and earth.' Psalm 115:15*
SUGGESTED FURTHER READING: Genesis 3:1–21

This is very sweet to those who fear God. To them it is peculiarly precious to know that they are blessed of the Lord, because they know they deserve to have been cursed. A sense of wrath due to sin imparts a rare sweetness to the divine favour. Did you ever hear the roar of Sinai's thunder in your ear? If so, you will never forget it to your dying day; and even in eternity it will impart an additional melody to the music of the cross. I would to God that some Christians were ploughed a little more before they were sown, for I notice that the flimsiness and superficiality of the religion which is common nowadays, arises mainly from the lack of deep self-knowledge and solemn personal conviction that they were themselves utterly lost and ruined. I fear many have made but poor students in the University of theology, because they were never well-grounded in the school of repentance. I am astonished that we should live to hear from a nonconformist pulpit that the fall of man was a fiction! I make bold to say that the religion of the man who could utter such a speech, is a fiction beyond all question. What does he know about the things of God, when he does not even know the things of man? Let him get back to his God in penitence and ask to be taught aright; for he who knows not the fall of man, does not know the uplifting by free grace. If he knows not the disease, he is a wretched physician and is sure to mistake the remedy. He who has once known the curse and smarted under it, loves the wine and oil of the blessing, for by it his bleeding wounds were staunched. The blessing of the Lord is as dew to the mown grass and as showers to the parched soil; it is life itself and the essence of heaven.

FOR MEDITATION: We cannot understand the scope of God's blessing unless we see it in its proper context. God sent his Son into the world to bless us by turning us away from our sins (Acts 3:26); the greatest blessing from God we can know is to have our sins forgiven, covered and not held against us (Romans 4:6–8).

A honeycomb

'For consider him that endured such contradiction of sinners against himself, lest ye be wearied and faint in your minds.' Hebrews 12:3
SUGGESTED FURTHER READING: 1 John 4:15–19

Somebody says, 'I am troubled about the three last things; I am afraid of death, judgment and hell.' Afraid of *death*? But if you will trust the Son of God who died for sinners, you need never be afraid to die. Your little child, when she has run about, wearied herself, and wants to sleep, is she afraid to fall asleep in mother's arms? And you, dear child of God, when you are weary with your work, you shall go and lay your head on Jesus and fall asleep, and it shall be just as easy and just as sweet as for your little ones to sleep on you. 'But I am afraid of judgment,' says one. *Judgment*? But your judgment is past already. Your sins were judged in Christ and punished in Christ, if you trust in him. The sins of all believers were brought before the bar of judgment, condemned and broken on the wheel in Christ. Let us go back to that famous passage by Paul; he pictures God's chosen people standing before the throne, and he cries, 'Who shall lay any thing to the charge of God's elect?' Who is afraid of judgment when nobody can lay anything to his charge? And then he goes on to say, 'Who is he that condemneth?' None can condemn but the judge; and who is he? 'It is Christ that died,' and can he that died for us condemn us? Impossible; he cannot belie himself. So you need not be afraid of judgment. 'But I am afraid of *hell*,' says one. Yes, and there is good cause to fear it; 'fear him which is able to destroy both soul and body in hell'; 'yea, I say unto you, Fear him.' But you need not fear hell if you trust in Jesus, for Christ has suffered the punishment of your sin, and as far as you are concerned hell is not. There are no flames of wrath for you; they spent themselves upon the Saviour.

FOR MEDITATION: The unbeliever has good reason to fear death (Hebrews 2:15), judgment (Hebrews 10:27) and hell (Luke 12:5), but the fear of such things should vanish when we are saved and delivered from their threat (John 5:24; Hebrews 2:14–15; 1 John 4:17–18).

The soul's crisis

'Jesus of Nazareth passeth by.' Luke 18:37
SUGGESTED FURTHER READING: Mark 8:34–38

What is it to be lost? To be cast away from the presence of God into hell, to have to suffer for ever all that the justice of God can demand and all that the omnipotence of God can inflict. If I have just a headache or a toothache for one brief hour, my patience can scarcely endure the torture; what must it be to suffer such pains for a century? What must it be to have ten thousand times worse pains than these for ever and ever? To be dejected in mind, to be despairing, to be disconsolate—how bewildered it makes men! They take the knife or the poison in a fit of insanity; it may be they cannot bear their lives because of their anguish and desperation. But all the pangs, racks and abandonment from which men suffer here are nothing to be compared with the woes and mental anguish of the world to come. Oh, the agony of a spirit doomed, forlorn, accursed, upon which God shall put his foot in awful wrath and lift it up no more for ever! And there, as you lie, tormented to the quick, you will have this to be your miserable portion—'I heard the gospel, but I would not heed it; Christ was put before me, but I would not acknowledge him; I was entreated to believe in his name and fly to him for salvation, but I hesitated, hung in suspense, demurred and at length denied him.' And all for what? For a little drink, a little dance, a little sin that yielded but slight pleasure, or for worldly gain, or for low and grovelling vices, or for sheer carelessness and gaiety! Lost! And for nothing! A sinner damned! He lost his soul, but he did not gain the world. He gained only a little frivolous pleasure; even that poor pittance he spent in an hour, and then he was for ever cast away! May it not be so with you.

FOR MEDITATION: In Jesus's parable the lost sheep represented 1% of a hundred (Luke 15:4) and much value, the lost silver 10% of ten (Luke 15:8) and more value, but the lost son 50% of two (Luke 15:11) and most value. Jesus came to seek and save the lost (Luke 19:10); there is much rejoicing when they are found (Luke 15:6–7,9–10,23–24,32). Are you still spiritually lost? It's serious.

N.B. In the early hours of the day on which this sermon was preached, a couple who had been attentive listeners to Spurgeon suffocated in their burning house.

SERMON NO. 906

Our watchword

'Let such as love thy salvation say continually, Let God be magnified.'
Psalm 70:4
SUGGESTED FURTHER READING (Spurgeon): Psalm 40:1–17

It is a great pity that so many professors have only a religion of feeling, and are quite unable to explain and justify their faith. They live by passion rather than by principle. Religion is in them a series of paroxysms, a succession of emotions. They were stirred up at a certain meeting, excited and carried away, and let us hope they were really and sincerely converted: but they have failed to become to the fullest extent disciples or learners. They do not sit at Jesus' feet; they are not Bereans who search the Scriptures daily to see whether these things be so: they are content with the mere rudiments, the simple elements: they are still little children and need to be fed with milk, for they cannot digest the strong meat of the kingdom. Such persons do not discern so many reasons for admiring and loving the salvation of God, as the intelligent, enlightened, Spirit-taught believer. I would to God that all of us, after we have received Christ, meditated much upon his blessed person, and the details of his work, and the various streams of blessings which leap forth from the central fount of Calvary's sacrifice. All Scripture is profitable, but especially those Scriptures which concern our salvation. Some things lose by observation and are most wondered at when least understood; but the gospel gains by study: no man is ever wearied in meditating upon it, nor does he find his admiration diminished, but abundantly increased. Blessed is he who studies the gospel both day and night and finds his heart's delight in it. Such a man will have a steadier and intenser affection for it, in proportion as he perceives its excellence and surpassing glory. The man who receives the gospel superficially and holds it as a matter of impression and little more, being quite unable to give a reason for the hope that is in him, lacks that which would confirm and intensify his love.

FOR MEDITATION: God's children should not be childish in the sense of remaining immature (1 Corinthians 14:20) or impressionable (Ephesians 4:14) in their thinking, but they should be childlike in the sense of being imitators of God (Ephesians 5:1) and inquisitive concerning his ways (Ephesians 5:8,10).

SERMON NO. 1013

Jesus no phantom

'And when the disciples saw him walking on the sea, they were troubled, saying, It is a spirit; and they cried out for fear.' Matthew 14:26

SUGGESTED FURTHER READING: John 13:36–14:3

I do not know whether you can think of death without a shudder. I am afraid there are not many of us who can. It is very easy, when we are rejoicing with all our brethren on Sundays, to sing—*'On Jordan's stormy banks I stand, And cast a wishful eye.'*

I am afraid we would rather live than die after all. A missionary told me the story of an old negro woman in Jamaica who used to be continually singing, 'Angel Gabriel, come and take Aunty Betsy home to glory', but when some wicked wag knocked on her door at the dead of night and told her the angel Gabriel had come for Aunty Betsy, she said, 'She lives next door.' I am afraid it may possibly be so with us, that though we think we wish the waves of Jordan to divide that we may be landed on the other shore, we linger on the bank shivering still. It is so. We dread to leave the warm precincts of this house of clay; we cast many 'a longing, lingering look behind.' But why is it? It is all because we realise the dying bed, the death sweat, the pangs and the glazing eye—we often realise what never turns out to be reality, but do not realise what are sure to be realities, namely the angelic watchers at the bedside, waiting to act as a convoy to bear our spirits up through tracts unknown of purest ether. We do not realise the presence of the Saviour receiving saints into his bosom that they may rest there until the trumpet of the archangel sounds. We do not really grasp the rising again—*'From beds of dust and silent clay, To realms of everlasting day.'*

If we did, then our songs about dying would be more true and our readiness to depart more abiding.

FOR MEDITATION: Walking by faith and not by sight relates to the death as well as to the life of the Christian (2 Corinthians 5:6–8). To see the death of the believer in its proper context we have to look behind the scenes. Take a glimpse at what was seen by Lazarus (Luke 16:22) and by Stephen (Acts 7:55–56).

SERMON NO. 957

Christ with the keys of death and hell

'I ... have the keys of hell and of death.' Revelation 1:18
SUGGESTED FURTHER READING: 1 Peter 3:18–22

As if to prove that he had the keys of the grave, Jesus passed in and passed out again, and he has made free passage now for his people, free entrance and free exit. Whether, when our Lord died, his soul actually descended into hell itself we will not assert or deny; the elder theologians all asserted that he did and hence they inserted in the Creed the sentence, 'He descended into hell', meaning, for many of them, hell itself. It was not till Puritanic times that this doctrine began to be generally questioned, when it was asserted, as I think rightly, that Jesus Christ went into the world of separated spirits, but not into the region of the damned. Well, it is not for us to speak where Scripture is silent, but why may it not be true that the Great Conqueror cast the shadow of his presence over the dens of his enemies as he passed in triumph by the gates of hell? May not the keepers of that infernal gate have seen his star and trembled as they also beheld their master, 'Satan as lightning fall from heaven'? Would it not add to Christ's glory if those who were his implacable foes were made to know of his complete triumph? At any rate, it was but a passing presence, for we know that he sped swiftly to the gates of heaven, taking with him the repentant thief to be with him that day in Paradise. Jesus had opened thus the grave by going into it, hell by passing by it, heaven by passing into it, heaven again by passing out of it, death again by rising from it into this world, and heaven by his ascension. Thus passing and repassing, he has proved that the keys are at his girdle.

FOR MEDITATION: The Lord Jesus Christ holds the keys not only of hell, of death and of heaven (Matthew 16:19), but also of our hearts (Acts 16:14). God alone can open the door of faith to us (Acts 14:27). It is our responsibility to take advantage of these facts while the doors remain open, because no one can reopen the doors once Christ has closed and locked them again (Revelation 3:7).

The universal remedy

'With his stripes we are healed.' Isaiah 53:5
SUGGESTED FURTHER READING: Luke 5:17–32

There are some saints who have *numbness of soul*: the stripes of Christ
can best quicken them; deadness dies in the presence of his death, and
rocks break when the Rock of Ages is seen as cleft for us.

'Who can think, without admiring?
Who can hear, and nothing feel?
See the Lord of life expiring,
Yet retain a heart of steel?'

Many are subject to *the fever of pride*, but a sight of Jesus in his
humiliation, contradicted of sinners, will tend to make them humble.
Pride drops her plumes when she hears the cry, 'Behold the man!' In the
society of one so great, enduring so much scorn, there is no room for
vanity. Some are covered with *the leprosy of selfishness*, but if anything
can forbid a man to lead a selfish life, it is the life of Jesus, who saved
others—himself he could not save. Misers, gluttons and self-seekers love
not the Saviour, for his whole conduct upbraids them. Upon some *the fit
of anger* often comes; but what can give gentleness of spirit like the sight
of him who was as a lamb dumb before her shearers, and who opened
not his mouth under blasphemy and rebuke? If any of you feel *the
fretting consumption of worldliness*, or *the cancer of covetousness*—for
such rank diseases as these are common in Zion—still the groans and
griefs of the Man of sorrows, the acquaintance of grief, will prove a cure.
All evils fly before the Lord Jesus, even as darkness vanishes before the
sun. Lash us, Master, to thy cross; no fatal shipwreck shall we fear if
fastened there. Bind us with cords to the horns of the altar; no disease
can come there: the sacrifice purifies the air.

FOR MEDITATION: The cleaning of the inside should affect the outside
(Matthew 23:26). If we claim to have been healed from the disease of sin
by the death of the Lord Jesus Christ, the sin in our lives should give way
to righteousness (1 Peter 2:24). We have a part to play in the ongoing
healing process (Hebrews 12:12–15), but if the symptoms show no sign of
abating, we ought to question our claims.

SERMON NO. 834

Overwhelming obligations

'What shall I render unto the LORD for all his benefits toward me?' Psalm
116:12
SUGGESTED FURTHER READING: Isaiah 38:9–20

We have reason to be very grateful for the measure of health which we
enjoy. 'It is indeed a strange and awful sensation to be suddenly reduced
by the unnerving hand of sickness to the feebleness of infancy; for giant
strength to lie prostrate, and busy activity to be chained to the weary
bed.' When the bones begin to ache, and sinews and tissues seem to be
but roads for pain to travel on, then we thank God for even a moment's
rest. Do you not know what it is to toss to and fro in the night and wish
for the day, and when the daylight has come to pine for the night? If there
has been an interval of relief, just a little lull in the torture and the pain,
how grateful you have been for it! Shall we not be thankful for health
then, and specially so for a long continuance of it? You strong men that
hardly know what sickness means, if you could be made to walk the
wards of the hospital and see where there have been broken bones, where
there are disorders that depress the system, maladies incurable, pangs
that rack and convulse the frame, and pains all but unbearable, you
would think, I hope, that you had cause enough for gratitude. Not far
from this spot there stands a dome—I thank God for the existence of the
place of which it forms a part—but I can never look at it, and hope I
never shall, without lifting up my heart in thanks to God that my reason
is spared. It is no small unhappiness to be bereft of our faculties, to have
the mind swept to and fro in hurricanes of desperate, raging madness, or
to be victims of hallucinations that shut you out from all usefulness and
even companionship with your fellow men. That you are not in St. Luke's
or Bedlam tonight, should be a cause for thankfulness to Almighty God.

FOR MEDITATION: Physical and mental health are great blessings which
cannot be taken for granted; those who enjoy good health ought to thank
God. Sadly not many bother (Luke 17:12–18). Consider the worshipful
attitude of Nebuchadnezzar when his reason returned (Daniel 4:34–37).

N.B. The nearby domed building in London to which Spurgeon
referred housed the Bethlem Royal Hospital (Bedlam) from 1815 to 1930
and is now the home of the Imperial War Museum.

SERMON NO. 910

A sharp knife for the vine-branches

'Every branch in me that beareth not fruit he taketh away: and every branch that beareth fruit, he purgeth it, that it may bring forth more fruit.' John 15:2

SUGGESTED FURTHER READING: Hebrews 12:5–11

Learn, beloved, especially you under trial, not to see an angry God in your pains, losses or crosses; but instead see a husbandman, who thinks you a branch whom he estimates at so great a rate that he will take the trouble to prune you, which he would not do if he had not a kind consideration towards you. The real reason is that more fruit may be produced, which I understand to mean more in *quantity*. A good man, who feels the power of the word pruning him of this and that superfluity, sets to work in the power of the Holy Spirit to do more for Jesus. Before he was afflicted he did not know how to be patient. He learns it at last—a hard lesson. Before he was poor he did not know how to be humble, but he learns that. Before the word came with power he did not know how to pray with his fellows, or to speak to sinners, or lay himself out for usefulness; but the more he is pruned, the more he serves his Lord. More fruit in *variety* too may be intended. One tree can only produce one kind of fruit usually, but the Lord's people can produce many; and the more they are pruned the more they will produce. There will be all kinds of fruits, both new and old, which they will lay up for their beloved. There will be more in *quality* too. The man may not pray more, but he will pray more earnestly; he may not preach more sermons, but he will preach them more thoroughly from his heart, with a greater unction. It may be that he will not be more in communion with God as to time, but it will be a closer communion; he will throw himself more thoroughly into the divine element of communion and will become more hearty in all that he does. This is the result of the pruning which our heavenly Father gives.

FOR MEDITATION: Does your life produce fruit in quantity (Mark 4:8; John 15:8), in variety (Galatians 5:22–23) and in quality (Ephesians 5:9; Colossians 1:10)? This should be the aim of every Christian, but God has made it clear that it will be a painful process (Hebrews 12:11).

SERMON NO. 774

The Paraclete

'I will pray the Father, and he shall give you another Comforter, that he may abide with you for ever.' John 14:16
SUGGESTED FURTHER READING: 1 Timothy 4:1–7

Honour the Spirit of God as you would honour Jesus Christ if he were present. If Jesus Christ were dwelling in your house you would not ignore him; you would not go about your business as if he were not there. Do not ignore the presence of the Holy Spirit in your soul. I beseech you, do not live as if you had not heard whether there were any Holy Spirit. To him pay your constant adorations. Reverence the august guest who has been pleased to make your body his sacred abode. Love him, obey him, worship him. Take care never to impute the vain imaginings of your fancy to him. I have seen the Spirit of God shamefully dishonoured by persons—I hope they were insane—who have said that they have had this and that revealed to them. There has not for some years passed over my head a single week in which I have not been pestered with the revelations of hypocrites or maniacs. Semi-lunatics are very fond of coming with messages from the Lord to me, and it may spare them some trouble if I tell them once for all that I will have none of their stupid messages. When my Lord and Master has any message to me he knows where I am, and he will send it to me direct and not by madcaps. Never dream that events are revealed to you by heaven, or you may come to be like those idiots who dare impute their blatant follies to the Holy Spirit. If you feel your tongue itch to talk nonsense, trace it to the devil, not to the Spirit of God. Whatever is to be revealed by the Spirit to any of us is in the word of God already—he adds nothing to the Bible, and never will. Let those who have revelations of this, that and the other, go to bed and wake up in their senses. I only wish they would follow the advice, and no longer insult the Holy Spirit by laying their nonsense at his door.

FOR MEDITATION: This is strong language! But offences against the Holy Spirit are treated very seriously in the Bible. If it is dangerous to blaspheme or speak against the Holy Spirit (Matthew 12:31–32) and to lie to the Holy Spirit (Acts 5:3–5), we ought to be careful not to dishonour or discredit his name. Things claimed to be said in the name of the Holy Spirit can come from a lying spirit instead (1 Kings 22:19–28).

Nunc dimittis [or Now lettest thou depart]

'Lord, now lettest thou thy servant depart in peace, according to thy
word: for mine eyes have seen thy salvation.' Luke 2:29–30
SUGGESTED FURTHER READING: Philippians 1:19–26

Every believer shall in death depart in the same sense as Simeon did. The
word here used is suggestive and encouraging: it may be applied either to
escape from confinement or to deliverance from toil. The Christian man
in the present state is like a bird in a cage: his body imprisons his soul.
His spirit, it is true, ranges heaven and earth, and laughs at the limits of
matter, space and time; but for all that, the flesh is a poor scabbard
unworthy of the glittering soul, a mean cottage unfit for a princely spirit,
a clog, a burden and a fetter. When we would watch and pray, we find full
often that 'the spirit indeed is willing, but the flesh is weak.' 'For we that
are in this tabernacle do groan'. The fact is, we are caged birds, but the
day is coming when the great Master shall open the cage door and release
his prisoners. We need not dread the act of unfastening the door, for it
will give to our soul the liberty for which it inwardly pines; and then,
with the wings of a dove, covered with silver, and its feathers with yellow
gold, though once it had lain among the pots, it will soar into its native
air, singing all the way with a rapture beyond imagination. Simeon
looked upon dying as a mode of being let loose, a deliverance out of
durance vile, an escape from captivity, a release from bondage. The like
redemption shall be dealt unto us. How often does my soul feel like an
unhatched chick, shut up within a narrow shell, in darkness and
discomfort! The life within labours hard to chip and break the shell, to
know a little more of the great universe of truth, and see in clearer light
the infinite of divine love. Oh happy day, when the shell shall be broken,
and the soul, complete in the image of Christ, shall enter into the
freedom for which she is preparing!

FOR MEDITATION: 'According to thy word'—consider the verses later listed
by Spurgeon as giving the believer an assurance of departing in peace
(Psalm 23:4; 37:37; 116:15: Isaiah 57:2; 1 Corinthians 3:22; 15:54;
Revelation 14:13). The death of the unconverted will also involve
departing, but it will be out of the frying pan into the fire (Matthew
25:41; Luke 13:27–28; Revelation 21:8).

SERMON NO. 1014

A most needful prayer concerning the Holy Spirit

'Cast me not away from thy presence; and take not thy holy spirit from me.' Psalm 51:11
SUGGESTED FURTHER READING: Revelation 3:14–22

Souls are not saved by systems, but by the Spirit. Organisations without the Holy Spirit are windmills without wind. Methods and arrangements without grace are pipes from a dry conduit, lamps without oil. Even the most scriptural forms of church-government and effort are null and void without the 'power from on high.' Remember too that the power of the church does not lie in her gifts. You might every one of you have all wisdom, and be able to understand all mysteries, and we might all speak with tongues, and be numbered among the eloquent of the earth, but our church might not flourish for all this. Gifts glitter, but are not always gold. Gifts may puff up, but they cannot build up if the Holy Spirit be not there. Strifes, divisions, emulations and jealousies are, through the evil of our nature, the very frequent consequences of the possession of great talents by a church, and these things are unmingled evils. Nor does the power of the church consist in her wealth. When the Spirit is with her, sufficient treasure is laid at her feet, 'and the daughter of Tyre shall be there with a gift;' but if the Spirit of God be gone, we might say of all the money that was ever poured into ecclesiastical coffers by those who sought to strengthen her therewith, 'Thy money perish with thee'. Gold avails nothing to a church devoid of grace; it only increases the evil which is corrupting within. O you boastful churches, you may gild your domes, you may make your pillars of alabaster and cover your altars with precious stones, you may clothe your priests in scarlet and in fair white linen, you may make your ceremonies imposing, your processions gorgeous and your music enchanting, but all this avails nothing if the Spirit of God be gone; all that remains to you is 'as sounding brass, or a tinkling cymbal.'

FOR MEDITATION: In the last days the world will be full of divisive, sensual people who do not have the Spirit (Jude 18–19); much the same can be said about many in the church who have the outward trappings but not the power of godliness (2 Timothy 3:1–5). A living relationship with the Holy Spirit is vital (2 Timothy 1:14; Jude 20).

SERMON NO. 954

A song at the well-head

'Then Israel sang this song, Spring up, O well; sing ye unto it: the princes digged the well, the nobles of the people digged it, by the direction of the lawgiver, with their staves.' Numbers 21:17–18
SUGGESTED FURTHER READING: Jeremiah 7:21–34

They digged the well 'by the direction of the lawgiver'. We must not serve God according to our fancies. The *Westminster Assembly's Catechism* well lays down idolatry to be 'not only the worship of a false God, but the worship of God, the true God, in a way which he has not prescribed.' Consequently, all ceremonies that are not commanded in Scripture are flat idolatry—it matters not what they are. Every mode of worshipping God which is not commanded by God, is neither more nor less than flat idolatry. The children of Israel, in their apostasy, did not set up another God. It is clear to every reader of the story of the golden calf, that they did not worship another god when they fell down before it. They worshipped Jehovah under the form of that golden calf, but it was a way of worship which God had never ordained, for he said he allowed no similitude nor likeness of himself to be attempted to be made, and therefore it was idolatry. And when men adore pieces of bread, they will tell you that they worship Christ under the form of that bread, but it is idolatry. It is a glaring breaking of the second commandment and, we doubt not, will bring destruction upon those who fall into it. In everything we do for God we must not forget to go to work in God's way. I hold that in revivalism, I have no right to adopt anything which I cannot go before God with and justify at the throne of God. I must not adopt a mode of procedure which I may think suits the place or is adapted to the times. Is it right? Let it be done. Is it wrong? Let it not be so much as thought of amongst the saints. We are never to 'do evil that good may come', nor to run over and above, or counter to the current of Scripture in order to work some doubtful good. We must dig the well according to 'the direction of the lawgiver'.

FOR MEDITATION: Is there any form of idolatry in your relationship with God? From idolatry those who worship God in spirit and truth (John 4:24) must abstain (Acts 15:20), disassociate (1 Corinthians 5:11), flee (1 Corinthians 10:14), separate (2 Corinthians 6:16–17), turn (1 Thessalonians 1:9) and keep themselves (1 John 5:21).

SERMON NO. 776

Sown light

'Light is sown for the righteous, and gladness for the upright in heart.'
Psalm 97:11
SUGGESTED FURTHER READING: Mark 10:23–31

Our best is yet to come, and the mercy that is to come will be always coming until life's end. There is a story told of Rowland Hill, which I have no doubt is true, because it is so characteristic of the man's eccentricity and generosity. Some one or other had given him a hundred pounds to send to an extremely poor minister, but, thinking it was too much to send him all at once, he sent him five pounds in a letter with simply these words inside the envelope—'More to follow.' In a few days' time the good man had another letter by the post, and letters by the post were rarities in those days; when he opened it there was five pounds again, with just these words—'And more to follow.' A day or two after there came another, and still the same words—'And more to follow.' And so it continued twenty times, the good man being more and more astounded at these letters coming thus by post always with the sentence—'And more to follow.' Now, every blessing that comes from God is sent in just such an envelope, with the selfsame message—'And more to follow.' 'I forgive you your sins, but there's more to follow.' 'I justify you in the righteousness of Christ, but there's more to follow.' 'I adopt you into my family, but there's more to follow.' 'I educate you for heaven, but there's more to follow.' 'I have helped you even to old age, but there's more to follow.' 'I will bring you to the brink of Jordan, and bid you sit down and sing on its black banks, on the banks of the black stream, but there's more to follow. In the midst of that river, as you are passing into the world of spirits, my mercy shall continue with you, and when you land in the world to come, there shall still be more to follow.' Light is still 'sown for the righteous, and gladness for the upright in heart.'

FOR MEDITATION: The world to come is the Christian's oyster (1 Corinthians 3:21–22). Can you look forward to the life to come (1 Timothy 4:8), the powers to come (Hebrews 6:5) and the city to come (Hebrews 13:14)? Or are you an unbeliever whose worst is yet to come in the form of the wrath to come (Matthew 3:7) and the judgment to come (Acts 24:25)?

SERMON NO. 836

A root out of a dry ground

'A root out of a dry ground.' Isaiah 53:2
SUGGESTED FURTHER READING: Psalm 44:1–26

These are said to be very horrible times—they always were since I have known anything of the world, and I suppose they always were in our fathers' time. We are always at a crisis according to some people. I am not about to defend the times; they are, no doubt, very bad, for the innumerable spirits of evil are bold and active, while good men seem to have lost their courage. We find amalgamations and compromises ad infinitum, and the precious truth of God is trodden as the mire of the streets. What about all this? Are we discouraged? Far from it. Bad times are famous times for Christ. When Wycliffe came, the times were dark enough in England, and therefore the morning star was the more welcome. When Luther came into the world, the times were almost as black as they could be and therefore good times for reformation! The times were dead enough when Wesley and Whitefield came: but they proved glorious days for the Lord to work in! And if you discern now that there is not much prayerfulness, nor much spirituality, nor much truthful doctrine, nor much zeal, do not fret; it is thoroughly dry soil, and now the root of grace will grow. John Bunyan once said that when he heard the young fellows swear so profanely in his parish, he used to think what men God would make of them when he converted them! Let us think of that. Suppose he saves those wretched priests who are trying to swallow down England, suppose he converts these profane rationalists, who almost deny God's existence—what penitent sinners they will make when he once breaks their hearts, and what preachers of the word they will be when he renews them. Let us have good hope. Our faith does not rise when people say the times are improving, nor do we despond when men denounce the times as bad. Eternity is the lifetime of God, and he will work out his purposes.

FOR MEDITATION: The fact that God can use physical means to bring water to dry places (Psalm 105:41; 107:35; Isaiah 41:18) ought to encourage us to look to him in faith when we find ourselves suffering from spiritual drought whether personally (Psalm 63:1; Isaiah 58:11) or nationally (Ezekiel 37:2–4,11–12).

Plain words with the careless

'When he saw Jesus, he cried out, and fell down before him, and with a loud voice said, What have I to do with thee, Jesus, thou Son of God most high? I beseech thee, torment me not.' Luke 8:28
SUGGESTED FURTHER READING: Acts 13:38-52

If we understand these words to be the exclamation of the evil spirit which demented this poor demoniac, they are very natural words, and one can very readily understand them, for the presence of Christ is such a great torment to the prince of evil that he might well cry out, 'art thou come hither to torment us before the time?' If we would put Satan to rout, we have only to preach the Lord Jesus in the power of the Spirit, for this is the hell of devils. Hence it is that he roars so much against gospel preachers: he roars because the gospel makes him smart. But if these words be looked upon as the language of the man himself, they are most extraordinary. In fact they are singularly mad and foolish, that we can only account for them by the fact that, though it was a man who spoke, yet the devil was in him; for surely none but a man possessed with a devil would say to Jesus, who alone could bless him, 'depart from me' or 'torment me not'. And yet there are tens of thousands of men in this world who are saying just the same thing. Thousands of persons appear to be far more anxious to escape from salvation than to escape from eternal wrath. They avoid heaven's love with scrupulous diligence, and the prayer of their life seems to be, 'Keep me, Lord from heaven! Prevent me ever being saved! Give me the full swing of my sins and let me live so as to ruin my soul!' Conduct most strange! Whence comes such folly? The desire and determination of some men to destroy themselves are fixed and resolute to the last degree. Their self-hate and their suicidal avoidance of mercy's thousand exhortations and entreaties are so extraordinary that, I repeat, we can only account for men being so besotted and maddened, by the fact that Satan has the mastery over them and leads them captive at his will.

FOR MEDITATION: Satan can be held responsible for blinding the minds of unbelievers and preventing them from seeing the light of the gospel of Christ (2 Corinthians 4:4), but unbelievers bear their share of responsibility for following the devil in their trespasses and sins and for continuing to disobey God (Ephesians 2:1-2).

SERMON NO. 778

The great attraction

'And I, if I be lifted up from the earth, will draw all men unto me.' John
12:32
SUGGESTED FURTHER READING: Mark 1:14–20

Believers working for Christ, learn from the text that if you would win
souls, you must draw them rather than drive them. Very few people are
bullied into heaven. The way to bring men to Jesus Christ is not by rough
words, black looks and continually warning them, but rather by gentle
invitations. Tenderly as a nurse with her child must we seek to win souls.
In the second place, if we would win souls, Jesus Christ must be our great
attraction. In the Sunday-school class, visiting from house to house, or
elsewhere, we must keep close to the text and the text must be the cross. I
must confess there is a very great sweetness to my soul in preaching about
Christ. I hope it is never a weariness to preach any part of divine truth,
but it is delight itself to preach up the Master: then we have to deal with
the heart of the matter. When we preach Jesus Christ, we are not putting
out the plates, knives and forks for the feast, but we are handing out the
bread itself. Now we are not, as it were, working in the field at the
hedging, the ditching and the sowing, but we are gathering the golden
sheaves and bringing the harvest home. If we want a hundredfold harvest,
we must sow seed which was steeped in the blood of Calvary; and, dear
friends, if you want to be drawn nearer to Christ yourselves, do not go to
Moses to help you, but get to Christ. Go to Christ to get to Christ. 'I, if I
be lifted up from the earth, will draw all men'—where?—'unto me.' Jesus
draws to himself. Recollect you have never experienced the fulness of the
drawings unless you are drawn to Christ. If you are only drawn to
holiness, or to the church, or to good experiences, you have not obtained
the fulness and soul of the matter. You must be drawn to Christ.

FOR MEDITATION: Consider the gracious and gentle terms associated with
the death of Christ. He died not only to draw all men to himself, but to
gather together the scattered children of God (John 11:51–52) and to
bring us to God (John 10:15–17; 1 Peter 3:18). Do you rely on the
attractive power of Christ crucified as you seek to reach others
(1 Corinthians 1:18,24; 2:2)?

The one thing needful

'But one thing is needful.' Luke 10:42
SUGGESTED FURTHER READING: Psalm 27:1–14

Let us remark that, though this is only one thing and so concentrated, yet it is also comprehensive and contains many things. Imagine not that to sit at Jesus' feet is a very small meaningless thing. It means *peace*, for they who submit to Jesus find peace through his precious blood. It means *holiness*, for those who learn of Jesus learn no sin, but are instructed in things lovely and of good repute. It means *strength*, for they that sit with Jesus and feed upon him, are girded with his strength; the joy of the Lord is their strength. It means *wisdom*, for they that learn of the Son of God understand more than the ancients, because they keep his statutes. It means *zeal*, for the love of Christ fires hearts that live upon it, and they that are much with Jesus become like Jesus, so that the zeal of the Lord's house eats them up. If we say that in an army the one thing needful is loyalty to the sovereign, we know what that means; for the loyal soldier will be sure to be obedient to his officers, and, if attached to his queen, he will be brave in the day of battle and do his duty well. If we said that the one thing needful in a family was love, we should not have required a small thing; for love will place husband and wife in their true position; love will produce obedience in children and diligence in servants. Let love permeate everything and other virtues will grow out of it, as flowers spring from the soil. So when we say that sitting at Jesus' feet is the one thing needful, we have not uttered a mere truism: it comprehends a world of blessings.

FOR MEDITATION: Those who are 'dull of hearing' end up needing a refresher course in the basics of the Christian faith (Hebrews 5:11–12); those who abide in Christ and his word will find that they receive all the teaching they need to give them a comprehensive spiritual education (1 John 2:27).

A singular but needful question

'*Wilt thou be made whole?*' *John 5:6*
SUGGESTED FURTHER READING: Hebrews 7:23–28

The perfection of our Saviour's manhood consisted in this, that he was 'holy, harmless, undefiled, separate from sinners'. He was *holy*, that is, in its root, the same thing as 'whole'; he was a complete, perfect, uninjured, undefiled, untainted man. He was whole towards his God. It was his meat and drink to do the will of God that sent him. Jesus as man was man as God would have man, perfectly conformed to his right position. He was as man came from the Maker's hand, without blot, without loss, without outgrowth of evil, and without the absence of any good thing; he was whole and holy. Hence he was *harmless*, never inflicting ill on others in word or deed; *undefiled*, never affected by the influences that surrounded him so as to become false to his God or unkind to man; undefiled, though blasphemy passed through or by his ear, yet it never polluted his heart; though he saw the lust and wickedness of man carried to its climax, yet he himself remained without spot and blameless. He was also *separate from sinners*, not drawing around him a Pharisaic cordon and saying, 'Stand by, for I am holier than thou,' but eating with them and yet separate from them, and never more separate than when his gracious hand touched them, and when he entered most deeply into sympathy with them in their sorrows. He was separate by his own mental elevation, moral superiority and spiritual grandeur. Now, would you wish to be like Jesus? Probably if you were, it would involve in you much of his experience; you would be laughed at, scoffed at and persecuted, and, unless providence restrained your foe, you also might be brought to the death: but taking Christ for all and all, would you be willing to be made like him, to have torn away from yourself much real evil, which you now admire, and to have implanted in you much real good, which perhaps at this moment you do not appreciate? Would you be willing now to be made whole?

FOR MEDITATION: In the expectation of being like Christ in the future (1 John 3:2), the Christian should aim to be like him now by being holy (1 Peter 1:15–16), harmless (Philippians 2:15), undefiled (James 1:27) and separate from sinners (2 Corinthians 6:17), while being amongst them in the world (1 Corinthians 5:9–10).

SERMON NO. 955

The coming resurrection

'Marvel not at this: for the hour is coming, in the which all that are in the graves shall hear his voice, and shall come forth; they that have done good, unto the resurrection of life; and they that have done evil, unto the resurrection of damnation.' John 5:28–29
SUGGESTED FURTHER READING: James 2:14–26

Those who search the Scriptures know that the mode of judging at the last day will be entirely according to works. Will men be saved then for their works? No, by no means. Salvation is in every case the work and gift of grace. But the judgment will be guided by our works. It is due to those to be judged, that they should all be tried by the same rule. Now, no rule can be common to saints and sinners, except the rule of their moral conduct, and by this rule shall all men be judged. If God does not find in you any holiness of life whatever, neither will he accept you. 'What', says one, 'of the dying thief then?' There was the righteousness of faith in him and it produced all the holy acts which circumstances allowed; the very moment he believed in Christ, he confessed Christ and spoke for Christ, and that one act stood as evidence of his being a friend of God, while all his sins were washed away. May God grant you grace so to confess your sins and believe in Jesus, that all your transgressions may be forgiven you. There must be some evidence of your faith. Before the assembled host of men there shall be no evidence given of your faith fetched from your inward feelings, but the evidence shall be found in your outward actions. It will still be, 'I was an hungred, and ye gave me meat: I was thirsty, and ye gave me drink: I was a stranger, and ye took me in: naked, and ye clothed me: I was sick, and ye visited me: I was in prison, and ye came unto me.' Take heed, then, as to practical godliness, and abhor all preaching which would make sanctity of life to be a secondary thing. We are justified by faith, but not by a dead faith: the faith which justifies is that which produces 'holiness, without which no man shall see the Lord'.

FOR MEDITATION: Without faith it is impossible to please God (Hebrews 11:6) and without holiness it will be impossible to see God (Hebrews 12:14), but there is cause for great assurance when faith and holiness are combined (Colossians 1:21–23; 1 Timothy 2:15; Jude 20–21,24).

All these things—a sermon with three texts

'And Jacob their father said unto them, Me have ye bereaved of my children: Joseph is not, and Simeon is not, and ye will take Benjamin away: all these things are against me.' Genesis 42:36
SUGGESTED FURTHER READING: 2 Chronicles 32:20–31

In the Greek annals there is an old story of a soldier under Antigonus who had a disease about him, an extremely painful one, likely to bring him soon to the grave. Always first in the ranks was this soldier, and in the hottest part of the fray; he was always to be seen leading the van, the bravest of the brave, because his pain prompted him to fight that he might forget it; and he feared not death because he knew that in any case he had not long to live. Antigonus, who greatly admired the valour of his soldier, finding out that he suffered from a disease, had him cured by one of the most eminent physicians of the day, but, alas, from that moment the warrior was absent from the front of the battle. He now sought his ease, for, as he remarked to his companions, he had something worth living for—health, home, family and other comforts—and he would not risk his life now as before. So when our troubles are many, we are made courageous in serving our God; we feel we have nothing to live for in this world, and by hope of the world to come we are driven to exhibit zeal, self-denial and industry; but how often is it otherwise in better times? For then the joys and pleasures of this world make it hard for us to remember the world to come, and we sink into inglorious ease. Master, we thank thee for our griefs, for they have quickened us. We bless thee for winds and waves, for these have driven us away from treacherous shores. 'Before I was afflicted I went astray: but now have I kept thy word.' Trials and troubles touch the life of our spirit because their endurance is strengthening.

FOR MEDITATION: Spurgeon's 'three texts' shared the words 'all these things'. Consider the ways in which, to use Spurgeon's headings, we can regard our trials and troubles negatively with *the exclamation of unbelief* (Genesis 42:36), or treat them positively by seeing their beneficial effects upon us through *the philosophy of experience* (Isaiah 38:16) and by conquering them through *the triumph of faith* (Romans 8:37).

SERMON NO. 837

Royal homage

'And cast their crowns before the throne.' Revelation 4:10
SUGGESTED FURTHER READING: 1 Corinthians 1:26–31

By this text we can know whether we are the way to heaven or not, because no man goes to heaven to learn for the first time heavenly things. We must be scholars in Christ's school here, or else we cannot be taken into Christ's college above. If you and I should walk into some great cathedral where they were singing, and ask to be allowed to sing in the choir, they would ask whether we had ever learnt the tune, and they would not let us join unless we had. Nor can we expect that untrained voices should be admitted into the choirs above. Now, dear brothers and sisters, have you learnt to cast your crowns at the Saviour's feet? Have you been professors of religion for some years, and been honoured in the Sunday-school class or in the ministry, and have you been enabled to maintain an upright character? Well, in some measure, you have a crown. Are you continually in the habit of casting that at his feet? Let me put it to you—have you anything that you call your own to boast of? Have you some good things that you have done that you could speak of? Could you say, like one of old, 'God, I thank thee, that I am not as other men are'? Have you been very good and industrious, very consistent and persevering, and do you feel you deserve a good deal of esteem and honour as an acknowledgment of your distinguished services? My dear friend, I am afraid you are learning a music that will never answer in heaven. There is no one in glory who ever says, 'I have done well: I deserve credit and honour.' Quite the reverse. There the one music is, 'Not unto us, O Lord, not unto us'. Have you learnt that? Is that your spirit every day?

FOR MEDITATION: Have you started to learn the songs sung by the redeemed in heaven (Revelation 14:3; 15:3)? The song of Moses (Revelation 15:3) concentrates on God—'The Lord is my strength and song, and he is become my salvation' (Exodus 15:2). You can join in now if you know that he was once angry with you and that his anger is turned away (Isaiah 12:1–2). 'This is my story, this is my song, Praising *myself* all the day long' is not the music of heaven.

The saints blessing the Lord

'Bless the LORD, *O my soul: and all that is within me, bless his holy name.' Psalm 103:1*
SUGGESTED FURTHER READING: Hebrews 12:11–23

If we can attain to constant praise now, it will prepare us for all that awaits us. We do not know what will happen to us between this and heaven, but we can easily prognosticate the aim and result of all that will occur. We are harps which will be tuned in all their strings for the concerts of the blessed. The tuner is putting us in order. He sweeps his hands along the strings; there is a jar from every note; so he begins first with one string and then goes to another. He continues at each string till he hears the exact note. The last time you were ill, one of your strings was tuned; the last time you had a bad debt, or trembled at declining business, another string was tuned. And so, between now and heaven, you will have every string set in order; and you will not enter heaven till all are in tune. Have you ever gone to a place where they make pianos, and expect to hear sweet music? The tuning-room is enough to drive a man mad, and in the factory you hear the screeching of saws and the noise of hammers, and you say, 'I thought this was a place where they made pianos.' Yes, so it is, but it is not the place where they play them. On earth is the place where God makes musical instruments and tunes them, and between now and heaven he will put all that is within them into fit condition for blessing and praising his name eternally. In heaven every part of the man will bless God without any difficulty. No need for a preacher there to exhort you; no need for you to talk to yourself and say, 'Bless the Lord, O my soul:' you will do it as naturally as now you breathe. You never take any consideration as to how often you shall breathe, and you have no plan laid down as to when your blood shall circulate, because these matters come naturally to you; and in heaven it will be your nature to praise God.

FOR MEDITATION: Christians are to make melody (literally 'play on a stringed instrument') in their hearts to the Lord (Ephesians 5:19), but we tend to be more like 'sounding brass, or a tinkling cymbal' (1 Corinthians 13:1) or poorly played pipes, harps and trumpets (1 Corinthians 14:7–8). On this side of heaven there needs to be a lot of tuning on God's part and a lot of practice on our part.

SERMON NO. 1078

The poor man's friend

'For he shall deliver the needy when he crieth; the poor also, and him that hath no helper.' Psalm 72:12

SUGGESTED FURTHER READING: Psalm 109:21–31

We begin life in a needy state. We are full of needs in our infancy and cannot help ourselves. We continue throughout life in a needy state. The very breath in our nostrils has to be the gift of God's goodness; 'in him we live, and move, and have our being'. As we grow old our needs become even more apparent. The staff on which we lean reveals to us our needs, and our infirmities all tell us what needy creatures we are. We need temporal things and we need spiritual things. Our body needs, our soul needs and our spirit needs. We need to be kept from evil; we need to be led into the paths of righteousness; we need on the outset that grace should be implanted; when implanted, we need that it be nurtured; when nurtured, we need that it be perfected and made to bring forth fruit. We are never a moment without need. We wake up, and our first glance might reveal our needs to us; and when we fall asleep it is upon a poor man's pillow, for we need God to preserve us through the night. We have needs when we are on our knees, else where would be the energy of our prayers? We have needs when we try to sing, else how should our uncircumcised lips praise God aright? We have needs when we are relieving the needs of others, lest we become proud of our almsgiving. We have need in preaching and need in hearing; we have need in working, need in suffering and need in resting. What is our life but one long need? All men are full of needs. But God's own special people *feel* this need. They not only confess it is so, but they know it experimentally. They are full of needs.

FOR MEDITATION: God knows what his children really need (Matthew 6:8,32) and can be relied upon to meet those needs (Philippians 4:19). Consider how great a comfort this was to David whenever he was burdened with a sense of how poor and needy he was (Psalm 35:10; 40:17; 70:5; 86:1).

The talking book

'When thou awakest, it shall talk with thee.' Proverbs 6:22
SUGGESTED FURTHER READING (Spurgeon): Psalm 119:161–176

I was assured the other day by a good man, with a great deal of alarm, that all England was going over to popery. I told him I did not know what kind of God he worshipped, but my God was a good deal bigger than the devil, and did not intend to let the devil have his way after all, and that I was not half as much afraid of the Pope at Rome as of the ritualists at home. But, mark it, there is some truth in these fears. There will be a going over to one form of error or another, unless there is in the Christian church a more honest, industrious and general reading of Holy Scripture. What if I were to say that most of you church members do not read your Bibles; would I be slandering you? You hear on the Lord's Day a chapter read, and you perhaps read a passage at family prayer, but a very large number never read the Bible privately for themselves; they take their religion out of the monthly magazine, or accept it from the minister's lips. Oh for the Berean spirit back again, to search the Scriptures whether these things be so. I would like to see a huge pile of all the books, good and bad that were ever written, prayer-books, sermons and hymn-books, all smoking like Sodom of old, if the reading of those books keeps you away from the reading of the Bible; for a ton weight of human literature is not worth an ounce of Scripture; one single drop of the essential tincture of the word of God is better than a sea full of our commentings and sermonisings, and the like. We must live upon the word, the simple, pure, infallible word of God, if we are to become strong against error and tenacious of truth. Brethren, may you be established in the faith, rooted, grounded and built up; but I know you cannot be unless you search the Scriptures continually.

FOR MEDITATION: In a world full of deceitful and empty talkers, we need to be taught by those who hold faithfully to the Bible (1 Timothy 4:1,6; Titus 1:9–10). But we still need to do our own homework (Acts 17:11); those who fail to do their homework usually get into trouble.

SERMON NO. 1017

Think well and do well

'For thy lovingkindness is before mine eyes: and I have walked in thy truth.' Psalm 26:3

SUGGESTED FURTHER READING (Spurgeon): Psalm 139:1–24

It is an encouraging fact, when we can honestly feel as before God that our thoughts are habitually exercised upon himself and upon divine truth; 'as he thinketh in his heart, so is he'. We may probably form a better judgment of ourselves from the tenor of our thoughts than from any other evidence. If all our thoughts go downward, downward we ourselves are going; but if there be some breathings towards the heavenly, some aspirations of our spirit towards the pure and perfect Father of Lights, then may we have hope that we also are ascending towards the heavenly places and shall dwell in them hereafter. David could urge, besides the secret evidence of his devout thoughts, the public proof of his holy acts—'I have walked in thy truth.' It would be vanity for a man to find evidence of a renewed heart in his private meditations, if those thoughts were not sufficiently deep to lead him to practical godliness. The thoughts become a valuable evidence because of their influence upon the life, but if they were so powerlessly superficial that our daily life was in no degree affected by them, they would be as salt that has lost its savour. If our actions are evil, it is vain to take comfort from our thoughts. If actions speak louder than words, they may well speak louder than thoughts. We must display outward holiness, otherwise our inward experience of grace exists only in pretence. Whatever may be your thoughts, if all your behaviour is according to the will of the flesh and not after the will of God, your thoughts are nothing; you have deceived yourself as to their tenor; they cannot be as you say they are, truthful, holy, devout and divine thoughts. Put the two together, holy thoughts and holy living, and you have sure evidences of a renewed nature; and if God has given you both of these, though you will probably confess that you have them not in the measure in which you would desire to have them, yet bless the grace that has so worked upon you.

FOR MEDITATION: The actions of God are consistent with his thoughts (Psalm 92:5); the same is true of man (Genesis 6:5). But by nature our thoughts and ways are not consistent with God's (Isaiah 55:8–9) and true repentance involves a turnabout in both areas (Isaiah 55:7).

SERMON NO. 956

The first cry from the cross

'Then said Jesus, Father, forgive them; for they know not what they do.'
Luke 23:34
SUGGESTED FURTHER READING: John 11:45–53

Notice that nothing is sought for these people but that which concerns their souls—'Father, forgive them'. And I believe the church will do well when she recollects that she wrestles not with flesh and blood, but with spiritual wickedness, and that what she has to dispense is not the law and order by which magistrates may be upheld or tyrannies pulled down, but the spiritual government by which hearts are conquered to Christ, and judgments are brought into subjection to his truth. I believe that the more the church of God strains, before God, after the forgiveness of sinners, and the more she seeks to teach sinners what sin is, what the blood of Christ is, what is the hell that must follow if sin be not washed out, and what is the heaven which will be ensured to all those who are cleansed from sin, the more she keeps to this the better. Press forward as one man, my brethren, to secure the root of the matter in the forgiveness of sinners. As to all the evils that afflict humanity, by all means take your share in battling with them; let temperance be maintained, let education be supported, let reforms, political and ecclesiastical, be pushed forward as far as you have the time and effort to spare, but the first business of every Christian man and woman is with the hearts and consciences of men as they stand before the everlasting God. Let nothing turn you aside from your divine errand of mercy to undying souls. This is your one business. Tell to sinners that sin will damn them, that Christ alone can take away sin; make this the one passion of your souls, 'Father, forgive them! Let them know how to be forgiven. Let them be actually forgiven, and let me never rest except as I am the means of bringing sinners to be forgiven, even the guiltiest of them.'

FOR MEDITATION: The Lord Jesus Christ came into the world to save sinners (1 Timothy 1:15) and to forgive their sins (Luke 7:37,48). Sinners flocked to hear him (Luke 15:1). If God in his goodness teaches sinners in the way (Psalm 25:8), those whom he has forgiven should also long for the conversion of others and teach them accordingly (Psalm 51:13; James 5:20).

SERMON NO. 897

Sins of omission

'Yet they obeyed not, nor inclined their ear, but walked every one in the imagination of their evil heart: therefore I will bring upon them all the words of this covenant, which I commanded them to do; but they did them not.' Jeremiah 11:8

SUGGESTED FURTHER READING (Spurgeon): Matthew 25:14–30

Consider what God thinks of omissions. Saul was ordered to kill the Amalekites and not to let one escape. He saved Agag and the best of the cattle, and for that, though he had positively done nothing but simply stayed his hand, the Lord put him away from being king over Israel. Ahab was commanded to kill Benhadad on account of innumerable cruelties. Benhadad was taken captive, but Ahab treated him with great leniency and, because he let him go, the result was that Ahab's life would go for his life. Non-obedience ruined Ahab. Our Lord Jesus Christ was the gentlest of all men, and yet there was one miracle which had a degree of vengeance in it; what was that? He stood under a fig tree, saw there leaves but no fruit and said, 'Let no fruit grow on thee henceforward for ever', as if to show that fruitless things provoked his anger, not so much brambles which bear their thorns, but fig trees which ought to bear figs and do not. Remember the parable of the talents. The man with one talent was condemned not for squandering his Lord's money, but because he had not increased it. So in God's opinion not doing good is sufficient to condemn men, even if they have not committed positive evil. When the Holy Spirit convinces men of sin, what is the special sin which he reveals? Adultery? Robbery? No, a sin of omission—'of sin, because they believe not on me'. Omitting to trust in Jesus is the master sin of which the Holy Spirit convicts the world. Remember that solemn question in Hebrews 2:3—'how shall we escape if we' what? Swear? Frequent the tavern? No, 'if we neglect so great salvation'? Lifelong neglect of salvation involves us in danger from which there is no escape.

FOR MEDITATION: Unbelievers express surprise at the foolish things Christians refuse to do (1 Peter 4:4). The Lord Jesus Christ expresses sadness at the wise things unbelievers refuse to do (Matthew 23:37–38), such as receiving him and trusting in him for salvation (John 1:11; 3:18). To fail to do what we know to be right is sin (James 4:17).

A summons to battle

'The time when kings go forth to battle.' 2 Samuel 11:1
SUGGESTED FURTHER READING: Proverbs 24:30–34

Read at your leisure the context of my text. David sent his servant Joab to contend with the Ammonites. Unhappy king! He had been called to fight the Lord's battles; he had been anointed king for the very purpose, to be a captain in Israel; but a fit of sloth had seized him, and true in David's case was the children's song, 'Satan finds some mischief still for idle hands to do.' The eyes that ought to have been looking on the foe, looked on Bathsheba; the heart that ought to have been stout against the enemies of Israel, softened with lascivious desires, and the king had a fall, not from the battlements of his house, but from the elevation of his purity and faith, from which he never altogether recovered and which has left the blackest stain upon his reputation. Such are the dangers of inaction to us all; it may not take precisely that form, for Satan knows how to adapt the temptation to each man's temperament and to each woman's case. I do believe it is before every Christian either to serve his God with all his heart, or to fall into sin. I believe we must either go forward or fall. The rule in Christian life is, if we do not bring forth fruit unto the Lord our God, we shall lose even our leaves and stand like a winter's tree, bare and withered. God grant you to make no ill choice in this matter, but to resolve that if you be overtaken in a fault, it shall not be because you travelled so slowly that sin could readily overtake you. I would remind you that in some form or other evil must come to you if you loiter; if you will not serve your Lord, neither shall you be established; if you will not bring forth fruit to his glory, neither can you expect the comforts of his gospel.

FOR MEDITATION: Idleness is a great enemy. Consider in Proverbs 6:6–11 the description of a sluggard (v.9), the destruction of a sluggard (vv.10–11), the distinction between a sluggard and the diligent (vv.6–8) and the direction to the sluggard (v.6). The experience of the idle servant in yesterday's suggested reading should be a warning to us (Matthew 25:18,24–30).

The vital force

'Now the just shall live by faith.' Hebrews 10:38
SUGGESTED FURTHER READING: 2 Timothy 4:1–8

Some people seem to imagine that there is a kind of finality in each stage of religious experience, as though we are to repent in the first dawn of our spiritual life, but afterwards we may leave off repenting, and account henceforth that this bitter cup of gall is emptied, no more to sting the conscience with remorse or move the heart to godly sorrow; whereas, I suppose, we shall pass through the pearly gates brushing away the last tear of repentance, always till then having need to mourn past sins and grieve for present frailties in penitential showers of grief. It seems to have been the fancy of others, that we are to stand as sinners once for all at the foot of the cross, look to Jesus and be lightened; but after that, we are to press to something higher, something yet beyond, a repose calm and undisturbed, free from rough winds and rude alarms. Surely such people do not know what the Christian's inner life is. Depend upon it, that as much at the last as at the first 'the just shall live by faith'. He that is ripest and nearest heaven has no more ground of confidence than he who only five minutes ago, like the dying thief, received the assurance of his pardon. The ground of the sinner's acceptance in the first moment of his faith is the finished work of Christ, and, after fifty years of earnest service, that must still be the sole cause of his acceptance with God and the only rock upon which his soul must dare to build. The act of simple faith, looking out of self and looking alone to Christ, is a thing for the penitent publican when first he smites on his breast; but it is also for the dying David, when he knows that the covenant is 'ordered in all things, and sure'. Thus it well becomes the maturest saint, with his last breath, to express his confidence in the God who pardons sin through the application of the precious blood.

FOR MEDITATION: Faith abides (1 Corinthians 13:13). As far as saving faith is concerned the Christian is to continue (Acts 14:22; Colossians 1:23), stand fast (1 Corinthians 16:13), grow (2 Thessalonians 1:3) and hold fast (1 Timothy 1:19; Hebrews 10:23). By God's grace it should be the norm for every Christian to claim in all humility 'I have kept the faith' (2 Timothy 4:7).

SERMON NO. 891

Self-humbling and self-searching

'Look not upon me, because I am black, because the sun hath looked upon me: my mother's children were angry with me; they made me the keeper of the vineyards; but mine own vineyard have I not kept.' Song of Solomon 1:6
SUGGESTED FURTHER READING: 2 Corinthians 7:5–12

Do you know what it is to fret because you have spoken an unadvised word? Do you know what it is to smite upon your breast, because you were angry? You were justly provoked perhaps, but still, being angry, you spoke unadvisedly. Have you ever gone to a sleepless bed, because in business you have let fall a word, or have done an action which, upon mature deliberation, you could not justify? Does the tear never come from your eye because you are not like your Lord, and have failed when you hoped to succeed? I would give little for your godliness, if you know nothing of this. Repentance is as much a mark of a Christian as faith itself. Do not think we have done with repenting when we come to Christ and receive the forgiveness of our sins by the blood that once did atone. No, we shall repent as long as we sin and as long as we need the precious blood for cleansing. While there is sin, or a proneness to any kind of sin, lurking in us, the grace of God will make us loathe the sin and humble ourselves before the Most High on account of it. Now, I think our text seems to say just this: there were some that admired the church. They said she was fair. She seemed to say, 'Don't say that; you don't know what I am, or you would not praise me.' There is nothing that brings a blush to a genuine Christian's face like praising him, for he feels, 'Praise such a heap of dirt as I am? Give any credit to such a worthless worm as I am? No, do not cast admiring glances at me! Do not say, "That man has many virtues and many excellences!"' 'Look not upon me, because I am black'.

FOR MEDITATION: On earth only a sinless Christian would need no more repentance, but there is no such person in existence (1 John 1:8–10). A Christian needs to go on repenting (Luke 17:3–4) and it is tragic when professing Christians appear to have 'advanced' beyond the desire to repent or have lost the willpower to do so (2 Corinthians 12:21).

SERMON NO. 990

Pleading

'But I am poor and needy: make haste unto me, O God: thou art my help and my deliverer; O LORD, make no tarrying.' Psalm 70:5
SUGGESTED FURTHER READING (Spurgeon): Genesis 32:9–32

Mere prayer sayers, who do not pray at all, forget to argue with God; but those who would prevail bring forth their reasons and their strong arguments, and they debate the question with the Lord. Those who play at wrestling catch here and there at random, but those who are really wrestling have a certain way of grasping the opponent, a certain mode of throwing and the like; they work according to order and rule. Faith's art of wrestling is to plead with God and say with holy boldness, 'Let it be thus and thus, for these reasons.' Hosea tells us of Jacob at Jabbok that 'there he spake with us', from which I understand that Jacob instructed us by his example. Now, the two pleas which Jacob used were God's precept and God's promise. First he said, 'O God ... which saidst unto me, Return unto thy country, and to thy kindred', as much as if he put it thus—'Lord, I am in difficulty, but I have come here through obedience to thee. Thou didst tell me to do this; now, since thou commandest me to come hither, into the very teeth of my brother Esau, who comes to meet me like a lion, Lord, thou canst not be so unfaithful as to bring me into danger and then leave me in it.' This was sound reasoning and it prevailed with God. Then Jacob also urged a promise: 'thou saidst, I will surely do thee good'. Among men it is a masterly way of reasoning when you can challenge your opponent with his own words: you may quote other authorities and he may say, 'I deny their force', but when you quote a man against himself, you foil him completely. When you bring a man's promise to his mind, he must either confess himself to be unfaithful and changeable, or, if he holds to being the same and being true to his word, you have him and you have won your will of him. Let us learn thus to plead the precepts, the promises and whatever else may serve our turn; but let us always have something to plead. Do not reckon you have prayed unless you have pleaded.

FOR MEDITATION: Consider some others who in prayer have quoted God's word in support of their pleas (Exodus 33:12–13; Numbers 14:17–19; 2 Samuel 7:25–27; 1 Kings 8:25–26,29; Nehemiah 1:8–9). Do you know God's word well enough to be able to attempt this?

Dei gratia [or, by the grace of God]

'To the praise of the glory of his grace.' Ephesians 1:6
SUGGESTED FURTHER READING: 1 Corinthians 15:1–10

Here needs a tongue far more fluent than mine; or rather here is wanted no tongue but a warm heart and grateful thought to sit down and contemplate. As many of you as have been bought with blood and washed in it, as many of you as have been taken from among men and made to be the Lord's own special people, I ask you now in silence to praise God while your mind surveys the whole plan of your salvation. Chosen before the earth was—grace, free grace; given into the hands of Christ to be his treasure—all of grace; redeemed with the heart's blood of Emmanuel, all out of his free favour to you; preserved when you were running into sin, slaves of Satan, mad on your idols, preserved in Christ Jesus by longsuffering grace; called with that voice which wakes the dead, and endowed with spiritual life, altogether of grace; adopted into the divine family, made partakers of the divine nature, because grace so willed it—what wonders are here! In your case it was grace of the most eminent degree. If you do not say so of your case, I must say so of mine. Above all the sons of men I humbly claim to be most indebted to the grace of God. But, I doubt not, you also claim the same. There were specialities about our character, peculiarities about our sin, and difficulties about our constitution which all tended to make it very remarkable that we should be the subjects of the divine love. Each one of us can say—

'What was there in me that could merit esteem,
Or give the Creator delight?'

Now, you will glorify God if you let your soul in silence muse at the foot of the throne of grace, and worship him of whose mercy you have so largely been made a recipient.

FOR MEDITATION: If you have experienced it, glory in the grace of God through which you have received faith (Acts 18:27), justification (Romans 3:24; Titus 3:7), salvation (Ephesians 2:5,8; Titus 2:11), everlasting consolation and good hope (2 Thessalonians 2:16).

SERMON NO. 958

A word with those who wait for signs and wonders

'This is an evil generation: they seek a sign.' Luke 11:29
SUGGESTED FURTHER READING: John 4:46–54

Some of you who are not believing are seeking signs which others have never had. I will give you an instance or two. There stood the prodigal son feeding the swine, so hungry that 'he would fain have filled his belly with the husks'; the thought crossed his mind, 'I will arise and go to my father'. What sign had he? He sets off to seek his father's face. What sign had he, I say? There does not appear to have been even an invitation sent, but he sought his father and he found forgiveness. Take another case. Christ has likened seeking souls to the widow who sought help of the unjust judge. She cried to him; she continued to cry to him, until she gained her suit; but what sign had she? If any sign, it was all negative, all from the opposite quarter, yet on she went. Look at the Canaanitish woman. She desired that her daughter might be healed. What sign had she? Christ said, 'It is not meet to take the children's bread, and to cast it to dogs'. Instead of a sign to help her it was a hard word to discourage her, but yet she won her suit. And why not you, my hearers, why not you? The poor woman who touched the hem of Christ's garment in the crowd, what sign had she of his willingness to help her? It was her own earnest, intense desire, and her faith in Jesus that made her touch the hem out of which the virtue came. Wait not then for signs to be given to you when they have not been given to others, but do as others have done, and obtain the like blessing.

FOR MEDITATION: Those who demand signs and wonders as a stimulus to repentance and faith in Christ usually turn out to be the very same people who murmur at God's word and reject it (Luke 16:29–31; John 6:30,35,41; 1 Corinthians 1:21–23). Any signs and wonders God may allow them to see are more likely to lead them astray (2 Thessalonians 2:9–11).

The head of the church

'He is the head of the body, the church.' Colossians 1:18
SUGGESTED FURTHER READING: Jude 1–5

The church is not to be regulated by the times. We are told by some that this age requires a different kind of preaching from that of a hundred years ago, and that in the time of the Puritans doctrines were suitable which are exploded now; the minister must keep abreast of the age; this is a thoughtful and philosophic period, and the preacher must therefore philosophise and bring forth his own thinking rather than 'mere declamation', which is the learned name for a plain declaration of the gospel of Jesus Christ. But, sirs, it is not so; our King is the same, and the doctrines he has given us have not been changed by his authority, nor the rules he has laid down reversed by his proclamation; he is 'the same yesterday, and today, and for ever'; let the times be polished or uncouth, let them become philosophical or sink into barbarism, our duty will still be the same, in solemn loyalty to Jesus Christ, to know nothing among men 'save Jesus Christ, and him crucified.' But the discoveries of science, we are told, have materially affected belief, and therefore we should change our ways as philosophy changes. No, it must not be so. This is a stumbling stone and a rock of offence against which he who stumbles shall be broken. We have the same King still, the same laws still, the same teaching of the word still, and we are to deliver this teaching after the same sort and in the same spirit. 'Always the same' must be our motto, always keeping close to Jesus Christ and glorifying him, for he and not the times, not the philosophy and not the wit of man, must rule and govern the church of God. If we shall do this, if any church shall do this, namely, take its truth from Jesus' lips, live according to Jesus' word, and go forward in his name, such a church cannot by any possibility fail, for the failure of such a church would be the failure of the Master's own authority.

FOR MEDITATION: To go by the teaching in some churches one could be forgiven for thinking that Christians need to be converted to the world rather than that the world needs to be converted to Christ. Christians ought to be turning the world upside down with the gospel (Acts 17:6) rather than allowing the world to turn them upside down with its ways and philosophies (Romans 12:2; Colossians 2:8).

SERMON NO. 839

A generous proposal

'Come thou with us, and we will do thee good.' Numbers 10:29
SUGGESTED FURTHER READING: Acts 9:23–31

It is the duty of every child of God to be associated with the Christian church, and surely it is part of our duty to instruct others to do what the Lord would approve of. Do not, therefore, hesitate to say to such as serve and fear the Lord, 'How is it that you remain outside the pale of the visible church?' 'Come thou with us, and we will do thee good'. So Moses did to Hobab. As it is a very kind and tender word, 'come thou with us,' let it be spoken *persuasively*. Use such reasoning as you can to prove that it is at once their duty and their privilege. Observe, Moses did not command, but he persuaded; nor did he merely make a suggestion or give a formal invitation, but he used an argument; he put it attractively—'and we will do thee good'. So, look the matter up; study it; get your arguments ready, seek out inducements from your own experience. Draw a reason, and then and thus try to persuade your Christian friends. Do it *heartily*. Observe how Moses put it from a very warm heart—'come thou with us'; 'give me thy hand, my brother;' 'come thou with us, and we will do thee good'. There are no 'ifs, ands and buts' or 'Well, you may perhaps be welcome,' but 'come thou with us'. Give a hearty, loving, warm invitation to those whom you believe to be your brethren and sisters in Christ. Do it *repeatedly* if once will not suffice. Observe in this case, Hobab said he thought he would depart to his own land and his kindred, but Moses returned to the charge and said, 'Leave us not, I pray thee'. How earnestly he put it! He would have no put off. If at first it was a request, now it is a beseeching almost to entreaty—'Leave us not, I pray thee'. And how he repeated the old argument, but put it in a better light—'if thou go with us, yea, it shall be, that what goodness the Lord shall do unto us, the same will we do unto thee.'

FOR MEDITATION: Though the term 'church membership' is absent from the Bible, it is clear that Christians in the early church had leaders over them (1 Thessalonians 5:12; Hebrews 13:7,17,24) and that discipline could be enforced by means of excommunication (1 Corinthians 5:2,13). Are you a church member? Do you encourage other Christians to come and do likewise?

SERMON NO. 916

God's foreknowledge of man's sin

'I knew that thou wouldest deal very treacherously, and wast called a transgressor from the womb.' Isaiah 48:8
SUGGESTED FURTHER READING: Romans 5:6–11

This truth is very important to us, because in the light of it our security is clearly manifest. I cannot understand how we can be perplexed with the thought that God will cast us away now we are his people, if it be true that all the sins we have committed since conversion were all present before his mind; for surely if there be a reason in our sin for God casting us away now, since he foreknew that sin, it would have been an equally valid reason for his never loving us at all. A man undertakes mining operations in a certain place; he says, 'I shall dig for iron.' He meets with great difficulties, hard rocks to bore through, and so on. He comes to this conclusion, 'If I had known of this labour and of the expense, I should not have sought for the metal here.' But suppose the man to be well aware of everything, and that he meets with nothing but what he foresaw, then you may depend upon it that the man means business, and having commenced operations, he will continue working till he obtains that which he seeks after. Our God can never be obstructed by a circumstance in us which can create surprise in his mind or throw his course out of his reckoning. He knew that we should be what we are, and he determined to save us in the teeth of all our rebellion; and since the divine determination was wisely made, the cost was all counted, and every circumstance taken into consideration, there can be no shadow of a fear that he will ever turn aside from his eternal purpose. Has he found me, as his child, to be exceedingly wilful? Will that tempt him to drive me from the family? He knew I should be wilful. It might have prevented his beginning to love, but, seeing he has begun, how can it make him cease from blessing? Let this be a comfort to you, when the evil of sin weighs most heavily upon your faith.

FOR MEDITATION: Jesus foreknew that the devilish Judas would betray him (John 6:70–71; 13:18–21,26–27), but also that his true followers would forsake and deny him. His response was to encourage them, not to threaten to disown them when it happened (Matthew 26:31–35; Luke 22:31–34; John 13:36–38)—'having loved his own which were in the world, he loved them unto the end' (John 13:1).

SERMON NO. 779

Beauty for ashes

'To appoint unto them that mourn in Zion, to give unto them beauty for ashes, the oil of joy for mourning, the garment of praise for the spirit of heaviness; that they might be called trees of righteousness, the planting of the Lord, that he might be glorified.' Isaiah 61:3
SUGGESTED FURTHER READING: John 9:1–25

Some of us were under such sadness of heart before conversion, through a sense of sin, that when we found peace, everybody noticed the change and said, 'Who has made him so happy, for he was just now most depressed?' When we told them where we lost our burden, 'Then said they among the heathen, The Lord hath done great things for them.' Remember poor Christian in *Pilgrim's Progress*. What heavy sighs he heaved, what tears fell from his eyes, what a wretched man he was when he wrung his hands and said, 'The city wherein I dwell is to be burned up with fire from heaven, and I shall be consumed in it, and, besides, I am myself undone by reason of a burden that lieth hard upon me. Oh that I could get rid of it!' Do you remember John Bunyan's description of how he got rid of the burden? He stood at the foot of the cross, and there was a sepulchre hard by, and as he stood and looked, and saw one hanging on the tree, suddenly the bands that bound his burden cracked, and the load rolled right away into the sepulchre, and when he looked for it, it could not be found. And he gave three great leaps for joy, and sang,

'Bless'd cross! bless'd sepulchre! bless'd rather be
The man that there was put to shame for me.'

If those who knew the pilgrim in his wretchedness had met him, they would have said, 'Are you the same man?' If Christiana had met him that day, she would have said, 'My husband, are you the same? What a change has come over you;' and when she and the children marked the father's cheerful conversation, they would have been compelled to say, 'This is the Lord's doing; it is marvellous in our eyes.'

FOR MEDITATION: Meeting the Lord Jesus Christ left a demonic man sane (Mark 5:15), a diseased woman healed (Mark 5:27–29) and a dead child alive (Mark 5:41–42). Has he rescued you from the deadly disease of sin and the devil's power (Ephesians 2:1–2)? Has anybody noticed?

Household salvation

'And they spake unto him the word of the Lord, and to all that were in his house. And he ... was baptized, he and all his, straightway. And ... he ... rejoiced, believing in God with all his house.' Acts 16:32–34
SUGGESTED FURTHER READING: 2 Timothy 1:1–7

Sometimes a good man has to go alone to heaven: God's election has separated him from an ungodly family, and, despite his example, prayers and admonitions, they still remain unconverted, and he himself, a solitary one, a speckled bird amongst them, has to pursue his lonely flight to the skies. Far oftener, however, the God of Abraham becomes the God of Sarah, and then of Isaac, and then of Jacob, and though grace does not run in the blood, and regeneration is not of blood nor of birth, yet very frequently God, by means of one of a household, draws the rest to himself. He calls an individual and then uses him to be a sort of spiritual decoy to bring the rest of the family into the gospel net. John Bunyan, in the first part of his *Pilgrim's Progress*, describes Christian as a lonely traveller, pursuing his road to the Celestial City alone; occasionally he is attended by a Faithful, or he meets a Hopeful; but these are casual acquaintances, and are not of his kith or kin: brother or child after the flesh he has none with him. The second part of Bunyan's book exhibits family piety, for we see Christiana, her children and many friends all travelling in company to the better land; and, though it is often said that the second part of Bunyan's wondrous allegory is somewhat weaker than the first, yet many a gentle spirit has found it sweeter than the first, and it has given to many a loving heart great delight to feel that there is a possibility, beneath the leadership of one of the Lord's Greathearts, to form a convoy to the skies, so that a sacred caravan shall traverse the desert of earth, and women and children shall find their way in happy association to the City of Habitations.

FOR MEDITATION: Christians have special responsibilities towards their families and relatives (Ephesians 6:4; 1 Timothy 5:4,8). Spurgeon says, 'Let Abraham's prayer be for Ishmael, let Hannah pray for Samuel, let David plead for Solomon, let Andrew find first his brother Simon, and Eunice train her Timothy.' What are you doing to help your relatives find Christ? Or are you the one who needs such help from your Christian relatives?

SERMON NO. 1019

Right replies to right requests

'If ye then, being evil, know how to give good gifts unto your children:
how much more shall your heavenly Father give the Holy Spirit to them
that ask him?' Luke 11:13
SUGGESTED FURTHER READING: Matthew 7:7–11

Turn to the parallel passage in the gospel of Matthew. Read Matthew
7:11—'If ye, being evil, know how to give good gifts unto your children,
how much more shall your Father which is in heaven give good things to
them that ask him?' Now note what our text says—'how much more shall
your heavenly Father give the Holy Spirit to them that ask him?' Is it not
clear then that the Holy Spirit is the equivalent for 'good things', and that
in fact when the Lord gives us the Holy Spirit, he gives us all 'good
things'? What a comprehensive prayer then is the prayer for the Spirit of
God! Dear friend, sit down with pencil in hand and a sheet of blank
paper before you, and write down all your spiritual needs. I will judge of
your wisdom by the length of your catalogue, for if you know yourself,
you will find you have not done yet; you are a great mass of needs. To
pray for all these things separately might seem a very long exercise. Just
take up your pencil, and do as schoolchildren do when they add up the
total of their sums; you will find it comes to this—the Holy Spirit. 'My
God, give me the Holy Spirit, and I have all.' 'But do we not need the
Saviour?' asks one. Truly, but where he comes the Holy Spirit takes of the
things of Christ and shows them to us. That is the great value of the
Holy Spirit. 'He shall glorify me', said Jesus. Wherever the Spirit of God
comes, there comes the blood of the atonement by which we are brought
near, and every spiritual blessing bought with blood is brought by the
Holy Spirit home to the soul. If you have the Spirit, he does not come
empty-handed. He comes loaded with all the treasures of the covenant.

FOR MEDITATION: Jesus promised his apostles that the Holy Spirit would
teach them all things and remind them of all the things he had told them
(John 14:26); they proved the reality of his presence as he supported their
witness to the saving work of Christ (Acts 5:32; 1 Peter 1:12). The Holy
Spirit alone searches and knows the things of God (1 Corinthians
2:10–11). Only if we have received the Holy Spirit, can we know the things
of God; otherwise they are foolishness to us (1 Corinthians 2:12–14).

SERMON NO. 959

The unrivalled friend

'A friend loveth at all times, and a brother is born for adversity.' Proverbs *17:17*
SUGGESTED FURTHER READING: 2 Timothy 1:15–18

It may happen that some of you may be found in a workshop or in some other place to which business brings you, where some dear child of God will be laughed at and ridiculed. That same man you would have cheerfully owned on the Lord's Day as your brother; you delighted to unite your voice with him in prayer, but now, while he stands in the midst of a ribald throng, will you own him, or rather, own Christ in him? They are making cruel jokes and vexing his gracious spirit; now it is possible that a cowardly fear may make you slink away to the other end of the shop, but, if you remember that 'A friend loveth at all times,' you will take up this man's quarrel as being Christ's quarrel, and you, as being part of the body of Christ, will be willing to share whatever insults may come upon your fellow Christian, and you will say, 'If you mock at him, you may mock also at me, for I also have been with Jesus of Nazareth, and him whom you scoff at I adore.' O let us never, by the love that Christ has borne to us, keep back a truth because it may expose us to shame. Let us never be such cowards as to equivocate with the word of God, because we may then live in silken ease and delicacy. These are not times in which one single particle of truth ought to be repressed. Whatever the spirit of God and the word of God may have taught you, out with it for Christ's sake, and whatever it may bring to you, bear that with joy. Since your Saviour bore far more for you, count it joy to bear anything for him. Be a brother born on purpose for adversity.

FOR MEDITATION: A friend in need is a friend indeed. Consider the faithful friendship of Onesiphorus towards the apostle Paul (2 Timothy 1:15–18). Note the shame he resisted (v.16), the search at Rome (v. 17), the service he rendered (v. 18), the suffering he risked, the sin he reproved (v. 15), the spirit he refreshed (v. 16) and, as the result of it all, the supplication and the salutation he received (v. 18; 4:19). Is your friendship comparable to this or are you more like Demas (2 Timothy 4:10) and others (2 Timothy 4:16)?

SERMON NO. 899

Do not sin against the child

'Spake I not unto you, saying, Do not sin against the child?' Genesis
42:22
SUGGESTED FURTHER READING: Mark 9:33–42; 10:13–16

Teachers of Sunday schools, you have voluntarily assumed a position, the
responsibility of which is not to be laid aside so long as you continue in
the office. I beseech you, 'Do not sin against the child'. He comes to you
to learn something weighty and of eternal consequence; do not be dull
and uninteresting; do not talk to him of unimportant matters; do not be
cold and sleepy over your work, but tell him of Jesus lovingly, simply and
earnestly. Do not lead him to feel that you have yourself no faith in what
you teach. Be so earnest that he may see conviction gleaming from your
eye, and may soon in return feel it flashing into his heart. Remember,
other teachers have been prayerful over their children; they have brought
their boys and girls to Jesus and have won a blessing from the Master—
will you not be prayerful too? If not, it were better for those children that
you had never been born, and that some better teacher had been set over
them. 'Do not sin against the child' therefore by cumbering the ground
and occupying a place which might have been far more profitably filled
by a more earnest spirit. In the weekday 'Do not sin against the child' by
conduct inconsistent with your profession. 'Do not sin against the child'
by neglecting him during the six days if you have opportunities for
visitation. Seek his good at all times; follow him with your prayers and
tears if you cannot with your personal visits and loving words. Let
importunate entreaties to him and fervent prayers to God go together, as
God gives you opportunity; and who knows whether God shall give you
his soul as a seal to your faithful ministry! Teacher, 'Do not sin against
the child' by failure in anything to which conscience calls you.

FOR MEDITATION: Being a direct source of temptation (Mark 9:42) is not
the only way of sinning against a child. Samuel took steps to avoid
sinning in respect of those under his pastoral care by ensuring that he
prayed for them and that he taught them aright (1 Samuel 12:23).

SERMON NO. 840

The upper hand

'For sin shall not have dominion over you: for ye are not under the law, but under grace.' Romans 6:14
SUGGESTED FURTHER READING: Psalm 19:7–14

To every true believer the promise is 'sin shall not have dominion over you'. It does not say that sin shall not dwell in you. We know that it will dwell in you while you dwell in this corruptible body. In the holiest man there is enough sin to destroy him if it were not for the grace of God, which restrains its deadly operation. You cannot turn the old enemy completely out; he lurks, like aliens in a city, ever ready to do mischief. Nor are you told that you shall never fall into sin. Alas! Some of those who have walked very near to God have yet fallen very foully. Need I mention such as David? May we never repeat in our lives the lapses that tarnished the reputation of such godly men! The word, however, is passed and the security is given, that 'sin shall not have dominion over you'. The fair and lovely dove may fall into the mire, but the mire has not any dominion over it, for she rises up as quickly as she can, and away she flies and seeks to cleanse herself at some crystal fount. As for the duck, put that into the mire, and the mire has dominion over its nature. So the believer may fall into sin that he hates, and defile his garments with uncleanness that he loathes. Let a sheep tumble into a ditch and it scrambles out again, but let the swine go there and it rolls in it, for the mire has dominion over its nature. There is nothing here to excuse you from watchfulness, no reason shown nor any pledge given that sin may not sometimes terribly overcome you. It may carry the war right into the province of your spirit and ravage it, and the whole of your nature may for awhile seem to be subdued, except the heart. Happily a limit is prescribed. Though the enemy may seem to conquer the territory of your manhood, yet it cannot establish a kingdom there.

FOR MEDITATION: The Christian has been delivered from the dominion of an evil ruler and transferred to the kingdom of a perfect ruler (Colossians 1:13) who has the upper hand (Luke 11:21–22; 1 John 4:4). By his faithfulness we too can have the upper hand over temptations to sin (1 Corinthians 10:13).

SERMON NO. 901

The secret spot

'Their spot is not the spot of his children.' Deuteronomy 32:5
SUGGESTED FURTHER READING: Genesis 13:8–18

You who are the children of God must have noticed a difference between your sins now and your sins as they once were; and you cannot but observe, day by day, if you look within, that grace has made a change even in those sins in which our evil nature exercises most influence. But, beloved, the best thing we can do is to keep as far away from evil as possible. We have no right to say, 'I may be a child of God, and yet do so-and-so.' No, the heir of heaven does not desire to approach the appearance of evil. I am much afraid for some of you who are asking, 'Is this wrong and that wrong?' Do nothing about which you have need to ask a question. Be quite sure about it, or leave it alone. Do you not know that inspired word, 'whatsoever is not of faith is sin'? That is, whatsoever you cannot do with the confidence that you are doing right, is sin to you. Though the deed may be right to other people, if you have any doubt about it yourself, it is evil to you. God grant, dear friends, that you may not be 'conformed to this world', but be 'transformed by the renewing of your mind'. If I knew that there was a pest-house anywhere in the country, I do not think I should want to build my house near it; I should not send for the physician and say, ' Sir, how far do you think the effect of pestilence might spread? I should like to get as near as I could without actually catching the disease.' 'No', you say, 'if there is a plot of land to be bought where there is no disease, there let my tent be pitched. It is best to dwell far off from evil.' O may God separate us from evil in this world, as we hope to be separated from it in the world to come!

FOR MEDITATION: By pitching his tent toward the wicked city of Sodom (Genesis 13:12–13), Lot had taken the first step towards dwelling in Sodom itself (Genesis 14:12) and accepting a position of importance in the gate of Sodom (Genesis 19:1). Even when Sodom was about to be destroyed by God, he was reluctant to move far away (Genesis 19:20). Contrast the Psalmist's desire for a clear-cut separation from the tents of wickedness (Psalm 84:10).

SERMON NO. 780

A prayer for the church militant

'Save thy people, and bless thine inheritance: feed them also, and lift them up for ever.' Psalm 28:9
SUGGESTED FURTHER READING: James 4:1–10

'Lift them up; O Lord, do not allow thy people to be like the world's people; lift them up for ever. The world lieth in the wicked one; lift them out of it; the world's people are looking after silver and gold, seeking their own pleasures and the gratification of their lusts; but, Lord, lift thy people up above all this; keep them from being 'muck-rakers' as John Bunyan calls the man who was always looking after gold; keep them from having their eyes always downwards; spare them from becoming carnal and sensual, lest they also become like others, devilish. O let thy grace lift thy people up, so that in whatever neighbourhood they may be found, they may be lights in the midst of a crooked and perverse generation.' This is a prayer for which we might all go down on our knees ten times a day for ourselves and for our fellow Christians, that God would elevate the general tone of true religion, that Christianity might become more powerful. I am not saying it is a fact, but I am sometimes afraid that the greatest mischief that there is in the world is an abundance of religious profession which is not genuine. You know very well how bad it is for trade when there is a great quantity of paper money about and not enough sterling bullion to back it up with; there is sure to come a panic and a crash. I am afraid that the Christian church issues a great deal of paper religion and has not enough bullion to back it up with. After all, in God's sight it is nothing but the solid gold that is worth having, and the paper profession will be burnt to ashes in the fire. May God 'lift up' his church and make her a truly golden church, that her piety may be a true bullion piety and that the circulation of the church may be a truly golden medium and not a mere bill and paper piety.

FOR MEDITATION: The people of the world can be expected to mind earthly things (Philippians 3:19), but the people of God can and should have their affections lifted from earthly things to things above (Colossians 3:1–2) and their motivation raised from earthly wisdom to the wisdom from above (James 3:15,17).

SERMON NO. 768

The Sun of righteousness

'In them hath he set a tabernacle for the sun, which is as a bridegroom coming out of his chamber, and rejoiceth as a strong man to run a race. His going forth is from the end of the heaven, and his circuit unto the ends of it: and there is nothing hid from the heat thereof.' Psalm 19:4–6
'The Sun of righteousness.' Malachi 4:2
SUGGESTED FURTHER READING: Matthew 17:1–8

You have probably looked upon the sun and said, 'This great orb, the lord of light and lamp of day, is like my Saviour; it is the faint image of his excellent glory whose countenance shines as the sun in its strength.' You have done well to seize on such a figure. What Milton calls the golden-tressed sun is the most glorious object in creation, and in Jesus the fulness of glory dwells; the sun is at the same time the most influential of existences, acting upon the whole world, and truly our Lord is, in the deepest sense, 'of this great world both eye and soul'; he 'with benignant ray sheds beauty, life, and joyance from above.' The sun is, moreover, the most abiding of creatures; and therein it is also a type of him who remains from generation to generation, and is 'the same yesterday, and today, and for ever.' The king of day is so vast and so bright that the human eye cannot bear to gaze upon him; we delight in his beams, but we should be blinded should we continue to peer into his face; even yet more brilliant is our Lord by nature, for as God he is a consuming fire, but he condescends to smile upon us with milder beams as our brother and Redeemer. Jesus, like the sun, is the centre and soul of all things, the fulness of all good, the lamp that lights us, the fire that warms us, the magnet that guides and controls us; he is the source and fountain of all life, beauty, fruitfulness and strength; he is the fosterer of tender herbs of penitence, the quickener of the vital sap of grace, the ripener of fruits of holiness, and the life of everything that grows within the garden of the Lord. Whereas to adore the sun would be idolatry, it is treason not to worship ardently the divine 'Sun of righteousness'.

FOR MEDITATION: 'For the LORD God is a sun and shield', the giver of grace, glory and good things to those who walk uprightly (Psalm 84:11). Even in his glorified appearance the Lord Jesus Christ puts the sun in the shade (Matthew 17:2; Acts 26:13; Revelation 1:16; 21:23).

Iconoclast [or, breaker of images]

'He removed the high places, and brake the images, and cut down the groves, and brake in pieces the brazen serpent that Moses had made: for unto those days the children of Israel did burn incense to it; and he called it Nehushtan. He trusted in the Lord God of Israel; so that after him was none like him among all the kings of Judah, nor any that were before him.' 2 Kings 18:4–5

SUGGESTED FURTHER READING: Philippians 3:12–16

Beloved brethren and sisters, exercise self-examination now for the next five minutes or so. How about your present position as a Christian? You feel probably after ten, twenty or thirty years of profession, very considerably in advance of what you were when you first came to Christ. Do you feel that you are? You can now see the imprudences of your early zeal, and you can look down with unmeasured pity upon those young people who know so little about the road to heaven, of which you know so much, and who have so little strength, of which you now have a very considerable share, and who are so little aware of the devices of Satan, against which you guard yourself so ably. Dear brother, are you really thus congratulating yourself upon your advanced position? Are you? Then permit a little image breaking there, for rest assured if we, any of us, come to put much value upon our attainments, we shall be very near to sliding into self-confidence, carnal security, and I know not what of mischievous pride. Beloved, are you stronger than you were? But does your strength lie anywhere else than where it used to lie, even in Christ? Are you wiser than you were? But have you any wisdom except that Christ is made unto you wisdom? Do you really think that twenty years' experience has changed your corruptions, that your passions have become extinct, that your tendencies to sin are not so strong as they were, and that in fact you have less need to watch and less need to depend simply upon the merit of Christ and the work of the Spirit? Do you think so? 'Wherefore let him that thinketh he standeth take heed lest he fall.'

FOR MEDITATION: Christians who suffer from delusions of spiritual grandeur invite ridicule (1 Corinthians 4:7–8) and betray how little they know themselves (Revelation 3:17). In all such cases an act of self-examination is urgently required (Galatians 6:3–4).

SERMON NO. 960

Moab is my washpot

'Moab is my washpot.' Psalm 60:8
SUGGESTED FURTHER READING: 1 Corinthians 10:1–13

The lives of many men are recorded in Scripture, not as excuses for our sins, much less as examples, but the very reverse. Like murderers in the olden times hung in chains, they are meant to be warnings. Their lives and deaths are danger-signals, bidding those who are pursuing a career of sin to come to a pause and reverse the engine forthwith. They are our washpot in that respect, that they warn us of pollution and so help to prevent our falling into it. When we learn that pride turned angels into devils, we have a lesson in humility read to us from heaven and hell. When we read of profane Esau, obstinate Pharaoh, disobedient Saul, apostate Judas or vacillating Pilate, we are taught thereby to shun the rocks upon they made eternal shipwreck. Transgressors of our own race are peculiarly suitable to act as warnings to us, for we ought ever to remember, when we see the sins of ungodly men, that 'such were some of' us. Whenever you see a drunkard, if you were once such, it will bring the tears to your eyes to remember when you too were a slave to the ensnaring cup, and you will thank God that his grace has changed you. Not as the Pharisee will you pretend to thank God, while you are flattering yourself, but with deep humiliation you will confess what grace has done. When we read in the newspaper a sad case of lasciviousness or any other breach of the laws of God and man, if we were once guilty of the like and have now been renewed in heart, it will make us blush; it will humble us and cause us to admire the power and sovereignty of divine grace. Now the blush of repentance, the shamefacedness of humility and the tear of gratitude are three helpful things, and all tend under God's grace to set us purging out the old leaven. Remember, believer, that there is no wretch upon earth so bad, that you were not once his equal in alienation from God and death in sin. In untoward acts there may have been much difference, but in the inner man how little!

FOR MEDITATION: Christians should imitate good and avoid the imitation of evil (3 John 11). Meditate upon the warnings issued by the evil examples of the fallen angels, the ungodly before the flood, the people of Sodom and Gomorrah, and even the Children of Israel whom God had rescued from Egypt (2 Peter 2:4–6; Jude 5–7).

SERMON NO. 983

Crowding to touch the Saviour

'For he had healed many; insomuch that they pressed upon him for to touch him, as many as had plagues.' Mark 3:10
SUGGESTED FURTHER READING: Ephesians 2:1–10

Do you know what it is to trust Christ? I do not know how to explain it better than by dwelling on the word itself—trust. It is a reliance, a dependence. It is leaning all your weight on Christ, giving up your own power and depending on him. Dr. Watts puts it thus:—

A guilty, weak, and helpless worm, On thy kind arms I fall;
Be thou my strength and righteousness, My Jesus and my all.'

But still people will not understand us. A young man once said to me, 'I want to know what I must do to be saved.' I reminded him of that verse. He said, 'Sir, I cannot fall.' 'You do not understand me,' said I. 'I do not mean a fall which needs any strength in you; I mean a fall caused by the absence of all strength.' It is to tumble down into Christ's arms because you cannot stand upright. Faint into the arms of Christ; that is faith. Just give up doing, give up depending upon anything that you are or do or ever hope to be, and depend upon the complete merits, finished work and precious blood of Jesus Christ. If you do this you are saved. Anything of your own doing spoils it all. You must give up relying upon your prayers, your tears, your baptism, your repentance and even your faith itself. Your reliance is to be on nothing but that which is in Christ Jesus. Those dear hands, those blessed feet, are ensigns of his love. That bleeding, martyred, murdered person is the grand display of the heart of the ever blessed God. Look to the Saviour's pangs, griefs and groans. These are punishments for human sin. This is God's wrath spending itself on Christ instead of the believer. Believe in Jesus and it is certain that he thus suffered for you. Trust in him to save you and you are saved. God grant you the privilege of faith and the boon of salvation.

FOR MEDITATION: Some trust in things (Psalm 20:7; 1 Timothy 6:17), some in false gods (Psalm 115:8), some in other people (Psalm 118:8–9; 146:3–4; Jeremiah 17:5–6) and others in themselves (Proverbs 3:5; 28:26; Luke 18:9; 2 Corinthians 1:9). The immediate contexts of all these verses redirect us to trust in the Lord instead.

SERMON NO. 841

Seeing Jesus

'We see Jesus.' Hebrews 2:9
SUGGESTED FURTHER READING: Hebrews 11:1–16

Rapid is the action of faith. Brethren, we know not where heaven may be, where the state, the place called 'heaven' is, but faith takes us there in contemplation in a single moment. We cannot tell when the Lord may come; it may not be for centuries yet, but faith steps over the distance in a moment, sees him coming in the clouds of heaven, and hears the trump of resurrection. It would be very difficult, indeed it would be impossible, for us to travel backward in any other chariot than that of faith, for it is faith which helps us to see the creation of the world 'when the morning stars sang together, and all the sons of God shouted for joy'. Faith enables us to walk in the garden with our first parents, and to witness the scene when God promised that the seed of the woman should bruise the serpent's head. Faith makes us familiar with patriarchs, and gives us to see the troubles and trials of kings. Faith takes us to Calvary's summit, where we stand and see our Saviour as plainly as did his mother when she stood sorrowfully at the foot of the cross. This day we can fly back to the solemn day of Pentecost and feel as if we could hear the mighty rushing wind, and see the cloven tongues sitting upon the chosen company; so swiftly does faith travel. And, best of all, in one moment faith can take a sinner out of a state of death into a state of life, can lift him from damnation into salvation, can remove him from the land of the shadow of death, where he sat in affliction and irons, and give him 'the oil of joy for mourning, the garment of praise for the spirit of heaviness'. O sinner, you can get at Christ in a moment of time. No sooner has your heart trusted Jesus, than you are with him, united to him.

FOR MEDITATION: Faith in the living God enables us to accept what he has done in the past (Hebrews 11:3) and to set our hopes upon what he is going to do in the future (Hebrews 11:13,16). Consider the apostle Paul as he testified to his faith in the past and future works of God (Acts 24:14–15).

Christus et ego [or, Christ and I]

'I am crucified with Christ: nevertheless I live; yet not I, but Christ liveth in me: and the life which I now live in the flesh I live by the faith of the Son of God, who loved me, and gave himself for me.' Galatians 2:20
SUGGESTED FURTHER READING: 1 Corinthians 15:45–49

Read the text over again. Here is the man, but here is the Son of God quite as conspicuously, and the two personalities are singularly interwoven. I think I see two trees before me. They are distinct plants growing side by side, but as I follow them downward, I observe that the roots are so interlaced and intertwined that no one can trace the separate trees and allot the members of each to its proper whole. Such are Christ and the believer. I see before me a vine. Yonder is a branch, distinct and perfect as a branch; it is not to be mistaken for any other; it is a branch, a whole and perfect branch, yet how perfectly it is joined to the stem and how completely is its individuality merged in the one vine of which it is a member! Now, so is it with the believer in Christ. There was one parent man who threw his shadow across our path and from whose influence we could never escape. From all other men we might have struggled away and claimed to be separate, but this one man was part of ourselves and we part of him—Adam the first, in his fallen state: we are fallen with him and are broken in pieces in his ruin. And now, glory be to God, as the shadow of the first man has been uplifted from us, there appears a second man, 'the Lord from heaven.' And across our path there falls the light of his glory and his excellence, from which also, blessed be God, we who have believed in him cannot escape: in the light of that man, the second Adam, the heavenly federal head of all his people, in his light we rejoice. Interwoven with our history and personality is the history and personality of the man Christ Jesus, and we are for ever one with him.

FOR MEDITATION: Read Romans 5:12–19. All are condemned to death with Adam, but only those who receive the Lord Jesus Christ can be said to have been crucified with him and raised to life with him. All who are in Adam die, but all who are in Christ are made alive (1 Corinthians 15:22).

SERMON NO. 781

The relationship of marriage

'Turn, O backsliding children, saith the LORD; *for I am married unto you.' Jeremiah 3:14*
SUGGESTED FURTHER READING: Hosea 2:16–3:5

The text is found addressed not to Christians in a flourishing state of heart, not to believers upon Mount Tabor, transfigured with Christ, not to a spouse all chaste and fair, and sitting under the banner of love, feasting with her Lord, but to those who are called 'backsliding children'. God speaks to his church in her lowest and most abject estate, and though he does not fail to rebuke her sin, to lament it, and to make her lament it too, yet still in such an estate he says to her, 'I am married unto you'. It is grace that he should be married to any of us, but it is grace at its highest pitch, the ocean of grace at its flood-tide, that he should speak thus of 'backsliding children'. That he should speak in notes of love to any of the fallen race of Adam is 'passing strange—'tis wonderful;' but that he should select those who have behaved treacherously to him, who have turned their backs to him and not their faces, who have played him false, although, nevertheless, his own, and that he should say unto them, 'I am married unto you', this is lovingkindness beyond anything we could imagine. Hear, O heaven, and admire, O earth; let every understanding heart break forth into singing; let every humble mind bless and praise the condescension of the Most High! Cheer up, poor drooping hearts. Here is sweet encouragement for some of you who are depressed and disconsolate, and who sit alone, to draw living waters out of this well. Do not let 'the noise of the archers' keep you from 'the places of drawing water' [see sermon no. 763—27 July]. Be not afraid lest you should be cursed whilst you are anticipating the blessing. If you trust in Jesus, if you have a vital interest in the once humbled, now exalted Lord, come with holy boldness to the text, and whatever comfort there be here, receive it and rejoice in it.

FOR MEDITATION: Paul had the heart and mind of Christ when he addressed wayward Christians as 'little children' (Galatians 4:19) and described Christ as their 'husband' (2 Corinthians 11:2), but he balanced these words of encouragement with serious misgivings and warnings (2 Corinthians 11:3; Galatians 4:20).

The throne of grace

'The throne of grace.' Hebrews 4:16
SUGGESTED FURTHER READING: Revelation 8:1–5

'Thou art coming to a king:
Large petitions with thee bring.'

We do not come in prayer, as it were, only to God's almonry where he dispenses his favours to the poor, nor do we come to the back-door of the house of mercy to receive the broken scraps, though that is more than we deserve; to eat the crumbs that fall from the Master's table is more than we could claim; but, when we pray, we are standing in the palace, on the glittering floor of the great King's own reception room, and thus we are placed upon a vantage ground. In prayer we stand where angels bow with veiled faces; there, even there, the cherubim and seraphim adore, before that selfsame throne to which our prayers ascend. And shall we come there with stunted requests, and narrow and contracted faith? No, it becomes not a King to be giving away pence; he distributes pieces of broad gold; he scatters not scraps of bread and broken meat as poor men must, but he makes 'a feast ... of fat things full of marrow, of wines on the lees well refined.' When Alexander's soldier was told to ask what he would, he did not ask stintedly after the nature of his own merits, but he made such a heavy demand that the royal treasurer refused to pay it and put the case to Alexander, who in right kingly manner replied, 'He knows how great Alexander is, and he has asked as from a king; let him have what he requests.' Take heed of imagining that God's thoughts are as your thoughts, and his ways as your ways. Do not bring before God stinted petitions and narrow desires, saying, 'Lord, do according to these,' but remember that as high as the heavens are above the earth, so high are his ways above your ways, and his thoughts above your thoughts; ask, therefore, after a godlike manner; ask for great things, for you are before a great throne.

FOR MEDITATION: It should not surprise us when unbelievers fail to ask or expect much of God (2 Kings 13:14–19; Isaiah 7:10–13; John 4:10), but it is a great shame when Christians do the same (James 4:2). Our asking and thinking can never begin to match God's ability and capacity to answer (Ephesians 3:20).

SERMON NO. 1024

New uses for old trophies

'King David's spears and shields, that were in the temple of the Lord.'
2 Kings 11:10
SUGGESTED FURTHER READING: 2 Peter 3:11–18

Texts of Scripture are sometimes used by adversaries of the gospel and turned against us. I know some ministers who, when they meet with a passage that they cannot immediately reconcile with the orthodox faith, alter the reading, or put a fresh sense on the words, or twist and turn it to suit their purpose. It is a bad plan; the texts of Scripture are to be taken as they stand, and you may rest assured they will always defend, never overturn, the faith once delivered to the saints. When I have seen a text sometimes in the hand of the enemy used against the deity of Christ, or against the doctrine of election, or against some other important and vital doctrine, I have not felt at all inclined to give up the text or think lightly of it. I rather admire those Americans in the South, who, when they had lost some guns, were asked by the commanding officer whether they had not spiked the guns before they gave them up to the foe. 'Spiked them? No,' said they, 'we did not like to spoil such beautiful guns; we will take them again tomorrow.' And so they did. I would not have a text touched. Grand old text! We honour you even while we cannot keep the field, or guard you from the aggression of the invader. But shall we spoil it or give it up as lost? Never; we will take it out of the hand of the enemy, use it for the defence of the gospel, and show that it does not mean what they think or answer the ends to which they would apply it. Are we baffled in attack, or do we lose ground in an argument? It is for us by more diligent study and closer research to take the guns, the good old guns, and use those which the enemy used against ourselves, to turn them round and use them against him. Depend upon it that the great temple of truth is not a house divided against itself.

FOR MEDITATION: We need not be afraid when the enemies of the gospel appear to get the better of us by throwing Scripture in our faces. Remember that they are talking out of the back of their heads from a position of ignorance (2 Peter 3:16). See John 7:40–42 for an occasion when opponents of Christ eagerly fastened upon a text in an ignorant attempt to undermine his claims.

SERMON NO. 972

The saint one with his Saviour

'He that is joined unto the Lord is one spirit.' 1 Corinthians 6:17
SUGGESTED FURTHER READING: Philippians 2:1–5

See here a *rebuke* for us. We have been joined to Christ, but have we been manifestly one spirit with him? Angry—was that Christ's spirit? Worldly—was that Christ's spirit? Frivolous, verging upon impropriety— was that Christ's spirit? Proud, dictatorial, slothful, repining, or unbelieving—was that Christ's spirit? If you can read this verse without a tear you are either better or worse than I; you are worse perhaps, for you do not feel the penitence you should; or you are better and have no need to confess the same faults which unhappily rise before my memory. I trust we have a measure of the spirit of Jesus, but does not our own spirit adulterate it dreadfully? A second practical word is one of *hope*. We want to have the same spirit as Christ. Well, our hope is that we shall have it, for we are joined to the Lord, and 'he that is joined unto the Lord is one spirit.' Are you not joined to Jesus, my brother, my sister? I know what you say—'I sometimes fear I am not.' Yes, but what do you add to that? You add, 'But I desire to be, and I do today renew my union with him by another act of faith and confidence in him. Dear Lord and Saviour, thou art my only hope; I at this hour embrace thy cross once more. I know thou savest sinners; I know that they who believe in thee are saved, and therefore I am saved; now being persuaded of this, I love thee. O that I could kiss thy feet where the nail prints are, and that my whole life could be a washing of those feet with my tears.' Since then you are joined to Christ, you are one spirit, and though it is not yet fully seen, it will be before long. There are better times coming; there are deeper degrees of grace for you yet; only persevere.

FOR MEDITATION: Being joined to the Lord and one spirit with him is not only a private matter. Its outworking is to be seen in the corporate unity of mind enjoyed by those who are joined to the Lord (1 Corinthians 1:10; Philippians 2:2,5). 'Is Christ divided?' (1 Corinthians 1:13).

SERMON NO. 961

The angelic life

'For in the resurrection they neither marry, nor are given in marriage, but are as the angels of God in heaven.' Matthew 22:30
SUGGESTED FURTHER READING (Spurgeon): Revelation 7:9–17

We shall be like the angels in heavenliness. Here we come to the vital meaning of the text. They are not married or given in marriage; they have other things to think of, and they have other cares and other enjoyments; they mind not earthly things, but are of a heavenly spirit. So is it with the blessed spirits before the throne. To eat and drink, to be clothed—these are things which fret their minds no more. To keep the house, to maintain the children, to thrust the wolf from the door—such anxieties never trouble celestial spirits. Brethren, this is one of the things which makes the great change so desirable to us, that after death our thoughts, our cares, our position, our desires and our joys will all be in God. Here we want externals, here we seek after carnal things; for we must eat and drink, and be clothed and housed. Here we must be somewhat hampered by the grosser elements of this poor materialism, but up yonder they have no needs like our own; they consequently have no desires of an earthly kind; their desires are all concerning their God. No creature drags them downward. They are free to bow before the Creator and to think alone of him, to 'Plunge into the Godhead's deepest sea, And bathe in his immensity.'

What a deliverance that must be! If now for a minute or two we soar to sublimer things and climb as upon the top of Pisgah to look down upon the world, we are called to descend again into the valley amid the noise and dust of the battle; but there for ever and ever we shall abide in the loftiness of heavenly things, absorbed with the glory which shall then be revealed.

FOR MEDITATION: The angels in heaven always behold the face of God (Matthew 18:10), consist of an innumerable company (Hebrews 12:22) and sing the praises of the Lamb of God (Revelation 5:11–12). Likewise the redeemed in heaven will behold Christ's glory and see God face to face (John 17:24; 1 Corinthians 13:12), consist of an innumerable multitude (Revelation 7:9) and sing the praises of God and the Lamb (Revelation 7:10; 15:3–4). Will you be one of them?

SERMON NO. 842

The pastor's parting blessing

'The grace of our Lord Jesus Christ be with you all.' Romans 16:24
SUGGESTED FURTHER READING: 1 Peter 5:5–12

'The grace of our Lord Jesus Christ be with you,' sons and daughters of poverty, to enable you to be patient, to sanctify your trials, to make your homes bright with the presence of the Lord, and to keep you from envy and murmuring. May your rooms be palaces to you, because the King visits you and feasts you with his love. May that same grace be with the few among us who may be said to be rich, for how much grace do the wealthy require, that they may be kept from the temptations which beset their position, and delivered from the cankering influence of riches! 'The grace of our Lord Jesus Christ be with you', that, consecrating your substance habitually to Christ, it may bring with it many comforts to your souls as well as to your bodies. 'The grace of our Lord Jesus Christ be with you', who are ripening for heaven; may it be light with you at eventide and may your rest be glorious. Though near to glory, you know that you are still dependent upon grace, and I trust you will abundantly enjoy it. 'The grace of our Lord Jesus Christ be with you', young beginners, who have just put on the harness. May you live long in the Christian church and serve your Master well. Amidst the temptations of youth and the trials of manhood, may you stand fast and glorify your Lord. Some of you are 'strong in the Lord, and in the power of his might.' 'The grace of our Lord Jesus Christ be with you' to keep you strong. If you have trodden down strength, and have had the hind's feet with which you have stood upon your high places, may you never lose your position, but maintain your joy. And as for you who are doubting and fearing, the timid ones of the flock—'The grace of our Lord Jesus Christ be with you' too, for 'he shall gather the lambs with his arm, and carry them in his bosom, and shall gently lead those that are with young.' 'A bruised reed shall he not break, and the smoking flax shall he not quench'.

FOR MEDITATION: Meditate on Acts 20:32, the apostle Paul's parting blessing to the Ephesian elders, in which he commended them 'to God, and to the word of his grace': note there what God's grace can do for us both in time and for eternity.

N.B. Spurgeon preached this sermon 'before leaving home for a journey.'

SERMON NO. 988

Saving knowledge

'Jesus answered and said unto her, If thou knewest the gift of God, and who it is that saith to thee, Give me to drink; thou wouldest have asked of him, and he would have given thee living water.' John 4:10
SUGGESTED FURTHER READING: John 3:16–18

The text uses the definite article—'If thou knewest the gift of God,' setting Christ's as God's gift beyond all other gifts. True, the light of the sun is the gift of God to us. There is not a piece of bread we eat, nor a drop of water we drink, that cannot be called the gift of God; but *the* gift which comprehends, excels and sanctifies all other gifts, is the gift of Jesus Christ to the sons of men. I wish I had the power to speak of this gift as I should do, but I am reminded by God's word that it is 'unspeakable'—'Thanks be unto God for his unspeakable gift.' I can comprehend God's giving the earth to the children of men, giving to Adam and his seed dominion over all the works of his hands; I think I can understand God's giving heaven to his people and permitting them to dwell at his right hand for ever and ever; but that God should give the only begotten, 'very God of very God', to take upon himself our nature, and in that nature actually to be 'obedient unto death, even the death of the cross', this we cannot understand, and even the angels with their mightier intellects cannot grasp it fully. They look into it, but as they gaze they desire to see more, for even they feel they cannot search this out to perfection. A depth unfathomable of divine love is there in the condescending lovingkindness which gave Jesus Christ to die for us when we were yet sinners. Beloved, it is an unrivalled gift. God has given to us such a treasure, that if heaven and earth were melted down, the price could not buy another like to him. All eternity cannot yield such a person as the Lord Jesus Christ. Eternal God, thou hast no equal, and becoming Son of man, thy condescension has nothing that can rival it. What a gift!

FOR MEDITATION: God is the giver of every good and perfect gift (James 1:17) and he knows how to give good things to his children (Matthew 7:11). Praise him for his very best and most perfect gift, given for us in the most complete way possible (Romans 8:32).

The secret food and the public name

'Thy words were found, and I did eat them; and thy word was unto me the joy and rejoicing of mine heart: for I am called by thy name, O LORD God of hosts.' Jeremiah 15:16
SUGGESTED FURTHER READING: 2 Timothy 2:15–26

'I am called by thy name, O Lord God of hosts.' Of course you are so called, if your profession is true. You were baptized 'in the name of the Father, and of the Son, and of the Holy Ghost', and you there and then accepted that name. You are a believer in Christ, and therefore you are rightly called a Christian. You cannot escape from it. By being a believer in Christ's name, you have Christ's name named upon you. Friend, consider what your obligations are! There was a soldier in the Macedonian army who was named Alexander; he was a coward; and he was called before the king, who asked, 'What is your name?' 'Alexander' he said. Then said the king, 'You must give up your name, or you must cease to be a coward.' So we call before us those who are Christians, and we say, 'What is your name? You are named with the name of Christ; therefore you must give up being covetous; you must give up being bad-tempered, worldly, slothful, lustful, or else you must give up Christ's name, for we cannot have Christ's name dishonoured any more than Alexander would have his name dishonoured.' You were spitting fire just now against that person who had irritated you. Suppose I had stepped in at that moment and said, 'You are called by the name of Christ!' What a colour would have risen in your face! Perhaps today you were talking the idlest stuff with vain persons; suppose some one whom you honoured and loved had laid his hand on you and whispered, 'What, you a Christian, talking like that?' How would you have felt? May we remember always that we are Christians, who therefore must always act up to the name that is named upon us. God grant you that in the power of the eating of God's word, you may be constrained to act always as becomes those upon whom the name of Christ is named.

FOR MEDITATION: Can it be said that everything you say and do is done in the name of the Lord Jesus (Colossians 3:17)? Is the name of the Lord Jesus Christ glorified in you (2 Thessalonians 1:12), or is God's name blasphemed by others because of your inconsistency (Romans 2:24; 1 Timothy 6:1)? The required standard is set out for us in 2 Timothy 2:19.

The life, walk, and triumph of faith

'And when Abram was ninety years old and nine, the LORD appeared to Abram, and said unto him, I am the Almighty God; walk before me, and be thou perfect. And I will make my covenant between me and thee, and will multiply thee exceedingly.' Genesis 17:1–2
SUGGESTED FURTHER READING: James 2:8–13

You must have all the graces, if you are to be a perfect man. I think I have known some Christians who have had all the graces except patience, but they never could be patient. The Lord says, 'walk before me, and be thou perfect' in patience. I have known some others who seemed to have almost every grace except the grace of forgiveness; they could not very readily forget any injury that had been done to them. Dear brother, you must get that grace, the grace of forgiveness, and walk before the Lord with that, or you will remain a mutilated character. A Christian's character is spoilt by the omission of any one virtue. And you must labour in the presence of God to have all these things, that they 'be in you, and abound'. Be in this sense perfect. And as we have all the graces, so we should seek to have exhibited in our lives all the virtues in the fulfilment of all our duties. It is a very sad thing when you hear of a Christian man that he is a very excellent deacon, that he is a very admirable local-preacher or Sunday-school teacher, but that he is a very unkind father. That 'but' spoils it all. A saint abroad is no saint if he be a devil at home. We have known men of whom it has been said that out of doors they were all that could be desired, *but* they were bad husbands. That 'but' mars the tale. It is the dead fly which has got into a very good pot of ointment and made the whole of it stink. Keep the dead flies out, brethren. By God's grace may your character be full-orbed! May God grant you grace to be at home and abroad, in the shop and in the chamber, and in every department of life, just that which a man should be who walks before the all-sufficient God.

FOR MEDITATION: What prevents you from having an all-round Christian character? Materialism (Matthew 19:20–21), partiality (James 2:9–10), your speech (James 3:2), a shortage of love (1 John 4:18) or something else? Perfection is something every Christian should aim at (Matthew 5:48; Philippians 3:12) and God has given us the Scriptures to help us towards that goal (2 Timothy 3:16–17).

SERMON NO. 1082

Our King our joy

'Let the children of Zion be joyful in their King.' Psalm 149:2
SUGGESTED FURTHER READING (Spurgeon): Habakkuk 3:17–19

At times our heart is bowed down because of the backslidings revealed in the moral and spiritual characters of our brethren. They did run well; what did hinder them? They were foremost once; where are they now? They were burning with zeal; why are they now so lukewarm? Where has their ardour gone? We hoped that they would be our joy and crown, but they have gone out from us because they were not of us. Moreover, we mourn that those who are truly saints do not exhibit the spirit of Christ so manifestly as we could desire; we see among them too little earnestness, too little holy jealousy. Well, if we cannot be joyful in our fellow citizens, we will be joyful in our King. When our heart is ready to break because we see so much of our labour lost, and so many tempted of Satan and turning aside, we will rejoice that the honour of our exalted King is still safe and his kingdom does not fail. This is an age—I fear I must say it—of very general declension in spiritual things. There is much profession of religion but little earnest contention for the faith, much talk of charity but little zeal for the truth, much boasting of high-toned piety but little vital godliness: yet if the famine in the church should grow worse and worse, till the faithful utterly fail, and rebuke and blasphemy abound, we must not cease to rejoice in the Lord. We ourselves have grave cause to complain of ourselves when we examine ourselves as before the Lord. Never pray we a prayer without wishing to have it forgiven as well as answered; our faith is frequently so weak that we scarce know whether to call it faith or unbelief; as for ourselves, we are a mass of flaws and infirmities. We might be very heavy if we thought only of our own personal barrenness, but we will be joyful in our King and sing again the royal song. There are no flaws in him, no imperfections in our Beloved, no coldness, no turning aside in him. Glory be to his name.

FOR MEDITATION: Spiritual joy in the Lord can and should triumph over all the trials and disappointments of the Christian life even when these involve rejection (Luke 6:22–23), tribulation (John 16:33), temptations (1 Peter 1:6) and suffering (1 Peter 4:13).

SERMON NO. 963

A new order of priests and Levites

'And I will also take of them for priests and for Levites, saith the LORD.*'*
Isaiah 66:21
SUGGESTED FURTHER READING: Galatians 1:11–24

I thank God, I do remember in my soul some dear brethren who have been made eminent ministers of the gospel, of whom if any one had said they would ever have preached the gospel, none would have believed it. Not to mention the living, go back to the early days of John Newton, an earnest preacher and famous evangelist, not to add a sweet poet. Almost a model for the ministry was John Newton, but once a blasphemer and injurious. Turn farther back to John Bunyan on the village green with his tip-cat on the Sabbath-day, with all a drunkard's vices and sins, and foul-mouthed in his profanity: yet John Bunyan became an eminent proclaimer of the gospel and the author of a matchless allegory which has served to guide many a pilgrim to heaven. Turn farther back to Luther, most earnest as a Romanist for all the letter of the law, diligent in every ceremony, superstitious to a high degree, yet afterwards the bold proclaimer of the gospel of the grace of God. Turn to Augustine, a youth of corrupt and vicious propensities according to his own confession and to the grief of his mother Monica, yet called by sovereign grace to be one of the fathers of the church and a notable exponent of sound doctrine. Look yet farther back to the apostle Paul, breathing out threatenings and slaughter against the disciples of the Lord, like a huge wild beast, making havoc of the church, but suddenly struck down and almost as suddenly raised up a new man and ordained 'not of men, neither by man, but by Jesus Christ, and God the Father' to be a chosen vessel unto Christ, to bear his name unto the Gentiles. 'I will also take of them', the most unlikely and unfit according to human judgment. 'I will also take of them for priests and for Levites, saith the Lord.'

FOR MEDITATION: If the Lord Jesus Christ could make apostles out of unlearned and ignorant fishermen (Matthew 4:18–22; Acts 4:13), a tax collector (Matthew 9:9; 10:3), a zealot (Luke 6:15) and the chief persecutor of the Christian church (1 Corinthians 15:8–9; 1 Timothy 1:12–13), there is no telling whom he may call to serve him in the Christian ministry.

SERMON NO. 992

Effectual calling—illustrated by the call of Abram

'They went forth to go into the land of Canaan; and into the land of Canaan they came.' Genesis 12:5
SUGGESTED FURTHER READING: Numbers 14:20–45

How many there are who set out to go to Canaan, but unto Canaan they come not! Some are stopped by the first depression of spirits that they meet with; like Pliable, they run home with the mud of Despond on their boots. Others turn aside to Self-righteousness. They follow the directions of Mr Worldly Wiseman and resort to Dr. Legality or Mr Civility, and Sinai falls upon them and crushes them. Some turn to the right hand with Hypocrisy, thinking that to pretend to be holy will be as good as being so. Others go on the left hand to Formality, imagining that sacraments and outward rites will be as effectual as inward purity and the work of the Spirit in their hearts. Many fall down the silver mine where Demas broke his neck. Hundreds get into Despair's castle and leave their bones there, because they will not trust Christ and so obtain eternal life. Some go far apparently, but, like Ignorance, they never go really and, when they come to the river, they perish at the very last. Some, like Turn-away, become apostates and are dragged away by the back door to hell, after all their professions. Some are frightened by the lions, others are tempted by By-path Meadow. Some would be saved, but must make a fortune. Many would be saved, but cannot bear to be laughed at. Some would trust Christ, but cannot endure his cross. Many would wear the crown, but cannot bear the labour by which they must attain to it. Ah, sons of men, you will turn aside to Madam Wanton and to Madam Bubble; you will be bewitched, but the beauties of the glorious Saviour, the lasting joys, the real happiness which he has to give, these are too high for you; they are above you and you reach not after them, or if you seek them for a while, 'The dog is turned to his own vomit again; and the sow that was washed to her wallowing in the mire.'

FOR MEDITATION: The failure of almost a whole generation of Israelites to reach the Promised Land is mirrored in the lives of many who fall short after appearing to be on their way to Heaven (Hebrews 3:16–4:2). Perseverance is essential (Hebrews 3:14). If John Bunyan had described you in *Pilgrim's Progress*, what name would he have given you? Would you have reached the Celestial City in the end?

SERMON NO. 843

The northern iron and the steel

'Shall iron break the northern iron and the steel?' Jeremiah 15:12
SUGGESTED FURTHER READING: 1 Corinthians 3:5–10

Some, no doubt, have had to labour all their lives, and have bequeathed to their heirs the promise whose fulfilment they had not personally seen. They laid the underground courses of the temple and others entered into their labours. You know the story of the removal of old St. Paul's by Sir Christopher Wren. A very massive piece of masonry had to be broken down, and the task, by pick and shovel, would have been a very tedious one, so the great architect prepared a battering-ram for its removal, and a large number of workmen were directed to strike with force against the wall with the ram. After several hours of labour, the wall, to all appearances, stood fast and firm. Their many strikes had apparently been lost, but the architect knew that they were gradually communicating motion to the wall, creating an agitation throughout the whole of it, and that, by and by, when they had continued long enough, the entire mass would come down beneath a single stroke. The workmen, no doubt, attributed the result to the one crowning concussion, but their master knew that their previous strokes had only culminated in that one tremendous blow, and that all the non-resultant work had been necessary to prepare for the stroke which achieved the purpose. Christian people, do not expect to see always the full outgrowth of your labours! Go on, serve your God, testify of his truth, tell of Jesus' love, pray for sinners, live a godly life, serve God with all your might, and if no harvest springs up to your joyous sickle, others shall follow you and reap what you have sown, and since God will be glorified, it shall be enough for you. Let no amount of non-success daunt you. Be uneasy about it, but do not be discouraged; let not even this iron break the resolution of your soul; let your determination to honour Jesus be as 'the northern iron and the steel'.

FOR MEDITATION: Even Moses did not live to see the fruit of his life's ministry, but had to leave it to Joshua (Deuteronomy 3:23–28) to see the fulfilment of God's promises to him (Joshua 1:1–3). Our work for God will be fruitful in due course, as long as we avoid giving up (Galatians 6:9).

Sermons from saintly death-beds

'And when Jacob had made an end of commanding his sons, he gathered up his feet into the bed, and yielded up the ghost.' Genesis 49:33
SUGGESTED FURTHER READING: 1 Kings 2:1–4

The taking away of eminent saints from among us should teach us to depend more upon God and less upon human instrumentality. I was reading the dying prayer of Oliver Cromwell, and one sentence in that man of God's last breathings pleased me exceedingly. It was to this effect, I think—'Teach those who look too much on thy instruments to depend more upon thyself.' Brave old Oliver was a man upon whom the whole nation rested; he could say with the Psalmist, 'The earth and all the inhabitants thereof are dissolved: I bear up the pillars of it.' In a time of terrible anarchy, when men had become fierce with fanatical prophesyings and wild with political passions, Oliver Cromwell's iron hand restored peace and kept a tumultuous land in order; and now, when he would be worst missed and could very ill be spared, he must depart, and this is his prayer, 'Teach them to depend less upon thy instrument and more upon thyself.' Frequently when a man is in the zenith of his power and people have said, 'That is the man whom of all others we could least afford to lose,' that very man has been taken away, that special light has been quenched and that particular pillar has been removed. The Lord would have all the glory given unto his own name. He has said it often in voice of thunder, but men will not hear it—'All power belongeth unto God.' He will honour and bless an instrumentality, for that is his mode of working, but he will not divide the crown with the most honoured agency; he will have all the glory redound unto himself; and by frequently breaking up his battle axes and weapons of war, he teaches his church that he can fight with his own bare arm and win the victory to himself without an instrument of warfare.

FOR MEDITATION: Consider Psalm 146:3–6. Though called 'a prince' by God (Genesis 32:28), Jacob also would have diverted our dependence away from mortal princes and towards the eternal God of Jacob. Read how Joseph later placed his own forthcoming death in its proper context (Genesis 50:24).

N.B. This sermon was prompted by the death of the eminent minister James Hamilton.

SERMON NO. 783

The church as she should be

'Thou art beautiful, O my love, as Tirzah, comely as Jerusalem, terrible as an army with banners.' Song of Solomon 6:4
SUGGESTED FURTHER READING: 2 Timothy 2:1–13

Ask yourself: 'An army, a company of warriors—am I one of them? Am I a soldier? I have entered the church; I make a profession; but am I really a soldier? Do I fight? Do I endure hardness? Am I a mere carpet-knight, a mere lie-a-bed soldier, one who is pleased to put on regimentals in order to adorn myself with a profession without ever going to the war?'

'Am I a soldier of the cross—a follower of the Lamb?'

Are you a soldier who engages in actual fighting for Jesus under his banner? Do you rally round it? Do you know the standard? Do you love it? Could you die in defence of it? Is the person of Jesus dearest of all things to you? Do you value the doctrine of the atoning substitution? Do you feel your own energy and power awakened in the defence of that and for the love of that? Ask the searching question. And then—'terrible'. Am I in any way terrible through being a Christian? Is there any power in my life that would condemn a sinner, any holiness about me that would make a wicked man feel ill at ease in my company? Is there enough of Christ about my life to make me like a light in the midst of the darkness? Or is it very likely that if I were to live in a house, the inhabitants would never see any difference between me and the ungodly? How many Christians there are who need to wear a label round their necks: you would never know that they were Christians without it! They make long prayers and great pretences, but they are Christians in nothing but the name. May our lives never be thus despicable, but may we convince gainsayers that there is a power in the gospel of Jesus Christ, and make them confess that they, not having it, are losing a great blessing.

FOR MEDITATION: Does your life and witness shine like a light in the midst of a crooked and perverse nation (Philippians 2:15–16)? Are you different enough to expose the works of darkness (Ephesians 5:11)? Or is your Christian life and witness a little bit too 'user-friendly' to make much of an impact upon others?

SERMON NO. 984

The touchstone of godly sincerity

'Will he always call upon God?' Job 27:10
SUGGESTED FURTHER READING: 1 John 3:19–24

I have great confidence in the sincerity of any Christian man who says habitually and truthfully, 'Lord, let me know the very worst of my case, whatever it is. Even if all my fair prospects and bright ideals should be but dreams, the fabric of a vision, and if yonder prospect before me of green fields and flowing streams should be but an awful mirage and on the morrow should change into the hot burning desert of an awful reality, so be it, only let me know the truth; lead me in a plain path; let me be sincere before thee, O thou heart-searching, rein-trying God!' Let us come before the Lord with such frank candour and ingenuous simplicity. Let as many of us as fear the Lord and distrust ourselves, take refuge in his omniscience against the jealousies and suspicions which haunt our own hearts. And let us do better still; let us hasten anew to the cross of Jesus and thus end our difficulties by accepting afresh the sinners' Saviour. When I have a knot to untie as to my evidence of being a child of God and I cannot untie it, I usually follow Alexander's example with the Gordian knot, and cut it. How cut it? Why, in this way—'You say, O conscience, this is wrong and that is wrong. You say, O Satan, that my faith is a delusion, my experience a fiction and my profession a lie. Be it so then; I will not dispute it; if I am no saint, I am a sinner; there can be no doubt about that! The devil himself is defied to question that. Then it is written that "Christ Jesus came into the world to save sinners", and to sinners is the gospel preached—"He that believeth on him is not condemned". I do believe on him; if I never did before I will now, and all my transgressions are therefore blotted out. And now, Lord, grant me grace to begin again, and from this time forth let me live the life of faith, the life of prayer.'

FOR MEDITATION: Whether we like it or not, God searches us and knows us (Psalm 139:1; Jeremiah 17:10; Hebrews 4:12–13), but it is a hopeful sign when we readily express an unconditional invitation for him to do so (Psalm 26:2; 139:23–24).

SERMON NO. 985

The essence of the gospel

'He that believeth on him is not condemned: but he that believeth not is condemned already, because he hath not believed in the name of the only begotten Son of God.' John 3:18
SUGGESTED FURTHER READING: John 12:35–46

The connection of our text will help us to form a judgment as to whether we are indeed believers in Jesus. Have you realised, by a true exercise of faith, what is meant by the fourteenth and fifteenth verses of the present chapter (John 3)? 'And as Moses lifted up the serpent in the wilderness, even so must the Son of man be lifted up: that whosoever believeth in him should not perish, but have eternal life.' As the serpent-bitten Israelite looked to the brazen serpent when it was uplifted, have you in the same way looked to Jesus and found healing through looking to him? By this you may judge yourselves. Have you been healed of the wounds of sin and quickened into a new and heavenly life? Have you in very deed made the crucified Saviour your soul's resting-place? In the verses which follow the text you find such words as these—'he that doeth truth cometh to the light'. Do you, as the result of having trusted in Christ, come to the light? Is it your desire to know God's truth, God's will, God's law and God's word? Are you seeking after the light and are you desirous that the works wrought in you should be seen to be the fruit of God's own Spirit? By this also can you judge yourself? It is vain to say, 'I trust in Christ,' if you have never looked to him with that same childlike look with which the Israelite looked to the brazen serpent, and equally vain for you to profess to be a believer in him, unless you desire the light. You may be in partial darkness still, as doubtless you are, but are you seeking more light, seeking God, seeking truth and seeking right? By this you shall know whether the Father has begotten you unto a new birth, whether you are to a certainty a new man, no longer a light-shunner but a light-seeker.

FOR MEDITATION: Our claims to trust in Christ have to stand up to examination (2 Corinthians 13:5). Not all faith is saving faith (1 Corinthians 15:2). Sometimes those who claim to believe in the Lord Jesus Christ fail this test (John 8:31–33,45; Acts 8:13,18–23).

The pilgrim's longings

'And truly, if they had been mindful of that country from whence they came out, they might have had opportunity to have returned. But now they desire a better country, that is, an heavenly: wherefore God is not ashamed to be called their God.' Hebrews 11:15–16

SUGGESTED FURTHER READING: James 1:1–12

Faith that is never tried is not true faith. It must be exercised sooner or later. God does not create useless things: he intends that the faith he gives should have its test and glorify his name. These opportunities to return are meant to try your faith, and they are sent to you to prove that you are a volunteer soldier. Why, if grace was a sort of chain that manacled you so that you could not leave your Lord, and if it had become a physical impossibility to forsake the Saviour, there would be no credit in it. He that does not run away because his legs are too weak, does not prove himself a hero; but he that could run, but will not run, he that could desert his Lord, but will not desert him, has within him a principle of grace stronger than any fetter could be, the highest, firmest, noblest bond that unites a man to the Saviour. By this shall you know whether you are Christ's or not. When you have opportunity to return, but do not return, that shall prove you are his. Two men are going along a road and there is a dog behind them. I do not know to which of them that dog belongs, but I shall be able to tell you directly. They are coming to a crossroad: one goes to the right, the other goes to the left. Now which man does the dog follow? He that is his master. So when Christ and the world go together, you cannot tell which you are following; but, when there is a separation, and Christ goes one way, and your interest and your pleasure seem to go the other way, if you can part with the world and keep with Christ, then you are one of his. After this manner these opportunities to return may serve us a good purpose: they prove our faith, while they try our character, thus helping us to see whether we are indeed the Lord's or not.

FOR MEDITATION: Disciples are not necessarily converted. Many of Jesus's disciples disputed his teaching (John 6:60), disbelieved (John 6:64) and departed from him (John 6:66). Contrast the evidence of true faith as voiced by Simon Peter (John 6:67–69). But beware—one who stayed with Christ was known by him to be a deceiver (John 6:70–71).

SERMON NO. 1030

Justification by faith—illustrated by Abram's righteousness

'And he believed in the LORD*; and he counted it to him for righteousness.'*
Genesis 15:6
SUGGESTED FURTHER READING (Spurgeon): Romans 4:1–25

It is a grand faith to trust in Jesus in the teeth of all your sins, and notwithstanding the accusations of conscience. To believe in him that justifies not merely the godly, but *the ungodly* (Romans 4:5), to believe not in the Saviour of saints, but in the Saviour of sinners, and to believe that 'if any man sin, we have an advocate with the Father, Jesus Christ the righteous', this is precious and is counted unto us for righteousness. This justifying faith was faith which dealt with a wonderful promise, vast and sublime. I imagine the patriarch standing beneath the starry sky, looking up to those innumerable orbs. He cannot count them. To his outward eye, long accustomed in the land of the Chaldees to midnight observation, the stars appeared more numerous than they would to an ordinary observer. He looked and looked again with elevated gaze, and the voice said, 'So shall thy seed be.' Now he did not say, 'Lord, if I may be the father of a clan, the progenitor of a tribe, I shall be well content; but it is not credible that countless hosts can ever come of my barren body.' No, he believed the promise; he believed it just as it stood. I do not hear him saying, 'It is too good to be true.' No; God has said it—and nothing is too good for God to do. The greater the grace of the promise, the more likely it is to have come from him, for good and perfect gifts come from the Father of lights. Beloved, does your faith take the promise as it stands in its vastness, in its height, depth, length and breadth? Can you believe that you, a sinner, are nevertheless a child, a son, an heir, an heir of God, a joint-heir with Christ Jesus?

FOR MEDITATION: Faith can come up against an extraordinary range of emotional obstacles including fear (Mark 5:36), unbelief (Mark 9:24), despair (Romans 4:18) and even joy (Luke 24:41)! But faith in the Lord Jesus Christ enables us to overcome our circumstances (1 John 5:4–5) whether things appear hopeless or too good to be true.

SERMON NO. 844

The thorn in the flesh

'And lest I should be exalted above measure through the abundance of the revelations, there was given to me a thorn in the flesh, the messenger of Satan to buffet me.' 2 Corinthians 12:7
SUGGESTED FURTHER READING: 2 Chronicles 16:7–14

It is no small matter when God sends a thorn in the flesh and it answers its end, for in some cases it does not. Without the sanctifying power of the Holy Spirit, thorns are productive of evil rather than good. In many people their thorn in the flesh does not appear to have fulfilled any admirable design at all; it has created another vice instead of removing a temptation. We have known some whose poverty has made them envious, others whose sickness has rendered them impatient and petulant, and others whose personal infirmity has rendered them perpetually fretful and rebellious against God. Dear brothers and sisters in Christ Jesus, let us labour against this with all our might, and if God has been pleased to put a fetter upon us in any shape or way, let us ask him not to allow us to make this the occasion for fresh folly, but, on the contrary, to bear the rod and learn its lessons. Pray that when we are afflicted we may grow in grace and in likeness to our Lord Jesus, and so bring more honour to his name. Does this not teach us all the solemn duty of being content, whatever our lot may be—content without the revelation if we are without the thorn, content with the thorn if we have the revelation, or content without either revelation or thorn, so long as we may have a humble hope in Jesus Christ our Saviour. What a happy people God's people are, and ought to be, when everything turns for their good, when even the thorn that was a curse becomes to them a blessing, and out of the lion comes forth honey. If the thorn be a blessing, what must the blessing itself be? If the smarts of earth heal us, what will the joys of heaven do for us?

FOR MEDITATION: The specific 'thorn in the flesh' to which the apostle Paul referred in 2 Corinthians 12:7–9 was not his only one. Read 2 Corinthians 11:23–28 and see how many other thorns in the flesh he endured; consider in 2 Corinthians 4:8–11 how such things distressed him, but could not destroy him. Why was he able to rise above all these things? The answer can be found in Philippians 4:11–13.

SERMON NO. 1084

The rose and the lily

'I am the rose of Sharon, and the lily of the valleys.' Song of Solomon 2:1
SUGGESTED FURTHER READING: John 8:12–20

It is our Lord who speaks: 'I am the rose of Sharon'. How is it that he utters his own commendation, for it is an old and true adage that 'self praise is no recommendation.' None but vain creatures ever praise themselves, and yet Jesus often praises himself. He says, 'I am the good shepherd', 'I am the bread of life', 'I am meek and lowly in heart', and in various speeches he is frequently declaring his own excellencies, yet Jesus is not vain! Scorned be the thought! Yet I said if any *creature* praised itself it must be vain, and that too is true. How then shall we solve the riddle? Is not this the answer, that he is no creature at all, and therefore comes not beneath the rule? For the creature to praise itself is vanity, but for the Creator to praise himself, for the Lord God to manifest and show forth his own glory is becoming and proper. Hear how he extols his own wisdom and power in the end of the book of Job, and see if it is not most seemly, as the Lord himself proclaims it! Is not God constantly ruling both providence and grace for the manifestation of his own glory, and do we not all freely consent that no motive short of this would be worthy of the divine mind? So then, because Christ talks thus of himself, since no man dare call him boastful, I gather an indirect proof of his deity, bow down before him and bless him that he gives me this incidental evidence of his being no creature, but the uncreated one himself. An old Scottish woman once said, 'He is never so bonnie as when he is commending himself', and we all feel it so: no words appear more suitable out of his own lips than these—'I am the rose of Sharon, and the lily of the valleys.'

FOR MEDITATION: The Lord Jesus Christ was accused of blasphemy when he made momentous claims concerning his person (Matthew 26:63–65; John 10:33–36) and his work (Luke 5:20–21). In the case of anybody else these accusations would have been totally justified, but in his case those abusing him were the ones who were blaspheming (Luke 22:63–65).

SERMON NO. 784

The sheep and their shepherd

*'My sheep hear my voice, and I know them, and they follow me.' John
10:27*
SUGGESTED FURTHER READING: Psalm 23:1–6

What sweet music there is to us in the name which is given to our Lord
Jesus Christ—'the good shepherd'! It not only describes the office he
holds, but it sets forth the sympathy he feels, the aptness he shows and
the responsibility he bears to promote our wellbeing. What if the sheep
be weak, yet is the shepherd strong to guard his flock from the prowling
wolf or the roaring lion. If the sheep suffer privation because the soil is
barren, yet is the shepherd able to lead them into pasturage suitable for
them. If they be foolish, yet he goes before them, cheers them with his
voice and rules them with the rod of his command. There cannot be a
flock without a shepherd; neither is there a shepherd truly without a
flock. The two must go together. They are the fulness of each other. As
the church is 'the fulness of him that filleth all in all', so we rejoice to
remember that 'of his fulness have all we received, and grace for grace.'
That I am like a sheep is a very sorry reflection, but that I have a shepherd
charms away the sorrow and creates a new joy. It even becomes a
gladsome thing to be weak that I may rely on his strength, to be full of
wants that I may draw from his fulness, to be shallow and often at my
wit's end that I may be always regulated by his wisdom. Even so does my
shame redound to his praise. Not to you, you great and mighty, who lift
your heads high and claim for yourselves honour, not for you is peace, not
to you is rest; but unto you, you lowly ones, who delight in the valley of
humiliation and feel yourselves to be taken down in your own esteem, to
you it is that the Saviour becomes dear, and to you will he give 'to lie
down in green pastures ... beside the still waters.'

FOR MEDITATION: Meditate on Psalm 23, a great Psalm. It speaks of great
possessions (v. 1), great peace (v. 2), a great pathway (v. 3), great
protection (v. 4), great provision (v. 5) and great prospects (v. 6). But there
is a great proviso—these blessings apply only to those who hear and
follow the good shepherd, only to those who can say, 'The LORD is *my*
shepherd'.

SERMON NO. 995

Living temples for the living God

'Thus saith the LORD *...; but to this man will I look, even to him that is poor and of a contrite spirit, and trembleth at my word.' Isaiah 66:1–2*
SUGGESTED FURTHER READING: Psalm 91:1–16

Those that are of this character secure a great blessing. God says he will *look* to them. That means several things. It means *consideration*. Whoever and whatever God may overlook, he will look upon a broken heart. This means *approbation*. Though God does not approve of the most costly building that is meant to be his house, he approves of everyone that trembles at his word. It means *acceptance*. Though God will accept no materialism in his worship, he will accept the sighs and cries of a poor broken spirit. It means *affection*. Be they who they may that do not receive God's help, a contrite spirit shall have it. And it means *benediction*—'to this man will I look'. I was reading the other day in an old author the following reflection as near as I can remember it. He says, 'There may be a child in the family that is very weak and sickly. There are several others that are also out of health, but this one is sorely ill. And the mother says to the nurse, "You shall see after the rest, but to this one will *I* look, even to this one that is so sore sick and so exceeding weak."' So God does not say to his angels, 'You shall look after the poor and the contrite; I have other things to do,' but he says, 'Go about, spirits, be ministering spirits to those that are stronger, and bear them up in your hands, lest they dash themselves against a stone; but here is a poor soul that is very poor: I will look after *him* myself. Here is a poor spirit that is very broken: I will bind that up myself. Here is a heart that trembles very much at my word: I will comfort that heart myself;' and so, he that 'telleth the number of the stars; he calleth them all by their names', *he* 'healeth the broken in heart, and bindeth up their wounds.' Out of special love to them he will do it himself.

FOR MEDITATION: Satan was not mistaken when he quoted the fact that angels exercise a caring ministry, but not long afterwards the Lord Jesus Christ rightly referred to his own superior caring ministry (Luke 4:10–11,18). He himself also steps in when under-shepherds fail (Ezekiel 34:4,10–11,15–16).

SERMON NO. 1083

Purging out the leaven

'Know ye not that a little leaven leaveneth the whole lump? Purge out therefore the old leaven, that ye may be a new lump, as ye are unleavened. For even Christ our passover is sacrificed for us: therefore let us keep the feast, not with old leaven, neither with the leaven of malice and wickedness; but with the unleavened bread of sincerity and truth.'
1 Corinthians 5:6–8
SUGGESTED FURTHER READING: Luke 22:54–62

If you do not walk in the light as Christ is in the light, it is not because he is not willing that you should walk in his light, but because you keep at a distance from him and so walk in darkness. Do you believe that the sad faces among God's servants are caused by their poverty? Some of the very poorest of saints have been the most joyful. Do you think they are caused by their sicknesses? Why, we have known people confined to the bed of sickness for twenty years, who have found a very heaven below in their chamber of languishing. What is it that makes God's people look so sad? It is the old leaven; 'let us keep the feast,' says the apostle, but it is useless to hope to do so while we keep the leaven. Perhaps there is one thing which we know to be our duty, but we have not attended to it; that one neglect will break up our festival. He that knows his master's will and does it not 'shall be beaten with many stripes.' Are these stripes to be given in the next world? I do not believe it; it is in this world that erring believers will be beaten, and very often depression of spirit, losses and bereavements happen to a Christian because he has knowingly violated his conscience by neglecting a duty or permitting a sin. Jesus will not commune with neglecters of his will. Jesus will have no leaven where he is. If you tolerate that which is nauseous to him, he will walk contrary to you. 'Can two walk together, except they be agreed?' I would with much affection press these considerations upon you.

FOR MEDITATION: Lagging behind Jesus can lead his followers to being amazed and afraid (Mark 10:32). Peter's experience should be a warning to us that following Jesus afar off (Mark 14:54; John 18:15–16) can so very easily end in tears (Mark 14:72). Chastening is initially a grievous thing (Hebrews 12:11).

SERMON NO. 965

A last look-out

'The time of my departure is at hand.' 2 Timothy 4:6
SUGGESTED FURTHER READING: Romans 13:8–14

If 'the time of my departure is at hand', I should like to be on good terms with all my friends on earth. Were you going to stop here always, when a man treated you badly, apart from a Christian spirit, you might as well have it out with him; but as we are going to stop such a little while, we may well put up with it. It is not desirable to be too ready at taking an offence. What if my neighbour has an ugly temper, the Lord has to put up with him, and so I may. There are some people with whom I would rather dwell in heaven for ever than abide with them half an hour on earth. Nevertheless, for the love of the brethren and for the peace of the church, we may tolerate much during the short time we have to brook with peevish moods and perverse humours. Does Christ love them, and shall not we? He covers their offences; why, then, should we disclose them or publish them abroad? If any of you have any grievances with one another, if there is any bickering or jealousy between you, I should like you to make it up tonight, because the time of your departure is at hand. Suppose there is someone to whom you spoke harshly, you would not like to hear tomorrow that he was dead. You would not have minded what you said to him if he had lived, but now that the seal is set upon all your communications one with another, you could wish that the last impress had been more friendly. There has been a little difference between two brothers, a little coldness between two sisters. Since one or other of you will soon be gone, make it up! Live in love, as Christ loved you and gave himself for you.

FOR MEDITATION: To part from others on bad terms is a sad thing, especially when we have happily worked alongside them in Christian service. Paul's memory of the sharp contention he had with Barnabas (Acts 15:39) may well be behind his pleas for arguing fellow-workers to agree in the Lord (Philippians 4:2–3). When the time of his departure was at hand, Paul was concerned not to be holding any grudges (2 Timothy 4:16).

SERMON NO. 989

Consecration to God—illustrated by Abraham's circumcision

'And when Abram was ninety years old and nine, the Lord appeared to Abram, and said unto him, I am the Almighty God; walk before me, and be thou perfect. And I will make my covenant between me and thee, and will multiply thee exceedingly.' Genesis 17:1–2
SUGGESTED FURTHER READING: 3 John 1–8

Immediately after God appeared to Abraham, his consecration was manifest, first, *in his prayer for his family.* 'O that Ishmael might live before thee!' Men of God, if you are indeed the Lord's and feel that you are his, begin now to intercede for all who belong to you. Never be satisfied unless they are saved too; and if you have a son, an Ishmael, concerning whom you have many fears and much anxiety, as you are saved yourself, never cease to groan out that cry, 'O that Ishmael might live before thee!' The next result of Abraham's consecration was that *he was most hospitable to his fellow men.* Look at the next chapter. He sits at the tent door and three men come to him. The Christian is the best servant of humanity in a spiritual sense. I mean that for his Master's sake he endeavours to do good to the sons of men. He is of all men the first to feed the hungry, to clothe the naked, and, as much as lies in him, to 'do good unto all men, especially unto them who are of the household of faith.' The third result was that Abraham *entertained the Lord himself,* for amongst those three angels who came to his house was the King of kings, the infinite One. Every believer who serves his God does, as it were, give refreshment to the divine mind. I mean this: God took an infinite delight in the work of his dear Son. He said, 'This is my beloved Son, in whom I am well pleased.' He takes a delight also in the holiness of all his people. Jesus sees 'of the travail of his soul,' and is satisfied by the works of the faithful; and you, as Abraham entertained the Lord, also entertain the Lord Jesus with your patience, your faith, your love and your zeal, when you are thoroughly consecrated to him.

FOR MEDITATION: Consecration to God is a command to the Christian (Romans 12:1). Consider some of the practical outworkings as listed in Romans 12—the use of spiritual gifts (vv. 6–8), love (vv. 9–10), serving the Lord (v. 11), prayer (v. 12) and hospitality (v. 13). Is your body consecrated to God? Or do you still regard it as your own private property (1 Corinthians 6:19–20)?

SERMON NO. 845

The water of life

'The woman saith unto him, Sir, give me this water.' John 4:15
SUGGESTED FURTHER READING: Revelation 22:1–17

The apostle John says he saw a 'river of water of life'. Nobody is afraid when there is a deep, broad, flowing river to draw from. Who fears to exhaust the Thames or drain the Danube by his thirst? Moreover, as John Bunyan reminds us, a river is free to everybody to drink. The source of it is private. Many rivers rise in a park or private grounds, but the river itself is public. As soon as it becomes a considerable stream, it becomes a public highway and a universal water-supply. It is free; it flows the way it wills. Rivers possess a sort of sovereignty; you cannot bid them flow in a straight line or order them by rules of geometry; they will have their own sweet will. If the river chooses to go by one town and not by another, it will have its way, try to stop it who may. But while it is sovereign in its course and direction, yet it is free for public use; the cattle come to drink and even a poor dog is not refused when he gets to the river's brink; if he wants to lap and cool his feverish tongue in the heat of the summer, who shall forbid him? And you, poor sinner, you shall find the grace of God free to you, for there is enough of it; it is up to the banks; no, it overflows the banks; there is a flood of it, such a flood that there never can by any possibility be any lack, though all men should come. Though ten thousand times ten thousand should come, there would still be found sufficient grace in Jesus to meet the case of all, for whom the Lord brings, the Lord can provide for in Christ Jesus. The grace of God is sovereign in its choice and discriminating in its course, but still it is free to all thirsty ones who long to partake of its everlasting fulness.

FOR MEDITATION: The abundance of water which flowed from the rock smitten by Moses quenched the thirst of a multitude in the wilderness (Numbers 20:11). But that is only a faint picture of the abundance of God's mercy (1 Peter 1:3) and grace (Romans 5:17; 2 Corinthians 4:15; 1 Timothy 1:14) which flows to us from the true rock, the Lord Jesus Christ (1 Corinthians 10:4), smitten for our sins on Calvary's cross (Isaiah 53:4–5).

Wanted, a guestchamber

'The Master saith, Where is the guestchamber, where I shall eat the passover with my disciples?' Mark 14:14
SUGGESTED FURTHER READING: Isaiah 57:15–19

Where is there room for him? He will bring the feast: the chamber is all he asks. Christ asks nothing good from you: he only asks the empty room in which he may spread the good things which he will bring with himself. The Master asks you not to prepare the feast, for you are penniless in your natural estate; you have nothing upon which he can feed, for you have not even food for your own soul; have you not spent your 'money for that which is not bread? and your labour for that which satisfieth not?' He asks an empty chamber—this is all. Room for the Saviour! Room for the Saviour to enter and dwell! It is not your virtues, your excellencies, nor anything good of you that he asks for, but simply the empty room in which you are willing to entertain him. The question is simply and alone, 'Where is the guestchamber?', not 'Where is the guestchamber that is sumptuously decorated and made fit for the great King?', nor, 'Where is the chamber that is glittering with gilded panels and tessellated pavements?' Jesus seeks no lofty chamber in which to lodge; if there be one of you who has a heart lofty and proud, Christ will not come to you, for all the splendours of your pretended goodness are faded and stained in his sight. He dwells not with the proud, nor with the great, 'but to this man will I look, even to him that is poor and of a contrite spirit, and trembleth at my word.' Are you guilty? Well, that need not keep the sin-atoning Priest away. Is the guestchamber of your heart all soiled and foul? Is it full of evils? Jesus Christ does not enquire concerning that; he only asks you if you are willing that he should come in and dwell there, and if you say 'Yes', it will be his business to cleanse the chamber and fit it for himself. Only, 'Where is the guestchamber?'

FOR MEDITATION: If the Lord Jesus Christ knocks at the door of bare and empty souls and will eat with those who receive him in (Revelation 3:17–20), he must have brought the feast with him; 'he … filleth the hungry soul with goodness' (Psalm 107:9). It is a tragedy to be under the delusion of self-sufficiency and to risk turning him away on that account (Revelation 3:17).

SERMON NO. 785

Heaven's nurse children

'*I taught Ephraim also to go, taking them by their arms.*' Hosea 11:3
SUGGESTED FURTHER READING: 1 Thessalonians 2:1–12

What a mercy it is that the Lord reveals to us his own truth by slow degrees! We ought never to expect our young converts to understand the doctrine of election and to be able to split hairs in orthodoxy. It is vain to overload them with such a precious truth as union with Christ or so deep a doctrine as predestination. Do they know Christ as their Saviour and themselves as sinners? Well then, do not try to make a child run; it will never walk if you do. Do not try to teach the babe gymnastics; first let it totter on and tremble forward a little way. 'I have yet many things to say unto you, but ye cannot bear them now', said the Saviour. Now, had certain reputedly wise men been there they would have said, 'Lord, let us hear it all; make full proof of it all; bring it all out: we can bear it—only try us.' But our Lord 'knew what was in man', and, therefore, he only brought out the truth little by little, line upon line, precept upon precept, and he does so experimentally with his children still. We do not know our own depraved hearts so well at first as we do afterwards. Both the disease and the remedy have to be more fully revealed to us by-and-by. Did we know at the first all that we shall know hereafter, we should be so overwhelmed with the abundance of the revelation that we should not be able to endure it; the Lord, therefore, lets in the light by degrees. If a person had been long famished, and you were to find him hungry, faint and ready to die, your instincts would say, 'Put food before him at once and let him have all he wants.' Yet this would be a ready enough way to kill him. If you are wise, you will give him nutriment slowly, as he is able to bear it. If you have been long in the dark and come into the light at once, your eyes smart and you cannot bear it; you need to come to it by degrees; and thus it is with the Lord's children.

FOR MEDITATION: God's menu for spiritual growth begins with milk as a starter (Hebrews 5:13; 1 Peter 2:2), followed by a second course of strong meat (Hebrews 5:14). It is unwise to begin too greedily, but just as inappropriate to be content with the starter when it is time to be well into the second course (1 Corinthians 3:1–2; Hebrews 5:11–12). Our knowledge of God is to increase, not remain static (Colossians 1:10; 2 Peter 3:18).

Soul winning

'He that winneth souls is wise.' Proverbs 11:30
SUGGESTED FURTHER READING: 1 Peter 3:1–16

We must school and train ourselves to deal personally with the unconverted. We must not excuse ourselves, but force ourselves to the irksome task till it becomes easy. This is one of the most honourable modes of soul-winning, and if it requires more than ordinary zeal and courage, so much the more reason for our resolving to master it. Beloved, we must win souls; we cannot live and see men damned; we must have them brought to Jesus. So be up and doing, and let none around you die unwarned, unwept and uncared for. A tract is a useful thing, but a living word is better. Your eye, face and voice will all help. Do not be so cowardly as to give a piece of paper where your own speech would be so much better. I charge you, attend to this for Jesus' sake. Some of you could write letters for your Lord and Master. To far-off friends a few loving lines may be most influential for good. Be like the men of Issachar, who handled the pen. Paper and ink are never better used than in soul-winning. Much has been done by this method. Could you not do it? Will you not try? Some of you, at any rate, if you could not speak or write much, could live much. That is a fine way of preaching, that of preaching with your feet—I mean preaching by your life, conduct and conversation. That loving wife who weeps in secret over an infidel husband, but is always so kind to him; that dear child whose heart is broken with a father's blasphemy, but is so much more obedient than he used to be before conversion; that servant at whom the master swears, but whom he could trust with his purse and the gold uncounted in it; that man in trade who is sneered at as a Presbyterian, but who, nevertheless, is straight as a line and would not be bribed to do a dirty action; these are the men and women who preach the best sermons; these are your practical preachers.

FOR MEDITATION: Christian witness ought to be proactive as well as reactive (Colossians 4:3–6). Deeds may suffice in the first place (1 Peter 3:1–2), but words will be needed sooner or later (1 Peter 3:15). Needless to say, our words and deeds must back each other up.

SERMON NO. 850

Joseph's bones

'By faith Joseph, when he died, made mention of the departing of the children of Israel; and gave commandment concerning his bones.'
Hebrews 11:22
SUGGESTED FURTHER READING (Spurgeon): Genesis 50:22–26

No man may be said to have real faith who is not concerned that faith may be found in the hearts of his fellow men. But, say you, 'What did Joseph do to encourage the faith of others?' Why, he left his bones to be a standing sermon to the children of Israel. We read that they were embalmed and put into a coffin in Egypt and thus they were ever in the keeping of the tribes. What did that say? Every time an Israelite thought of the bones of Joseph, he thought, 'We are to go out of this country one day.' Perhaps he was a man prospering in business, laying up store in Egypt; but he would say to himself, 'I shall have to part with this; Joseph's bones are to be carried up; I am not to be here for ever.' And then while it acted as a warning, his body would serve also as an encouragement, for when the taskmasters began to afflict the people and their labour was increased, the despondent Israelite would say, 'I shall never come up out of Egypt.' But others would say, 'Joseph believed we should; there are his bones still unburied. He has left us the assurance of his confidence that God would in due time bring up his people out of this house of bondage.' It seems to me that Joseph had thought of this device as being the best thing on the whole he could do to keep the Israelites perpetually in remembrance that they were strangers and sojourners, and to encourage them in the belief that in due time they would be delivered from the house of bondage and settled in the land that flowed with milk and honey. True faith seeks to propagate herself in the hearts of others. She is earnest, eager and intense, if by any means she may scatter a handful of holy seed that may fall in good soil and bring forth glory to God.

FOR MEDITATION: Faith in others can be promoted in various ways. Sometimes it will be helpful to encourage it (Mark 11:22; Acts 14:22; Ephesians 6:16; 1 Timothy 6:12). At other times it may be necessary to examine it (Luke 8:25; 2 Corinthians 13:5). It will always be good to exemplify it (1 Timothy 4:12; 2 Timothy 3:10) as Joseph did. Do you share the apostle Paul's concern for healthy faith in others (1 Thessalonians 3:5–8)?

Jesus, the King of truth

'Pilate therefore said unto him, Art thou a king then? Jesus answered, Thou sayest that I am a king. To this end was I born, and for this cause came I into the world.' John 18:37
SUGGESTED FURTHER READING: Luke 1:26–33

'To this end was I born, and for this cause came I into the world'. To set up his kingdom was the reason why he was born of the virgin. To be King of men it was necessary for him to be born. He was always the Lord of all; he needed not to be born to be a king in that sense, but to be king through the power of truth it was essential that he should be born in our nature. Why so? Firstly, because it seems unnatural that a ruler should be alien in nature to the people over whom he rules. An angelic king of men would be unsuitable; there could not exist the sympathy which is the cement of a spiritual empire. Jesus, that he might govern by force of love and truth alone, became of one nature with mankind; he was a man among men, a real man, but a right noble and kingly man, and so a King of men. Secondly, the Lord was born that he might be able to save his people. Subjects are essential to a kingdom; a king cannot be a king if there be none to govern. But all men must have perished through sin, had not Christ come into the world and been born to save. His birth was a necessary step to his redeeming death; his incarnation was necessary to the atonement. Moreover, truth never exerts such power as when it is embodied. Truth spoken may be defeated, but truth acted out in the life of a man is omnipotent through the Spirit of God. Now, Christ did not merely speak the truth, but he *was* truth. If he had been truth embodied in an angelic form, he would have possessed small power over our hearts and lives; but perfect truth in a human form has royal power over renewed humanity. Truth embodied in flesh and blood has power over flesh and blood. Hence, for this purpose was he born. So when you hear the bells ringing out at Christmas, think of the reason why Jesus was born.

FOR MEDITATION: 'Where is he that is born King' (Matthew 2:2)? The King of kings dwells in unapproachable light (1 Timothy 6:15–16), was born to dwell among us (John 1:14), and can dwell in our hearts now through faith (Ephesians 3:17). Those who reject his rule face serious consequences (Luke 19:14,27). Have you received the King?

SERMON NO. 1086

Good cheer for Christmas

'And in this mountain shall the LORD *of hosts make unto all people a feast of fat things, a feast of wines on the lees, of fat things full of marrow, of wines on the lees well refined.'* Isaiah 25:6
SUGGESTED FURTHER READING: John 6:25–35

We have nearly arrived at the great merry-making season of the year. On Christmas Day we shall find all the world in England enjoying themselves with all the good cheer which they can afford. Servants of God, you who have the largest share in the person of him who was born at Bethlehem, I invite you to the best of all Christmas fare, to nobler food than makes the table groan—bread from heaven, food for your spirit. How rich and abundant are the provisions which God has made for the high festival which he would have his servants keep not now and then, but all the days of their lives! God, in the verse before us, has been pleased to describe the provisions of the gospel of Jesus Christ. Although many other interpretations have been suggested for this verse, they are all flat and stale, and utterly unworthy of such expressions as those before us. When we behold the person of our Lord Jesus Christ, whose 'flesh is meat indeed,' and whose 'blood is drink indeed', when we see him offered up upon the chosen mountain, we then discover a fulness of meaning in these gracious words of sacred hospitality—the Lord shall make 'a feast of fat things … of fat things full of marrow'. Our Lord himself was very fond of describing his gospel under the selfsame image. He spoke of the marriage-supper of the king, who said, 'my oxen and my fatlings are killed, and all things are ready:' and it did not seem as if he could even complete the beauty of the parable of the prodigal son without the killing of the fat calf and the feasting, music and dancing. As a festival on earth is looked forward to and looked back upon as an oasis amid a desert of time, so the gospel of Jesus Christ is to the soul its sweet release from bondage and distress, its mirth and joy.

FOR MEDITATION: The Lord Jesus Christ, who could turn water into the best wine (John 2:10–11), provides his followers with spiritual water which removes spiritual thirst and springs up to eternal life (John 4:14), and with spiritual food which endures unto eternal life (John 6:27). To be relieved of spiritual thirst and hunger we have to come to him and trust in him (John 6:35; 7:37–39).

SERMON NO. 846

King's gardens

'The king's garden.' Nehemiah 3:15
SUGGESTED FURTHER READING (Spurgeon): Matthew 26:36–46

How long is it since you have been to a prayer-meeting? Shall I stop and let you count? Well, you have not been just lately, because it is Christmas-time. But it was not Christmas-time last October, and yet you were not there then. Some of you very seldom go at all. If you are lawfully detained at home, I would never ask you to come, or upbraid you for minding your home duties, for you have no right to leave legitimate business that ought to be done to come. But I am certain that some of you are idle and might come if you liked. I pray the Lord to send you a horsewhip in the shape of trouble in your conscience till you do come, for it very much weakens us all in our prayers when numbers decline; and whenever people come to despise weeknight services, be sure of it, farewell to the vital power of godliness, for weeknight services are very, very much the stamp of the man. Any hypocrite will come on a Sunday, but a man does need to take some interest in religious services to be found mingling with the people of God in prayer. Am I to believe that some of you do not care whether souls are saved or not? Am I to believe that some of you, church members, have no care whether our ministry is blessed or not? Am I to believe that you continue members of a church in which you take no interest? Am I to believe that it is nothing to you whether Christ is crowned or despised? I will not believe it, and yet your absence from the meetings for prayer tends to make me fear that it must be so. I beg you to correct yourselves in this matter, and as the King's garden wants rain and sunshine, and we cannot expect to have it without prayer, let us not forsake 'the assembling of ourselves together, as the manner of some is'.

FOR MEDITATION: Does the business of Christmas push the things of God into second place in your life? Christ's command to seek first the kingdom of God and his righteousness (Matthew 6:33–34) is particularly appropriate to the questions and worries such as 'What shall we eat? or, What shall we drink? or, Wherewithal shall we be clothed?' (Matthew 6:31) which can easily govern our Christmas preparations.

The hexapla of mystery [or, the six fold mystery]

'And without controversy great is the mystery of godliness: God was manifest in the flesh, justified in the Spirit, seen of angels, preached unto the Gentiles, believed on in the world, received up into glory.' 1 Timothy 3:16
SUGGESTED FURTHER READING: Matthew 1:18–25

'God was manifest in the flesh'. I believe that our version is the correct one, but the fiercest battles have been held over this sentence. It is asserted that the Greek word *theos* is a corruption for *os*, so that, instead of reading 'God was manifest in the flesh,' we should read, 'who was manifest in the flesh'. There is very little occasion for fighting about this matter, for if the text does not say 'God was manifest in the flesh', who does it say was manifest in the flesh, a man, an angel or a devil? Does it tell us that a man was manifest in the flesh? Assuredly that cannot be its teaching, for every man is manifest in the flesh, and there is no sense whatever in making such a statement concerning any mere man and then calling it a mystery. Was it an angel then? But what angel was ever manifest in the flesh? And if he were, would it be at all a mystery that he should be 'seen of angels'? Is it a wonder for an angel to see an angel? Can it be that the devil was manifest in the flesh? If so, he has been 'received up into glory', which, let us hope, is not the case. Well, if it was neither a man, nor an angel, nor a devil who was manifest in the flesh, surely he must have been God; and so, if the word be not there, the sense must be there, or else nonsense. We believe that, if criticism should grind the text in a mill, it would get out of it no more and no less than the sense expressed by our grand old version. God himself was manifest in the flesh. What a mystery is this, a mystery of mysteries! God the invisible was manifest; God the spiritual dwelt in flesh; the infinite, uncontained, boundless 'God was manifest in the flesh'.

FOR MEDITATION: Whatever theologians may contend, the fact remains that 'God was manifest in the flesh'. In the original Greek text the Lord Jesus Christ was described just before his birth as '*the* God with us' (Matthew 1:23) and a week after his resurrection was addressed by Thomas, without any correction, as '*the* God of me' (John 20:28). Is he with you as your God and Saviour?

SERMON NO. 1087

The great mystery of godliness

'And without controversy great is the mystery of godliness: God was manifest in the flesh, justified in the Spirit, seen of angels, preached unto the Gentiles, believed on in the world, received up into glory.' 1 Timothy 3:16
SUGGESTED FURTHER READING: Luke 2:8–20

Did you ever hear of angels hovering around the assemblies of philosophical societies? Very interesting papers are sometimes produced speculating upon geological facts; startling discoveries are every now and then made as to astronomy and the laws of motion; we are frequently surprised at the results of chemical analyses; yet I do not remember ever reading even in poetry that angelic beings have shown any excitement at the news. The fact is that the story of the world's history and all the facts about this world are as well known to angels as the letters of the alphabet are to us; all our profound sciences and recondite theories must seem utterly contemptible to them. Those august minds which have been long ago created by God, and preserved from defilement by his decrees, are better able to judge of the importance of things than we are; and when we find them deeply interested in a matter, it cannot be of small account. Concerning an incarnate God it is said, 'which things the angels desire to look into.' Their views of God's manifesting himself in the flesh are such that over the mercy seat they stand with outspread wings gazing in reverent admiration, and before the throne they sing, 'Worthy is the Lamb that was slain'. The doctrine of incarnate Deity may be folly to the Greeks, and the boastful wiseacres of this world may call it commonplace, but to angels it is an ever flowing fount of adoring admiration. They turn from every other sight to view the incarnate Redeemer, regarding his condescending deed of grace as a bottomless ocean of mystery, a topless steep of wonder. Jesus was 'seen of angels,' and they still delight to gaze upon him.

FOR MEDITATION: Angels attended Jesus throughout his life. They announced his birth (Matthew 1:20–23; Luke 1:30–35; 2:10–14), oversaw his infancy (Matthew 2:13,19–20), helped him after his temptations (Mark 1:13), strengthened him before his death (Luke 22:43), proclaimed his resurrection (Matthew 28:5–7; Luke 24:23) and will be with him when he comes again (Matthew 13:41; 16:27; 24:31; 25:31; 2 Thessalonians 1:7). The way they treat you then depends on how you treat him now.

Joy born at Bethlehem

'And the angel said unto them, Fear not: for, behold, I bring you good tidings of great joy, which shall be to all people. For unto you is born this day in the city of David a Saviour, which is Christ the Lord.' Luke 2:10–11
SUGGESTED FURTHER READING: Matthew 2:1–12

Holy joy is the joy of heaven, and that, be sure, is the very cream of joy. The joy of sin is a fire-fountain, having its source in the burning soil of hell, maddening and consuming those who drink its fire-water; of such delights we desire not to drink. It would be worse than damned to be happy in sin, since it is the beginning of grace to be wretched in sin, and the consummation of grace to be wholly escaped from sin and to shudder even at the thought of it. It is hell to live in sin and misery; it is a deep lower still when men can fashion a joy in sin. God save us from unholy peace and from unholy joy! The joy announced by the angel of the nativity is as pure as it is lasting, as holy as it is great. Let us then always believe concerning the Christian faith that it has its joy within itself, and holds its feasts within its own pure precincts, feasts whose viands all grow on holy ground. There are those who tomorrow will pretend to exhibit joy in the remembrance of our Saviour's birth, but they will not seek their pleasure in the Saviour: they will need many additions to the feast before they can be satisfied. Joy in Emmanuel would be a poor sort of mirth to them. In this country too often, if one were unaware of the name, one might believe the Christmas festival to be a feast of Bacchus or of Ceres, but certainly not a commemoration of the Divine birth. Yet there is cause enough for holy joy in the Lord himself and reasons for ecstasy in his birth among men. It is to be feared that most men imagine that in Christ there is only seriousness and solemnity, and to them consequently weariness, gloom and discontent; therefore, they look out of and beyond what Christ allows, to snatch from the tables of Satan the delicacies with which to adorn the banquet held in honour of a Saviour. Let it not be so among you.

FOR MEDITATION: In Christ we can possess a great joy which does not depend on outward circumstances (1 Peter 1:6–8). How much better to emulate Moses and choose 'rather to suffer affliction with the people of God, than to enjoy the pleasures of sin for a season' (Hebrews 11:25), even if only for the Christmas season.

SERMON NO. 1026

The sages, the star, and the Saviour

'Where is he that is born King of the Jews? for we have seen his star in the east, and are come to worship him.' Matthew 2:2
SUGGESTED FURTHER READING: 2 Corinthians 8:1–9

After worshipping, the wise men presented their gifts. One broke open his casket of gold and laid it at the feet of the new-born King. Another presented frankincense, one of the precious products of the country from which they came; others laid myrrh at the Redeemer's feet; all these they gave to prove the truth of their worship. They gave substantial offerings with no grudging hand. And now, after you have worshipped Christ in your soul and seen him with the eye of faith, give him yourself, your heart and your substance. Why, you will not be able to help doing it. He who really loves the Saviour in his heart, cannot help devoting to him his life, his strength, his all. With some people, when they give Christ anything or do anything for him, it is dreadfully forced work. They say, 'the love of Christ ought to constrain us.' I do not know that there is any such text as that in the Bible, however. I do remember one text that runs thus—'the love of Christ constraineth us'. If it does not constrain us, it is because it is not in us. It is not merely a thing which ought to be; it must be. If any man loves Christ, he will very soon be finding out ways and means of proving his love by his sacrifices. Go home, Mary, and fetch the alabaster box, and pour the ointment on his head, and if any say, 'To what purpose is this waste?' you will have a good reply; you have had much forgiven, therefore you love much. If you have gold, give it; if you have frankincense, give it; if you have myrrh, give it to Jesus; and if you have none of these things, give him your love, all your love, and that will be gold and spices all in one. Give him your tongue and speak of him; give him your hands and work for him; give him your whole self. I know you will, for he loved you and gave himself for you. The Lord bless you, and may this Christmas be a very memorable day.

FOR MEDITATION: In the midst of all the giving and receiving of Christmas presents let us not forget the priority of giving ourselves to the Lord who gave himself for us (2 Corinthians 8:5,9); 'present your bodies a living sacrifice, holy, acceptable unto God' (Romans 12:1).

SERMON NO. 967

Christ—the fall and rise of many

'And Simeon blessed them, and said unto Mary his mother, Behold, this child is set for the fall and rising of many in Israel; and for a sign which shall be spoken against.' Luke 2:34
SUGGESTED FURTHER READING: 1 Peter 2:2–8

The great practical doctrine before us is this, that wherever Jesus Christ comes, with whomsoever he may come in contact, he is never without influence, never inoperative, but in every case a weighty result is produced. There is about the holy child Jesus a power which is always in operation. He is not set to be an unobserved, inactive, slumbering personage in the midst of Israel; but he is set for the falling or for the rising of the many to whom he is known. Never does a man hear the gospel without rising or falling under that hearing. There is never a proclamation of Jesus Christ (and this is the spiritual coming forth of Christ himself) which leaves men precisely where they were; the gospel is sure to have some effect upon those who hear it. Moreover, the text informs us that mankind, when they understand the message and work of Christ, do not regard them with indifference; but when they hear the truth as it is in Jesus, they either take it joyfully in their arms with Simeon, or else it becomes to them 'a sign which shall be spoken against'. 'He that is not with me is against me; and he that gathereth not with me scattereth abroad.' Where Christ is no man remains a neutral; he decides either for Christ or against him. Given a mind that understands the gospel, you have before you also a mind that either stumbles at this stumbling-stone, being scandalised thereby, or else you have a mind that rejoices in a foundation upon which it delights to build all its hopes for time and for eternity. Observe, then, the two sides of the truth—Jesus always working upon men with marked effect, and, on the other hand, man treating the Lord Jesus with warmth either of affection or opposition, an action and a reaction being evermore produced.

FOR MEDITATION: God's word will not return to him void (Isaiah 55:11), but affect us for better or worse (2 Corinthians 2:15–16). The Saviour's birth, which brought joy to so many, left King Herod troubled, furious and murderous (Matthew 2:3,13,16). Have you been drawn nearer to Christ this Christmas, or have you finished with him for another year?

Joyful transformations

'I will make darkness light before them, and crooked things straight.'
Isaiah 42:16
SUGGESTED FURTHER READING: Lamentations 3:1–27

Child of God, if God will thus make all your darkness light and all your crooked things straight, do not forestall your troubles. They are darkness now; leave them alone and they will turn to light. They are crooked now; well, leave them to ripen and God will make them straight. Some fruit which you gather from your trees is of such a nature that if you were to try and eat it in the autumn, it would be very sour and would make you very unwell; but just store it up a little and see how luscious and juicy it becomes! It is a pity to destroy the fruit and pain yourself by premature use! It is just so with your troubles; they are all darkness now; do not meddle with them but leave them till God has ripened them and turned them into light. Yonder man is employed in carrying sacks of flour every day. He carries so many hundredweight each time, and in the day it comes to tons; and so many tons a day will come to an enormous amount in a year. Now, suppose on the first of January this man were to calculate the year's load and say, 'I have all that immense amount to carry; I cannot do it:' you would remind him that he has not to carry it all at once; he has all the work-days of the year to carry it in. So we put all our troubles together and cry, 'However shall I get over them?' Well, they will only come one at a time, and as they come, the strength will come with them. A man who has walked a thousand miles, did not traverse the thousand miles at a step, nor in a day, but he took his time and did it; and we must also take our time and with patience we shall accomplish our work. A fine lesson for us all is that word *wait, WAIT.*

FOR MEDITATION: Are you taken up with the problems and opportunities you are likely to face in the New Year? The Bible tells us not to worry about the future, but to make sure that we bring God into all our circumstances now (Matthew 6:33–34; James 4:13–15).

SERMON NO. 847

Timely reflections

'Now is our salvation nearer than when we believed.' Romans 13:11
SUGGESTED FURTHER READING: 1 Peter 1:3–9

The apostle measured from one fixed point to another fixed point. If you have two shifting points, you cannot say you are now nearer this or that. If the time of our believing was not a fixed and definite moment, but a thing which may be put here or there, we could not reckon from that; and if the time of our emancipation from this body and our complete salvation were unsettled, precarious, a point that moves, a sort of planetary star, we could not say we are getting any nearer to it. But the apostle takes a fixed point. There is a man saved; he has believed in Christ. That day he believed in Christ, that very minute (he may not know what minute, but God knows), that very second, at that tick of the clock in which he trusted in Christ, he became a new man, old things were passed away and all things became new. Henceforth that is a fixed and definite point in that man's history from which to date. And there is another point, settled by God in the divine decree, never to be removed, neither to be ante-dated nor post-dated, a moment when those that believe shall be with Christ where he is, and shall be like him, and shall behold his glory for ever. Now, between these two points you and I, if we have believed, are sailing; and at the close of the year it seemed appropriate for me to haul up the log and note where we are on the sea that rolls between these two blessed points, and to congratulate my fellow-believers that now we are nearer the eternal port by the space of many years than when we first slipped our cable, hauled up the anchor and began to sail towards the haven of everlasting rest; 'now is our salvation nearer than when we believed.'

FOR MEDITATION: If we have remembered to seek the Lord and to call upon him while he is near (Ecclesiastes 12:1; Isaiah 55:6), we can look forward to the approaching day of completed salvation (Isaiah 56:1; Luke 21:28) instead of the approaching day of judgment (Zephaniah 1:14–16).

The essence of simplicity

'Jesus heard that they had cast him out; and when he had found him, he said unto him, Dost thou believe on the Son of God? He answered and said, Who is he, Lord, that I might believe on him?' John 9:35–36
SUGGESTED FURTHER READING: Isaiah 55:1–7

I saw in Pompeii on a shop door the motto, 'Buy and you shall have', and I could not help thinking that if I were walking the streets of the New Jerusalem, I should have seen a very different notice—'come, buy wine and milk without money and without price.' If there could be a shop in which all the goods were to be had without money and without price, would you quarrel with the shopkeeper and petition for an Act of Parliament to shut his shop up and say it was wicked, because you would rather go on the old terms and pay for all you have? Not a bit of it. Yet why is it you stand out against free grace's golden motto, 'Trust in Christ and you shall have'? Here is instantaneous, perfect, everlasting pardon, sonship through Christ, safety on earth, glory in heaven, and all for nothing, the free gift of a gracious God to undeserving sinners who trust in Jesus! Would that men would leave their foolish reasonings and believe in Jesus Christ. Today upon this choice may hang everlasting things to many of you. The anniversary of the season has almost come round, when I was in a similar condition, when I knew myself to be ruined and undone, and heard, for the first time with true understanding, that word, 'Look unto me, and be ye saved, all the ends of the earth.' I knew how it stood that morning. And I do trust that now many a heart will say, 'I will simply rest my soul's salvation upon Christ the Son of God, who is the only Saviour of the lost: I will never from this day hope to be a self-saved man, nor look to anything but to him who on the tree endured the wrath of God on behalf of as many as believe on him.'

FOR MEDITATION: God's free gifts can never be bought, earned or deserved. We are simply required to receive by faith the Saviour (John 1:12) and with him the Holy Spirit (Acts 2:38), the forgiveness of sins (Acts 5:31), justification (Romans 5:16), righteousness (Romans 5:17) and eternal life (Romans 6:23).

N.B. In late October and through November Spurgeon had toured Southern France and Italy. A letter from Rome, dated 5 November 1872, is attached to sermon no. 1080.

SERMON NO. 1088

A song, a solace, a sermon, and a summon

'For his mercy endureth for ever.' Psalm 136:1–26
SUGGESTED FURTHER READING: Matthew 18:21–35

'His mercy endureth for ever.' Then, let our mercy endure. Have you during this year or at any previous time offended another or been offended, so that there is any ill-will in your mind between you and anyone? Then may I ask you, as this is a most fitting day at the close of the year, to end it at once? Even if we feel we have been grossly ill-treated or insulted, yet now let the token of reconciliation be given by every one of us. Recollect, you Christians *must* do it, or you are not Christians. You are nothing better than deceitful hypocrites if you harbour in your minds a single unforgiving thought. There are some sins which may be in the heart and yet you may be saved, but you cannot be saved unless you are forgiving; 'if ye forgive not men their trespasses, neither will your Father forgive your trespasses.' Those are Christ's own words. If we do not choose to forgive, we choose to be damned. Now, there is a good deal of lying about this. People will say, 'Yes, I will forgive it, but I cannot forget it.' You mean you do not forgive it. Everything like enmity must be renounced if you would be saved. When Mr Wesley was going out to America with General Ogilvie, he heard a great storming and raging going on in the cabin: it was the general scolding his servant. He said, 'I had so many bottles of Cypress wine put on board for me, the only wine I am allowed to drink, and that villain has drunk it all himself. I have put him in irons and I am going to send him on board a man-of-war to be flogged, for I never forgive.' 'Well,' said Mr Wesley, 'I hope you never sin.' The inference was so irresistible that the general said, 'Here, you sir, take my keys. I forgive you this time.' If we would be forgiven, let us forgive.

FOR MEDITATION: If it is wrong to let the sun go down on our anger (Ephesians 4:26), it can never be right to carry grudges over into a New Year. The right attitudes to adopt and maintain are found in Ephesians 4:32.

The joy of the Lord, the strength of his people

'The joy of the Lord is your strength.' Nehemiah 8:10
'Also that day they offered great sacrifices, and rejoiced: for God had made them rejoice with great joy: the wives also and the children rejoiced: so that the joy of Jerusalem was heard even afar off.' Nehemiah 12:43
SUGGESTED FURTHER READING: Malachi 3:6–10

What day is that in which the church of God now makes 'great sacrifices'? I have not seen it in the calendar of late; and if men make any sacrifice they very often do it in a mode which indicates that they would escape the infliction if they could. Few make great sacrifices and rejoice. You can persuade a man to give a considerable sum; a great many arguments at last overcome him, and he does it because he would have been ashamed not to do it, but in his heart he wishes you had not come that way but had gone to some other donor. That is the most acceptable gift to God which is given rejoicingly. It is well to feel that whatever good your gift may do to the church, or the poor, or the sick, it is twice as much benefit to you to give it. It is well to give, because you love to give, as the flower which pours forth its perfume because it never dreamed of doing otherwise, or like the bird which quivers with song because it is a bird and finds a pleasure in its notes, or like the sun which shines not by constraint but because, being a sun, it must shine, or like the waves of the sea which flash back the brilliance of the sun because it is their nature to reflect and not to hoard the light. Oh to have such grace in our hearts that we shall joyfully make sacrifices unto our God. The Lord grant that we may have much of this; for the bringing of the tithes into the storehouse is the way to the blessing, as says the Scripture: 'Bring ye all the tithes into the storehouse, that there may be meat in mine house, and prove me now herewith, saith the Lord of hosts, if I will not open you the windows of heaven, and pour you out a blessing, that there shall not be room enough to receive it.'

FOR MEDITATION: God has blessed the Christian with every spiritual blessing in Christ (Ephesians 1:3); having freely received so much, the Christian can enjoy even greater blessing by freely giving to others (Matthew 10:8; Acts 20:35). What are you planning to give in the New Year?

SERMON NO. 1027

Subject Index

Summary of Subject Index

Subject Index

Index of original texts and suggested further readings (Spurgeon's complete texts are identified below by an asterisk *).

Scripture Index

1. Location of numbers (in order of appearance)

Agricultural Hall, Islington (5)

742–746 (24/3/1867—21/4/1867)

The Metropolitan Tabernacle, Newington (356)

747–749, 751–755, 757, 759–766, 769–810, 812–840, 842–861, 863–1110

Camden Road Chapel (1)

758 (30/6/1867)

Surrey Chapel, Blackfriars Road (2)

767, 768 (undated evenings)

Westminster Chapel (1)

811 (Wednesday evening 13/5/1868)

Bloomsbury Chapel (1)

841 (15/11/1868)

2. Time of numbers

The time of most sermons is given on the title page; that of the undated sermons is in most cases indicated by internal references. Most of the sermons were preached on the **Lord's Day** in the **morning**; the exceptions are as follows:—

Sunday evening (21)—778, 790, 802, 808, 809, 816, 826, 857, 869, 882, 922, 930, 932, 933, 936, 946, 952, 962, 972, 1070, 1076

Thursday evening (16)—773, 776, 806, 823, 835, 876, 886 (correctly dated but wrongly attributed to the Lord's Day), 929, 977, 991, 1042, 1054, 1056, 1062, 1077, 1086

Undated evenings, probably Sunday or Thursday (32)—762, 765–768, 770–772, 777, 850, 892, 901, 903, 904, 906, 910, 916, 988–990, 1022, 1023, 1025, 1030, 1079–1081, 1083, 1085, 1092, 1102, 1108

Undated & untimed (probably Sunday or Thursday evenings) (23)—796, 832, 891, 900, 902, 905, 983–986, 992–997, 1002, 1007, 1016, 1021, 1037 (possibly on Sunday evening 22/10/1871 if a reference to 'last Sunday night' points to posthumously published no. 3047, preached on 15/10/1871), 1082, 1097

Wednesday evening (1)—811

3. Sermons preached on behalf of societies

Baptist Missionary Society (Young Men's Association in aid of)—806 (Thursday 16/4/1868); 876 (Thursday 15/4/1869)

London Missionary Society (Annual Sermon to Young Men)—811 (Wednesday 13/5/1868)

Baptist British & Irish Missionary Society—929 (14/4/1870)

Baptist Young Men's Missionary Association—977 (Thursday 21/4/1870)

4. Notably used sermons

None are mentioned in the preface to volume 13, the last volume for which Spurgeon provided such an introduction.

5. Contents of volumes used in this compilation

Vol. 13	nos. 742–9, 751–5, 757–787
Vol. 14	nos. 788–847
Vol. 15	nos. 848–861, 863–907
Vol. 16	nos. 908–967
Vol. 17	nos. 968–1027
Vol. 18	nos. 1028–1088
Vol. 19	nos. 1089–1110 (to 4 May 1873)